D0331252

THE ATLANTIC FRONTIER

THE
Atlantic Frontier

Colonial American Civilization

[1607-1763]

By Louis B. Wright

GREAT SEAL BOOKS

A division of Cornell University Press

ITHACA, NEW YORK

PRINTED IN THE UNITED STATES OF AMERICA
BY THE VAIL-BALLOU PRESS, INC.

*To five honest fishermen and lovers of history,
companions of the high altitudes*

FRANK N. RUSH

DAN S. HAMMACK

A. W. BUELL

ROBERT G. CLELAND

FREDERICK HARD

". . . that pleasure which is most comely, most honest,
and giveth the most liberty to divine meditation, . . . is
the Art of Angling, which having ever been most hurtlessly
necessary hath been the sport or recreation of God's saints,
of most holy fathers, and of many worthy and reverend
divines both dead and at this time breathing. . . . And
now for the inward qualities of the [angler's] mind . . .
The first and most especial whereof is that a skilful angler
ought to be a general scholar."

GERVASE MARKHAM, *The Pleasures of Princes,
or Good Men's Recreations* (1614).

Preface

THIS volume attempts to give a brief account of the growth of civilization in the thirteen colonies which became the United States. Although bookshelves groan with histories which explain the settlement of the colonies, that complex and fascinating theme is still unexhausted. Fresh research is constantly turning up information which makes reinterpretation necessary and desirable.

The present volume seeks to interpret the political, social, and intellectual development of the colonies in regional groups by providing a succinct narrative of their settlement and progress until they were firmly established. The necessity for compression obviously makes it impossible to give a detailed account of the political history of each colony, but it is hoped that enough is given to suggest the main trends. Since the formative years in each colony determined in a large measure the characteristics and qualities developed in later periods, the main emphasis is placed upon the early history of each regional group. The concluding chapter suggests the later development of the colonies as a whole and indicates the influences which finally brought them into a union opposed to the mother country.

Since the reader, it is hoped, will desire further and more detailed information about various aspects of colonial life, a selected bibliography for each chapter is provided.

The author is indebted to Miss Gracia Manspeaker and Mrs. Ruth Buffington for making the index, and to members of the Huntington Library staff for help in the preparation of the volume.

L.B.W.

Prefatory Note

IN order to make available material long out of print, it has seemed desirable to authorize this reissue. Conditions of republication have made extensive revision impossible. A few obvious errors that came to light in the original edition of 1947 have been corrected.

Louis B. Wright

The Folger Library
June 20, 1959

Contents

Illustrations

THE ATLANTIC FRONTIER

CHAPTER ONE

The Old World Background

NEWS travelled slowly in 1486, but in the coast towns of Portugal and Spain rumors were afloat that soon would be heard as far away as Venice, Genoa, Bristol, and London. Sailors were telling strange tales of a Portuguese navigator, one Bartholomew Diaz, who in that year had sailed first southwesterly and then eastward until he had reached a fabled land—perhaps the mythical Kingdom of Prester John. What Diaz had done was to round the Cape of Good Hope and bring to the consciousness of Europe the possibility of a profitable sea route to India and the riches of the Orient.

For nearly three quarters of a century before Diaz's momentous voyage, Portuguese seamen had been driving their little ships farther and farther into the South Atlantic. Inspired by their royal leader, Prince Henry the Navigator, who himself never strayed far from home, they made landings on the Madeiras and the Azores, and pushed down the west coast of Africa, where they enriched themselves with gold, and ivory, and black slaves. More important than all else, these sailors lost some of their fear of unknown seas. Diaz, who had sailed farther into the southern sea than any predecessor, had not slid into the great whirlpool popularly supposed to suck venturesome ships into its lethal vortex; he had not even lost his tackle in the whirling winds believed to make navigation impossible in that waste of water; and he had encountered neither boiling seas nor fearsome monsters, though some of his crew spoke of mermaids.

Within ten years after Diaz had caught a mist-shrouded glimpse of East Africa, a Genoese in the employ of Spain, Christopher Columbus, had made the epochal voyage of 1492 which spanned the Atlantic to the West Indies; Vasco da Gama had completed the voyage of 1497–98 which brought Portuguese traders at last by sea to the shores of India at Calicut; and John Cabot, a Genoese naturalized as a citizen of Venice, entered the employ of the Tudor king, Henry VII, and made the voyage of 1497 which explored the coast of Newfoundland or Nova Scotia and gave England a claim of discovery which she would later invoke in demanding a share of North America.

Among the rank and file of plain men in Europe, these events made small stir. Even Columbus himself scarcely knew what he had accomplished and died in the belief that he had reached the outskirts of Asia instead of the verge of a vast new world. But in a few chancelleries political leaders sniffed the scent of fresh lands for conquest; a few great merchants perceived that commerce would presently receive an infusion of profits beyond the dreams of an old man's avarice; and a horde of adventurers—sea-rovers, rascals, feudal knights-errant born out of time, buccaneers, traders, plain seamen, and scholars, dabblers in the emerging science of geography—all swarmed into vessels bound for the Western Sea.

Though Columbus may not have suspected a new continent to the West, his successors soon realized that a barrier of enormous extent lay between them and the coasts of China and Japan. Obviously this land mass was virgin territory to be had for the taking, and Spain, resurgent with vitality, was in no mood to lose a chance for aggrandizement. Because the Pope asserted the authority of disposing of newly discovered lands, Spanish ambassadors hurried to the Vatican to advance the claims of Ferdinand and Isabella to whatever portions of Heathenesse might lie across the seas.

The Old World Background

Therefore, in 1493, with the ease that comes to ecclesiastical authority, His Holiness, Alexander VI, a Spanish pope, called for his pen and at a stroke divided the world. All territory one hundred leagues west and south of the islands of Cape Verde fell to Spain; Portugal received anything east of the line. Curiously, Spain was not altogether pleased with this generous donation, for she wanted specific concessions in India—which Alexander VI shrewdly failed to mention—and Portugal screamed that the Spanish pope had given away her birthright. Whereupon, after a season of wrangling, the two nations agreed to draw another line across the map, this time three hundred and seventy leagues west of the Cape Verde Islands, a compromise which gave Portugal the hump of South America and enabled her to gain a foothold in Brazil.

If this apportionment of the western world satisfied Spain and Portugal, the rest of Europe conspired to disregard it. Indeed, a generation later, His Catholic Majesty Francis I of France spoke with scorn of the division, expressing a desire of first reading the will of Father Adam to see how he had partitioned the patrimony of his descendants. Having sent this ironic message to his brother of Spain, Francis I dispatched Jacques Cartier of St. Malo to explore the Gulf of St. Lawrence and to hoist the standard of France over a portion of the New World.

Thus within a little more than forty years after Columbus had first sighted land in the Caribbean, the elements of future European competition for a share of Father Adam's legacy were discernible. Although Portugal was concentrating her major activity in Africa, India, and the Far East, she claimed a place in the American sun. Spain was vigorously pursuing the path of empire in Central and South America. Before the sixteenth century was a third gone, her conquistadors had pillaged the wealth of Montezuma and the Incas, and her governors and viceroys had established Spanish power and authority from Mexico to Patagonia. France would soon penetrate the fisheries and forests of the far north. England was yet powerless to assert her rights, but Cabot's first voyage gave her a legal pretext to dispute with France for possession of North America. One day Holland would throw off the domination of Spain and rise as a maritime power capable of colonizing the valley of the Hudson. Even Sweden, still sleeping among her Baltic pines, would wake a century later and send people to settle on American shores. The race for empire in America which began in 1493 with Alexander VI's partition of the world, would continue for more than three centuries and become one of the most persistent influences in determining the lives and minds of men in the New World.

Colonial America was necessarily a projection of Europe across the Atlantic. The Ethiop does not change his skin nor the leopard his spots by going on a journey—at least, not immediately. Portuguese, Spaniards, Frenchmen, Englishmen, Scots, Irishmen, Dutchmen, and Swedes retained their habits, their manners, and their customs long after they had left their native heaths. Change they did, but they changed gradually, and the transformation was at first scarcely visible. As in the plant world, transplantation is a strengthening process. Weak and sickly specimens die, but the survivors grow with renewed vigor. So it is with peoples and their ideas. Many European stocks and many European ideas, transplanted to America, took on fresh life and flourished as never before.

The portion of North America which later became the United States was so dominantly English in its background that other elements in its composition are frequently overlooked. Yet even in those colonies most exclusively English the settlers were far from homogeneous in their origins. As late as 1700, Daniel Defoe in *The Trueborn Englishman* ridiculed the pretensions of his chauvinistic countrymen to racial purity. From time out of mind their island had been a destination, first for invaders and then for refugee outlanders;

The Old World Background

this traditional mixing of English blood with other races had
received a fresh stimulus in the sixteenth century:

> *Dutch, Walloons, Flemings, Irishmen, and Scots,*
> *Vaudois, and Valtolins, and Huguenots,*
> *In good Queen Bess's charitable reign,*
> *Supplied us with three hundred thousand men:*
> *Religion—God, we thank thee!—sent them hither,*
> *Priests, Protestants, the devil, all together.*

Defoe's lines might have been applied with greater accuracy to the thirteen British colonies in North America. Englishmen, Welshmen, Scots and Irishmen supplied diverse elements within the framework even of strictly British settlements. By the end of the seventeenth century, immigrants from continental Europe had also found their way into hundreds of British communities and mingled with the descendants of the first settlers.

Early in the century, French Huguenots came in small numbers, usually from England, where many had been domiciled since the time of the massacre of St. Bartholomew's Eve (1572). After the Revocation of the Edict of Nantes (1685), these Protestant refugees came by the shipload—to Virginia, the Carolinas, Pennsylvania, New York, and even a few to New England where the name of Paul Revere would one day bring honor to his Gallic ancestor. A scattering of other Latin peoples came—a handful of Italian craftsmen, a small number of Spanish traders, an occasional Portuguese fisherman or sailor—but French Protestantism contributed the main body of Latin stock.

Symbolic of New York's later characteristics was the polyglot nature of that colony, even as early as the mid-seventeenth century, when the Hudson valley was still New Netherland under the sway of the Dutch. Intent upon trade, the Dutch asked few questions about a settler's religion or race. Jews, for example, early found prosperity in New Amsterdam, as they did in Newport, Rhode Island—another center of toleration. By 1646 eighteen languages could be heard along the Hudson, says one chronicler of American immigration, "and the population included Dutch, Flemings, Walloons, French, Danes, Norwegians, Swedes, English, Scotch, Irish, Germans, Poles, Bohemians, Portuguese, and Italians." On the borders of New Netherland Swedes and Finns had already settled in the region later to be called New Jersey. The melting pot of later generations was already beginning to simmer.

By the end of the seventeenth century, Pennsylvania had also become a colony of many languages and peoples. Quakers of other than English heritage found their way to William Penn's refuge, and non-Quakers of various beliefs and nationalities added to the diversity. Within a generation after the turn of the century, nearly twenty thousand Germans, chiefly from distressed areas of the Rhineland, were happily farming the valleys and uplands of Pennsylvania. From there Germans drifted into other colonies until the backcountry as far south as the Carolinas had a share of Teutonic stock.

European people, different as they were, had certain common qualities and traditions, but in the New World they came in contact with two races totally different from anything they had previously known. Indians and Negroes were utterly alien to everything European and stood apart, but both profoundly affected the civilization transplanted from the old world.

A Dutch ship brought the first fateful cargo of Negro slaves to Virginia in 1619. Within a century, Negro slavery would revolutionize the agricultural economy of Virginia and neighboring colonies. New England merchants would also get rich on the traffic in Africans; Peter Faneuil of Boston, who gave to the city a hall known as the "cradle of American liberty," was only one of many who purchased their estates with the profits from slave ships. Colonists of the seventeenth and eighteenth centuries little realized that the black bondservants whom they bought and sold so eagerly would subtly influence their own lives, and the lives of their sons after them to the seventh and seven times the seventh generation.

The Indians within the colonies were a disturbing problem to the peace and consciences of Europeans. Pious folk earnestly debated whether the redskins were children of God or the devil. If of the devil, they might be destroyed in good conscience and their land appropriated to Christian use. This view had much in its favor. A few charitable souls, like gentle John Eliot, the missionary, believed that Christ in his mercy meant to save even Indian souls, and to reserve at least a portion of land for their sustenance. The College of William and Mary provided for the bringing up of a handful of Indian youths in good learning, and a few other schools likewise gave instruction to the heathen, but in general, the good Indian in the seventeenth century, as in the nineteenth, was a dead Indian. William Penn's peaceful, just, and successful dealings with the Indians stand out as the most brilliant exception to a general practice.

The English colonists' attitude toward non-English people varied from colony to colony and was subject to modifications brought about by time, but one condition, prevailing until well past the middle of the eighteenth century, enormously affected colonial thinking. Across the whole of the north and northwest stretched a vast imperial domain controlled by France. No man knew the precise extent of French dominion. That nation sent its emissaries into the dark forests beyond the Alleghenies; its explorers traced the inland streams and floated down the Mississippi to its mouth; French fur traders and enterprising *coureurs de bois* smoked the peace pipe with western Indians who told them of an illimitable land that extended to the setting sun; and Jesuit priests, black-gowned invincibles, carried the symbols of both the cross and the *fleur-de-lis* among Indians never before reached by Europeans.

Contacts of Protestant colonists on the Atlantic seaboard with the Catholic French of Canada were unfriendly and during a large part of the time actively hostile, for every political struggle which involved England and the continental powers found a quick reflection in the American wilderness. Puritans of New England and Calvinistic Dutchmen in New York hated the French Jesuits of Canada with a venom beyond theological difference; the priests of the forest, Protestants believed, used their influence with the Indians to incite them to fall upon outlying Dutch and British settlements, a warfare which made the frontier hideous with bloodshed and burning homesteads. The weary years of struggle with France, which only ended in 1763, conditioned Protestant English colonists to an ingrained hatred of most things French and all things Catholic—a heritage which had a long sequel in American history, particularly in New England.

On the southern borders of English America was another Catholic power, Spain. Spanish tentacles reached upward from St. Augustine to the borders of South Carolina and as late as the mid-eighteenth century threatened the youngest colony, Georgia. Territory claimed, or thinly occupied, by Spain extended around the Gulf of Mexico to make contact with the French in the lower Mississippi Valley. English America appeared to be permanently restricted to a narrow fringe along the eastern seaboard despite grandiloquent charters granting land from the Atlantic Ocean to the Great South Sea—wherever it might be found to the westward.

The conventional attitude of Protestants in the English colonies toward Spain and Spaniards was much the same as their opinion of France and Frenchmen. They hated them and told tales of their Machiavellian wiles and cruelty. Stories of the ferocity of Pedro Menéndez de Avilés, founder of St. Augustine, long circulated in the southern colonies. That stout soldier of the Inquisition in 1565 fell upon a hapless settlement of French Huguenots who had found refuge on the St. John's River in Florida. Over two hundred, including the great seaman and colonist, Jean Ribaut, the Spaniards put to the sword—and won a hearty commendation from Philip

The Old World Background

II. Centuries afterward, children in the deep South heard stories about ghosts of Spanish victims shrieking through the woods on stormy nights, and dwellers along the coast were familiar with the legend of a phantom ship piloted by Jean Ribaut.

To what extent in after years the border conflicts influenced British Americans in their attitude toward foreigners and Catholics, no one can say. But clearly the feuds of early generations subtly conditioned colonial minds and left a heritage of hate and suspicion that long endured.

Whatever the mixture of nationalities and races in the thirteen colonies, the dominant influence ultimately was British. Even in New York and Pennsylvania, which contained the largest proportions of continental Europeans, the English language, English law, and many English customs and habits of thought finally prevailed except in isolated pockets. The vitality of English culture in the seventeenth and eighteenth centuries was such that in time it assimilated all other cultures, not without undergoing some modification, to be sure, but without being radically changed. That is not to say that every colonial was translated into an Englishman abroad, but that the essential qualities of society were derived from the English tradition.

The legacy of the sixteenth and early seventeenth centuries (a period which we can agree, for want of a more definite label, to call the English Renaissance) was an inheritance whose influence has been too little understood and appreciated in the appraisal of colonial American life. Many ideas and ideals which moulded the characters of Englishmen in this period were equally effective in determining the traits of Americans, and they retained their potency in America long after they had lost their greatest influence at home. The Renaissance ideal of the gentleman, for example, with its insistence upon the development of man's complete personality and the obligations and responsibilities that went with privilege, remained a powerful factor in the development of the agrarian aristocracy of Virginia, Maryland, and the Carolinas generations after the English gentry had lost many of their Renaissance qualities. The kind of yeomanry, middle class, and gentry that evolved in England in the Renaissance determined to a considerable degree the quality of society that developed in the thirteen colonies in the seventeenth and eighteenth centuries. A comprehension of the social and intellectual development of Renaissance England, therefore, is essential to a proper understanding of colonial America.

No factor was more significant for the future than the growth in strength and power of English commoners under the Tudors when the plain people of England acquired an economic independence and a liberty of thought and action greater than that enjoyed by any other people in Europe, not even excepting the Dutch. Although the evolution of English liberties, economic and political, had its origin in the dim past back of the sixteenth century, the remarkable progress made during the reign of Elizabeth, from 1558 to 1603, had a tremendous effect on the development of modern English-speaking civilizations.

The sixteenth and seventeenth centuries saw tremendous stress and strain throughout Europe, as every nation in some measure underwent political, social, and religious upheaval. England did not escape the general unrest, and the progress made in this period came not from the opportunities conferred by halcyon calm and a beneficent government but rather from the vigor engendered by struggle.

When Henry Tudor on Bosworth Field in 1485 snatched the crown fallen from the anointed brow of Richard III and clapped it upon his own head, the only assurance of keeping it there lay in the hope of winning favor with the English populace. The accession of Henry VII, whose claim to the throne was none too strong, marked the end of feudal aristocracy and the beginning of a greatly increased significance of the lesser gentry, the middle class, and the yeomanry— classes that would give Britain its strength and character in the centuries to come. Henry was fortunate in that many of the great houses which had disputed authority with the crown for generations past had died out in the disorders of that internecine struggle called the Wars of the Roses. Mindful of this heaven-sent advantage, the Tudors were careful to court the favor of lesser—but more numerous—common folk, and to create only such nobles as would be subordinate to the reigning house. If England in the nineteenth century could be described as a nation of shopkeepers, the beginnings of the transformation in social structure must be sought in Tudor policy; neither Henry VIII nor Elizabeth, for all of their readiness to believe in the divinity that doth hedge a king, ever forgot that power resides in the people—and the public purse. If we would understand the men and women who could conquer an intractable wilderness along the western Atlantic, we must not be content with a study of the Stuarts and their times. The key is to be found in the evolution of the common people of Tudor England.

From the accession of Henry VII to the death of Elizabeth in 1603, England changed from a war-shattered and ruined medieval state, hardly fit to be called a nation, to a power strong enough to challenge the imperial Hapsburgs and threaten the wealth and strength of mighty Spain. This emergence from the darkness of feudalism into the bright sun of European power was accompanied by growing pains that wracked the whole social body of England. Time after time in the critical years of the sixteenth century, the nation's future trembled in the balance, and disaster threatened to engulf the little island and her people. Doubt often assailed even the most optimistic of patriots. When doting Mary Tudor in 1555 placed England at the feet of her husband, Philip II of Spain, none would have believed that thirty years later corsairs encouraged by Mary's sister, Elizabeth, would be harrying Philip's galleons from the seas, that the fires which had alternately burned Protestants and Catholics would be out, and that England would be basking in unwonted prosperity.

Plain Englishmen in those years of change bore stout hearts and developed tough minds. The spirit of independence, inherited from ancestors who had struggled for their rights against both lords and kings, grew with the years. Eager for peace and anxious to be loyal to just rulers, these Englishmen were not the sort to be complacent toward tyranny. It behooved the Tudors, therefore, to cultivate the good opinion of the multitude. Although Henry VIII might callously send wife or friend to the block, he was ever mindful to appear before his subjects as honest King Harry; and while Elizabeth the queen might play a political game of courtship with the decadent princes of France, she was shrewd enough to flatter her people by announcing that she had wed the realm of England. The great Tudors had a sixth sense, utterly lacking in the Stuarts, which kept them in touch with the people. Like successful politicians in any age, they recognized the strength of the public and knew how to turn it to their advantage. Under them, the rights and privileges of the people suffered no diminution, and the pride of Englishmen in their country and in their own accomplishments waxed strong.

The social structure of sixteenth century England, like unto no other in Europe, offered an opportunity for the development of a sturdy, independent, and freedom-loving people. In contrast to France or Spain, for example, the class stratification was not rigid. Indeed, such was the flexibility that definitions of English classes cannot be given with the clarity and simplicity beloved of academic precisionists. The people themselves refuse to be pigeon-holed neatly. A yeoman's son might achieve the honors and appellation of a gentleman; while the daughter of a country gentleman might think it no stain to her breeding to match with a worthy farmer, designated yeoman. Rich merchants and tradesmen enjoyed the luxuries and some of the privileges of aristocracy and often bought landed estates which gave them the technical basis of gentility. And by the same token, the younger sons of many proud county families were pleased to apprentice themselves to a tradesman, who would teach them the way to prosperity and independence.

The Old World Background

The secret of this social flexibility was law and custom: the law of primogeniture which gave only to the eldest son the title and estate which supported it. By custom, younger sons had to shift for themselves, and daughters from time immemorial have had to make good matches where they could. Snobbery of course was not unknown, but a society that experiences the constant ebb and flow of various bloods cannot discriminate in favor of a single stream that is blue.

Differences in the economic status of various elements of the yeomanry, middle-class, and gentry were not so great as to make a chasm between the classes. Many a yeoman, possessed of a productive freehold, hired laborers, made money, invested in livestock and lands, and was better off in this world's goods than some of his neighbors of ancient lineage and gentle blood. Merchants and tradesmen varied of course from poverty to riches, but as a group they received in the course of the century an enormous increase in wealth. Many of the gentry—families who had held landed estates for a generation or longer and could claim coat armor at the college of heralds—bestirred themselves to improve their methods of farming and grazing in order to increase their incomes in an era of change and rising prices. Economically there were no insuperable barriers to the mingling of the substantial classes in English society. Some even on the highest levels of the aristocracy were not far removed from the farm, sheep-cote, or counting house. The Earl of Arundel could twit the first Lord Spencer with his yeoman origin, but it was characteristic of English pride that Spencer could retort that while his ancestors were keeping sheep, the noble earl's were plotting treason. In the flux of Elizabethan society, the significant fact was that both extremes were moving toward the middle.

The sixteenth century was an era of tremendous expansion in England's trade, as it was for most of Europe. When the Portuguese developed the sea route to India and the Orient they unwittingly set in motion fundamental changes in European commerce. For the first time, traders could pay for Oriental products in kind and not in gold or silver. That meant, not only an outlet for European products, but more precious metal for circulation at home. As silver mines in eastern Europe became more productive and the gold and silver hoards of Mexico and Peru filtered into commerce, all of Europe experienced a creeping inflation which caused many maladjustments but nevertheless stimulated trade. Money jingled in pockets that had rarely before heard the tinkle of silver. For the commercial groups, and for everyone with something to sell, the increase of money made for an improvement in the standard of living, or at least gave the illusion of prosperity. As always, persons living on rents, on fixed incomes, and persons dependent upon fixed or customary wages, suffered most. At the top and bottom of society, the inflation hit hardest; for the middle class it was an elixir and a stimulant.

For time untold, English wool had been a commodity of international trade. Chaucer saw the wool packs move out of the port of London for Ghent and Bruges and the same vessels bringing back fine Flemish fabrics made by the craftsmen of the Low Countries. But tyranny in the fifteenth century sent some of these Flemings to England where they taught their hosts to weave something better than the native coarse homespuns. When the Spanish Terror again drove Flemings from their homes, Elizabeth welcomed the refugees to London, Norwich, and other towns. But she required each Flemish weaver to train at least one English apprentice. During the sixteenth century, woolen goods of English manufacture rivalled the best woven in Flanders and became an article in demand as far away as Aleppo, Calicut, or the court of Ivan the Terrible.

The growth of the woolen industry changed the face of England and helped to develop those shop-keeping qualities which became her strength and pride. Weaving in the sixteenth century was for the most part a cottage industry, widely diffused throughout England, and especially important in East Anglia, the Midlands, and parts of the West

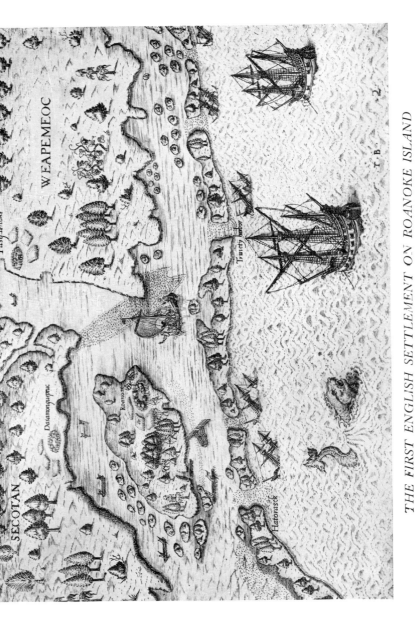

THE FIRST ENGLISH SETTLEMENT ON ROANOKE ISLAND

From the Huntington Library copy of Theodor DeBry, *Admiranda Narratio Fida Tamen . . .* (Frankfurt, 1590).

FROM WILDERNESS TO CIVILIZATION

"A Design to Represent the Beginning and Completion of an American Farm or Settlement," drawn by Gover-

The Old World Background

Country. The clack of looms in countless villages and hamlets was sweet music to the traders whose strings of packhorses were a common sight on country highways. But since the hungry looms required an ever increasing quantity of wool, sheep-raisers began to enroach on soil hitherto given over to tillage. Outcries against the enclosure of common lands and the fencing of estates which had formerly given employment to many farmers occupy a large place in the literature of complaint and give the impression that all England was being ruined by the greed of wool-growers.

That the enclosure of sheep pastures did throw many farmers and farm laborers out of work, there can be no question —and that fact is important in accounting for the impulse driving many of the dispossessed in the seventeenth century to seek farms in the American wilderness—but the distress caused by enclosures in the reign of Elizabeth was more than offset by the diffusion of prosperity among townsmen and countrymen alike as they took up the trade of weaving or some of the subsidiary occupations of the clothing industry. Nevertheless, during the late sixteenth and seventeenth centuries, farmers who could not find tillable soil, laborers who would not adjust themselves to the new opportunities of industry and commerce, and various nondescript unemployables swelled the throng of vagabonds and sturdy beggars who wandered about the countryside and gave color to the belief that England suffered from an excess of population crying out for habitations in the New World.

But the vast increase of opportunity in the crafts and trades, with the upsurge of pride in achievement among these independent workers, helped to obscure any distress caused by the displacement of farmers and the maladjustments that inevitably follow shifts of economic balance. Paralleling the satires against wicked enclosers, one finds ballads, pamphlets, plays, and novels extolling the happy life of apprentices, journeymen, and master craftsmen, all of whom are working for their own advancement and England's prosperity. As courtiers and gentlemen had a voice in Edmund Spenser, so lesser folk found a Homer in Thomas Deloney, the novelist and ballad writer, or in Thomas Heywood, the playwright. When Deloney set forth in 1596 his tale of the honest clothier, Jack of Newberry, and in 1597 his chronicle of *The Gentle Craft*, "showing what famous men have been shoemakers in time past in this land, with their worthy deeds and great hospitality," he put into print a view of English tradesmen which made popular reading for a century afterward. Not without significance was the description of the fifteen pictures hanging in Jack of Newberry's parlor "whereby he encouraged his servants to seek for fame and dignities," for they were the likenesses for the most part of noble Grecians and Romans who had risen from low to high estate: Aelius Pertinax, emperor of Rome, whose father had been a weaver; Iphicrates, an Athenian general, son of a cobbler; Agathocles, king of Sicily, who himself had turned the ancestral potter's wheel; even Marcus Aurelius, descended from a clothier; and many more of similar origin. The moral was clear. Tradesmen under Elizabeth could regard the world as their oyster if they practiced the virtues of industry and thrift. Deloney's fictional narratives of honest craftsmen breathe a fresh optimism. His people look out upon the world unafraid and speak their minds with democratic freedom. Their descendants in the Atlantic empire would be heard in a rising tempo.

Elizabethan labor practices and policy made for a large measure of industrial democracy, albeit, by modern standards, one that was highly paternalistic. The system of apprenticeship established by the Statute of Artificers of 1563 provided a means for the vocational education of any industrious youth and the eventual graduation of that youth into the ranks of the master craftsmen. The essential provisions of the Statute of Artificers, with occasional modifications, remained in force until the Industrial Revolution. Under this statute, apprentices were bound to serve a master for seven years and in return obtained technical training which enabled them at the end of their service to accept employment

The Old World Background

as journeymen or to set up as masters themselves. Every apprentice was potentially a master of men, and in practice the majority became independent craftsmen and many became employers. The factory system developed only to a limited degree, and Elizabethan England had no proletarian pool of labor without a voice in the management of industry. The freedom created by the Elizabethan industrial system determined the character of Englishmen who would be equally insistent upon political liberty.

The encouragement of trade and the expansion of overseas commerce were among the Elizabethan government's cardinal policies that would continue into later reigns and become dominant motives for colonization. Shrewdly Elizabeth began her reign by taking the advice of a merchant and banker, Thomas Gresham, and restoring to face value the coinage which had been debased by Henry VIII. With faith restored in a fluid medium of exchange, trade rapidly increased at home and abroad.

The search for new markets for English goods became intense in the later years of the sixteenth century and has never relaxed from that day to this. England's fortunes depended upon an adequate outlet for cloth, hats, caps, shoes, cutlery, and an ever increasing variety of other manufactured articles. Although one cannot minimize the spirit of adventure which lured many mariners to sea, the cold fact remains that some of the most romantic expeditions had as their objectives the vent of merchandise in far places: on the Baltic coast, in the Levant, in Persia and India, and on the inhospitable shores of the New World.

Enterprising Englishmen had long before the sixteenth century set up trading stations on the Continent; since the early fifteenth century the socalled "English nations" of the Merchant Adventurers had enjoyed extra-territorial rights in the Low Countries. From the English nation at Bruges William Caxton returned to England in 1476 to introduce the art of printing and to begin a career dedicated to the popularization of learning for the understanding of common men. In effect, the Merchant Adventurers abroad and their apprentices were self-governing colonies and the lessons they learned in commerce and government made easier the evolution of colonial government in the New World.

As early as 1553 an enterprising pioneer, Sir Hugh Willoughby, sought a new route to the Orient—and possibly trading privileges in Russia—by attempting a Northeast Passage around Archangel. Although the expedition met with disaster and Willoughby himself perished, one of his captains, Richard Chancellor, survived to have an audience with Ivan the Czar and to pave the way for the merchants of the Russia (or Muscovy) Company, which was chartered in 1554. Such was the Czar's favor that he guaranteed to the English merchants practical self-government within his domains. In the first year of Elizabeth's reign, Anthony Jenkinson, agent of the Russia Company, made the first of six expeditions across Russia to the Caspian Sea and thence into Persia. From that time onward, no place on earth was too distant or too difficult to stir the hopes of British traders.

Ambitious Elizabethan merchants had no mind to let the Portuguese, or any other foreign nation, monopolize the Oriental trade. Jenkinson's reports of the riches to be had in the regions to the east whetted the appetite of others. Since the dim past, Genoese and Venetians had made themselves rich by supplying western Europe with the products of the Mediterranean countries and the lands that lay beyond. Englishmen now looked with longing upon that trade. There were dangers to be sure. Fierce Moslem pirates from the ports of Barbary lay in wait and even ventured as far as the English Channel; Spanish warships in the Bay of Biscay and off Gibraltar made access to the blue waters of the Mediterranean a voyage of doubt; and the Great Turk controlled the favored destinations. But in 1579, William Harebone risked the journey to Constantinople and obtained from Sultan Murad III permission for English merchants to trade in any part of the Levant; in 1581 Queen Elizabeth issued letters patent to Harebone and his associates authorizing commerce with Turkey and with other parts of the East. In the years to come, under various charters, the Levant (or Turkey) Company brought to England luxuries in the form of silks, dates, raisins, drugs, and spices, and transported cloth, tin, and other English goods to Aleppo, to Bagdad, and even to faraway Agra, capital of the Indian Mogul.

By developing shipping and improving the quality of merchant vessels, the Levant Company contributed to the further advancement of overseas expansion. Englishmen were learning how to circumvent Fate and the Spaniards by building sturdy oaken ships which outsailed and outfought their rivals. So great was the pleasure of the Queen at their success that she and the Privy Council received members of the company in audience and commended them for their stout ships and the service they had rendered the kingdom.

The group destined to have the most profound influence upon English commerce—and the development of the empire beyond the seas—was the East India Company, which received its charter from the Queen on the very last day of the sixteenth century. The initial subscribers represented a cross section of the substantial classes of England and included nobles and knights, churchmen and great merchants, and some simpler folk with money to invest. The company's charter gave it the globe for its province, with the privilege of trading and buying lands without limitation in Africa, Asia, and America. In practice, however, the company concentrated its major activities in India and the East Indies.

For the first twelve years each of the East India Company's voyages was a separate financial venture for which stock was individually subscribed and profits taken without regard to other expeditions; but that procedure proved troublesome, and in 1612 the company became a true joint-stock company with profits and losses pooled from all ventures.

The emergence of the East India Company under the governorship of Sir Thomas Smythe, alderman of London, marks the beginning of a business expansion which was vastly accelerated in the first quarter of the seventeenth century. Smythe himself was connected with the most important enterprises of his day and in his own person reflects the quality of the new capitalism destined to establish England's power in the East and West. Pious and sincere, he believed that God had a special care for England's interest. Under his guidance, the East India Company operated with a high sense of national and religious destiny, albeit with a close attention to profits. The two objectives were not incompatible, and Smythe, like many of his Protestant contemporaries, felt that he was serving both God and his country by outwitting the Portuguese and the Spaniards and establishing English outposts in India and the New World.

Without seapower, which gradually developed under the Tudors, England could never have pushed her commercial tentacles into Asia, Africa, and America. The Royal Navy, like the Church of England, owes its foundation to Henry VIII, but while the Church was virtually an accident, the navy was the result of careful forethought. Before his time, such seapower as England possessed was part merchantman and part pirate—a quality retained in some degree throughout the sixteenth century—but Henry added to his informal navy a professional fleet, better rigged and better gunned than any warships afloat. An innovation of his shipbuilders was broadside armament with heavy, muzzle-loading cannon firing through portholes. This improvement vastly increased the firepower of English vessels, and that, combined with their greater mobility, gave the navy an enormous advantage over the traditional oared galleys which were still the main dependence of other nations. One of Henry's vessels, known as the "Great Harry," remained for years a byword for size and power.

England retained under Elizabeth the lead in design and navigation of warships. Sir John Hawkins, about 1577, began to build even more effective ships by increasing length and adding to the firepower of their broadsides. The fast and graceful ships of Elizabeth's navy could—and did—sail rings around the clumsy galleons of Spain.

Equally important as the improvement in ship-design was the evolution of the English sailor and the daring which he developed. The typical Elizabethan ship captain was a curious combination of buccaneer and pious Protestant, who looked upon Catholic Spain as a natural enemy and a source of profit. The common sailors were not very different from their commanders. Indeed, one of the qualities which distinguished English ships from most others in this period was the sturdy independence of their sailors and the equality of the men before the mast. Francis Drake, who ordered gentlemen and mariners in his ships to reef the same sails, was not the only commander to insist upon the democracy of work and danger. To the proud Spaniards could be left highfalutin and feudal notions of class distinctions, which landsmen might still accept, but which had no place at sea; and it was Spain's foolish class distinction between sailors and soldiers in her ships that helped to spell her ruin.

Along the west coast of England, and in the great port of London, youths watched the trim ships riding at anchor and dreamed of seafaring careers rich in honor and profit. Great names rang in their ears. Of these the best known were those famous cousins, John Hawkins and Francis Drake, both in due time knighted for their exploits.

Hawkins, from a West Country family of seamen, was responsible for a new and devious trade that in the two centuries following would put millions of pounds in British pockets and determine the quality of a large segment of American society. For Hawkins discovered the profits from "black ivory," the Negro slave trade from the coast of Guinea to the West Indies.

The Portuguese had long exploited the west coast of Africa, where they trafficked with local Negro kings for slaves, elephant tusks, and gold. News of the riches from this trade percolated into English port towns and aroused the cupidity of adventurous captains. More than one Portuguese vessel fell a prey to English pirates who were at times perplexed over the disposal of their human freight. It remained for John Hawkins, in 1562, to point the way which many a British ship would take in the years to come. In October of that year he sailed directly for Sierra Leone, loaded slaves, and took them to Hispaniola [Haiti] in open violation of the laws of Spain. But regardless of regulations decreed by Philip II, the planters of Hispaniola needed labor and would have willingly bought servants from any Englishman—or the devil. Hawkins received in exchange for his Negroes a valuable cargo of sugar, pearls, ginger, and cow hides—all saleable commodities on the European market. Thus began a triangular trade, which, with various modifications, continued until the British Empire abolished the slave traffic in 1807.

So successful was the voyage of 1562 that Hawkins was a made man, and two years later the Earl of Leicester, the Earl of Pembroke, and the Queen herself gave their support to similar expeditions. The Queen lent Hawkins a fine ship, the "Jesus of Lübeck"; the squadron of four vessels, which included the "Solomon," presently overtook and added "John the Baptist"—surely as well-named a fleet of slavers as ever touched the Guinea coast. After loading, the ships were becalmed, but since Hawkins was a devout man of religion, he prayed, and, in the words of one of his seaman, "Almighty God, who never suffereth his elect to perish," sent a fair wind that wafted the ships to the shores of Venezuela, where in January, 1565, the commander forced the Spaniards at gunpoint to purchase his Negroes. This voyage so profited the investors that Hawkins received a coat-of-arms with a crest bearing a "demi-Moor, proper, in chains."

Although Spain might protest against the illegality of exploits like Hawkins', and the Queen of England might officially deny responsibility for a set of piratical rogues, the English public applauded such deeds. Hawkins, Drake, and other buccaneers never lacked mariners, or financial backing from great merchants and noble lords. Negroes, readily sold to willing planters and miners in New Spain, and gold and silver seized on land and sea, brought easy money to common sailors and wealth to ship captains and their backers. Every returning treasure ship meant a new crop of legends which multiplied and stimulated afresh English interest in the New World.

Most epochal of the voyages was Francis Drake's circumnavigation of the globe, the first in which a commander returned to tell his own story, for Magellan, who had anticipated Drake's feat, lost his life in the Pacific. The expedition consisting of five vessels sailed from Plymouth Harbor on December 13, 1577. Drake's flagship, the "Pelican"—a name later changed to "Golden Hind" in compliment to a patron, Sir Christopher Hatton, whose crest bore that emblem—was the only vessel to make the entire voyage.

Sailing across the South Atlantic and along the coast of South America, Drake reached the Straits of Magellan at the end of October, 1578. Sixteen days later he entered the Pacific Ocean, which he himself had first seen five years before from a tree top in Panama. But instead of calm seas and favorable winds, the expedition encountered storms that would have discouraged weaker spirits. For fifty-two days they fought gales which swept them back almost around Cape Horn. The little squadron was hopelessly scattered; one ship was sunk and another made sail for England. Drake at last sighted the coast of Chile and, moving north, began a season of pillage the like of which no buccaneer had previously seen. Fat ships loaded with silver fell to his men; rich treasure towns lay sleeping in the sun waiting to be sacked. By the time Drake had cleared the west coast of Mexico, loot weighed down the "Golden Hind." From cabin boy to captain, every mariner felt secure in a fair share of wealth. Even the chaplain, Master Francis Fletcher, rejoiced in the spoil, for he had been allowed the altar silver at the sack of Santiago.

Somewhere on the coast of California Drake made a landing in July, 1579, the first contact of an Englishman with the western reaches of the North American continent. Indians flocked to the shore and listened with pleasure, Parson Fletcher reported, to the singing of Psalms and instruction in the Protestant religion.

Since all Spanish America would be on the watch in case Drake tried to return by Cape Horn, his only choice was to sail west. Touching the Philippines, Celebes, and other islands of the East—and narrowly escaping disaster—the "Golden Hind" at last reached England on September 26, 1580. In the following spring, Queen Elizabeth stepped aboard the little ship at Deptford and dubbed the commander knight. Thus the Queen signified to Spain—and to all of her own realm—the royal approval of successful adventures in any part of the world.

Hawkins, Drake, and a score of others of lesser name spread the renown of English seamen far and wide. More important, they stirred their own countrymen to look out from the little island upon a world which might be exploited for England's advantage. When Philip II, in 1588, at last decided that the time had come to crush this nest of heretics and interlopers, English seapower was already too strong.

Late in July, 1588, news reached London and the channel ports that a Spanish fleet, invincible in strength, was descending upon the English coast; at this word swift greyhounds of the sea assembled from the creeks and havens of the West Country. Then, with the help of a providential storm, Queen Elizabeth's little ships dispersed King Philip's huge Armada. For days they harried the unwieldy galleons, through the Channel, into the North Sea, and around Scotland to the shores of Ireland where some of the survivors went aground. When the toll of that battle was counted, the might of the Hapsburgs was broken and England could take her place as a world power. The Armada victory was one of the decisive battles of the world. Its outcome determined not only the destiny of England, but the future of North America, as events in the reign of Elizabeth's successor would demonstrate.

The Old World Background

The persistent hostility between England and Spain through most of the sixteenth century, characterized by the bitterest of political and religious antagonism, created the matrix which shaped many of the ideas that dominated English thinking for generations. Beginning with Henry VIII's desire for a divorce from a Spanish wife, Katherine of Aragon—a divorce the Pope refused to grant, not out of scruples, but from fear of Spain—events moved rapidly to cut England free of papal authority, to establish the King as supreme head of the Church, to draw future lines of conflict with Spain, and to bring in the Reformed religion as the faith of the mass of Englishmen.

Since papal interference had always aroused resentment in England, Henry's cunning in making the quarrel one between King and Pope—and a Pope subservient to Spain—swung the public to his side. Once having thrown down the gage of battle, Henry had to see it through, and England presently saw the strange spectacle of the sovereign who had written learnedly against Luther—Henry, the "Defender of the Faith"—turning monks and nuns out of their abbeys and giving aid and comfort to anti-clericalists among the rising commercial classes—the elements from whom a century later would come the most ardent Puritans. But Henry was not a wholehearted advocate of the Reformation. Indeed, he insisted upon conformity to most of the old theology and in 1539 approved the Six Articles which reaffirmed the doctrine of Transubstantiation, the confessional, and a celibate clergy. Dissenters courted death at the stake in Smithfield.

But the door was open for the New Religion. Henry himself expediently encouraged Archbishop Cranmer to translate the prayer book into English and to order the English Bible spread wide in every parish church. A public that could freely read the Scriptures would soon make its own interpretations. Already the influence of the priest as the intermediary before God was weakening. Soon the humblest weaver or shoemaker would feel capable of making his own petition to the Almighty—and of arguing as loudly as any bishop about religion. When the masses of men—and women—began to con the Scriptures and to prophesy, a way was blazed that eventually led to theological chaos more confusing than the diversity of tongues at Babel.

The strength of the English Reformation in the sixteenth century, however, lay in its acceptance by the commonality of citizens and its fusion with the rising spirit of nationalism. Even though many Englishmen still loved the sonorous Latin and the forms and rituals of the Roman church, adherence to Rome came more and more to be identified in popular thinking with hostile and alien powers, particularly the power of Spain. The Catholic interlude under Mary Tudor and her Spanish consort served only to confirm the average Englishman's suspicion that bondage to Spain and the retention of the Roman church were one and the same thing.

Queen Elizabeth, a shrewd ruler who knew better than most how to fit her policies to the temper of the people, never allowed the Reformation to get out of hand. Although Protestant refugees from all of Europe found asylum in her kingdom, bringing with them every variety of Reform belief, and theological differences among her own subjects were rife, Elizabeth made her Established Church elastic enough to maintain a reasonable conformity. Opposition to the authority of bishops, a distaste for vestments and ritual, and sundry other objections identified with Puritanism arose in her time, but the Queen by her personal tact and the diplomacy of her churchmen managed to keep a relative harmony between Church, State, and people.

Despite its apparent success, however, Elizabeth's policy of compromise, the celebrated *via media*, merely postponed the day of religious turmoil and ultimate revolution. Indeed, her compromises nurtured a spirit of independence and made impossible the enforcement of rigid conformity when her successors, the stiff-necked Stuarts, tried to pursue that illusory goal. The truth is that Pandora's box was open and no power could put back the thoughts on religion that took hold of the minds of men. The path from Cranmer's churches with their open Bibles led straight to Scrooby, and Delft, and finally to Plymouth and Boston in New England.

The religious transformation which England underwent in the sixteenth century was paralleled by other subtle and far-reaching changes in the intellectual habits and attitudes of Englishmen who reacted in their own way to that general European movement called the Renaissance. This term means many things to many men; scholars still engage in furious and sometimes acrimonious debate about the nature of the Renaissance, its origins and its characteristics, but, call it what we will, no one can refute the fact of a tremendous intellectual upheaval which by the end of the sixteenth century had stirred all of western Europe.

Some stimulus working in the minds of Italians, Frenchmen, Germans, Spaniards, or Englishmen produced various manifestations of a new spirit in art, music, literature, learning, and the whole complex of social relationships. Western Europe, which even in the dimmer times of the Dark Ages had never completely forgotten the heritage of Greece and Rome, now turned with fresh interest to the classics of antiquity as a source of instruction, delight, and wisdom. Plato was rediscovered; Aristotle attained greater stature; and metaphysicians set about reconciling the ancient philosophers and poets with their own Christian tradition. Like the Latin culture of the Middle Ages, the Renaissance spirit was European rather than characteristic of any one nation, but its qualities varied from country to country.

The ferment which produced the great art of Italy in the fifteenth and early sixteenth centuries acted more slowly in England as a leaven for literature and scholarship. The glory of the English Renaissance was the literature produced in the reign of Elizabeth: the epic poetry of Edmund Spenser, the rich cadences of Christopher Marlowe, the dramatic blank verse of William Shakespeare, the graceful sonnets of a Philip Sidney or a Walter Raleigh, and the prose and verse of a score of other writers, who, in a less distinguished age, would have shone as stars of the first magnitude. The literary brilliance of the Elizabethans outlived the Queen who gave her name to the age, and the afterglow of that period lasted far into the seventeenth century. In some respects, John Milton was more nearly an Elizabethan than a seventeenth-century Puritan.

In no other period has English literature combined so much of distinction in imagination with such high qualities of ethical purpose. If the Italian Renassiance was predominantly pagan—a point about which there is room for debate—the English Renaissance was primarily Christian and ethical in influence. The writings of English humanists like Sir Thomas Elyot and Roger Ascham, or the *Faerie Queene* of Edmund Spenser, reflect the fusion of classical and Christian traditions to produce a rationale of conduct both idealistic and eminently practical. Neither literature nor learning was an end in itself. Poets, teachers, and philosophers had as their goal the instruction of man so that he might be a proper member of society and a useful servant of the state.

But the state also was not an end in itself. The state, as ideally conceived by learned writers in the English Renaissance, was a hierarchy headed by a prince who insured order and justice between the component parts of society. Every man owed his service to the prince, each in his degree, so that all might bask in the sun of benign justice and develop those virtues implicit in his character. This conception was aristocratic, but the doctrine of aristocracy in the English Renaissance sternly taught that responsibility inevitably went with privilege. The notion of the duties and obligations of the privileged orders was emphasized by English Renaissance writers and became a tenet which gave strength and justification to incipient aristocracies established here and there in the colonies.

Learning in the English Renaissance enjoyed a prestige which was later transmitted to America as a zeal for education almost religious in its intensity. Elizabethan Englishmen were convinced of the utility of scholarship, for learning had not taken refuge in the cloister and it had for its purpose the production of good citizens and worthy leaders. "William Cecil," someone has pointed out, "might have remained a college don and crowned his life with an edition of Aristotle's *Politics;* instead he applied ancient wisdom (not without help from Macchiavelli) to practical statesmanship"—and made a success of Elizabeth's reign. The application of the wisdom of the ancients—and the moderns—to the world in which Renaissance Englishmen lived was proof of the vitality of their theories of education.

Of all the repositories of wisdom, pillaged by the Elizabethans for their education, none supplied more practical works of instruction than histories, ancient and modern. The rediscovery of the classics focussed attention once more upon the ideas of Greek and Roman writers who had treated historical themes, particularly those political problems which perennially are closest to every day life. The orations of Demosthenes and Cicero, the histories of Thucydides, Livy, and Tacitus, the examples of human nobility in Plutarch, and even the narratives of imperial wickedness in Suetonius supplied material for the inculcation of virtue and good citizenship. A translator of Euclid's geometry in 1570, one Henry Billingsley, a London merchant, observed that "the reading likewise of histories conduceth not a little to the adorning of the soul and mind of man, a study of all men commended; by it are seen and known the arts and doings of infinite wise men gone before us. In histories are contained infinite examples of heroical virtues to be of us followed, and horrible examples of vice to be of us eschewed." Two centuries later, an American, Thomas Jefferson, would accord classical history a similar importance in the instruction of man and would himself forego the reading of newspapers for the pleasure of re-reading Tacitus. The extent of the political lessons which Englishmen at home and in the colonies obtained from the contemplation of the virtues of republican Rome can never be definitely ascertained, but we can be sure that Englishmen reinforced their native traditions of liberty with classical examples and theories.

The Atlantic Frontier

Readers who discovered in history a practical utility applied the same purposefulness to other branches of literature and learning. In our own preoccupation with the esthetic values of the literature of the English Renaissance we are likely to forget that essentially it was didactic in purpose, designed to instruct as well as to delight. Art merely for art's sake would have been incomprehensible to Spenser, Shakespeare, or Milton. Political, practical, ethical, religious, or cosmic lessons occupied the minds of Renaissance writers and were not lost upon their readers. Later, when settlers in the English colonies along the Atlantic seaboard faced existence in a limitless wilderness they turned to writers of the immediate as well as the distant past for practical help in preserving the traditions of a civilized way of life.

The sixteenth century in England was a period of preparation—intellectual, spiritual, and material—for the expansion and development that took place in the seventeenth. Men's minds had been stirred as never before and the spirit of inquiry abroad in the land would increase until no holy of holies would be sufficiently sacrosanct to escape the curiosity of minds in search of truth. Traditional explanations of the physical universe no longer sufficed. Copernicus and Galileo, Thomas Digges and Francis Bacon, paved the way for scientific speculation and skepticism infinite in their implications. Continued exploration of the globe not only established geography as a science, but stimulated imaginations in every walk of life. Discoveries in physics led to further speculation as well as to mundane applications in the improvement of navigation. Characteristic of the practical approach of Englishmen was William Gilbert's treatise on magnetism in 1600 which began with a consideration of the mariner's compass and concluded with suggestions anticipating later discoveries in electricity. The new learning, both practical and speculative, permeated England and freed men's minds. "Tell me, who made the world," Marlowe has Faustus ask of the devil —a query blasphemous to the orthodox who conned their catechisms but pregnant with implications of the curiosity which an Elizabethan dared to admit.

The questioning spirit bold enough to inquire into the origins and workings of the physical universe would not let other things alone. When Milton sought in *Paradise Lost* to justify the ways of God to men, he was arguing a cause that had long occupied the thinking of his countrymen. Already in the sixteenth century men were not only asking about the relations of God to man but, more immediately, they were demanding an answer to inquiries concerning the ways of God's prelates and civil magistrates. Characteristically the Englishman in his questioning got down to cases. Not only did he speculate about the origins and workings of Church and State, but he began to agitate for specific reform and concrete improvements.

Someone has said that an Englishman is both afraid and embarrassed by an abstraction but fears no fiend or devil if visible. Perhaps for that reason sixteenth-century reformers in the church picked on such visible tokens as vestments and ceremonies as an object of attack, symbols which loomed in importance as Puritanism increased in the next reign. Similarly in the state, agitators complained of specific problems like the poor laws, taxes, and monopolies and talked little about abstract liberty. Nevertheless the individual's freedom to worship in accordance with his conscience and the right to enjoy just governance at the hands of civil authorities were much on the minds of the sixteenth century. The courage and will to defend these rights gathered strength under Elizabeth and rose to plague the obstinate Stuarts.

The accession of James I in 1603 marks the beginning of an era of realism and bourgeois progress fraught with momentous consequences for both England and America. In this age, colonization overseas begins, not, as in Spain, through the agency of government, but as a result of investments by men in search of profits. If the poet Spenser represents the romantic ebullience of an age of adventure and lyrical hope, the prose of Francis Bacon, calculating and pragmatic, is typical of the transition to the more matter-of-fact seventeenth century when the market place comes into its own.

James I was not a sovereign to excite the enthusiasm of poets, but the people welcomed him. To the populace he meant stability and security against civil strife at home and war abroad, for James was a declared man of peace. Within a year after his accession, he composed England's differences with the ancient enemy Spain—a peace which he was careful to keep. Although the King himself had small knowledge of business or economic processes, his peaceful succession to the throne reassured the commercial classes. Business men in Cheapside nodded approvingly and expressed the belief that the monarch was a "safe" man who would keep the country on an even keel. After the romantic idealism of the 1580's and 90's, which had been followed by a period of uncertainty and depression, the prosy dullness of James Stuart was precisely what the nation wanted. As so often in history, the reaction from a rarefied atmosphere of national enthusiasm was the desire for the unexciting and the commonplace, a condition which a colossal example of mediocrity in a later day described as "normalcy." James I was commonplace and comforting to men in the market place. Capital which had remained uninvested during the uncertain years of Elizabeth's decline now came out of hiding. Moneyed men sought new opportunities for trade and looked with fresh interest toward North America.

Although Spain traditionally had regarded the New World as virtually a private preserve, her strength in the early seventeenth century did not permit the assertion of ancient contentions with all of her former arrogance. When Englishmen finally made settlements in North America, her opposition was not sufficient to do more than frighten for the moment the timid king. After generations of delay, England was ready to take her place among the colonial powers.

The Old World Background

To give direction to the tremendous surge of trade and expansion the nation had a virile and intelligent middle class which had grown to power under the Tudors and had now become assertive. No aspect of seventeenth century society was more significant for the future quality of civilization in English America than the strength and ideology of this middle class.

As in the previous century, the class lines of the Stuart period remained fluid but roughly divisible into familiar classifications. At the top were the nobles, who stood apart, and the country gentry, composing the aristocracy; at the bottom were the hired laborers of the farms and towns, small farmers or husbandmen who earned their livelihoods by the labor of their own hands, and the artisans and lesser craftsmen of the towns; in between were the trading groups, the men of business and commerce, headed by the great merchants, and trailed by the shopkeepers, small tradesmen, and the more well-to-do craftsmen, the owners and operators of a variety of small but growing industries. Members of the learned professions, preachers, doctors, and lawyers, might come from any class and were usually assimilated either into the lesser gentry or the middle class depending largely upon their individual positions and areas of activity. Defying strict classification were the prosperous and independent yeomen who sometimes intermarried with the gentry. Of greater importance was the fact that England had no caste system: the constant flow of individuals from one class to another prevented that; there was no distinct military group and no class had a monopoly of preferment in the Church.

The middle class was numerous, strong, and rapidly increasing. The fact that Englishmen had small opportunity in the seventeenth century to attain honor or wealth by the sword forced enterprising young men to choose less exciting but more rewarding occupations in business. Trade, however, was not without the appeal of adventure, and Englishmen learned to look upon service with the East India Company, or with one of the corporate bodies organized for trade and settlement in America, with the gusto that Frenchmen or Spaniards regarded careers in the army. England was on its way to becoming a nation of shopkeepers indeed, but shopkeepers of a superior quality.

The predominance of London in the early seventeenth century was an important factor in the development of middle-class influence. London was the focal point of government, of social and intellectual life in the kingdom, of printing and the distribution of books, of communications and news, and of trade, both domestic and foreign. No other city approached it in commercial importance or in the number and wealth of its citizens. Out of the country's total population in 1603 of not more than four and a half million, London and its immediate environs counted close to two hundred and twenty thousand, and it was rapidly growing despite recurrences of the plague and proclamations of the king against crowding to the city. By comparison, even such enterprising towns as Bristol, Plymouth, and Norwich were yet scarcely more than villages.

Despite a considerable number of the gentry who swarmed to London for social or political reasons, the bulk of the population belonged to the middle class. And nowhere at that time, unless in Holland, was there a more intelligent and articulate bourgeoisie. Enterprising, shrewd, keen, and alert, Londoners of the seventeenth century were profoundly concerned with education, self-improvement, and the advancement of their intellectual as well as their financial status. Ambitious Americans of the nineteenth and twentieth centuries would have understood the aspirations and methods of their spiritual ancestors.

London in the early years of the seventeenth century was an exciting place. Its shops were filled with the produce of the world: rich silks from China, drugs and spices from the East Indies, tobacco and new herbs, guaranteed to cure all ailments, from America, glassware from Venice, rugs and silver ornaments from Persia and India, furs from Russia or North America. Through the Royal Exchange, built by Sir

The Old World Background

Thomas Gresham, strode an endless procession of men, most of them still young, who had seen the far places of the earth and had tall stories to tell. Reports swept the town of the immense profits from a single cargo of pepper or of wealth to be had in a few years' trade overseas. Every provincial apprentice in England dreamed of going to London where he would make his fortune and perhaps in time wear about his neck the Lord Mayor's golden chain.

A great city, populated by men with alert and active minds, is a favorable milieu for the development of vigorous opinions. By constant association with a shifting, multifarious, and stimulating populace, the London citizen sharpened his wits and improved his intellect. From the printing presses poured a steady stream of books and pamphlets on every conceivable subject which he read for what they might teach him, or, at times, for entertainment. From the ranks of London's citizens came many of the writers who supplied the printers with copy, and the city's population attained an importance and influence far in excess of its numerical strength. Though Oxford and Cambridge were the seats of learning, London was actually the intellectual capital, and its middle class reflected the quality of the city.

The ideology of London's citizens, especially their concepts of religion and ethics, had a profound influence upon the rest of the nation and ultimately upon the colonies overseas. Protestantism, which had become firmly established as the official religion of England in the reign of Elizabeth, had been steadily swinging toward Puritanism, and by the reign of James I, London had become a hotbed of nonconformity. Preachers in the rich city churches, supported by their congregations, spoke boldly against the bishops and refused to observe rituals and ceremonies which seemed to them relics of superstition. While Puritanism in varying degrees was growing in East Anglia, the Midlands, and in other parts of England, Jacobean London became an articulate voice demanding that the body of the Church be purged of "Popish corruption." Although the city's preachers generally remained technically in the fold of the Church of England, they displayed a sympathy for nonconformity which in another generation would split the ecclesiastical establishment and bring a king to the executioner's block.

The political consequences of Puritanism with its constantly accelerating trend toward independency were obvious to King James who dourly summed up the situation by grumbling, "No bishop, no king." In a manner hard for a twentieth-century American to comprehend, religion was inseparably bound up with politics throughout the sixteenth and seventeenth centuries, and by the time of the first Stuarts, the dissensions within the ranks of Protestants raised political issues affecting the lives of every citizen. In the political ascendancy of Puritanism, with all of its implications for colonial America, the resurgent middle class, centered in London, had the loudest voice and wielded the greatest power.

The social and ethical views of these middle-class Puritans not only helped shape the thinking of seventeenth century England but became the cornerstone of bourgeois civilization transmitted to America. Much has been written about the influence of Calvinistic religion upon the rise of capitalism. Since Max Weber at the beginning of the present century published his famous treatise on capitalism and the Protestant ethic, social historians have had a field day debating the merits of his thesis and trying to determine the part Calvinism —or Puritanism—played in the rapid development of commercial society. Although the capitalistic spirit was not a monopoly of the Calvinists, the English middle class did find Puritan ethics notably congenial. The mercantile groups evolved a creed of success which emphasized the same ascetic qualities glorified by Puritan preachers. From their masters on week days and from preachers on Sunday, apprentices heard commendations of diligence, sobriety, honesty, and thrift. If strict predestinarians could not promise that the practice of these prudential virtues would insure a seat at the right hand of Abraham, they nevertheless conveyed the notion that conspicuous adherence to the code would be evidence of election. Moreover, a code which permitted no extravagant follies, no sins that wasted either time or money, and kept its adherents everlastingly at the job in hand would almost inevitably guarantee material success. God would smile upon the diligent and pious apprentice who in time would become a great merchant with money to lend and apprentices of his own to guide along the same straight and narrow road to prosperity. Given a normal amount of intelligence and an even break of luck, the seventeenth century business man who austerely practiced the prudential virtues could scarcely avoid success in his vocation. There was not much else for him to do.

Preachers in their sermons, writers of handbooks on behavior, fathers in advice to their sons, all emphasized the gospel of work. Diligence in one's vocation became a cardinal principle of conduct. The avoidance of idleness was a moral issue upon which the salvation of the soul, and, incidentally, one's earthly success, might depend.

The glorification of work as an end in itself, so useful to middle-class Puritans, was not confined to them but permeated much of the social theory of the seventeenth century. Indeed, bourgeois ethics in general subtly colored even aristocratic treatises on conduct. Richard Brathwaite, a country gentleman himself, in his treatise entitled *The English Gentleman* (1630), at times sounds for all the world like a London merchant moralizing on behavior, for Brathwaite set out to produce a godly and succesful man equipped with the Christian virtues of his day. Far different was the earlier Renaissance rationale of conduct for the gentlemen, a system which emphasized the complete development of a well-rounded personality. By Brathwaite's time, however, some of the accomplishments necessary to the earlier aristocrat were no longer prized. More admired than a versatile and charming personality was the grave man, eternally vigilant to make the best use of his time. The gentry were not exempt from the compulsions so commended by bourgeois Puritans.

Brathwaite stresses this point: "Men in great place (sayeth one) are thrice servants; servants of the sovereign, or state; servants of fame; and servants of business: so they have no freedom, neither in their persons, nor their actions, nor in their times." The necessity of devoting all of one's time to the service of family, church, and commonwealth finds constant iteration among moralistic writers in this period. A gospel of work with this additional social implication was an inspired doctrine vouchsafed a people destined to create new commonwealths in the wilderness of America.

The social importance of the English country gentry in the seventeenth century was almost as significant for later developments in America as was the rise of the middle class. The two groups in fact were not so far apart in their thinking as we have sometimes believed. Puritanism gained favor in manor houses, especially in East Anglia, no less than in market places. Country gentlemen were sometimes even more austere in their adherence to the Puritan creed than their brethren of London or Norwich; furthermore, many of the social views of both Puritans and Anglicans had much in common. Protestantism, of whatever persuasion, modified the theories of conduct distilled from Renaissance treatises like Castiglione's *Book of the Courtier* and emphasized the negative virtues of self-denial as well as the positive good of public service.

The constant flow of younger sons of country squires into the ranks of the mercantile classes and the reverse tendency which induced well-to-do tradesmen to buy land and retire to the country, or to marry the daughters of aristocrats, served to mix the middle class and gentry inextricably. Since the minor aristocracy could not stand aloof from members of their own families and freeze into a caste, one hears little nonsense from the seventeenth-century gentry about despising trade. In an era of gradual inflation when fixed rents grew smaller and smaller in real purchasing power, the gentry could not help envying the adaptable middle class, participating when possible in its prosperity, and, incidentally, sharing many of its points of view.

For generations the gentry had been the backbone of government in rural England—a tradition which made self-government in colonial America a reality from the very first. The Tudors had ruled England successfully through the justices of the peace chosen from substantial county families. The prestige of these officials was high; their sense of responsibility both to the people and the sovereign was great; and, for all of Shakespeare's satire of Justice Shallow, they were generally competent. When their legal learning was deficient, they depended upon their commonsense—a quality in English justice which has distinguished it from that day to this.

The evolution of a class of natural leaders, selected from a sort of middle-class gentry, kept the administration of government in the hands of men still close to the soil. If the squires were not always precisely tribunes of the people, their own interests were sufficiently identified with the good of their tenants and neighbors to make them genuine representatives of popular government. Shrewdly the Tudors knew that they must retain the love of the country's natural leaders if they were to flourish and govern happily. Because the Stuarts signally lacked this perception and the capacity for retaining the co-operation of either the gentry or middle class, they eventually blundered into civil war.

The country gentry united with progressive members of the middle class to oppose encroachments upon traditional English rights attempted by James I and his son Charles I. Over the centuries, from the granting of Magna Charta onward, Englishmen had gradually increased their liberties. Backed by the common law—that great body of legal precedents accumulated through the years—the people were accustomed to seek legal redress in the courts and in Parliament against injustices from the sovereign or his officers. This notion of the supremacy of the common law would be taken to America and play a great part in the colonists' insistence upon their rights as inheritors of the legal tradition. The squires and the middle class found in Parliament a training ground for political leadership which, by the mid-seventeenth century, gave them power sufficient to depose royal authority, but it was characteristic that they dethroned and executed Charles I by due process of law. To the intelligence and courage of the minor gentry in Parliament during the first half of the seventeenth century, the House of Commons owed much of its prestige. These men represented the best in the Renaissance ideal of leadership, modified by middle-class and Puritan concepts of earnest application to duty. They believed that a citizen had an obligation to be learned and to utilize his learning, if need be, in defense of the common rights of Englishmen. Their political creed became the doctrine of the wisest of colonial leaders.

Seventeenth-century Englishmen realized the inseparable connection between political liberty and freedom of the mind. Long before John Milton gave classic expression to the ideal in *Areopagitica*, plain men had been putting its doctrines into practice. In few other periods has the average man placed so high a premium upon learning, and rarely has an age produced so many lawyers, preachers, and men of everyday affairs who exemplified the learned ideal. Their learning, based upon an understanding of the wisdom of the ancients, was not narrowly professional but was intensely purposeful.

At the beginning of the next century, a French traveller, Louis de LaHontan, who had observed Englishmen on both sides of the Atlantic, remarked: "I enjoy in England a sort of liberty that is not met with elsewhere. For one may justly say that of all the countries inhabited by civilized people, this alone affords the greatest perfection of liberty of the mind, for I am convinced that the English maintain it with a great deal of tenderness. So true it is that all degrees of slavery are abhorred by this people, who show their wisdom in the precautions they take to prevent their sinking into a *fatal* servitude." This ideal of the freedom of the mind, carefully nurtured and combined with the notion of learning for a purpose—the purpose of serving society as well as one's self—was carried to the New World where it helped to assure an intelligent body of leaders capable of establishing and defending the tradition of liberty.

The motives which first sent Englishmen overseas to seek homes in the unfriendly forests of Virginia and New England were as complex as the society which had developed in England by the end of the first third of the seventeenth century, a society whose qualities would largely determine the nature of American culture for generations to come. If England had ever been homogeneous in social structure and mental attitude, that condition was long since past. The tendency of society all through the Tudor and Stuart periods was to develop differences, to produce a spirit of individualism, sometimes to break into separate fractions. Although this quality was implicit in the very thesis of the Protestant's independent and individual relation to God, religion was not the only explanation of the diversity of attitudes in the seventeenth century. Almost as important was the Renaissance educational heritage emphasizing the cultivation of the individual personality. Politically, socially, and intellectually, Englishmen were growing constantly more individualistic—and more independent. The air tingled with an electrical restlessness felt in all of England. Few communities were so isolated that they did not react to changes taking place in their fluid world. The atmosphere of the age stimulated men to take speculative risks. They were not afraid to adventure their persons, their purses, their minds, and even their immortal souls in pursuit of ends deemed good. For many men —and women—for one reason or another, this pursuit led across the stormy waters of the Atlantic.

The sheer spirit of adventure must not be overlooked in accounting for the impulse that drove Englishmen overseas. Since the great days of buccaneering, the New World had been a land of romantic fascination. During the peaceful years of James's reign, youths whose fathers might have signed on the "Golden Hind" to raid the Spanish Main had to find other outlets for their energies. The more prosaic business of joining a colonial enterprise was not without its appeal. Many a youth went to Virginia or New England for no other reason than to escape a humdrum life at home. What proportion of settlers, old and young, consisted of this type of adventurer we can never know, but on every English and American frontier they have always been numerous. Much has been made of religious persecution as a cause of English migrations overseas. No one can deny that religious reasons were strong with certain groups, but we have over-emphasized English persecution as a motive. So firmly fixed is this idea that we have created a popular legend that English America was peopled by refugees, fleeing for their lives and liberties, who set about establishing the principles of toleration when they reached these shores. In reality there was much less active persecution under the first two Stuarts than we have been led to believe, and the refugees, like most people in the seventeenth century, had no patience with toleration. The very fact that religious quarrels were so rife, repression so difficult, and conformity so ill-enforced argues the lack of violent religious persecution. The truth is that England enjoyed, even under the relatively severe exertions of Archbishop Laud, more freedom of conscience than any country in Europe except Holland. But Protestantism, which had no rigid Inquisition to hold heretics in check, inevitably produced sectaries to whom any restraint was anathema. Ecclesiastical authorities under both James I and his successor silenced some preachers for violating their oaths to conform to the Anglican ritual. An occasional sectary landed in jail for what was regarded as disorderly conduct in failing to observe the established religious decorum. But regulations which English dissenters hated as oppression would have seemed to an Italian or a Spaniard of that day a fantastic dream of license, if not of freedom.

Annoyance of nonconforming folk there was in abundance, and to independent spirits persistent annoyance became tyranny and persecution. Objections to regulation were sufficient indeed to induce many earnest souls to leave England for Holland or the New World where they hoped, usually in vain, to worship undisturbed by schismatics within the fold and oppressors without. Officially the government encouraged emigrants for religious reasons to settle in the dominions beyond the seas, and it is worthy of note that the government rarely pursued them with objectionable regulations. In time both Protestant and Catholic dissidents would find refuge under the British flag in America.

The most impelling single motive which induced emigrants to leave England was the desire for land and all that the possession of broad acres implied. Land hunger frequently was joined with other considerations—the lure of adventure, the desire for religious freedom, or any number of a multitude of frustrations at home—but the emigrant's brightest dream was the vision of becoming a landed proprietor. Even the poorest servant, who sold himself into a four-years' bondage to pay his passage, had a hope of ultimately settling upon a piece of ground which he would own in fee simple.

Americans, brought up in a country where anyone for a modest sum can purchase at least a small farm or a building lot, have difficulty comprehending the value which the seventeenth-century Englishman, of whatever degree, placed upon the possession of land. Most English soil was tightly held; and for such land as could be bought, the demand was great. Younger sons of the gentry, left without landed estates under the law of primogeniture, purchased holdings when they could. Rich merchants and tradesmen with money to invest eagerly sought country estates, the symbol of social prestige. Under the dual stimulation of inflation and an ever-increasing demand, land prices rose during the first half of the seventeenth century until only the well-to-do could buy, at exorbitant rates, desirable country property.

The scarcity of purchasable land and the throngs of unemployed wanderers in Jacobean England gave rise to a popular notion that the country was over-populated and required an outlet for its surplus people. An island which today supports a population of more than forty-one million can scarcely have been burdened with less than five million souls, but the shifts in the balance between agriculture and industry had temporarily displaced many farmers and other laborers, who gave the impression of an excess of indigent people. Periodic financial depressions, notably between 1619 and 1624, also magnified the indications of impending calamity and convinced observers that settlements overseas were the only solution of acute—and permanent—unemployment.

Propagandists outdid themselves in commending the establishment of colonies in America. Poets, ballad writers, pamphleteers, and preachers took up the theme. Verily in North America Eden might be rediscovered. The fertility of the soil exceeded that in the valleys of the Nile or Euphrates. Every plant needful and pleasant flourished there. Fish, fowl, and beasts of the field seemed especially created for man's pleasure and profit. The climate was benign and the air wholesome. "Many that have been weak and sickly in old England, by coming hither have been thoroughly healed and grown healthful and strong," wrote the Reverend Francis Higginson from Massachusetts in 1630. Such was the softness of the air that he himself, who had "not gone without a cap for many years together, neither durst leave off the same, have now cast away my cap and do wear none at all in the day time." Though Higginson, ironically, died of tuberculosis within a year, his words must have encouraged prospective emigrants.

Preachers and other writers pointed out that colonization overseas would be a stroke for both God and King—as well as a direct profit to the individual settler. By taking the gospel message to heathen Indians, colonists would win the favor of the Almighty. By establishing outposts in America against England's enemies, they would perform a patriotic service. The new settlements would consume the goods of English merchants, furnish a ready supply of commodities useful to the mother country, and provide homes and farms for every needy person. This doctrine rang from press and pulpit.

One of the most persuasive books on colonization—one now almost forgotten—came from the pen of the Reverend Richard Eburne, vicar of Henstridge in Somerset, who published in 1624 *A Plain Pathway to Plantations*, commending in particular a settlement in Newfoundland and advocating in general a program of expansion overseas. Although the depression which had been responsible for considerable unemployment in the previous five years was really caused by a constriction of credit by the merchants and money-lenders of London, Eburne interpreted it as a result of luxury, extravagance, and sloth induced by an era of peace and prosperity. Life in the colonies would correct the tendency to idleness which had been growing, he believed, and restore to Englishmen their former virtues of diligence and thrift. The standard of living had improved, especially for urban and industrial groups, and Eburne remarked, quite correctly, that "Englishmen above many others are worst able to live with a little." To his countrymen, who had become accustomed to the good things of this world, the author held out the hope of renewed prosperity, combined with wholesome virtue, in the plantations across the sea.

The ordinary Englishman's refusal to be content with a little, as Eburne hints, resulted in a great stir of action during times of depression. The fundamental health of the economic system rather than its decay explains the vigor of emigrants who went abroad to carry a little of England with them. "Imagine all that to be England where English men, where English people, you with them, and they with you, do dwell," admonished Richard Eburne, anticipating Rupert Brooke by three centuries. "And it be the people that makes the land English, not the land the people. So you may find England, and an happy England too, where now is, as I may say, no land." When times got hard, seventeenth-century citizens were too virile to accept distress supinely; they were men of action, with minds of their own, willing and able to make another England, improved and happier, in realms that waited their conquest.

Whether discontent was caused by grievances against the religious establishment, distress in the pocketbook, or plain restlessness, the Englishman, like his descendant in nineteenth-century America, had a remedy. He could begin a new life in a frontier society to the west, where he would carry his dream of a better world.

A Frenchman naturalized in America at the end of the colonial period, one who called himself Hector St. John de Crèvecoeur, gave a classic definition of an American, a definition often quoted but eternally charming: "He is an American who, leaving behind him all his ancient prejudices and manners, receives new ones from the new mode of life he has embraced, the new government he obeys, and the new rank he holds. He becomes an American by being received in the broad lap of our great *Alma Mater*. Here individuals of all nations are melted into a new race of men, whose labours and posterity will one day cause great changes in the world. Americans are the western pilgrims, who are carrying along with them that great mass of arts, sciences, vigor, and industry which began long since in the east; they will finish the great circle." Though true in essence, de Crèvecoeur's statement is in part misleading. The immigrant did not undergo an immediate sea-change; he was not, in the language of the Scriptures, born again; he did not leave behind him all his prejudices, manners, and customs. On the contrary, he brought to the New World a full panoply of ancient ideas and concepts, some of which flourished with renewed vigor in fresh soil. And though he was a part of all he had met, he was not a bond-slave of the past. Though the crystallized experience of a cycle of Europe lay behind him, he was ready—slowly—to adapt his traditional belief to the conditions of a new life. The immigrants of Virginia, New England, Pennsylvania, New York, or any of the other colonies, were a varied and complex lot, who, in time, were

INDIAN LIFE IN VIRGINIA

(A) chief's house (B) place for solemn prayers (C) ceremonial dance (D) feast spread (E) tobacco plants (F) watchman to scare birds from corn fields (G) corn growing (H) squash field (K) ceremonial fire (L) water supply

From the Huntington Library copy of Theodor DeBry, *Admirando Narratio Fida Tamen . . .* (Frankfurt, 1590).

LOADING TOBACCO AT A PLANTER'S WHARF

From the Huntington Library copy of Thomas Jeffreys, *Atlas* (1776).

The Old World Background

fused into Americans as described by de Crèvecoeur. But in the seventeenth century they were like Adam and Eve at the end of *Paradise Lost*:

> *The world was all before them, where to choose*
> *Their place of rest, and Providence was their guide.*

CHAPTER TWO

Patrician and Yeoman in the Chesapeake Bay Colonies

FOR a decade preceding the crisis of the Spanish Armada, two opposing views of England's immediate destiny in the New World struggled for dominance in English politics. Prudent, cautious, realistic Lord Burleigh headed a faction of "little Englanders," who sought to increase the nation's prosperity and stability by working out a *modus vivendi* with Spain and encouraging trade with the Continent. Burleigh, who understood more clearly than most of his contemporaries the inability of Elizabeth's government to finance expensive military outlays, feared that any English attempt to demand a place in the American sun would precipitate a disastrous war; furthermore, he had no stomach for vague schemes of settling plantations across three thousand miles of stormy ocean. The sound business enterprise of the cloth merchants, with their profitable trade to the Low Countries and Germany, was more to his liking. Burleigh's group opposed, at least for the time being, any effort at colonial expansion overseas and any undue provocation of Spain. Arrayed against these conservatives was another faction, composed of younger and more adventurous spirits—men like Sir Walter Raleigh, Sir Francis Walsingham, Sir Humphrey Gilbert, Francis Drake, and Richard Hakluyt—who burned with rage against Spain and demanded that England snatch a portion of the good earth on the American mainland. In the opinion of these men, the future of England was at stake. The country must procure outposts against Spain in the western ocean or be content with a humble place in European politics.

The ablest spokesman and propagandist for this group of incipient imperialists was Richard Hakluyt, a parson who made the doctrine of colonial expansion a religion and preached the belief that it was part of the divine plan for England to seize an empire in North America. Shrewdly and sincerely Hakluyt argued that England had an obligation before God to carry the message of the Protestant gospel to the Indians as a countermeasure against the Catholic faith spread by Spain. Appealing to every prejudice of his Protestant countrymen, and emphasizing every theme of self-interest, Hakluyt kept up a persistent demand for colonies overseas.

The first expedition seriously to attempt an English colony in America was led by Sir Humphrey Gilbert, supported by his half-brother, Sir Walter Raleigh, who supplied one ship. Arriving on August 5, 1583, at St. John's harbor, Newfoundland—already the dwelling place of a rough and polyglot group of fishermen—Gilbert took possession and proclaimed that henceforth the religion of the place would conform to the rites of the Church of England. His plan was to return with a complement of settlers. Despite the Anglican bias of the leader, Gilbert's expedition had the backing of certain English Catholics who hoped to establish in Newfoundland a refuge for their co-religionists. Unhappily, Gilbert's ship went down on the homeward voyage, and the colony never materialized.

Though Gilbert's adventure failed, the germ of the colonial idea remained alive. Raleigh was determined to establish in the North Atlantic region a colony of Englishmen who would be profitable to both promoter and commonwealth, and would serve as a bulwark against the encroachments of Spain in North America. Raising money among his friends and dipping into his own pocket, he sent out an exploring expedition in 1584 under Philip Amadas and Arthur Barlow, who, on their return, reported the sight of fruitful and goodly lands which they had claimed in the name of the Queen. Their investigation had taken them into Pamlico and Albemarle Sounds, and along the coast of North Carolina. So glowing was their account that Queen Elizabeth was pleased to call the territory Virginia in honor of her maiden state. For two decades this name would apply to all the land from Florida to Newfoundland.

In the spring of 1585, Raleigh sent out a fleet of seven vessels under the command of his cousin, Sir Richard Grenville, to take possession of vague and undefined Virginia. Among the hundred men who went along as settlers were John White, an artist who painted the first accurate pictures of the Indians, and Thomas Hariot, who wrote the first eye witness account of Virginia. Ralph Lane was named governor. The spot selected was Roanoke Island, at the upper end of Pamlico Sound, and there the colonists built their huts.

Although the terms of Raleigh's charter granted him sovereign powers, certain provisions were pregnant with meaning for English America. The settlers and their descendants, the charter declared, "shall and may have all the privileges of free denizens, and persons native of England." The proprietor might establish such laws and ordinances as seemed best for the government of his colony, "so always as the said statutes, laws, and ordinances may be as near as conveniently may be agreeable to the form of the laws, statutes, government, or policy of England." These simple phrases, plain and undramatic, meant that emigrants when they took ship would carry with them the legacy of the common law and all the liberties and privileges which Englishmen had won for themselves over the centuries. Future charters granted to other colonial promoters would carry those essential guarantees against absolutism.

If Walter Raleigh appeared as a bright star in Elizabeth's galaxy, he was in reality a man born to trouble. All his grandest schemes came to naught. Among the earliest of the disasters that darkened his career were the misfortunes of his Virginian enterprises. After a miserable year on Roanoke Island, the first colony was glad to give up and go home when a fleet commanded by Francis Drake anchored in the sound. Two weeks after their departure, Grenville returned, found the colony gone, and himself departed leaving fifteen men as a token of English possession. Raleigh sent out another group of colonists in the spring of 1587 under the governorship of John White, the artist. They too settled on Roanoke Island and had for company only the ghosts of the fifteen men left by Grenville, not one of whom had survived. After a month Governor White sailed for England to procure additional help and supplies. Among the settlers at Roanoke he left his own daughter, Eleanor, wife of Ananias Dare, and their baby, Virginia Dare, the first white child born in English America. Nearly four years elapsed before the governor or any other Englishman came back. Ships intended for the succor of the colony went off privateering, or were held at home to defend England against the Spanish Armada. When White finally reached Roanoke in March, 1591, the colony had disappeared, leaving as a clue the letters "CRO" cut in the bark of a tree and the word "Croatoan" carved on a post. From that day to this, no one has solved the mystery of the "lost colony." Raleigh had spent his money to no effect. Courtiers of the Tudor Queen were not destined to found an empire.

Raleigh's efforts, however, were not altogether in vain. Without his pioneering, the English public might not have been ready to support later and more successful enterprises. And two incidental consequences of his activities, seemingly trivial at the time, would have far-reaching results. Ralph Lane brought back the white potato—or so it is said—and Raleigh cultivated it on his Irish estate. In time the lowly potato would transform the food economy, not only of Ireland, but of large parts of Europe. Raleigh also popularized, if he did not introduce, the smoking of tobacco; the vogue of that weed would bring prosperity to later colonies in the region where he had tried to make a settlement.

The first English colony to survive owed its support to the enterprise of London merchants who were instrumental in organizing the Virginia Company of London in 1606. A second corporate body called the Virginia Company of Plymouth was created at the same time. The two groups were authorized to choose domains in "Virginia," by that time conceived to include the territory from the Cape Fear River in North Carolina to the forty-fifth parallel of latitude in Maine. The southern portion would be the special province of the London company.

From Raleigh's time onward promoters had kept alive colonial aspirations. As early as 1589, Raleigh himself had turned over certain of his chartered rights to a syndicate of London merchants who included Sir Thomas Smythe, later a prime mover in the Virginia Company. A year after James I, in 1604, made peace with Spain, the Earl of Southampton and Sir Thomas Arundel dispatched Captain George Weymouth to explore the American coast with a view to establishing a Catholic refuge there. Weymouth landed on the coast of Maine in May and captured five Indians whom he brought back to England and taught enough words to praise the climate and richness of their country, a feat worthy of the ingenuity of modern realtors. Sir Ferdinando Gorges and Sir John Popham, through the Plymouth Company, busied themselves in an effort to establish a colony in Maine and at least succeeded in stimulating public interest. In the meantime, the French through the Canada Company had seriously undertaken the exploration of the land to the north, and Samuel Champlain set out in 1606 on the first of his expeditions. A rising fever of speculation and activity stirred men's pulses on both sides of the English Channel in the early years of the seventeenth century. Soon America was on the minds of innumerable investors and adventurers.

The Virginia Company of London found it easy in 1606 to raise funds and enlist men for its first endeavor. Late in

Patrician and Yeoman on the Chesapeake

December of that year it had three ships, loaded with supplies, tied up at the Blackwall dock. A motley group numbering slightly more than one hundred men in search of adventure rather than homes in the wilderness went aboard, and the vessels, commanded by Captain Christopher Newport, dropped down the Thames to begin one of the longest and most tedious trans-Atlantic crossings on record. Sea-weary but undaunted, at last near the middle of May, the voyagers sailed into the smooth waters of the James, and selected a haven, far up the river, where they could anchor in six fathoms and tie up to the trees of a shady peninsula. A soft breeze blew from the land, bees droned lazily in the plum bushes, and the air was fragrant with flowers and the odor of strawberries. This surely was the promised land. The men carried their stores ashore and erected a fort. In honor of their sovereign they named the spot Jamestown. After a few weeks Captain Newport bade farewell to the settlers and sailed for home. On his return he reported to Lord Salisbury that the country was "excellent and very rich in gold and copper." Captain Newport also bore a letter from the governing council in the colony to the Virginia Company declaring the goodness of the land and imploring reinforcements and supplies lest the "all devouring Spaniard lay his ravenous hands upon these gold showing mountains, which if we be so enabled he shall never dare to think on."

Only a few of the first immigrants looked upon Virginia as a place of permanent abode. They still had the Elizabethan dream of quick riches from gold and precious stones. The majority of the adventurers were denominated "gentlemen," and hardly more than a quarter could be described as artisans and laborers. Most distinguished, in point of birth, was George Percy, eighth son of the Earl of Northumberland, whose *Observations* provides one of the earliest accounts of the colony. Unhappily for genealogists who prize legends of nobility, he did not remain to establish his line in Virginia. Intent upon discovering mountains of gold, or pearls and rubies believed to be common in the sands of the rivers, the immigrants showed small inclination for the drudgery of cutting trees and tilling the soil. Moreover, they were undisciplined and contentious. Of the seven men named to the ruling council, some had already quarreled with the others before landing. At length after many disputes Captain John Smith emerged as a dominant spirit capable of enforcing discipline and organizing the group into something approaching a civil society. Some of the gentlemen, volunteering for hard labor, set a good example to the others. During the second year Captain Smith could praise a few of the gentlemen-woodchoppers, though he admits that blistered hands caused many a blasphemous oath. To improve their manners, he decreed that for each oath an offender should have a can of cold water poured down his sleeve. Thus Captain Smith maintained the proprieties and got a certain amount of work out of his band of gallants.

Despite quarrels, starvation, and the constant threat of attacks from the Indians, the little colony survived. Smith himself was captured by braves of the Indian ruler Powhatan and barely escaped with his life. Whether he was rescued dramatically by Powhatan's daughter Pocahontas as he described later in his *General History of Virginia* (1624) is a moot question, but the tale at least made a colorful legend. Corn and game bought from the Indians kept the settlers alive during more than one period of crisis. A few reinforcements from England added a little to the strength of the colony.

The Virginia Company in 1609 received a new charter providing for the appointment of a governor in place of the colony's ruling council; it chose Lord Delaware for the post. Hopes for the prosperity of the enterprise were renewed. Delaware delayed his own departure but sent Sir Thomas Gates to rule temporarily in his stead. Gates' expedition of nine ships, with over six hundred men, women, and children, met with storms and disaster. One vessel was sunk; another containing Gates himself foundered in the Bermudas, but the crew and passengers made shore, and a year later, in two pinnaces of their own building, reached Jamestown. Seven of the ships with approximately four hundred passengers landed at Jamestown in August, 1609. Shortly after the fleet's arrival, Captain John Smith received so serious an injury in a powder explosion that he returned to England. The winter of 1609–10 almost saw the end of the colony. The new arrivals had not brought enough food for subsistence, and supplies from the Indians failed. Fearing the savages, the settlers dared not venture far beyond their palisades in search of game or fuel. During the cold months of January and February, they burned the hewn clapboards of their huts and lived on mice, rats, and such roots as they could dig. Desperate in this "starving time" a few miscreants turned cannibal and rifled new made graves. One man murdered his wife and salted her body away like pork. Without the strong hand of John Smith the settlers sank into primitive chaos and waited dismally for the end.

At last, in May, 1610, Sir Thomas Gates arrived from Bermuda. Of the five hundred or more immigrants, he found only about sixty embittered survivors who demanded to be taken from the accursed place. Gates agreed to embark with them for Newfoundland in the hope of finding aid among the fishing fleet, but on the way down the James he met Lord Delaware with a relief expedition. They turned back and once more undertook to establish themselves on the verge of the forest. Although grief and misfortune afflicted them at intervals in later years, English settlers never again deserted the soil of Virginia.

From 1607 until 1624, the colony of Virginia was a business enterprise operated by a stock company for profit— or so the shareholders hoped. Sir Thomas Smythe, the first treasurer of the Virginia Company, was also governor of the East India Company and an officer in other corporations. Impressed by the enormous profits made in early voyages of the East India Company, stockholders in the Virginia Company dreamed of similar riches. Their hopes were kept at a high level by a campaign of publicity more intense and shrewd than any the country had previously experienced. Pamphleteers and preachers were enlisted in the cause. No less a person than Dr. John Donne, the poet and dean of St. Paul's, received stock in the company for his advocacy of the enterprise. Others, less conspicuous but more gifted than the metaphysical dean in the lucid style of advertisers, offered their pens and their pulpits. With one accord the clergy praised Virginia as a commonwealth destined to establish English Protestantism in the New World, to be a fortress against Spain, and to become a source of ultimate profit to the shareholders, whom they urged to have patience. Congregations were hardly through talking about Sunday's sermon before the Virginia Company placed a copy of it in the hands of some printer. If shareholders received no dividends to tuck into their purses, they at least had many hopeful assurances of God's blessing upon their endeavors.

But more than fair words and noble intentions of benefiting the commonwealth of England were required for successful colonization. Lacking knowledge of what commodities from Virginia would prove economically profitable, the Virginia Company had to learn from costly experience. By trial and error, it also had to discover that its system of land tenure, a sort of joint-ownership by the early settlers, would never provide incentives necessary to make enterprising colonial citizens, nor would employees hired by the company prove adequate for pioneering.

Officers and shareholders in the Virginia Company at first thought that their ships would return laden with saleable products, as the East India Company's vessels had brought back rich cargoes of pepper, spices, and silk. The early immigrants, therefore, had instructions not only to look for gold and precious stones, but to make ships stores and procure with all speed other vendible commodities. Instead of planting crops and planning for their own subsistence, workers among the early colonists were required to spend their energy in hewing clapboards and spars, making pitch and soap ashes, digging sassafras roots (believed to have curative virtues), and searching for any other products which might turn a profit on the London market. For a long time, armchair economists insisted that Virginia would be a source for raw silk if silk-worm culture could be introduced. With inexhaustible forests to supply fuel, they also believed that iron smelters and glass works ought to flourish. To that end, the Company sent to Virginia a few skilled workers who actually produced both glass and iron in small quantities but never at a profit.

An experiment made by John Rolfe in 1612 ultimately revolutionized the economy of Virginia and the whole contiguous region. In that year he produced and cured a crop of tobacco palatable to European tastes. Although Rolfe's marriage to Pocahontas immortalized him in legend, his cultivation of tobacco provided a more material basis for his fame. His first shipment of Virginia tobacco reached the London market in 1614, and within a decade this weed gave promise of becoming a steady and profitable source of revenue. Before the century was out, tobacco culture would determine the quality of the economic, the social, and even the intellectual life of Virginia and Maryland.

The key to enduring success of the English settlements in Virginia, and elsewhere in North America, was tied up in the restrictions on free ownership of land. The Virginia Company perceived this slowly. When the landless multitudes of England realized that eventually they might become the possessors of estates of their own, on which they could grow tobacco enough to assure themselves a livelihood and a competence, prospective settlers needed little further persuasion.

The first move to alter the land system occurred in 1613–14 when Governor Thomas Dale gave every old settler three acres of arable land for his own use, subject to certain rents and service. Though Dale is remembered for the harshness of his laws and discipline, the colony under his administration took on new life. Farmers cultivated their private acres with such diligence and success that never thereafter were they in danger of starvation. The company in 1616 took another step in the direction of private ownership of land. To subscribers of as much as £12, 10 s., to the stock, the Company offered fifty acres of land in perpetuity subject only to a nominal fixed rent. Two years later the offer of land was extended to every person who would undertake to transport himself and his family to Virginia. The immigrant could expect to receive fifty acres for himself and every member of his household, including servants. A man with a wife and eight children, for example, was thus certain of an initial home site of five hundred acres. This "head right" system, which proved successful despite abuses, persisted in Virginia and in other colonies through most of the seventeenth century.

But try as it would, the Virginia Company never achieved prosperity, though it is believed to have spent nearly £200,-000 in trying to establish the colony on a paying basis. By subscription and lottery, it repeatedly sought to raise new money for the enterprise, and though it kept the settlements on the James from collapsing, it could not wring a profit either from the exploitation of natural resources or from its ventures in capitalistic farming. Quarrels within the company, mismanagement and lack of focus of its activities, and disasters in Virginia make a doleful tale of frustration.

Factional dissensions among the shareholders resulted in the election, in 1619, of Sir Edwin Sandys as treasurer in place of Sir Thomas Smythe, who had served since the Company's organization. Nineteenth-century historians of Virginia were wont to see in this change of officers a great victory for the "liberal" party—the party of representative government—but the research of later scholars has proved that the fundamental reason for the change, as so often in the history of corporations, was a vociferous dissatisfaction over the management's failure to produce dividends. Although Sandys showed great energy in his administration, profits remained just as elusive and dissension just as rife, and he followed Smythe into the discard when the Earl of

Patrician and Yeoman on the Chesapeake

Southampton was elected treasurer in 1620. Finally, in 1624, King James annulled the Company's charter. Henceforth Virginia was to be a royal province.

The first representative assembly in Virginia met in Jamestown on July 30, 1619, a date important in the history of American democratic institutions. On that day in the little church in Jamestown, Governor George Yeardley and his council, and twenty-two burgesses—two elected from each of eleven settlements—met to make laws for the colony. Martial rule which had been put into force by Governor Dale was repealed, and statutes based on English common law were enacted. From this time forward Virginians jealously guarded the privilege of holding their own legislative assembly; despite later encroachments of royal governors and the Council of State (which came to have the dual powers of an upper house and a supreme court), the House of Burgesses became an instrument of self-government and a school for the democratic process.

Overly patriotic historians have seen in the assembly of 1619 a rebellion against English tyranny engineered by Sir Edwin Sandys the liberal, but that interpretation is sheer romanticism. Actually the assembly met to establish for the colony of Virginia the tradition of common law which the English government since Raleigh's charter had acknowledged as the right of settlers who lived abroad under the flag of England. The instructions drawn up for Governor Yeardley in November, 1618, six months before Sandys became treasurer, provided for the assembly. Although Sandys, who was a liberal spirit, it is true, clearly exerted his influence in behalf of reform, Sir Thomas Smythe was also instrumental in the preparation of Yeardley's instructions, which dealt more extensively with plans to broaden the base of land tenure than with politics. These instructions, described by the assembly of 1619 as the "great charter," loomed in nineteenth-century imaginations as an American Magna Charta; but though the instructions were significant, they were only an expression of a private company's policies and not a fun-

[61]

damental document of state. Nevertheless, when King James took over the Company, Virginians continued to hold a legislative assembly—at first without official notice or guarantees. Like the common law of England, however, representative government in Virginia gradually established itself by precedent and became an example to the other colonies.

The type of society which evolved in Virginia—and a little later in Maryland—was exclusively agrarian. In England, promoters of colonies worried over the refusal of immigrants to settle in towns, but the reasons for the dispersal were obvious. The cultivation of tobacco, which had proved the one profitable commodity, required fresh and fertile land. Soil on which tobacco had grown for several years became so exhausted that it would produce only weak and spindling stalks. Farmers were obliged therefore to have sufficient acreages to insure new ground for their crops. Since the best sites were on the creeks and rivers, where transportation was easy, planters quickly scattered up and down the numerous waterways until they were strung out over most of the tidewater region. Here and there could be seen a cluster of houses, but no towns dotted the country. Although Jamestown was the capital, it had only a church and a few houses. It was not even a central shipping point, for planters along the rivers built their own docks where vessels from London or Bristol unloaded supplies and took aboard the annual crops of tobacco, usually packed in hogsheads.

Planters quickly adapted themselves to a system of trade at long range. London, Bristol, or some other English port was their market town. An English merchant there acted as factor for the sale of their tobacco and purchasing agent for every article required from the European market. These merchant-factors were often friends and counsellors who performed such necessary duties as selecting a silk dress or a pair of earrings for the planter's wife or advising about a proper English school for his children. When the children were sent to England, the merchant took them in and was responsible for their welfare until they were properly enrolled at school.

Since there were no market towns in Virginia and Maryland, small farmers throughout the seventeenth century depended upon the larger planters to serve as middlemen in the sale of their tobacco and the purchase of goods abroad. After the development of shipping in the New England colonies, an occasional trading vessel from that region visited the Virginia rivers, but the bulk of the tobacco trade remained in the hands of the great planters, who maintained plantation storehouses. Sometimes English ship captains bought tobacco in small lots directly from farmers or bartered goods which they brought along for trade. Oftener than the authorities liked to believe, Dutch or English smugglers loaded tobacco and sailed away to the Continent with an illicit cargo which could be sold without paying the duties imposed by the English government.

The greediness of settlers for rich land in outlying regions made them extremely vulnerable to Indian attack, but for several years after the marriage of Pocahontas and John Rolfe, Virginians believed that this union had cemented a permanent friendship with the savages. That dream was shattered on Good Friday, 1622, when a concerted attack on the farms and plantations along the James River nearly destroyed the colony. More than three hundred men, women, and children were slain outright, and hundreds of others were forced to abandon homes, which the Indians immediately burned. The whites retaliated with a war of vengeance. Plans for Christianizing and educating the Indians no longer appealed to white men. For several years sporadic fighting went on. Each summer the whites organized expeditions to destroy the Indians' corn crops and drive them deeper into the forests of the interior until at last the Indians gave up the struggle and made peace. Another outbreak occurred in 1644, when the Virginia Indians, employing the same stealthy tactics as in 1622, fell on the outlying settlements and massacred more than five hundred persons. But after bloody retaliation by the whites, they again sued for peace. Not even these disasters kept settlers from pushing ever farther into the wilderness in search of tobacco lands.

The immigrants who came to Virginia in the first half of the seventeenth century were a varied lot, inspired by sundry motives, but most of them were men and women who hoped to better their economic lot in a new land. Some were sons of merchants or other substantial citizens who could afford enough capital to buy fairly extensive landed estates. These landholders made the nucleus of the first ruling class, a hierarchy of planters who would become increasingly powerful as the years went on. The number of immigrants from the ranks of aristocratic English families could be counted on one hand. A sardonic historian has commented that Virginians in search of ancestral clues might investigate the calendars of Newgate Prison more profitably than the records of the peerage.

The majority of immigrants came as indentured servants. Between 1635 and 1680, the number of white servants of this class averaged between 1000 and 1600 per year. To masters paying their transportation, they contracted to serve from four to seven years. At the expiration of their servitude, they became free citizens of Virginia and could acquire land on easy terms. Many of them in time became well-to-do landowners and masters of servants themselves. But in the early years of the colony, before the introduction of Peruvian bark as a specific against malaria, the mortality among laborers was frightful, and in some localities scarcely one in five survived the first year.

Many Englishmen regarded the transportation of criminals to America as a satisfactory means of solving the penal problem and supplying the colonies with labor. Although English judges sentenced a considerable number of convicts to servitude in Virginia, twentieth-century Americans need not fear too greatly the taint of ancient felony in their ancestry, for the death rate among the weakened jailbirds was excessive; many were under life sentences; and the few who lived to attain their freedom could rarely find wives, such was the scarcity of women. Most of the convicts were not felons at all but debtors, political prisoners, and other victims of misfortune. During the Puritan regime Oliver Cromwell shipped some prisoners of war to the colonies, and after the Restoration, royalists could think of no punishment more fitting for recalcitrant dissenters than transportation to the plantations.

Although religious motives played almost no part in the early settlement of Virginia, religion was far less neglected in the colony than has been supposed. One of the first buildings erected in Jamestown was a church, where the first parson, the Reverend Robert Hunt, read the service of the Church of England. The Established Church became the official religion of the colony, but conformity was enforced only spasmodically. When New England Puritans in 1642 sent three preachers to Virginia to minister to the Calvinists there, the House of Burgesses passed a law requiring the clergy to conform to the Church of England and instructing the governor and council to expel all dissenters from Virginia. But even in the face of the law, one of the Puritan preachers long remained in Virginia gathering a harvest of Calvinist souls. And the landowners—who in the end represented the law—were too eager for tenants and laborers to permit the deportation of useful citizens, whatever their private beliefs.

In the neighboring colony of Maryland, religion was more diverse and more vexing to the authorities, though Maryland began by granting toleration to all believers in the divinity of Christ.

The settlement of Maryland offers many contrasts to the early development of Virginia. Instead of being a manifestation of the new spirit of commercial enterprise, Maryland represents the return to a feudal and baronial ideal of land tenure and government, the most extreme of the proprietary colonies in America.

Maryland owed its name and existence to the land-hunger of George Calvert, created Baron Baltimore in the Irish peer-

[65]

age in 1625. Like many a seventeenth-century aristocrat, his dignities outweighed his purse, and he looked to land grants, first in Ireland and later in America, as a means of recouping his fortune. Receiving by royal grant the peninsula of Avalon in Newfoundland, Calvert, in 1627, took his family and a party of settlers to that foggy island, where he remained for two years. But the cold mists of Newfoundland were too much for him, and he sought temporary refuge in Virginia. A yearning for land there met with objections from that colony, for Calvert was a Catholic with exalted ideas of a proprietor's rights and privileges. When the Virginians ordered him to take the oath of supremacy, he departed for England. From King Charles, he finally procured a territory extending from the fortieth degree of north latitude to the south bank of the Potomac River. In tribute to Queen Henrietta Maria, he named his principality Maryland.

George Calvert died in 1632 before he could send settlers to Maryland, but the charter passed to his son Cecilius, who became Lord Proprietor. Naming his brother Leonard governor, he recruited between two and three hundred colonists and embarked them in two ships, the "Ark" and the "Dove." On March 25, 1634, they landed at a small island in the Potomac and named it St. Clement's. There Father Andrew White, a devoted Jesuit, celebrated the first mass offered in that part of the world, and afterwards conducted the Catholics in a procession to erect a cross hewn from a great tree "as a trophy to Christ our Savior."

George Calvert had wanted to make the colony a place where his Catholic countrymen might find freedom from the persecution which they suffered at home, but religion was not his, or his successors', first concern. They were intent upon creating estates which would return a handsome profit. To that end, Protestants as well as Catholics were encouraged to settle in Maryland, and the passengers on the "Ark" and the "Dove" were of various faiths. So careful was the proprietor to avoid dissension that he instructed his governor and commissioners "to preserve unity and peace amongst all the passengers on shipboard, and that they suffer no scandal nor offence to be given any of the Protestants, whereby any just complaint may hereafter be made by them in Virginia or in England, and that for that end, they cause all acts of Roman Catholic religion to be done as privately as may be, and that they instruct all the Roman Catholics to be silent upon all occasions of discourse concerning matters of religion, and that the said governor and commissioners treat the Protestants with as much mildness and favor as justice will permit. And this to be observed at land as well as at sea."

Although Lord Baltimore, in the interest of his pocketbook, might plead for harmony between Catholics and Protestants, that state of bliss was not to be found in the seventeenth century. Before the settlers reached the Potomac, disputes had occurred on board, and the seeds of future quarrels were planted. Virginians, who looked upon the new settlers with hostility, circulated a tale among the Indians that the newcomers were Spaniards bringing fire and sword to destroy them. A little later, trouble makers from Virginia crossed into Maryland to stir up the Protestants against their Catholic overlords. All was not harmonious even among the Catholics, for the Jesuit priests complained against the stinginess of Lord Baltimore because he refused to lay out money in their support.

But despite an increasing tendency to dissension, the colony prospered. The first settlers soon moved from St. Clement's to a site named St. Mary's on the mainland, where the governor placated the Indians by fairly buying their holdings. Other immigrants arrived and pushed farther up the waterways until plantations dotted the tidewater country of Maryland. Catholics made St. Mary's their principal center, while Protestants showed a liking for the region around Providence, later called Annapolis.

The charter by which Charles I conferred upon the Calverts and their heirs forever the princely domain of Maryland declared that the Lord Proprietor should hold his territory—nearly ten million acres—"in free and common soccage" after the manner of the county palatine of Durham. Since the Lord Bishops of Durham for centuries had been virtually supreme within their principality, the proprietors of Maryland found themselves absolute lords; indeed, the official title conferred by the charter was "Absolute Lord and Proprietary of Maryland and Avalon, Lord Baron of Baltimore." In this high style, Lord Baltimore was empowered to rule the land and people of Maryland. He could make any laws he wished, "with the advice, assent, and approbation of the freemen of the province," so long as these laws were consonant with the laws of England. He could fix rents, establish manors, levy duties and taxes, and exact any obligations of service that suited him. The King even relinquished his right to pardon criminals. For all of this property and regal power, the King required the payment of only two Indian arrows annually in token of fealty.

In social structure and in government, Maryland was aristocratic in the ancient tradition still familiar to Englishmen of the seventeenth century. Settlers in Maryland could not own their land. They were tenants of the House of Calvert, but not all of them were tenants in the same degree. Relatives and friends of the Calverts received baronial manors with all the panoply of manorial customs, courts baron, and courts leet inherited from the medieval system of land tenure. These estates might be awarded for life, or for three lifetimes, or for longer, so long as the holders paid to the proprietor his quit-rents. The lords of the manors assumed the responsibility of settling their estates with tenants from whom they in turn exacted rents; they were also planters in their own right, using as laborers indentured or hired servants and Negro slaves.

In addition to the great planters, the proprietor leased farms to hundreds of yeoman families who grew their crops of tobacco and corn by the sweat of their own brows. The back country was gradually peopled with poor Germans, Scots, and other landless folk who obtained from the Calverts leaseholds which they in time came to regard as their own.

Patrician and Yeoman on the Chesapeake

The Calverts ruled Maryland with all the prerogatives of kings—albeit with frequent complaints and occasional uprisings of their subjects. Unrest was so acute in 1688 that when news of the Glorious Revolution reached Maryland, malcontents rose against the proprietary government and received recognition from William and Mary, who established a royal government in the colony but permitted the Calverts to retain their rents and revenues. The capital was removed from Catholic St. Mary's to Protestant Annapolis. Although the proprietorship was restored in 1715 and continued in effect until the Revolutionary War, the traditional feudal system had long since declined. The independence of frontier society, whatever its technical structure, was not favorable to the retention of feudal trappings.

For all of their pretensions to absolutism, the proprietors of Maryland could not circumvent the stubborn belief of Englishmen in the guarantees of personal liberty established by common law and the natural rights of subjects to participate in government through representative assemblies. Though the proprietary charter granted the Calverts regal privileges, it did require the establishment of a popular assembly, which, however, was not permitted to initiate legislation. The Lord Proprietor made the laws and sent them to the assembly for approval or disapproval. But from the early assemblies—the first dating from 1635—the representatives of the people asserted the right to make laws for themselves. The history of the relations between the assembly and the proprietor is the story of a continued struggle to curb the authority of the Calverts, even though the assembly itself was prevailingly aristocratic in composition. After the repercussions of 1688, the Maryland assembly increased in dignity until it became in the eighteenth century one of the proudest and most stubborn defenders of parliamentary authority.

Immigrants to Maryland, as to other colonies in America, came to better their condition, and they did not willingly accommodate themselves to an outworn feudal system of land tenure, any more than they accepted without protest an absolutist government. Only by compromise, and by making tenancy approximate ownership, were the Calverts able to maintain their proprietary system and collect their rents and fees—a revenue that bore lightly on individual Marylanders, but in its totality provided a rich income for the proprietors.

Despite the differences in government and in the systems of land tenure, Virginia and Maryland developed civilizations much alike. Both were exclusively agrarian, with a dominant ruling class of great planters; both had a back country into which yeoman farmers gradually filtered. Both suffered the handicaps of a one-crop system—a bondage to tobacco. Before the mid-eighteenth century, the culture of both colonies was profoundly affected by Negro slavery.

If the ruling planters were not aristocratic in origins, they quickly adapted the manner and style of the English gentry, many of whose characteristics they consciously imitated. The tradition of the English gentleman, as developed during the sixteenth and seventeenth centuries, went far toward shaping the society which dominated Virginia and Maryland for more than two centuries, and the quality of that society had a significant and pervasive effect upon the destiny of America.

Much ink has been wasted in romantic descriptions of the "cavaliers," as novelists and genealogists have delighted to call the well-to-do planters of tidewater Virginia and Maryland. If fiction writers could be believed, these colonial aristocrats were a gay and gracious folk, forever idling in an ambrosial paradise, with an occasional duel to break the monotony of their well-bred pleasures. The truth is that the gentry of the seventeenth century, and the somewhat more substantial aristocracy of the eighteenth, were a singularly hard-working group who had little time for idle frivolities and rarely, if ever, favored duels. Although they developed the most cultivated society on the North American continent prior to the Revolution, they were singularly devoid of the foppery and idle pastimes commonly attributed to cavaliers.

Patrician and Yeoman on the Chesapeake

Wealthy planters began to rise above the common level of other immigrants before the middle of the seventeenth century. For example, Captain Samuel Matthews, a trader, early acquired large tracts of land above Newport News and established a manor almost equal to an independent village. "He hath a fine house," says an account of 1649, "and all things answerable to it. He sows yearly store of hemp and flax, and causes it to be spun; he keeps weavers, and hath a tan-house, causes leather to be dressed, hath eight shoemakers employed in their trade, hath forty Negro servants, brings them up to trades in his house. He yearly sows abundance of wheat, barley, &c. The wheat he selleth at four shillings the bushel, kills store of beeves, and sells them to victual the ships when they come thither; hath abundance of kine, a brave dairy, swine great store, and poultry; he married the daughter of Sir Thomas Hinton, and in a word, keeps a good house, lives bravely, and [is] a true lover of Virginia; he is worthy of much honour." This reads like a description which Thomas Deloney might have written of some contemporary of bourgeois Jack of Newberry. No silken grandee was Samuel Matthews, but he was a landowner wealthy enough to match with the daughter of a London knight.

Although Samuel Matthews was not a cavalier by any definition, he was typical of the new aristocracy setting itself up in the wilderness. Like the English country gentry whom they imitated, these Virginians took their social responsibilities seriously. They became justices of the peace, colonels of the militia, and members of the vestry in the parish churches; they served in the legislative assembly, and, if especially influential, Virginians became members of the Council of State. Though they may have had as much of selfishness and greed as most of human kind, they at least inherited a tradition of social responsibility from the theory and practice of English gentlemen. Furthermore, the duties which this new aristocracy assumed required intelligence and a degree of learning. Its members, therefore, were concerned to provide for the education of their own and their neighbors' children lest they grow up barbarous in the wilderness; and they gathered libraries in order that they might draw upon the reservoirs of accumulated knowledge. These seventeenth-century pioneers, intent upon establishing their families on a solid foundation in the new country, realized that mere material possessions were insufficient for the full life which they envisioned for themselves and their heirs.

The members of the ruling class in Virginia and Maryland were not identical in their political, social, and religious views, but they all shared similar ambitions of establishing family dynasties in the manner of the English county families. Whatever their background—whether traders, merchants, adventurers, or sons of the lesser gentry at home— once they came into possession of broad acres of tobacco land, they quickly transformed themselves into an aristocracy. But it was a fluid aristocracy, determined by the ability to obtain and develop land sufficient to maintain them in dignity rather than upon any pretensions of birth. Although the higher planter group soon became acutely conscious of class distinctions, in pre-Revolutionary days they never developed into a caste. As in England, there was a constant ebb and flow in the ranks of the upper class, as small planters grew prosperous and worked themselves into a better station, or as old planters fell on evil days and lost their possessions.

The yeomen farmers, always an important group in the economy of Virginia and Maryland, were not without political influence, for they often sat in the popular assemblies and found their way into the lesser political offices. But despite their greater numerical strength, they lacked the power to override the owners of the larger estates or the lords of manors in Maryland. Nevertheless their outspoken independence of spirit served as a constant warning to the oligarchy of wealthier planters that they might not encroach too far upon the rights of freemen.

The greatest period of opportunity for the yeomen was in the years before the Restoration of Charles II. During most of that earlier period, tobacco brought a fair price. But when Charles returned to his throne, he set about enforcing the navigation laws forbidding trade between the colonies and foreign countries except through England, and in English ships. Although the first navigation act had been passed in 1651, it was never very rigidly enforced, and the colonies had enjoyed the benefits of trade with Holland. Dutch ships brought goods from the Low Countries and paid three pennies a pound or better for tobacco. But the navigation act of 1660, which the English authorities enforced with vigor, curtailed Dutch trade and sent tobacco prices tumbling. Soon tobacco was bringing only a half-penny a pound, and at times it went down to a farthing. To make matters worse, imports from England cost more than the goods of Holland.

From 1660 onward, the farmer who depended on the labor of his own hands, or had only the help of his wife and children, found himself struggling against odds often insuperable. Well-to-do planters owned most of the best land. When their tobacco fields became exhausted after six or seven years, they could clear wood land and grow crops on new ground. The poorer farmers, who had no fresh soil, were obliged to strike out for the hinterland, where they could find homesteads, or give up the struggle and hire out as laborers.

The poor white man in the colonies after 1660 also faced the competition of slave labor. Since about 1619, Negroes had been known in Virginia, but white indentured servants predominated until after the Restoration when Charles II's charter of the Royal African Company in 1672 stimulated the slave trade. After this company's monopoly was broken in 1697, African slavery received a further impetus from a horde of ship-owners who brought Negroes to the colonies. New Englanders found Africans a profitable commodity, and a few Virginians engaged in the traffic. William Byrd I, for example, had a slave ship and sold Negroes to his fellow planters. By the end of the seventeenth century, slavery was well established in Virginia and Maryland, and by 1725

Negro slaves had become the chief source of labor on the larger plantations.

From this time onward, the social structure of Virginia and Maryland took on the characteristic qualities which it would retain until the War Between the States. At the top was the well-to-do class of planters, supported by slave labor, monopolizing political power and the best of the tidewater land. They built the great houses, adopted an aristocratic manner of life, and maintained communication with the world of cultivation overseas. Next to them were farmers who found their hope of prosperity in fresh soil of the frontier counties. With an occasional hired servant, or sometimes a slave or two, many small landowners worked out their salvation in the backwoods. Least prosperous of the farmers were those who struggled for an existence in the tidewater region in competition with slave-owning planters. Their lot was little, if any, better than that of the tenants, the hired white laborers, and the artisans who found employment on the plantations. From the ranks of the small farmers and laborers came a constant flow of bankrupts, failures, and ne'er-do-wells who filled the back country and made up the inhabitants of that Lubberland which William Byrd II discovered over the border in North Carolina.

Neither Virginia nor Maryland developed a trading class or anything approaching industry until very late in the colonial period. Planters who traded directly with London or Bristol merchants set up plantation storehouses and sold goods to their less opulent neighbors, but they never made store-keeping their chief activity. William Byrd I sold rum, guns, and iron pots to the Indians, bought furs and other Indian commodities, and made a fat profit from these transactions, but he remained primarily a planter. No Virginian or Marylander had any disposition to despise the emoluments of trade, but while their land was sufficiently fertile to produce comfortable revenues, they had small compulsion to follow the more exacting pursuits of the marketplace. Once the pattern of traffic between the Chesapeake Bay region and England was established, landless folk, who might have achieved prosperity in trade, found no opportunity. Not until near the end of the period did Virginia and Maryland have an appreciable number of local traders and merchants, and then only the persistent and thrifty Scots made headway.

The evolution of a stable, intelligent, and vigorous landed class in Virginia and Maryland early led to the growth of a spirit of independence and the establishment of a tradition of self-government which had important consequences in the later history of the country. The owners of plantations in Virginia or the holders of manors in Maryland were quick to resent arbitrary acts of petty tyranny from a royal governor or the encroachments of a lord proprietor. If the great planters themselves were at times proud, arbitrary, and grasping, nevertheless, over the years, they demonstrated a remarkable degree of public interest and a great capacity for governing themselves in accordance with the traditions of English common law. Although competition for land and power precipitated more than one upheaval in Virginia and Maryland, these very disturbances gave the colonists experience in handling their own affairs, for crises would not wait upon the slow passage of messages and instructions from London. Colonists soon learned to take matters into their own hands and hope for the eventual approval—or forgetfulness—of the central authority in England.

The Virginia colony was still young when its leaders rose against an arbitrary governor and expelled him, because of his contempt of the Council of State as much as for his highhanded disregard of the law. This governor, Sir John Harvey, had flouted the rights of the people in 1634 by drafting a planter's servant to work as ship's carpenter for one of the Governor's favorites. When news of this breach of the Virginia statutes reached members of the Council, they solemnly demanded an explanation from Harvey. Samuel Matthews, who was leader and spokesman for the Council, later reported that he had heard Harvey "in open court revile all the Council and tell them they were to give their attendance as assistants only to advise with him." Not content with verbal rebuffs, the Governor knocked out the teeth of one Councillor and threatened others with the gallows. Such behavior would not be tolerated by freemen. In the spring of 1635, the Council seized Harvey, forcibly placed him in his chair, and made him listen to a recital of grievances read by Samuel Matthews. Backed by armed musketeers, the Council shortly thereafter arrested Harvey, placed him on board a ship bound for London, and elected a governor, Captain John West, in his stead.

Because the King could not brook disrespect of the crown's representative, he sent Harvey back. Although the vengeful governor determined to ruin his enemies, particularly Matthews whom he vowed to despoil until he was not "worth a cow tail," the Councillors survived to maintain their rights and to bring Harvey eventually to trial for his misdeeds. Significantly, the Governor's opponents proceeded by due process of law and at last induced the Privy Council in England to appoint another governor, Sir Francis Wyatt, who was succeeded in 1642 by Sir William Berkeley.

The love of power and the zeal for the acquisition of land were not always tinctured with noble patriotism and a desire to resist oppression. Isolated from the curbs of any immediate authority, planters sometimes ruled their domains like potentates. One of the most ambitious and scheming of the landholders was William Claiborne, the lord of Kent Island in Chesapeake Bay. He arrived in Virginia in 1621 and at various times from 1637 to 1660 served as the colony's secretary of state. In August, 1631, he established an Indian trading post and a plantation on Kent Island which he made the center of a little principality. Since his territory was embraced by the charter granted to Lord Baltimore, he soon found himself in conflict with the proprietor of Maryland. Because Claiborne was charged with inciting the Indians against the Maryland colonists, Governor Leonard Calvert made war upon the Kent Islanders and in 1637, during Claiborne's absence in England, brought the island under his authority. This petty war on the frontier excited partisans on both sides, and Claiborne bided his time.

Claiborne saw in the Puritans who had found refuge in tolerant Maryland an instrument to work his revenge upon the Catholic proprietor. Taking advantage of the unrest caused by news of the Puritan rebellion in England, Claiborne, in alliance with a Puritan shipmaster named Richard Ingle, invaded Maryland in the autumn of 1644 and captured St. Mary's. Leonard Calvert, the governor, took refuge in Virginia while Claiborne, Ingle, and their Puritan cohorts for two years made merry with Catholic property in Maryland. Old Father Andrew White, a Jesuit who had come with the first party of colonists, was sent in irons to England, charged with treason. The Lord Proprietor despaired of regaining his rights.

But Governor Berkeley, who had no love for Claiborne and less for the Puritan rabble, helped Calvert recruit a little army in Virginia. With these troops, late in 1646, Calvert drove out the interlopers and resumed his authority over Maryland.

Governor Berkeley and his Anglicans in Virginia had no intention of recognizing the rule of Parliamentarians in England. When news of the execution of Charles I reached the shocked Virginians, they affirmed their adherence to the house of Stuart. Richard Lee I is said to have chartered a Dutch ship at his own expense and gone to Brussels to procure a new commission for Governor Berkeley from Prince Charles, now proclaimed Charles II by his devoted followers.

Although Parliament frowned upon the doings of Berkeley and his Royalists, not until 1652 did it get around to exerting its authority. In the spring of that year, Parliamentary commissioners aboard a frigate reached Jamestown to accept the surrender of Virginia. One of these officials was William Claiborne of Kent Island, now an ardent Parliamentarian and still hot for the conquest of Romish Maryland. Berkeley would have resisted, but he was persuaded by his Council that compliance was the better part of valor. The House of

Burgesses in April elected a Puritan, Richard Bennett, governor and assumed the prerogatives formerly held by the King. Virginia to all intents was now a self-governing republic, but life was little changed, for the commonwealth had already grown accustomed to controlling its internal affairs. Two other planters, by election of the House of Burgesses, served as governor during the Interregnum: Edward Digges and stout old Samuel Matthews. When Matthews died shortly before King Charles returned to the throne in 1660, the House of Burgesses dutifully elected their former royalist governor, Sir William Berkeley, who all the while had been quietly living on his own plantation at Green Spring. The King pleased Berkeley by sending him a royal commission.

Maryland, thanks to a mixed population of various religions and the trouble-making of William Claiborne, enjoyed no such peaceful settlement of its affairs during this period. To stop the mouths of agitators who complained that Maryland was a nest of Papists seeking the destruction of Protestants, the Maryland Assembly in 1649 passed an "Act Concerning Religion" designed "to preserve mutual love and amity among the inhabitants of the Province." It guaranteed freedom of worship to all believers in Jesus Christ and forbade anyone to call another a Puritan, a Papist, a Jesuit, or any similar term applied in opprobrium. But this precaution was not enough to stave off Puritan activities against the Lord Proprietor, particularly when stirred up by Claiborne, who after 1652 was again influential in Virginia.

Though Lord Baltimore made an earnest effort to insure peace and toleration in his colony, he was ahead of his time. The seventeenth century was not yet ready for so much humanity. The Puritans in Maryland were responsible for inserting in the Act Concerning Religion provisions for the harsh punishment of heretics and blasphemers—interpreted to include all who did not believe in the Trinity. And before long, the Puritans, who had always outnumbered the Catholics, were zealously restricting the liberties of their Romish brethren. The first Protestant governor, William Stone, in 1648 swore not to molest any Roman Catholic, but he was ejected from his office by Claiborne and Bennett, serving as Parliamentary Commissioners, and in the autumn of 1654, the Maryland Assembly, now dominated by Puritans, repealed the Act Concerning Religion and passed another more in keeping with their dispositions. It forbade freedom of worship to any who believed in "popery or prelacy" and took from them the right to vote. The intolerances of the Long Parliament found reflection in Maryland, and in the spring of 1655 Maryland also repeated in miniature the English civil war. With the help of a New Englander named Roger Heaman, captain of the ship "Golden Lion," the Puritans captured St. Clement's Island and other Catholic territory. Filled with the zeal of Prophets of Jehovah, they smote their adversaries hip and thigh, devoted Catholic property to the good use of Protestants, forced the priests to flee to Virginia, condemned ten Papists to the gallows, and succeeded in executing four before the fervor of religious vengeance burned itself out. But by this time Oliver Cromwell had heard the complaints of Lord Baltimore and upheld his rights. Although the Lord Proprietor had yet to quell the rebellion of a rascally governor named Josias Fendall, whom he had appointed in 1656, the worst was over, and Maryland again learned the ways of peace in 1660 under the governorship of Philip Calvert, half-brother of the proprietor. But the diversity of peoples in Maryland made for an uneasy peace at best, and grumbling frontiersmen in the backwoods counties were a constant threat to the established authority.

Successful as were the ruling classes of Virginia and Maryland in adapting the patterns of an old social order to new conditions in an illimitable wilderness, the effort created strains and tensions which left their mark on both colonies. As indentured servants achieved their freedom and took up land, and as farmers in the frontier counties extended their holdings, they became more and more impatient with the political monopoly enjoyed by the tidewater gentry. A part of the unrest in Maryland can be attributed to the unwillingness of frontiersmen to submit to an obsolete manorial system, however lightly its restrictions were applied.

The rebellion led by Nathaniel Bacon in Virginia in 1676 was in a measure a result of popular discontent with the ruling clique. Although the gentry of Virginia and Maryland might invoke fewer privileges than their counterparts in England, the classes under them were far less subservient than the lower orders at home. Land, the very basis of freedom, lay beckoning in the wilds to every man with stout arms and heart. The New World was not the place for the growth of that doctrine of degree which had been long accepted by Europe as part of the divine plan.

The causes of Bacon's Rebellion in Virginia are now obscure and were not clearly understood even by contemporaries. That it was the spontaneous uprising of a courageous people against the tyranny of the royal governor and his favorites—a class war led by a dashing knight errant intent upon righting the wrongs of the oppressed—is more romantic than accurate, but there is enough truth in that interpretation to make it credible.

Nathaniel Bacon, only twenty-six when he matched his strength against Governor Berkeley, had been educated at Cambridge and had travelled on the Continent. A few years before his rebellion, he arrived in Virginia, acquired a plantation at Curle's Neck on the James, and—such was his wealth and influence—took a seat on the exclusive Council. Certainly here was no landless agitator, and there is little indication that he "chafed under the wrongs" of the people. The facts are that the hotheaded youth first took up arms in a simple effort to avenge the death of an overseer who had been slain by marauding Indians.

Indians in the spring of 1676 were wreaking a terrible vengeance upon the white settlers along the borders of Virginia and Maryland. Equipped with muskets, and with powder and shot, sold them by traders like William Byrd and even Governor Berkeley himself, the savages were slaughter-

THE RAW MATERIAL FOR NEW ENGLAND'S RUM

Engraving of a sugar mill in the West Indies, from the Huntington Library copy of Jean Baptiste Du Tertre, *Histoire Generale des Antilles* (4 vols., Paris, 1667–71).

THE PREPARATION OF TOBACCO

From the Huntington Library copy of the *Universal Magazine* for November 1750.

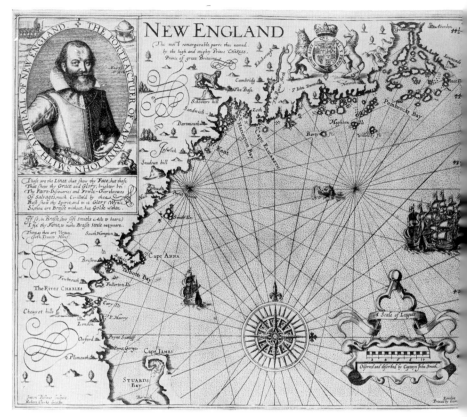

CAPTAIN JOHN SMITH'S MAP OF NEW ENGLAND

From the Church copy in the Huntington Library of John Smith, *A Description of N[ew]
England* (1616).

ing farmers in the outlying districts. Berkeley would do nothing to stop the massacres and obstinately refused to call out the militia, partly, it was said, because he did not want to disturb his own traffic in beaver skins, partly because he feared an uprising of the people if they should be called to arms. Certainly the frontier counties seethed with unrest and discontent. Tobacco prices had been falling until a farmer could scarcely make enough to keep soul and body together. Moreover, a high poll tax had recently been imposed, and frontiersmen especially grumbled because the House of Burgesses had sat, like the Long Parliament, for years without a new election. Conditions were ripe for an explosion when Bacon entered the scene.

Without waiting for the Governor's approval, Bacon gathered a force of armed men and led them successfully against the Indians. His courage and decisiveness made him at once a popular hero, not only with the small farmers on the frontiers, but with substantial planters and traders as well, many of whom had suffered from the Indian forays. For example, when William Byrd I found that incursions of northern Indians were interfering with his own Indian trade, he made common cause with Bacon against the invaders and deserted him only when he began to talk about reforms.

Before long, with Bacon as a leader, Berkeley's enemies were demanding sweeping changes. A new House of Burgesses was elected and included Bacon among its members. This assembly extended the franchise to all freemen and eased the burden of taxes. But friction between Berkeley and Bacon increased, and soon Virginia was split between warring factions. Berkeley fled to the Eastern Shore of Virginia, and Bacon captured and burned Jamestown rather than let it fall into the Governor's hands after he returned to the attack. When the fiery old governor fled again to the Eastern Shore, Bacon established himself in Berkeley's house at Green Spring and prepared to reform the government. At this moment of triumph Fate struck down the young leader. During a trip into Gloucester County, he contracted a fever and died. His followers buried him secretly, and one mourned his loss in one of the best poems of the colonial period:

> *Death, why so cruel ! what, no other way*
> *To manifest thy spleen but thus to slay*
> *Our hopes of safety, liberty, our all,*
> *Which through thy tyranny with him must fall*
> *To its late chaos ? . . .*
> *Here let him rest, while we this truth report,*
> *He's gone from hence unto a higher court*
> *To plead his cause, where he by this doth know*
> *Whether to Caesar he was friend or foe.*

Signs and portents, according to a contemporary narrative, had foretold disaster on the eve of Bacon's rebellion. A comet streaming like a horsetail swept across the evening sky; flights of pigeons darkened the heavens and broke down the trees; and a plague of flies "an inch long and big as the top of a man's little finger, rising out of spigot holes in the earth," devoured the new leaves in the tree tops and departed. All of these things, Virginians believed, were warnings of troubles to come. The rebellion and its aftermath proved that their fears were justified.

After Bacon's death, his "army" melted away and returned to their farms and plantations. Governor Berkeley, bitter in his old age and violent with rage at his humiliations, came back from the Eastern Shore bent upon revenge. Whenever he could, he caught and hanged rebel leaders until Charles II, hearing of the orgy of executions in Virginia, remarked that the "old fool has hanged more men in that naked country than I have done for the murder of my father." Greedily the irate governor confiscated the property of his victims and turned their wives and children out of doors. Such behavior shocked even the indolent government of Charles II into action. The King sent a commission to make a report, presently recalled Berkeley, and appointed Herbert Jeffreys in his place. The seething cauldron of revolt gradually simmered down.

Patrician and Yeoman on the Chesapeake

To interpret Bacon's Rebellion as a forecast of the American Revolution or as clear proof of the development of the American system of democracy on the frontier, is hardly accurate, but this conflict was an omen of things to come. It was an indication of the spirit of independence engendered among settlers in a region where the acquisition of landed freeholds was easy; it was a declaration that the whole body of freemen would demand the rights which Englishmen were guaranteed under the common law; and it was a warning that the aristocratic system imitative of the English country gentry would have to be adaptable and on guard against political corruption if it hoped to survive.

The upheaval which stirred Virginia was not confined to that colony but rumbled through the frontiers of Maryland. Josias Fendall, smarting under the humiliation of defeat after a previous attack on the authority of the Lord Proprietor, became the leader of a new agitation. He had the support of another malcontent John Coode. These men, whom Lord Baltimore described as "rank Baconists," won the backing of discontented frontiersmen, notably Protestants, who were violently opposed to the continuation of the proprietary system with its quitrents and customary duties. For years these men kept the border regions of Maryland in an uproar. Charged with plotting to seize the Lord Proprietor (then a resident of Maryland) and members of his Council, Fendall was arrested and exiled in 1681. On the eve of the Glorious Revolution of 1688, he died.

John Coode, described in the records as a debauched and profane person, though a deacon and a priest of the Church of England, outlived Fendall and continued his feud with Lord Baltimore. He was one of the leaders of a revolt against the proprietary government, precipitated by news of the accession of William and Mary, and helped to set up the royal government in Maryland. But no change of government made good citizens of trouble-makers like John Coode. Finally convicted of embezzlement and blasphemy in 1696, he earned the undying hostility of Governor Francis Nicholson, who managed to suppress him until his death in 1709.

Both Virginia and Maryland reached a new maturity in the last decade of the seventeenth century and "came of age" as settled and stable regions. Already second- and third-generation inhabitants were assuming places of influence in the colonies. Out of the turmoil of the earlier years had come the experience which gave the colonies a capacity for managing their own affairs.

The Glorious Revolution of 1688, which brought constitutional changes affecting the later history of England, had a profound influence upon the colonies. Although Virginia and Maryland would have incompetent and arbitrary governors in the years to follow, the days when they feared for their basic liberties were over. The later Stuarts had regarded the colonies as personal pawns to be used as they saw fit. Charles II, for instance, in a moment of careless generosity had given the Northern Neck—that portion of Virginia between the Rappahannock and the Potomac Rivers—to several of his favorites, and a little later he gave away the whole of Virginia to Lord Culpeper and the Earl of Arlington, who were to be the lords proprietors. The expense incurred by the colony in sending representatives to London to beg the King to reconsider, and the tax levied to buy off these lordly patentees, helped to cause the unrest which brought on Bacon's Rebellion. In the end, the King rescinded the patent to all of the colony, but Culpeper eventually became governor of Virginia and established his right to the Northern Neck. His grandson, Thomas, sixth Baron Fairfax, at length inherited the domain and came to live in the colony. Robert Carter of Corotoman was agent for the Fairfax proprietary, and young George Washington served as its surveyor. Like Culpeper, the other Stuart governors who came after Berkeley—Herbert Jeffreys, Sir Henry Chicheley, and Francis, Lord Howard of Effingham—were abitrary and self-seeking, characteristic of their time and the dynasty which they represented. Though Virginia ever proclaimed its loyalty to the Stuarts, the colony owed little except misfortune to that house. The accession of William and Mary marked the beginning of a new and better age.

The power of assemblies in Virginia and Maryland had grown with the years, and had roughly paralleled the increase in prestige of Parliament. After 1688, they became the great bulwarks of the people against external encroachments. Royal governors or royal proprietors found it increasingly difficult to exert arbitrary power against the stubborn will of these law-making bodies who could—and often did—support their own agents in London to protest against unfavorable policies or injustices. The fact that great planters—the aristocratic ruling class—often found it expedient to make common cause with lesser folk in the assemblies against outside despotism helped to keep the colonial governments from hardening into oppressive aristocracies. Although class distinctions and class tensions increased in the eighteenth century, the popular assemblies served as restraining forces and preserved a semblance of representative government.

The late seventeenth and early eighteenth centuries saw the further evolution of the planter class into a responsible and cultivated society. Great houses multiplied along the rivers; slave quarters increased; more tobacco ships lay each autumn off the capes; and the volume of trade and traffic each year grew more important—for Virginia and the British Empire.

The time had come when colonists thought of themselves, not as Englishmen in an alien land, but as Americans. Significant of this development was a pamphlet, *An Essay upon the Government of the English Plantations on the Continent of America,* published in London in 1701. Its author—possibly Robert Beverley or perhaps his father-in-law William Byrd I—signed his work with the phrase, "By an American." This American, who declared himself a citizen of Virginia, refuted misinformation about Virginia and Maryland, circulated by the English government in dealing with colonial problems. The author's detailed suggestions for improving the relations between the mother country and the colonies, if adopted, might have prevented the breach of 1776. More than a half-century before Benjamin Franklin's proposal, he advocated a plan of union. Where a few years before the wildcat and bear roamed the aboriginal forest, a reflective and cultivated citizen now sat in his study and wrote a document on the science of governing the commonwealths of British America.

As thoughtful planters contemplated the intellectual status of Virginia in the last decade of the seventeenth century, they realized the need of a college. As long before as 1619, a college had been projected, but the calamities of the early years stopped its development. At last, in 1691, the colony seemed ready to foster higher learning. In that year the colonial government sent a memorial to London requesting aid in the establishment of a college. The Reverend James Blair, commissary or ranking official of the Church of England in Virginia, made a personal appeal to the Lords of the Treasury; he emphasized the value of the college in training ministers to save the souls of the colonists. "Souls!" exclaimed Sir Edward Seymour, one of the treasury officials, "Damn your souls! Make tobacco!" But despite Seymour's objection Blair, a determined Scot, obtained a charter from their Majesties in 1693 and named the college William and Mary in their honor. Both Virginia and Maryland were to share in the college's support and enjoy its benefits.

The site chosen was Middle Plantation, soon to be called Williamsburg, and there the cornerstone of the first building was laid in 1695. Although in its early years the college was little more than a grammar school, five students had sufficiently advanced by May 1, 1699, to take part in a festival of learning. Each delivered an oration before Governor Francis Nicholson, the Council, the House of Burgesses, and assembled citizens. The college, the orators asserted, would be the means through which Virginia would grow in intellectual grace. "Methinks we see already that happy time," the last speaker declared, "when we shall surpass the Asiaticans in civility, the Jews in religion, the Greeks in philosophy, the

Egyptians in geometry, the Phoenicians in arithmetic, and the Chaldeans in astrology. O happy Virginia!"

The College of William and Mary was a symbol of the desire of the colonists to perpetuate the learning of the past and to give their sons the benefits of a classical education. With the help of the college, one of the orators of 1699 maintained, Virginians would be able to converse with the most excellent men of all ages, with Plato, Aristotle, Seneca, Cicero, Livy, Tacitus, and many other writers of infinite wisdom. In the next century, one of the college's most distinguished alumni, Thomas Jefferson, would echo the orator's praise of classical culture with the fervor of a Renaissance scholar. The quality of the learning desired by colonial Virginians perhaps had a greater influence in producing a trained leadership than the quantity of education in later ages. Certainly the zeal for traditional learning was more than a meaningless gesture to ornamental cultivation.

When Governor Francis Nicholson was governor of Maryland in 1694, he urged the establishment of a free school and set in motion plans which matured in 1701 with the founding of King William's School (eventually St. John's College) at Annapolis. Nicholson also moved the capital to Annapolis, which henceforth became the center of intellectual life in the colony.

Adequate provision for elementary education was a problem never solved in a region lacking the concentration of towns. The farms and plantations of Virginia and Maryland were too far apart for the community schools of more compact settlements. Planters sometimes joined with their nearest neighbors and hired tutors to teach all the children in reach; in the more thickly settled areas, a few neighborhood schools provided instruction; but in general the individual planter was obliged to assume the cost and responsibility of hiring tutors. The children of poorer families had to go without formal education, though a surprising number acquired the rudiments of learning from their parents.

Some of the wealthier planters sent their children, even

their daughters, to England for schooling. The misgivings with which a parent saw a child sail on a tobacco ship can scarcely be imagined today. Many did not survive the experience, for the diseases of childhood, as well as the dreaded smallpox, took their deadly toll. William Fitzhugh, dwelling in frontier Stafford County, planned in 1690 to send his son and heir, then less than five years old, to England, but found a Huguenot minister who undertook to teach him French and Latin. When the boy was a little over eleven, Fitzhugh finally sent him to Bristol in the care of the merchant who handled his tobacco. With the instructions specifying a good school where the lad could continue his French and Latin, the father adds a touching note that he is to have "now and then a little money to buy apples, plums, etc." The classical education which Fitzhugh prescribed for his son was not wasted, for the child grew up into one of the enlightened members of the ruling class in the eighteenth century, the master of the plantation known as Eagle's Nest.

Upon their libraries planters depended for much of their contact with the world of cultivation. Fitzhugh, writing to a correspondent in England, observes that "some of the newest books, if they be ingenious, will be mighty acceptable, as will likewise a full account of the news." The books which he ordered were various and characteristic of the taste displayed by the planter group: histories, books of conduct, pious works, Greek and Latin classics (in translation), treatises on law and government, natural science and medicine. Planters gathered their libraries for use, not ostentation; their correspondence indicates the frequent exchange of books, so that each plantation collection served as a kind of lending library.

The zeal for the preservation and perpetuation of the older traditions of culture finds few better illustrations than in William Fitzhugh. On his backwoods plantation, he made himself the kind of gentleman whom the English Renaissance would have comprehended and approved: a well-rounded personality, learned as well as gracious, intensely conscious of his duty to church and state, serious but not solemn, a man whose sense of dignity never prevented the full enjoyment of and participation in the world about him.

Although Fitzhugh died in 1701 when he was barely fifty, he had earned the respect of his contemporaries for deep learning in the law, and he was in constant correspondence with his fellow Virginians about legal problems. With quotations from Magna Charta, Sir Edward Coke's *Institutes*, and many early authorities, sometimes reinforced by a classical allusion, he defended the innate right of Virginians to freedom and justice under the traditional law of England. Before statute law can be interpreted properly, he insists, one must know the common law, "the only guide"; and he adds that a knowledge of the common law "is only to be learned out of ancient authors (for out of the old fields must come the new corn) contrary to opinion of the generality of our judges and practicers of the law here." Fitzhugh's commendation of the precedents of law and ancient authorities was symbolic of the respect which he had for the whole cultural tradition. Stafford County lay on the verge of the endless forest, but Fitzhugh made his domain an outpost of English civilization.

Many other planters shared Fitzhugh's cultural aspirations and exemplified the qualities which he represented and commended. His friend and client, Ralph Wormeley, the very embodiment of rules of conduct laid down in Henry Peacham's *Compleat Gentleman*, came nearest to being the fabled type of cavalier. His plantation house at Rosegill on a bluff overlooking the Rappahannock was a baronial seat where he entertained lavishly, surrounded by a host of retainers. But though Wormeley was noted among "the gay part of the gentlemen" in his section, his amusements did not interfere with his duties to the colony which he served capably and honestly as secretary of state, nor did they prevent his devotion to literature. The library at Rosegill contained approximately three hundred and seventy-five titles covering a wide range of interest: religion, law, statecraft, history, science, medicine, learning, classical literature, more recent belles-lettres, and music. Like many of his colleagues, he possessed Richard Allestree's *The Whole Duty of Man*, Jeremy Taylor's *The Rule and Exercises of Holy Living* and its sequel on holy dying, Richard Hooker's *Of the Laws of Ecclesiastical Polity*, and sermons by some of the most notable Anglican preachers. Religion, even with the gayest of these Virginia planters, was an organic part of their lives, and they gave their support to the church as a part of decorum required for decency and order in society.

In his devotion to learning and to the service of the state, Richard Lee II, ancestor of many famous Lees of later generations, was a belated Elizabethan. When he was buried in 1714 in the family graveyard at Mount Pleasant, Westmoreland County, the good Latin epitaph carved upon his tombstone announced to posterity that Richard Lee, gentleman, while a magistrate "was a zealous promoter of the public good" and that "he was very skilful in the Greek and Latin languages and other parts of polite learning." Before Lee's death Governor Spotswood described him as "a gentleman of as fair character as any in the country for his exact justice, honesty, and unexceptionable loyalty in all the stations wherein he has served in this government." A grandson later reported that Richard Lee was so devoted to learning that he "spent almost his whole life in study and usually wrote his notes in Greek, Hebrew, or Latin . . . so that he neither diminished nor improved his paternal estate . . . He was of the Council in Virginia and also other offices of honor and profit, though they yielded little to him." An heir might regret his ancestor's failure to utilize opportunities for material aggrandizement, but others can applaud Lee's integrity and devotion to public service and learning.

Less averse to the profits of office than Richard Lee, Robert Carter of Corotoman—known for his pride and the extent of his possessions as "King" Carter—accumulated more than three hundred thousand acres of land before his death in 1732. As agent for the Fairfaxes, proprietors of the

Northern Neck, he had great opportunities for personal gain and overlooked none of them, though there is never a suggestion of anything less than scrupulous honesty in his stewardship.

In his attitude toward every aspect of life, Carter was typical of the realistic, practical type of aristocrat that Virginia developed in this period. He and his group valued the tradition of gentility and were eager to perpetuate the best elements in that tradition, but they were never fooled by romantic notions of aristocracy and were unhampered by any suggestions of an aristocratic code obsolete or alien to the practical necessities of Virginia. For example, the code-consciousness and the fripperies of the French aristocracy of the period would have been dismissed by Robert Carter as arrant nonsense. As he constantly reiterated, he was a plain-dealing man, albeit one acutely conscious of his class. But his class-consciousness did not prevent his being an industrious and astute businessman, for shrewd oversight of his tobacco sales, his purchases of commodities or securities, his land transactions, and the multifarious details connected with his great plantations were a part of the responsibilities of his kind. His letters of advice to his sons drive home his ideas of what a Virginia youth should learn. He was extremely suspicious of the vanities of London and advised his son John to "mind less the pleasures of the town" and stick closer to his duties. One of his worries about his wards, the sons of his friend Ralph Wormeley, was that they would learn foolish extravagance and acquire vain notions in their English school. The Virginia planter, aristocrat though he might be, was of necessity strongly imbued with qualities usually attributed to the bourgeoisie.

Carter's attitude toward religion and the Established Church was characteristic of his class. Very significantly he disapproved of High Church tendencies as ill-adapted to the needs of Virginia. Though some English prelates of the time regarded the latitudinarian tendencies of the Virginia church as a scandal, Carter and others stood firm in their views. A letter concerning the education of his sons, then in England, is revealing. "The health of my sons and their improvement in learning and manners is one of the greatest blessings I can meet with in this world," he writes. "Let others take what courses they please in bringing up their posterity, I resolve the principles of our holy religion shall be instilled into mine betimes; as I am of the Church of England way, so I desire they should be; but the highflown up top notions and the great stress that it laid upon ceremonies, any farther than decency and conformity, is what I cannot come into the reason of. Practical godliness is the substance; these are but the shell."

The care which Robert Carter lavished upon the upbringing of his children bore fruit, for his family became one of the most influential in the whole region. They firmly believed in the value of classical education and were not content to be provincials. Of all the offices which Robert Carter himself held, he was proudest of being rector of the College of William and Mary and had a record of that honor inscribed on his tombstone.

The planter-society which had developed by the beginning of the eighteenth century was self-conscious, proud, and vigorous. Far from complacent, it was eager for self-improvement and zealous in the pursuit of intellectual and spiritual development—a fact often forgotten in later histories. Few more ornamental members of colonial society can be found than William Byrd II, owner of the great plantation house at Westover, the friend and correspondent of British noblemen. And yet Byrd's private diary reveals a lifetime's devotion to methodical study which would have been a credit to a professional scholar.

An entry for May 26, 1710 is typical: "I rose at 5 o'clock and read two chapters in Hebrew and some Greek in Anacreon. I said my prayers and ate milk and strawberries with Captain Posford for breakfast. He told me that a ship was arrived with Negroes and offered his service to fetch my wine from Williamburg . . . I read some Italian in the evening and took a walk about the plantation. I scolded at G-r-l for telling a lie. I said my prayers and had good health, good thoughts, and good humor, thanks be to God Almighty." Day in and day out, Byrd read his stint of Hebrew and Greek, interspersed occasionally with Latin, Italian, or French. Sometimes in the midst of exacting duties he applied himself to writing: a bit of translation, some verses, or the revision of a narrative of his own experiences. His *History of the Dividing Line*—an account of the survey of the boundary between Virginia and North Carolina in 1728— is one of the most urbane pieces of writing in the colonial period.

Byrd's brother-in-law, Robert Beverley, was proud of being a Virginian and proud of the country which he represented. A garbled account of the colony, designed for inclusion in a history of British America, coming to Beverley's notice during a visit to England in 1703, stirred him to write his own *History and Present State of Virginia,* published in 1705, the first history of the colony written by a native. Though Beverley was caustic and critical about the shortcomings of his contemporaries, particularly of the royal governors, his *History* demonstrates a high degree of devotion to Virginia and a new sense of native patriotism.

As the sense of social stability increased in the eighteenth century, the tidewater region lost the rough quality of its earlier frontier settlements. Though the planters were usually busy and hard-working people, they began to emphasize the comforts and amenities of a settled and more leisurely life. There was visiting and entertainment in the great houses, and the capitals of both Virginia and Maryland sparkled with a show of fashion, especially during sessions of the legislative assemblies.

The capital of Virginia was moved in 1699 from marshy and malarial Jamestown to Middle Plantation, a more wholesome spot, which had its name changed in honor of the King to Williamsburg. At first the legislative assembly met in the college building; but soon a capitol was erected at the opposite end of the broad center street, named in honor of the Duke of Gloucester; additional streets were laid out; a fine house was built for the governor; and other houses multiplied. Within a few years the capital began to take on the appearance of a thriving little town, something Virginia had never had before. Governor Nicholson had been responsible for moving the capital, but its chief growth occurred during the administration of Governor Alexander Spotswood, a capable administrator who did much to advance the development of Virginia.

From the issuance of its first charter, Virginia had laid claim to all the land to the westward as far as the Great South Sea (the Pacific Ocean), but few had ever penetrated the mountain barrier which lay beyond the falls of the rivers, and no one knew the distance to the western sea. Governor Spotswood, who was interested in iron mining and in the development of the back country, led an expedition over the mountains at the end of August 1716 and opened the valley of the Shenandoah. Although the implications of this expedition were momentous, few gayer cavalcades have ever ridden through the woodlands of America. Participants included a goodly number of planters, among them Robert Beverley, the historian, and John Fontaine, a Huguenot diarist who recorded the events. When they reached the summit of the Blue Ridge Mountains on September 5, they stopped to drink healths to King George I and all the royal family—as many as they could remember. On the next day, when they crossed the "Euphrates"—as they called the Shenandoah—and claimed the land beyond in the King's name, they again celebrated: "We had a good dinner, and after it we got the men together, and loaded all their arms, and we drank the King's health in champagne, and fired a volley; the Princess' health in burgundy, and fired a volley; and all the rest of the royal family in claret, and a volley. We had several sorts of liquors, viz., Virginia red wine and white wine, Irish usquebaugh, brandy, shrub, two sorts of rum, champagne, canary, cherry, punch, water, cider, etc."

Patrician and Yeoman on the Chesapeake

If the future of the valley of Virginia looked rosy to the convivial explorers on the Shenandoah that September day, their imaginations could hardly have perceived the complete significance of the thrust westward which the expedition symbolized. From this time onward, hardy settlers would begin a transmontane movement which would never end until they had indeed reached the Great South Sea.

Since 1685 when the revocation of the Edict of Nantes made French Protestants once again subject to religious persecution, landowners in the colonies had dreamed of settling their estates with Huguenot refugees. Many of the Frenchmen came to the Chesapeake Bay region. The first William Byrd was instrumental in persuading a group to settle on the upper James River at Manakin Town, and Huguenots soon became an important immigrant group. Scottish Presbyterians followed the Huguenots. Because many of these Scots came from settlements in Ulster, they were known as Scotch-Irish. A little later German Protestants—Lutherans, Mennonites, Calvinists, and Dunkers—came in search of farm lands and freedom. Some drifted southward down the river valleys from Pennsylvania; others came directly to Virginia and Maryland. Governor Spotswood himself settled a colony of Palatine Germans on the Rapidan River and called the locality Germanna. By the mid-eighteenth century the back country of Virginia and Maryland was populous with the farms of thrifty and hard-working immigrants—German, French, and Scottish. This region was also the economic salvation of farmers fleeing the distress brought by worn-out land and low-priced tobacco in the tidewater country. In the red hills they learned to grow wheat and cattle. If the produce of their land brought them little cash, they knew how to subsist comfortably and well on what they raised. The back country was beginning not only to develop a new system of farming but also to produce a new race of freemen, economically as well as spiritually independent of the older regions.

Humble farmers were not the only ones who found the

lands of the interior attractive. Peter Jefferson, an enterprising surveyor who had married an aristocratic Randolph, settled in the hill country of Albemarle County. For a bowl of punch he bought from William Randolph four hundred acres, the homesite of Shadwell, where Thomas Jefferson was born in 1743. Four years after the future president's birth, Thomas sixth Lord Fairfax came to live on his proprietary lands in Virginia and in 1752 established himself in the Shenandoah Valley at a hunting lodge which he named Greenway Court. There the only resident peer in America lived in rustic simplicity and performed the traditional duties of justice of peace and commander of the local militia.

Though tidewater people gradually moved into the foothills, the majority of the settlers in the interior of Virginia and Maryland were vastly different from the aristocrats of the lowlands. Most of them depended upon their own labor, for few could afford slaves. Living on the edge of the Indian country, their cabins were their fortresses, and they relied for protection on their own sharp eyes and trusty muskets. By necessity they became a sturdy and self-reliant people who proved their mettle in the Revolution.

The religious and spiritual quality of these frontiersmen differed greatly from the lowlanders. The Church of England had been the established church of Virginia from the beginning. In Maryland, the Reverend Thomas Bray, an ardent Anglican missionary remembered now for the libraries which he collected for the colonies, succeeded in 1702 in having the Church of England established as the state religion of Maryland. Charles Calvert, fifth Lord Baltimore, to whom the proprietary rights of Maryland were restored in 1715, was an Anglican, his father Benedict having been converted from Catholicism. The great planters of tidewater Maryland were usually Anglicans or Catholics. But the frontiersmen of both Virginia and Maryland for the most part belonged to Calvinistic or evangelical groups with a sprinkling of Quakers and a somewhat larger number of German pietists. They had no sympathy with state support

of the Established Church or with the ceremonies of Angli-
canism and resented the payment of taxes to support the
Established Church. Thus it was no mere chance that later
the most articulate spokesman for the hill country, Thomas
Jefferson, should have been the author of the bill in the
Virginia assembly for the separation of church and state.

Already discernible before the Revolution were lines of
cleavage between the old and new, the East and West, the
settled regions of the Atlantic seaboard and the inland frontier. Though their differences would be dramatic, each
region in time would subtly influence the other, for men did
not live in utter isolation even on the eighteenth-century
frontier. As pioneers moved ever westward, they carried
forward something of the older civilization and established
in fresh soil traditions which were a part of their common
inheritance. Many of these western pilgrims would return to
tell their stories and excite the imaginations of stay-at-homes.
Men from the western country would also make their voices
heard in political debate combatting the inertia of mere age
and convention. Complacency would have small quarter in
the vigorous society which an expanding country generated.
The movement into the foothills of the Alleghenies and beyond, which began a slow transformation of the economy
and qualities of Virginia and Maryland, was a *Drang nach
Westen* of tremendous import for the future history of the
whole of English America.

CHAPTER THREE

Piety and Commerce in the New England Commonwealths

NO region in America has inspired such an enormous body of legend as New England. No term carries such a variety of connotations and meanings as the word "Puritan." Few themes in the history of that region lying north of the Hudson Valley can be treated without stepping into a controversy, past or present.

As ancestor worshippers in Virginia created the fiction of a cavalier society, so filial New Englanders fostered the myth of the pious perfection of their colonial progenitors. The eloquence of innumerable orators before the Pilgrim Society persuaded many that the men and women of Plymouth planted the seeds of religious freedom and American liberty. Equally earnest advocates of Massachusetts Bay declared the virtues of citizens of that commonwealth, described as the true bringers of light to forested darkness. To thousands of Americans, the story of colonial New England conjures up a single picture, the portrait of the stolid grey Puritan of St. Gaudens' statue, grave and humorless, intent upon the Ten Commandments. Others remember only of the story of the first Thanksgiving, of a solemn Pilgrim in the image of Governor Carver with a blunderbus under one arm and a turkey under the other, preparing for that initial American festival.

Inevitably the legendary concept of New England produced iconoclasts who sought to discount the worth of the Puritans, to prove them uncharitable hypocrites given over to secret sins, unholy greed, and grim intolerance. More friendly revisionists contented themselves with painting the Puritans as a much maligned folk who mingled their piety with a singular devotion to learning and literature, a people to whom an occasional bit of gaiety in dress and social intercourse was more than welcome.

Americans have inherited a set of conventional notions about the Pilgrims and the Puritans, and many retain images left by the verses of Felicia Hemans or Henry Wadsworth Longfellow. In legend and in fact, the thrifty settlers of New England have made such a deep impression upon American life that they deserve a more realistic appraisal than they have often received.

While Virginia and Maryland were establishing an agrarian society with a ruling class of wealthy planters, New England was developing trade and commerce and doing honor to the great merchants and masters of shipping. In time New England would have an aristocracy of trade, as the Chesapeake Bay region had an aristocracy of the soil. Neither section showed the less favored of mankind much sympathy or consideration. The acquisition of this world's goods was the measure of man's success, and in New England prosperity was also regarded as a token of God's favor, perhaps as a sign of spiritual election.

New England's civilization was inevitably commercial, as the South's was inevitably agrarian. In the beginning the determining factor was geographical rather than human, though before long the people of each region began to accentuate the qualities which their vocations dictated, and to believe that their peculiar genius lay in trade or in agriculture, as the case might be. New England's soil, except in rare spots in the river valleys, is thin and poor, and a backbone of rocky hills lies much nearer the coast than do the foothills in the South; thus the fall line of the rivers stopped navigation to the interior and prevented the kind of dispersal which took place in the South. But as was their habit, New Englanders soon turned this handicap to their advantage by harnessing the waterpower and establishing mills where they ground wheat and corn, or sawed lumber for export. The indentations in the coast made excellent harbors; good timber growing to the water's edge was an invitation to shipbuilding; and the teeming fish of the sea from Boston Bay to Newfoundland provided a source of profit as old and as respectable as the Apostles.

Settling in villages and towns around the numerous harbors, New Englanders quickly adopted an urban existence in contrast with the plantation life in Virginia and Maryland. Common pasture land and common woodlots served the needs of townsmen who often acquired small farms nearby. Farming was usually carried on as an adjunct of some trade or business and did not become the exclusive preoccupation of New Englanders. Going out each morning and returning each evening, farmers followed a practice common in English villages since the Middle Ages and took comfort in neighborly proximity to each other. Compactness made possible the village school, the village church, the town meeting, and frequent communication—all factors which had an immense influence on the quality of the developing civilization. Sharing similar hardships, cultivating the same kind of rocky acres, following simple trades and crafts, facing always the same misty sea, New Englanders rapidly acquired characteristics which marked them as a people apart. The qualities of the typical Yankee of later generations began to develop soon after the settlements were established.

Motives prompting Englishmen to show an interest in the northern coast of America were the same as those which induced settlements in Virginia and the West Indies: the desire for landed estates, the hope of trade, the lingering belief that gold might be found in the new country, and a professed zeal to carry the Protestant gospel to the heathen Indians. Since the reign of Henry VIII, Englishmen had taken a leading part in the fishing industry off Newfoundland, but if fishermen visited the coast of New England in the sixteenth century, they left no permanent trace. In 1602, one Bartholomew Gosnold made an unlicensed trading trip to what was then called North Virginia, in violation of Raleigh's patent for trade and colonization. His observation of the abundance of fish in the coastal waters opened the eyes of his countrymen and gave a name, Cape Cod, to a famous point of land. A year later, another inquisitive sea captain, Martin Pring, probed the coast, cast anchor in Plymouth harbor, and returned to give a favorable account of the country. A third expedition, in 1605, financed largely by the Earl of Southampton and Sir Ferdinando Gorges and led by Captain George Weymouth, brough back a valuable cargo of furs and sassafras and five kidnapped Indians. Sir Ferdinando took charge of three of these Indians and taught them to speak English. Their commendation of the north country so stirred their patron and mentor that he determined to send colonies overseas. For the rest of his long life, Gorges dreamed of riches from plantations in the New World—and spent an untold fortune in the effort to establish settlements in New England.

The charter under which the Virginia Company of London made the settlement at Jamestown provided for two companies, one of London and one of Plymouth. The London company was to have the right to colonize between latitudes 34 and 41 degrees; the Plymouth company similar rights between latitudes 38 and 45 degrees. Where the territory overlapped, neither company was permitted to make a settlement nearer than 100 miles of the other company's settlements.

The leading spirits of the Plymouth company were Sir Ferdinando Gorges and Sir John Popham, lord chief justice of England. Fired with hope of profits, they fitted out two ships in the spring of 1607 and on May 31, watched them sail away from Plymouth. Under command of George Popham, a brother of Sir John, and Raleigh Gilbert, son of Sir Humphrey Gilbert, one hundred and twenty prospective colonists were bound for the coast of Maine, where their settlement would not conflict with the claims of the London company. At this time Englishmen, for reasons unknown, believed that the climate of Maine was salubrious and that all the fruits and spices of Eden would grow there. The expedition reached the river Sagadahoc, now called the Kennebec, in August, and on the nineteenth they went ashore near the river's mouth and established a fort. Before the chill of early autumn foretold the hardships of winter, the little group was already quarreling. Popham, past seventy and unwieldy with fat, proved incompetent as governor, and Gilbert was reported to be jealous and headstrong, "a loose-liver" and possessed of "little zeal in religion." During the hard winter, Popham died, and in the following summer Gilbert returned to England, taking with him all the colonists. During their stay the settlers had built a ship which they named the "Virginia," and had collected a cargo of valuable furs. Though the first English colony in the north ended in failure, the experience showed some of the potentialities of the region: a rich trade in furs, a limitless source for ship's stores in the forests, and codfish innumerable offshore. Figs and dates, cinnamon and nutmeg, they decided, were not likely to be found in the Maine woods. Though the belief in the tropical fruitfulness of northern America died hard, from this time forward, promoters regarded the region more realistically. For several years after the collapse of the colony at Sagahadoc, no other attempt at settlement was made, but English fishermen made frequent visits and dried codfish there each summer.

Among the visitors was Captain John Smith, who proved an ardent propagandist as well as a shrewd observer. Smith's departure from Jamestown by no means ended his interest in America. During the spring and summer of 1614 he commanded two ships which touched the coast of Maine and explored the territory to the south in search of gold, copper, furs, whales, and fish. Whales were elusive and the metals nonexistent, but while his crews fished for cod and dried their catch, Smith with eight or nine others ranged the coast in a small boat trading for beaver, marten, and otter skins. When he returned to England, he wrote and published *A Description of New England; or, The Observations and Discoveries of Captain John Smith (Admiral of that Country) in the North of America in the Year of Our Lord 1614, with the Success of Six Ships That Went the Next Year, 1615 . . . With the Proof of the Present Benefit This Country Affords . . .* (1616). Included with the book was a map which bore a handsome portrait of the "admiral" and a legend declaring that place names had been given to "the most remarkable parts" by "the high and mighty Prince Charles, Prince of Great Britain." In the back of the little volume, inserted like an errata sheet, was a table of old and new names to enable the reader to make his own adjustment because "the book was printed ere the Prince His Highness had altered the names."

Although Smith had little encouragement to offer gold-hunters, he painted a vivid picture of the riches of the country in staple products and stressed the wholesomeness of the air; ". . . of all the four parts of the world that I have yet seen not inhabited," he observed, "could I have but means to transport a colony, I would rather live here than anywhere; and if it did not maintain itself, were we but indifferently well-fitted, let us starve." The main staple, he insisted, was fish, a commodity which had made the Hollanders rich and could bring similar prosperity to Englishmen. Drawing a lesson from the diligence of Dutch fishermen, he commented: "This is their mine, and the sea the source of those silvered streams of all their virtue."

John Smith's words were more prophetic of the future of New England than even he could have dreamed, and his recommendation of the country to "men that have great spirits but small means" would soon be heeded more earnestly than he knew. Smith's *Description* gave currency to the name New England which henceforth was the designation of that territory.

Sir Ferdinando Gorges in 1620 tried to rejuvenate the moribund Virginia Company of Plymouth, usually known simply as the Plymouth company. But he sought a new type of organization, a group of aristocrats instead of merchants, who would control the land granted them as proprietors in the manner of Lord Calvert's later grant to Maryland rather than as stockholders. In June 1621, he succeeded in getting a patent to the northern territory formerly granted to the Plymouth company. The incorporators of the new group, forty noblemen and landed gentlemen, were called the Council for New England. They were privileged to make sub-grants to colonists, establish plantations, make laws, organize a central government for all of New England, and in short, to rule in place of King and Parliament in New England. The Council also had the exclusive right to fishing in northern waters. This provision was bitterly contested by Virginia and other interested groups. Finally, when the Council for New England had proved a failure and Gorges received a new charter in 1639 to the "Province of Maine," a stipulation guaranteed freedom of fishing to all the King's subjects, and access to the shore for salting fish and drying nets.

Long before the English had established a permanent settlement in New England, Frenchmen had explored and claimed a vast territory to the north which they called New France. New France overlapped New England, and conflicting claims, as well as rivalry in the Indian trade, made Englishmen and Frenchmen natural enemies for more than a century and a half. The voyage in 1609 of Henry Hudson, an Englishman in the employ of the Dutch, gave that enterprising nation the Hudson valley and a nebulous claim to adjacent territory. Far to the south, English settlements in Bermuda pointed the way to the colonization of Barbados and the sugar islands of the West Indies; this development would lay the foundation for a trade which one day would make New England prosperous. Great events were shaping in the first two decades of the seventeenth century, but as yet New England was the resort of only itinerant fishermen and traders.

The first permanent settlement owed nothing to the activities of Gorges and his aristocratic brethren of the Council for New England, but had its inception in the restlessness of a small group of English religious zealots resident in Holland. They belonged to a sect of left-wing Puritans who believed that the Established Church could never be reformed to their liking and that their only hope lay in withdrawal. These Separatists were a small minority among the Puritans. In August 1609, a congregation of Separatists in the village of Scrooby, Nottinghamshire, annoyed because their conforming neighbors had them investigated by the ecclesiastical authorities, managed to flee England for tolerant Holland. Leaders of the group who ultimately settled at Leyden were William Brewster, a bailiff of the Archbishop of York, William Bradford, a well-to-do farmer's son, and John Robinson, their minister, a graduate of Cambridge.

After a decade in Holland, the English Separatists were eager to move again. They could not complain of Dutch hospitality or tolerance, but they were disturbed because in closely settled Holland, they could not remain apart, unspotted from the world. "But that which was more lamentable," explains William Bradford in his *History of Plymouth Plantation*, "and of all sorrows most heavy to be borne, was that many of their children . . . were drawn by evil examples into extravagant and dangerous courses, getting the reins off their necks and departing from their parents. Some became soldiers; others took upon them far voyages by sea; and others some worse courses tending to dissoluteness and danger of their souls to the great grief of their parents and dishonor of God." Moreover the truce between Spain and Holland was about to expire, and the Separatists feared a return of the Spanish terror. Last but not least of their reasons, says Bradford, was an "inward zeal . . . of laying some good foundation . . . for the propagating and advancing the gospel of the kingdom of Christ in those remote parts of the world; yea, though they should be but even as stepping stones unto others for the performing of so great a work."

The discontent of the Leyden Separatists led them to enter into negotiations with the Virginia Company of London for land in the New World. Hearing of their desires, Thomas Weston, a London promoter, offered them land under a charter which he and certain others held from the Virginia Company in the name of John Peirce and his associates. After tedious discussions, a minority of the Leyden group decided to accept Weston's offer and emigrate. Under their agreement, they would be sharers in a joint-stock company. The labor of each settler for seven years would purchase one share of stock in the partnership; other shares could be bought for £10 per share by either the London promoters or the settlers.

Though these terms seemed hard to the men of Leyden, in July 1620, a contingent of about thirty-five sold their possessions, bought a rotten little craft misnamed the "Speedwell," and embarked for Southampton; there they expected to fall in with the "Mayflower," a vessel chartered by Weston to take over eighty additional recruits. Most of these were employees hired by Weston, and some at least had no strong religious interests. Among them was Miles Standish, who went along as a military man and captain of the guard. After many disagreements and false starts, the voyagers abandoned the leaky "Speedwell," and all who were still resolved to go transferred to the "Mayflower," which weighed anchor on September 16, 1620. The prospective settlers numbered one hundred and one souls. Before they set foot on land, they had lost one by death and added two by birth—infant boys named appropriately Oceanus Hopkins and Peregrine White.

Late in November the "Mayflower," instead of making a landfall in Virginia, touched Cape Cod. Sick and sea-weary, the Pilgrims determined to abandon their patent and settle in New England. Though they had no legal right to land in that area, the shore was inviting, and they thanked God, says Bradford, because he had once again "set their feet on the firm and stable earth, their proper element." Upon that element they decided to stay.

To give some semblance of legality to their decision—and to quell certain rebellious spirits who threatened "that when they came ashore they would use their own liberty, for none had power to command them, the patent they had being for Virginia"—the Pilgrims drew up their now famous compact. It was a model of brevity, and, as it turned out, it remained for many years the fundamental instrument of government for the little democracy which it established without any other authority than the wishes of the signers. The forty-one men who subscribed their names to the document agreed "solemnly and mutually in the presence of God and one another [to] covenant and combine ourselves together into a civil body politic for our better ordering and preservation and furtherance of the ende aforesaid; and by virtue hereof to enact and constitute, and frame such just and equal laws, ordinances, acts, constitutions, and offices from time to time as shall be thought most meet and convenient for the general good of the colony, unto which we promise all due submission and obedience." They confirmed John Carver as their governor.

After several weeks of exploration by sea in the "Mayflower's" shallop, as well as by land, they at last discovered Plymouth harbor and chose as the site for their settlement an abandoned Indian cornfield. Though the Pilgrims did not know it yet, a plague—perhaps influenza or small-pox—had decimated all the Indian tribes along the seaboard. Using the "Mayflower" for quarters, the Pilgrims began work on the first house on December 25, 1620. The hardships of the winter were enough to discourage the stoutest hearts; before spring nearly half the company lay in the burial ground. Luckily, however, they had escaped Indian attack. Indeed, the savages who had survived the plague proved friendly. By a freak of chance, two Indians in the neighborhood, Samoset and Squanto, could speak English, and through them the settlers made a treaty with a tribal chief Massasoit. The Pilgrims attributed it to the providence of God that Samoset, who had learned his English from fishermen, and Squanto, who had been in England—probably one of the five kidnapped by Weymouth—were waiting in the wilderness to help them in their time of distress.

The settlement at Plymouth survived. When the "Mayflower" sailed for home in April, not one of the settlers returned, though many must have waved farewell with grave misgivings. By autumn, with health restored, the settlers gathered their scanty harvest and celebrated with a feast, washing down roasted venison, wild duck, clams, cornbread, and other substantial fare with wine made from native grapes, "very sweet and strong." Thus they began the tradition of Thanksgiving which President Lincoln in 1863 declared a national holiday.

The Pilgrims during the first autumn also discovered the profits of the fur trade. A party in the shallop, commanded by Captain Standish, went as far as Boston harbor and traded with the Massachusetts Indians for beaver and otter skins. That trade would prove their salvation in the years to come. "In fact," observes James Truslow Adams, "the Bible and the beaver were the two mainstays of the young colony. The former saved its morale and the latter paid its bills; and the rodent's share was a large one." When the little ship "Fortune," sent out by the London partners, arrived in November, the Pilgrims sent home a cargo of oak timbers and furs valued at £500.

Although Plymouth colony gradually increased, it never became large or very prosperous, and it had small importance in the development of the rest of New England. At the end of the first seven years, William Bradford—perennially governor after Carver's death in April 1621—and seven other Pilgrims bought out the London shareholders in the original joint-stock and distributed the land and cattle among the residents. This action freed the colony from the constant pressure of shareholders in London seeking to squeeze a profit from their investments.

By 1637, Plymouth's population had grown to a mere 549. Its people—plain farmers and artisans—were content with a life of patriarchal simplicity and were more concerned about their crops and the scarcity of beaver pelts than about education, literature, or the arts. In religion they were devoted to a pietistic faith, founded on the Bible as they read it, and most of them were innocent of theological knowledge or interest. In church government they firmly believed in the autonomy of the local congregation. Congregationalism, which became the prevalent form of church government in New England, owed something to the example of Plymouth, but other forces helped to bring about its establishment. "The Pilgrim Fathers stand rather as an emblem of virtue than a moulding force in the life of the nation," declares Charles M. Andrews, one of the wisest of New England's historians.

The symbolic quality of the Pilgrims, their heroism and faith, exerted a powerful influence upon nineteenth-century imaginations. To one man among the Pilgrims, William Bradford, we owe much of the modern interest in the little settlement. Bradford's narrative history, which he himself unostentatiously labelled "Of Plymouth Plantation," is one of the classics of colonial literature. It has the simplicity and dignity of John Bunyan and an easy grace and charm found in few other early New England writers. Since its first publication in 1856, it has focussed attention upon Plymouth and made the story of the Pilgrims better known than that of other settlements of greater economic and political significance.

While the Pilgrims were struggling for existence at Plymouth, adventurers of various sorts were making their way to New England, sometimes to the embarrassment of the Separatists, who found themselves the neighbors, and at times even the unwilling hosts, of sundry sorts of visitors. In the restless seventeenth century, not even three thousand miles of storm-tossed ocean could keep Plymouth a haven separate from the world. Thomas Weston, the erstwhile financial backer of the Pilgrims, sent over a rival colony in 1622. Fifty or sixty of this company, described as "rude and profane fellows," landed at Plymouth and had to be housed and fed by the Pilgrims until they could continue to Wessagusset, the site of modern Weymouth. Mismanagement brought them to the verge of starvation, and they dispersed the next year.

Of greater interest was a plantation attempted by a certain Captain Wollaston who settled in 1625 at Passonagessit, about where Quincy now stands, and named the spot Mt. Wollaston. Among Captain Wollaston's company was one Thomas Morton, Gent., lawyer of Cliffords Inn, a frolicsome spirit given to song and merriment. Though his career at Merry Mount—as he renamed Mt. Wollaston—was a scandal to his neighbors, against the somber background of traditional New England his gaieties almost glitter.

"Morton became Lord of Misrule and maintained, as it were, a school of atheism," disapproving William Bradford asserts. "And after they had got some goods into their hands and got much by trading with the Indians, they spent it as vainly, in quaffing and drinking both wine and strong waters in great excess, as some reported, £10 worth in a morning. They also set up a May-pole, drinking and dancing about it many days together, inviting the Indian women for their consorts, dancing and frisking together (like so many fairies or furies rather) and worse practices, as if they had anew revived and celebrated the feasts of the Roman goddess Flora, or the beastly practices of the mad Bacchanalians." This was not all. Morton showed ribald disrespect for his pious neighbors and lampooned them unmercifully. "Morton likewise, to show his poetry," Bradford continues, "composed sundry rhymes and verses some tending to lasciviousness and others to the detraction and scandal of some persons, which he affixed to this idle or idol May-pole."

Piety and Commerce in New England

Shocked at the carryings on at Merry Mount—and disturbed with greater reason because Morton and his crew were trading guns and shot to the Indians for beaver skins—the Pilgrims joined with a half dozen or more trading posts to stop the free life at Merry Mount by arresting its head. Early in June 1628 a corporal's guard under Captain Standish besieged Morton in his house and persuaded him to surrender without bloodshed. He was shipped off to England, but, as Bradford gloomily recounts, "nothing was done to him, not so much as rebuked, for ought was heard," and the next year Morton was back in his old haunts. Happily for the peace of the community, "some of the worst of the company were dispersed." Morton lived to write a narrative of these events under the title of the *New English Canaan*, published in London in 1632, which ridiculed the Pilgrims, especially his sometime jailer, "Captain Shrimp," as he disrespectfully called Miles Standish, whose pomp was greater than his stature.

A plan for settling New England, marvelous in pretentiousness, was devised during the winter of 1622–23 by Sir Ferdinando Gorges and his associates of the Council for New England who still believed that fortunes would be made by carving great estates out of rocky New England. Sir Ferdinando's son Robert was named governor general; Francis West was appointed admiral of New England; and an Anglican clergyman, the Reverend William Morrell, was chosen to head the Established Church in that unlikely wilderness.

Arriving in September, Gorges and a numerous company settled down in the houses left vacant six months before at Wessagusset when Weston's half-starved settlers dispersed. The winter was dismally cold, the company quarrelsome, and the prospects gloomy. When spring came, Governor Gorges left for home as did many of his group. Parson Morrell stuck it out another year and then decided that New England was not ripe for English episcopacy. Some of Gorges' people eventually found a friendly haven in Virginia.

A few stouthearted fellows remained for years in the vicinity. One of these, William Blaxton, a non-conforming Anglican preacher, built a house and planted an apple orchard on what was later called Beacon Hill, Boston, but after the Puritans occupied the region, he found solitude under his apple trees less inviting. Disturbed by the intolerance of the magistrates, he was constrained in 1635 to remove to Rhode Island giving a cogent reason for his departure: "I came from England because I did not like the Lord Bishops, but I cannot join with you because I would not be under the Lord Brethren."

The settlement which was to play the most important part in the development of New England—and of the nation—was composed of those Puritans who proved so distasteful to the Anglican orchardist on Beacon Hill. Numerically as well as in education and talents, the group who occupied the Massachusetts Bay region surpassed all others who had attempted to gain a foothold on the American mainland.

Reasons for the mass migration to Massachusetts Bay in the decade after 1630 must be sought in the troubled state of England in those years. This period saw the attempt by Charles I and Archbishop Laud to assert the supremacy of the King and the bishops over Parliament and the people. From March 2, 1629, until November 3, 1640, the King ruled without calling a Parliament. During this time, Laud, who became Archbishop of Canterbury in 1633, labored unceasingly to root out nonconformity in the Established Church. His enemies believed and asserted that he was rapidly moulding the English church in the pattern of Rome and eventually would return to the Catholic fold. Laud on his part believed that opposition to the ritual and customs of the Established Church, as exemplified by the behavior of Puritan clergy and laymen alike, would bring chaos to both Church and State. He was determined to use the authority of the King to maintain conformity.

The Puritans, who had been growing with vigor since

CHURCHES ON THE BOSTON HORIZON

AN EARLY VIEW OF NEWPORT

From eighteenth century engravings in the Huntington Library collection.

A VIEW OF NEW AMSTERDAM

From a seventeenth century engraving in the Huntington Library collection.

the 1560's, were the most numerous element in the Church of England when Charles I became king in 1625. The term Puritan means many things to many men, but in this time it was a general designation for those who objected to the authority of the bishops and opposed ritualism that smacked of the Roman Catholic liturgy. The Puritan group believed that essential truth in matters of church government, as well as in customs and ritual, was to be found by searching the Scriptures and not by heeding the promulgations of the bishops. The Puritans were merely carrying out the logic implicit in the fundamental doctrine of Protestants. The Puritan insistence on the supremacy of the Scriptures as the source of all truth and authority, and the corollary belief in the individual's ability to discover truth for himself, opened the way for an infinite variety of dissenting opinion.

In the first half of the seventeenth century, dissenters from the middle-of-the-road church which had seemed acceptable to most Englishmen during the reign of Elizabeth were a mixed lot, though the name Puritan is usually given to all types of Calvinists who refused to conform to the Established Church. The Puritans ranged from nonconformists within the Church to Anabaptists and Separatists who would have no part in the Establishment. They included Presbyterians, who wanted a centralized church organization but no bishops; Independents, who believed in the freedom of the individual congregation; and a varied assortment of Calvinistic sectarians whose political and religious views were both unorthodox.

The majority of those who came to Massachusetts Bay in the first waves of migration were conservative Puritans who had hoped to "purify" the Church without separating from it. Though they had become dissatisfied with the trend of Laud's efforts to induce conformity, few had actually suffered penalties. But they feared the future. America seemed in the 1630's to offer a refuge from an unhappy religious condition at home as well as a means of recovering from economic distress which depressions had brought to many landowners and to some of the middle class, especially in East Anglia, where the Puritans were strong.

The bright picture, painted by the Virginia Company and Gorges' propagandists, of prosperity to be achieved in America had not been wasted on dissatisfied Puritans. Stories brought back by fishermen who yearly visited American shores encouraged a belief in the goodliness of the north country. Already some hundreds of Englishmen were living in scattered outposts from Plymouth to northern Maine. Migration to New England had ceased to be an untried adventure. Consequently a plan devised during the summer of 1629 by John Winthrop and a group of his fellow Puritans to remove to Massachusetts Bay was far from quixotic. By the end of 1630 more than two thousand participants in this new enterprise had arrived and were busily establishing themselves in the Boston area.

Through an involved set of circumstances, a fishing station, occupied at Cape Ann late in 1623, became the forerunner of the Massachusetts Bay colony. When the Cape Ann venture failed, some of the fishermen moved down the coast to Naumkeag (later Salem). Hoping to save something from the collapse of the undertaking, the investors chose one of their own number, John Endecott, to go over in 1628 as governor of the tiny Salem community. With him went sixty new emigrants. From the Council for New England Endecott and his colleagues had obtained a patent for territory between the Merrimac and the Charles rivers.

Certain evidence suggests that before Endecott left England, he and his brethren were hatching a deep plan for something bigger than a plantation under the proprietorship of Gorges' Council for New England. At any rate by some miracle—perhaps by the intervention of the Earl of Warwick, who was friendly to the Puritans—Endecott and twenty-five others, on March 4, 1629, obtained a royal charter incorporating the Massachusetts Bay Company and granting that company land already held by the Council for

New England. This grant, in clear violation of Gorges' rights, was the source of bitter litigation, but Gorges was not able to have the charter annulled.

Although the incorporators of the Massachusetts Bay Company included men of various religious interests, the Puritans gained control before the first year had passed. Almost immediately they voted that control of the company would not be vested in a board of governors in England but should be forever in the hands of the members of the company who themselves were venturing to America. Unlike any other stock company yet organized for colonization, the corporation itself would emigrate and be self governing in the new land, subject only to the English crown. The colonists' most precious possession was the charter, which they took with them in the first ship.

The man who did most to shape the affairs of the company was John Winthrop, lord of the manor of Groton in Suffolk and a lawyer of prominence, who was chosen governor in the autumn of 1629. Despondent because of debts and the unfavorable state of business, politics, and religion, he had decided to leave England forever. Many of his kinsmen, friends, and neighbors shared his hope of a better world overseas where neither grasping creditors nor high-handed ecclesiastical courts would trouble them. Not all of the prospective colonists were in financial distress, but all looked forward to improving their condition.

Most of the Winthrop connection were devout Puritans. Like Winthrop, many of the other leaders came from substantial county families and had influential connections. Isaac Johnson, for example, was the brother-in-law of the Earl of Lincoln; to honor his wife, Lady Arbella, the flagship of the immigrant fleet of 1630 bore her name. Other men of substance in the early Puritan migration included Winthrop's brother-in-law, Emmanuel Downing (whose son George gave his name to London's Downing Street), Richard Saltonstall, John Humphry, Thomas Dudley, Simon Bradstreet, and numerous others.

Most of the leaders were educated men. Winthrop himself was a matriculate of Trinity College, Cambridge; the clergymen who came were largely Cambridge men, for the most part from Emmanuel College. These men of means brought their servants and helped less prosperous friends to join in the enterprise. Theirs was no shoe-string affair; making the first mass migration from England to America, they were determined to succeed. Among the emigrants were a large number of yeomen and artisans. The majority were probably Puritans, but by no means all belonged to the precise sect. Many simply saw what they thought would be an opportunity for a profitable venture and took a chance on life with the saints. In the years which followed saints and sinners were often a trial to one another.

Near the end of March 1630 Winthrop and three sons sailed from Southampton in the "Arbella." The rest of his family came later. Four ships made up the flotilla, bound for Salem, and seven other vessels followed shortly thereafter. By the end of the year seventeen ships had landed two thousand colonists who scattered over the Boston area and established themselves in many separate communities. The Great Migration continued for the next ten years; before it was over, nearly twenty thousand men, women, and children, with their chattels and possessions, had entered Massachusetts Bay. Many died, and when New England's Zion proved something less than Paradise, many went home to nurse their disillusion, but most of the immigrants set their minds and hands to the stern business of making a living and moulding a commonwealth suitable for the elect of God.

Before leaving England, Winthrop and others signed a paper declaring that they had no intention of separating from the Church of England. They probably believed sincerely at this time that they would simply set up the church in New England in a purified state, but colonial conditions altered the fact of communion with the Established Church at home, whatever might be the theory. Mere physical distance from the central ecclesiastical authority was a disruptive influence, even in strongly Anglican colonies like Virginia. Where the majority of the population hated the established hierarchy as well as the traditional ritual, the assertion of being a part of the Church of England was pure fiction.

A body of strong-minded clergymen in Massachusetts Bay saw to it that the church as they interpreted it in New England was vastly different from the church over which Archbishop Laud presided. While pretending to be part of the Established Church, the congregations of Massachusetts Bay recognized no authority other than God and his word revealed in the Scriptures. The true church was composed only of God's elected saints. Membership in the church therefore depended upon proof of election. Proof consisted of the convincing testimony before the whole congregation by each aspirant to church membership that he or she had experienced a personal conversion and conviction of salvation. Those who had not undergone this experience were excluded from membership with the elected saints. Church membership was consequently an exclusive privilege of a minority—the Puritan elite—for even in that religious age only a minority of the population received the blessed assurance of salvation. Upon church members the unconverted could look with envy and yearning because they enjoyed special benefits on earth as well as the prospect of heaven.

During the first decade of immigration at least sixty-five preachers arrived in Massachusetts Bay, and by 1645 the colony had twenty-three separate congregations. The Massachusetts clergy came with a high sense of destiny to lead the flocks of God's elect to the New Jerusalem. The preachers were a learned group, deeply versed in theology, and many could search the Scriptures in Hebrew or Greek as readily as they could in English. Two-thirds of them were graduates of Cambridge University, and the majority of these had had some connection with that great nursery of Puritanism, Emmanuel College. Since the Puritans regarded the Scriptures as the ultimate source of truth, they naturally looked to their most learned expositors of the Bible, the preachers, for wisdom and advice in things secular as well as things spiritual. Thus inevitably, the clergy came to occupy a position of preponderant influence in society.

The development of a theocracy in New England was a logical consequence of the theological convictions of the leaders. Although they were in essence Calvinistic, they had made some striking additions to the doctrines of the Genevan lawyer, principally in what is called their "covenant theology." They recognized three covenants: The Covenant of Grace or the invisible church of the saints known only to God; the Church Covenant or the visible church composed of such as may be deemed saints by their personal conviction and blameless lives; and the Civil Covenant or ruling body of civil authority.

If in theory church and state occupied separate places, in practice they were one and indivisible. "Theoretically God set up ministers to declare his will and magistrates to execute it," Herbert W. Schneider declares in a lucid book, *The Puritan Mind;* "ministers had authority to counsel, advise, and admonish; magistrates to command, judge, and punish. But in reality the civil compact was merely the physical enforcement and public advancement of whatever the churches desired. Religion was not a department or phase of social life; it was the end and aim of all life; and to it, consequently all institutions were subordinated."

To the Old Testament the secular authorities looked for their fundamental law, and, as one religious historian has observed, the clergy constituted themselves "the supreme court set up rightly to interpret it." For at least two generations in Massachusetts Bay the preachers were more powerful than the civil magistrates and were in fact the supreme court of civil authority. What was "delivered in the pulpit was soon put into an order of the court," a contemporary commented of John Cotton, and the same could be said of other influential ministers.

For years John Cotton was the brightest star in the galaxy of New England's preachers. A fellow of Emmanuel College, a vicar of St. Botolph's in Boston, Lincolnshire, he had preached the farewell sermon over Winthrop's party when they sailed from Southampton. Finally, in 1633, he too fled Laud's England and came to Boston in New England to become the Puritan pope of that commonwealth. Of the reverence in which he was held, Roger Williams remarked with faint irony that many "could hardly believe that God would suffer Mr. Cotton to err." When he died in 1652, it was remembered that a comet had previously appeared in the skies, and its slow dimming was taken as a signal of God's intention to remove the brightest of his earthly luminaries to celestial glory.

Naturally when the fathers of the Bay colony in 1636 came to frame a body of laws, they would consult Mr. Cotton, and just as naturally he would submit a set of statutes based on the Ten Commandments entitled *Moses His Judicials*. Despite a belief in Master Cotton's infallibility, his code leaned too heavily on Leviticus, even for the saints, and they next turned to another preacher, the Reverend Nathaniel Ward of Ipswich, who had formerly been a practicing lawyer. He devised an instrument which blended nicely the Old Testament, Magna Charta, and the precedents of common law as revealed by Sir Edward Coke's *Reports*. Ward's compilation, called the "Body of Liberties," was pleasingly legalistic, satisfactorily pious, and severe enough to commend it to the conservative magistrates and elders. Though liberals disliked the code because it concentrated power in the hands of a few, it was accepted for a trial period of three years. In 1647 the general court ordered a new compilation, published as *The Book of the General Laws and Liberties . . .* (1648), which served as an alphabetical handbook of laws in existence in Massachusetts Bay.

A system of government, theocratic and authoritarian, rapidly evolved in Massachusetts Bay as the clergy and the lay leaders of the Puritans realized their opportunities. Though the colony's political action was based on the charter, the leaders departed from the letter of its provisions whenever conditions demanded. The members of the company who elected Winthrop the first governor also provided for a deputy governor and a court of seven assistants, or magistrates as they were generally called. In the beginning this small group distributed land, made the laws, and enforced the regulations under which the colony operated. Winthrop, himself an aristocrat, had searched the Scriptures without finding any warrant or authority for democratic government, and was anxious for a small and highly select body to retain control over the multitude. Neither in Winthrop nor in any of the other leaders was there a glimmer of faith in the capacity of the humble and unlettered to take part in government.

Though Winthrop and the magistrates may have wished to make their authority self-perpetuating, the charter provided for elections by the "freemen" of the company, who were to meet at four general courts each year. The question now arose as to who constituted the freemen. Since obviously the generality of people could not all be considered freemen, the magistrates in the autumn of 1630 issued an invitation to everyone who felt that he ought to be included as a freeman of the company to hand in his name—certainly an informal way of handling a difficult problem. Some suspicion that freemen might have more responsibilities than privileges perhaps kept many settlers from applying, for only one hundred and eight turned in their names; some of these had been on the ground before the Puritans arrived and were Anglicans in religion.

Because the Puritan leaders were displeased at any dilution of their power, within a year they took a step which placed authority entirely in the hands of the pious. After a meeting of the general court of May 31, 1631, it was decreed that no man could be a freeman, with the right to vote, who was not a member of one of the churches in the jurisdiction of the colony. Thus church membership became a prerequisite for the right to vote, and the franchise was restricted to the small body of saints. The majority of the population, disfranchised because they could not qualify for church membership, had no voice in the central government.

From a colony controlled by a company charter, Massachusetts Bay quickly developed into a holy commonwealth, in reality self-governing but governed by a small ruling class —an aristocracy of the pious. In the background was the charter of privileges—which few men had seen—and across the ocean was the King of England to whom Massachusetts paid scant lip service. For a time Winthrop and his assistants governed like the patriarchal judges of Israel, but Massachusetts was too full of individualists to make their arbitrary rule satisfactory even to all of the elders.

Opposition to Winthrop's rule came to a head at a meeting of the general court in the spring of 1634 when a group of freemen led by Israel Stoughton demanded to see the charter, which revealed that the general court had the only power to legislate. Winthrop's excuse for the exercise of this power by the governor and assistants alone was that the general court had become too unwieldy. To remedy the condition, provision was made for each of the towns to choose two or three deputies to represent the freemen of these towns in three meetings of the general court. The fourth, or May meeting, was election day, and the freemen all were expected to vote in person or by proxy. The general court also established its right to levy taxes and raise money and to distribute the public lands.

From this beginning the legislative assembly evolved, with a lower house composed of the deputies and an upper house of magistrates. But such is the irony of politics that the completion of the legislative system depended upon the outcome of a celebrated trial involving the possession of Mrs. Richard Sherman's white sow, which, she claimed, Robert Keaynes, a Boston merchant, had penned up. Charges and counter charges were made until finally the merits of the case were forgotten in the greater argument over whether the magistrates could veto a decision of the deputies in the general court. The clergy and conservatives of Winthrop's type stood out for the veto to keep the commonwealth from falling into the chaos of what Winthrop called "a mere democracy," but in the end the deputies won a partial victory, and after 1644 the magistrates and deputies sat as separate houses. Each could disapprove the actions of the other.

From the first, the rule of the Puritan oligarchy was distasteful to many of the politically submerged, and at times the dictation of the clergy was too much even for the church members. When John Cotton, who ever yearned to impart his political wisdom, preached a sermon in 1634 proving that magistrates had a vested right in their offices and God meant for them to be reelected so long as they walked righteously in their vocations, the freemen responded by voting out of office Cotton's candidate, Governor Winthrop, and electing Thomas Dudley in his stead. The choice was not a victory for liberalism, however, for Dudley was a narrow bigot without Winthrop's grave kindness of spirit. The oligarchy a little later established a life council of magistrates, including both Winthrop and Dudley, but the experiment proved unpopular and was soon abandoned.

Despite occasional setbacks, the clergy and conservative laymen fastened an iron grip on Massachusetts Bay and retained their hold for the better part of the seventeenth century. In the phrase of that day, the magistrates were "the nursing fathers" of the church, and the clergy were the advisers of the magistrates. With a zeal unsurpassed by Archbishop Laud—or the Spanish Inquisition—the theocracy grimly determined to maintain conformity of religion in Massachusetts Bay. The erstwhile nonconformists, once established in power in New England, would brook no deviation from *their* established church. Heretics in theology or politics stood in danger of banishment for the first offense; later the death sentence was invoked against Quakers for returning from banishment. Unorthodox opinions were a danger to both church and state, as the *Laws and Liberties* of 1648 made clear in prescribing banishment for Anabaptists and such schismatics, "which opinions if connived at by us are like to be increased among us and so necessarily bring guilt upon us, infection, and trouble to the churches, and hazard to the whole commonwealth."

But no law can bind the mind of every citizen, or curb the tongue of the inspired zealot, as the Puritans ought to have known better than most. Though their laws might threaten punishments prescribed in Leviticus, some men—and some women—would speak their minds, and, if necessary, suffer for their consciences. One of the early nonconformists was a double trial to the Puritans because he was a minister of blameless life, a brilliant man, skillful in debate, and learned in the law, having had as his guardian the great common lawyer Sir Edward Coke. This man was Roger Williams, of Pembroke College, Cambridge, who came to New England early in 1631. Though he was clearly a godly minister, the magistrates soon knew that he would be a "trouble-maker"—the phrase with which authoritarians always damn dissenters from their views.

Williams, destined to play a great and noble part in the development of liberal ideas in America, declined a call from the Boston church because at this time it still maintained the fiction of communion with the Church of England and was thus guilty, in Williams' opinion, of compounding corruption. He went instead to Salem and from thence to Plymouth, in search of a pure and separate church. By 1634 he was back at Salem, which accepted him as pastor though a general court complained against him. Williams had already antagonized the ruling class by insisting that meetings of the clergy and their interference in politics threatened the freedom of individual congregations. More heinous than this offense was a question which he raised concerning the right of white settlers, under their charter, to take the Indians' land.

Because both in England, and elsewhere in New England, enemies of the Puritans were attacking the legality of their charter and their commonwealth, the leaders were peculiarly sensitive to criticism from within the colony, criticism which might get back to the authorities in England and add color to the charges made by the Bay colony's enemies. Moreover, the question of Indian lands was a sore one, for not everyone was easy in his conscience on that score, and the less said about it the better.

Opinion varied as to whether the Indians were children of the devil who might be exterminated and their land appropriated, or whether they were heathen waiting for salvation who might profitably give up their lands in exchange for a celestial heritage. Many inclined to the infernal view. Even William Bradford, less bloodthirsty than some, could describe the massacre in 1637 of more than four hundred Pequots burned in their fort at Mystic, in terms reminiscent of an Old Testament prophet exulting in the slaughter of the worshippers of Baal: "Those that scaped the fire were slain with the sword; some hewed to pieces, others run through with their rapiers, so as they were quickly dispatched, and very few escaped. It was conceived they thus destroyed about 400 at this time. It was a fearful sight to see them thus frying in the fire, and the streams of blood quenching the same, and horrible was the stink and scent thereof. But the victory seemed a sweet sacrifice, and they gave the praise thereof to God who had wrought so wonderfully for them, thus to enclose their enemies in their hands, and give them so speedy a victory over so proud and insulting an enemy."

Some viewed captive Indians as a useful commodity in trade to be exchanged for more tractable African slaves. Emmanuel Downing writing to John Winthrop in 1645 points out the advantages of war with the Narragansett Indians: "A war with the Narragansett is very considerable to this plantation, for I doubt whether it be not sin in us, having power in our hands, to suffer them to maintain the worship of the devil which their paw waws [pow wows] often do. Secondly, if upon a just war the Lord should deliver them into our hands, we might easily have men, women, and children enough to exchange for Moors [Africans], which will be more gainful pillage for us than we conceive, for I do not see how we can thrive until we get into a stock of slaves . . ."

For Williams to question the right of Christians to take land from devil-worshipping heathen, and for him to cast doubt upon the wisdom of the elders in meeting together to keep church and state in unified harmony, constituted an offense of such gravity that he was hailed before ministers and magistrates for examination, and in October 1635 the general court sentenced him to banishment for spreading "new and dangerous opinions against the authority of the magistrates." During the six weeks allowed to settle his affairs, Williams persuaded some of the Salem congregation to remove with him to Narragansett Bay to form a colony there, but when this news reached the magistrates, they sent to arrest him. A colony of heretics on their southern flank was not what they wanted. With only his cloak for protection, Williams fled through the snow-drifted woods to find a refuge among friendly Indians in Rhode Island. Soon he established a colony where men might believe as they wished and church and state would be forever separate.

Congratulating themselves on being rid of this pestilent heretic, the magistrates next turned their attention to an even more annoying troublemaker, in this case a brilliant woman, Mrs. Anne Hutchinson, wife of a merchant, William Hutchinson, and the mother of fourteen children. Mrs. Hutchinson, who had been in John Cotton's congregation in England, reached Massachusetts Bay in 1634. Soon she was holding meetings in her home, analyzing and explaining the sermons of the local ministers. But Mrs. Hutchinson was more than a pious reporter. She was a mystic holding that the individual by contemplation and illumination can come into direct contact with the divine. Furthermore, she revealed a belief in a covenant of grace, meaning a religion of divine love, as opposed to the covenant of works, meaning a religion of moralism and law requiring the visible demonstration of virtue by action. It was more important, she insisted, to be filled with the holy spirit than to devote one's efforts to external manifestations of good works. Among the New England preachers, the only ones of whom she approved entirely were John Cotton and her brother-in-law John Wheelright.

Mrs. Hutchinson's teachings, somewhat akin to the Quaker belief in the inner light and to the faith of other pietists, was at odds with the legalistic Calvinism of the Puritans. She was also a grievous offender on other scores. She was a woman, and it was presumptuous for her to meddle with theological matters. Furthermore, she made the cardinal mistake of gaining a following. Even Master Cotton nodded a vague approval at her praise of his preaching until it became dangerous to befriend her. Young Harry Vane, elected governor of the colony in 1636, was her friend. Besides these, a host of others, especially in Boston, eagerly accepted her religion of kindness and love instead of the cold legalism of the orthodox leaders in the Bay, whose gloomy hatred of all other faiths led them into various types of fanaticism. With his own hands sour John Endecott had lately cut the cross from English flags on ships in Boston harbor lest this symbol be construed as popish.

In the opinion of the rulers of the colony, Mrs. Hutchinson was corrupting religion and undermining the state, and she must be silenced and punished. Believers in her teachings were described as Antinomians, that is to say, heretics. Especially obnoxious was the Reverend John Wheelright, who early in 1637 was found guilty by the general court of sedition and contempt of authority. The clerical party then bent its efforts to defeating Vane for reelection as governor, and it succeeded in returning Winthrop to office. A meeting of twenty-five preachers, the magistrates, and other laymen, who met to discuss the heretical state of the colony, listed eighty-two offending beliefs "some blasphemous, others erroneous, and all unsafe." The stage was now set for the sacrifice of the chief victim. Mrs. Hutchinson was called before the general court, which had been stacked with her opponents by an illegal election.

The court sat at Newtown lest the more liberal atmosphere of Boston contaminate the proceedings. More than forty members, assisted by advising clergymen, were present when the frail woman, whose only offense was teaching a religion of divine love, was called to the bar of judgment. Among other things she was charged with traducing the magistrates and ministers, but they could submit no proof. Badgered by her inquisitors about the source of her doctrines, she finally declared that she spoke by direct revelation from God. With that, John Cotton, looking for a way to disavow an admirer who had become an embarrassment, asserted that she was deluded, and Thomas Dudley, the deputy governor, added that her delusion was of the devil. Her conviction was of course a foregone conclusion despite a stout defense by William Coddington, later an important figure in the development of Rhode Island, and William Colbourn, delegate from Boston. Mrs. Hutchinson was sentenced to banishment, and the court declared her "a woman not fit for society." When she asked why she was being banished, Governor Winthrop, usually kind and just according to his lights, gave a surly answer: "Say no more, the court knows wherefore and is satisfied."

Posterity has not been satisfied with that answer, nor were many contemporaries in the Bay colony. John Wheelright and Mrs. Hutchinson were forced to seek refuge elsewhere, but their influence lingered, as did that of Roger Williams. Though the clerical party for the time was supreme, and the Reverend John Wilson gloated as over a victory won against the pagans, the spirit of unrest was abroad among the unchurched multitude as well as among many godly freemen. A day would come when, even in Massachusetts Bay, the clergy would not sit at the right hands of the civil magistrates, but that day was not yet.

A few years later another troublesome spirit in the person of Dr. Robert Child arose to plague the oligarchy and pose the greatest danger to their leadership since the colony's settlement. A travelled and cultivated man, a doctor of medicine from Padua, and an ardent Presbyterian, Child in the autumn of 1645 induced six colleagues to join with him in remonstrating to the general court over tyrannical conditions in the colony. They demanded that the administration of justice conform to the laws of England, that the franchise be extended to all English subjects, and that churches which so desired be permitted to adopt the Presbyterian system. Coupled with the demand was the threat of an appeal directly to the English Parliament for a redress of grievances. At this moment the Long Parliament ruled England, and within Parliament the Presbyterian faction controlled. If Dr. Child and his Remonstrants reached England with their complaints, the charter might be endangered, the congregations might find themselves controlled by presbyteries, and the colony made subservient to the English Parliament. This was a thought to give the ruling elders the shudders. Accordingly they hailed the Remonstrants before the general court and levied fines of from ten to fifty pounds against them. When Dr. Child tried to go to England to present his case, they seized and searched him, confiscating his papers which they interpreted as seditious. The general court in 1647 finally levied a fine of £200 against him. Since one of the Remonstrants had got away to England, the court appointed Edward Winslow of Plymouth as agent and sent him to England to confute any charges of maladministration in Massachusetts Bay. Winslow was successful in circumventing Child's complaints, and the matter dropped.

If Anne Hutchinson's mild doctrines of grace had annoyed the Puritans, the Quakers' more intense faith in divine illumination as the sole guide to life drove them to a fury of persecution. Every belief of the Quakers was in opposition to the orthodox doctrines of the Massachusetts theocracy, and particularly obnoxious was the Quaker objection to "a hireling ministry." With holy dread, the ruling elders anticipated the arrival of Quakers upon the sacred soil of the Bay colony and took steps to prevent their flourishing. The first Quaker problem arose in July 1656 with the arrival from

Piety and Commerce in New England

Barbados of two Quakeresses, Mary Fisher and Ann Austin. Since the authorities had witchcraft on their minds, having just hanged a witch, one Ann Hibben, they ordered the Quaker women stripped stark naked and their bodies examined minutely for tokens that might denote them as witches. Finding nothing that would give an excuse for another hanging, they imprisoned the women in a cell without light and five weeks later deported them to Barbados.

John Endecott, in whose soul no spark of charity ever glowed, warned the next Quakers to arrive that they might "stretch a halter" and a little later proved his words no idle threat. Believing their laws too lax, the general court in October 1656 decreed that any ship captain bringing in Quakers should be fined £100; that Quakers themselves should be imprisoned, whipped, and put at hard labor; and that anyone who defended them should be fined and for a third offense, banished. For attempting to aid two Quaker women starving in prison, an old man, Nicholas Upshall, was fined £20 and sent wandering on foot toward free Rhode Island in the dead of winter.

Spurred by the persuasions of two zealous preachers, John Norton and Charles Chauncy, the general court in 1658 made the death penalty legal for Quakers who persisted in returning after banishment. Previously the laws had permitted only tortured imprisonment, whippings and mutilations. William Brend, an old man, for instance, endured prison with irons locking his neck and heels together for sixteen hours; on the following day his jailers gave him one hundred and seventeen strokes with a tarred rope, cutting the flesh on his bare back to ribbons, and leaving him unconscious. When the populace of Boston made an uproar over this cruelty, Parson Norton defended the jailer and the justice of the sentence. When two Quakers were unable to pay their fines, the treasurer sold their two children into bondage and shipped them out of the colony. Finally, in a climax of persecution, in October 1659, Endecott and his fellow judges sent to the gallows three Quakers, William Robinson, Marmaduke Stevenson, and Mary Dyer. With a rope about her neck, Mary Dyer saw her two companions hanged and then heard her sentence commuted to banishment. But the spirit of martyrdom possessed her, and she returned to Boston in the spring of 1660 to bear witness against the unjust law and was forthwith hanged. Though the clergy and the magistrates approved these cruelties, the people were stirred as never before against the tyranny of the theocracy. Something called public opinion was slowly gathering force against the powers of priestcraft and oppression.

Unwanted by the leadership, often unrecognized for what it was, by the back door, a measure of democracy crept into Massachusetts Bay. The town meetings, famous as the nurseries of popular government, helped to perpetuate many traditions of English municipal independence and gave a certain amount of experience in self-government to the majority of the population. Though the towns of Massachusetts Bay developed around the church congregations and looked up to the local pastor as their high priest, the whole population, whether church members or not, by the very exigencies of frontier life, had to share in civic obligations and to some degree in consultative meetings. Despite the desire of the Puritan elders to hold a tight rein on authority, the *Laws and Liberties* of 1648 specified that non-freemen had the right to attend town meetings, courts, and councils and to present petitions in person or in writing, to make complaints, and otherwise to raise pertinent issues.

Even though non-freemen—that is, non-church members —could not vote, they at least could make a stir in their own communities and exert an increasing influence upon those who could vote. As the population of Massachusetts Bay grew, the proportion of church members diminished. In a struggle to keep power in the hands of godly folk by broadening the base of church membership, the churches adopted in 1662 what is known as the Half-Way Covenant, which provided that children of church members, even though they had not experienced conversion, might be admitted to the church and thus qualify as freemen. These unregenerate church members were not admitted to the sacrament of the Lord's supper, but they could vote as freemen of the commonwealth. The Half-Way Covenant was a symbol of the gradual weakening of theocratic control, but the forces of liberalism, often defeated before by the pious oligarchy, would have many battles still to fight.

During the years when the iron laws of the Puritans were strongest in Massachusetts Bay, many immigrants, finding the yoke of the clergy too heavy to bear, fled to neighboring communities and helped in the development of the rest of New England. Those who suffered banishment for their consciences' sake became involuntary additions to other settlements. Unwittingly the leaders of Massachusetts Bay by their narrow intolerance contributed to the development of neighboring colonies, notably Rhode Island.

After a hard winter among the Rhode Island Indians following his flight from Salem in January 1636, Roger Williams bargained with the savages for a parcel of land and began a settlement which he named Providence. Soon other fugitives from the Puritan magistrates found refuge there. Williams divided the land among the settlers, and they made a compact which clearly stated that civil authority would have jurisdiction only in civil matters and no civil law would compel a man's conscience. The separation of church and state and the guarantee of liberty of conscience became one of the cardinal principles of the government of Providence.

In Williams' conception, all faiths—Protestants or Catholics, Turks or Jews—should have the right of freedom of worship without penalty from any authority. To many in the seventeenth century this belief in liberty of conscience looked like starry-eyed folly, but Williams, in a famous letter to the town of Providence in 1655 showed that he was both a liberal and a man of common sense: "There goes many a ship to sea," he declared, "with many hundred souls in one ship, whose weal and woe is common, and is a true picture of a commonwealth or human combination or society. It hath fallen out sometimes that both Papists and Protestants, Jews and Turks, may be embarked in one ship; upon which supposal I affirm that all the liberty of conscience that ever I pleaded for, turns upon these two hinges —that none of the Papists, Protestants, Jews, or Turks, be forced to come to the ship's prayers for worship, nor compelled from their own particular prayers or worship if they practice any. I further add that I never denied that, notwithstanding this liberty, the commander of this ship ought to command the ship's course, yea, and also command that justice, peace, and sobriety be kept and practiced both among the seamen and all the passengers. If any of the seamen refuse to perform their services, or passengers to pay their freight; if any refuse to help, in person or purse, toward the common charges or defence; if any refuse to obey the common laws and orders of the ship, concerning their common peace or preservation; if any shall mutiny and rise up against their commanders and officers; if any should preach or write that there ought to be no commanders or officers, because all are equal in Christ, therefore no masters nor officers, no laws nor orders, nor corrections, nor punishments;—I say, I never denied but in such cases, whatever is pretended, the commander or commanders may judge, resist, compel, and punish such transgressors according to their deserts and merits."

Not anarchy but democracy was Williams' ideal. His devotion to freedom of conscience did not prevent the expression of his own opinion, but he would not allow his prejudice to color his sense of justice. He did not like Quakers, for example, partly because of their refusal to cooperate in civil and military responsibilities, and he carried on an acrimonious debate with John Fox and his colleagues, but he offered Quakers a haven in Providence and defended their right to liberty.

Williams was an advanced thinker for his time, and his influence spread beyond New England. When he went to England in 1643 to obtain a charter which would legalize the settlement of Rhode Island, he found a political conflict raging between Presbyterians and Independents. He lent his influence to the Independents, and the publication in London the next year of his tract, *The Bloody Tenent [Tenet] of Persecution for Cause of Conscience*, gave support to their cause and helped defeat the Presbyterians in 1648.

Providence Plantation, which Williams had established, grew into an agrarian community composed of hardworking farmers who planted corn and tobacco and raised hogs, cattle, and sheep. Although the settlers never became very prosperous, they raised a surplus of farm products and managed to carry on a trade with the other colonies.

Meanwhile other settlements were developing. William Coddington, one of Mrs. Hutchinson's disciples and later a Quaker, with Roger Williams' help, bought from the Indians the island of Aquidneck and in 1639 established himself and a group, including Mrs. Hutchinson and her husband, at Portsmouth. They elected Coddington judge in the Old Testament sense, and established freedom of worship. But before a year had passed, the Hutchinsons tired of Coddington's leadership, and with the support of Samuel Gorton, a free lance in theology, they made a new civil compact which did not include Coddington as their head. Whereupon he moved to the opposite end of the island and established Newport. Gorton was too much of an individualist to dwell in peace with the Hutchinsons, and he too soon found it expedient to leave Portsmouth. Eventually he bought land of the Indians at Shawomet, which he renamed Warwick in 1648 in honor of the Earl of Warwick, chief of the Parliamentary commission on plantations, who gave him a letter commanding Massachusetts Bay and other colonies to leave him undisturbed in his possessions.

Though the leaders of these four Rhode Island communities all had different theological views, they agreed on liberty of conscience and the separation of church and state. Finally, in 1644, through the influence of Roger Williams they obtained from Parliament a charter uniting them as Providence

Plantations in the Narragansett Bay. The communities agreed to form a sort of federation with an assembly made up of representatives from each town. This assembly would elect annually a president and four assistants. But legislation had to be initiated and ratified by the towns. The system of local control varied with each town, Providence being the most democratic. There the heads of families met every two weeks to consider matters concerning the public welfare. Only women, children, and bachelors were excluded from voting. The Rhode Island assembly of 1647 voted to outlaw trials for witchcraft and imprisonment for debt. It also reduced the number of offenses punishable by death. Rhode Island applied for a new charter in 1663 from Charles II, because a charter from Parliament would have no standing in the eyes of the Restoration government. This charter incorporated the democratic provisions of the first one and was so satisfactory that it remained the basis of Rhode Island's jurisprudence until 1842.

With all of their liberty of conscience and democracy—perhaps because of it—Rhode Islanders were not free of contentions. The communities were wracked with constant disputes, particularly over land titles, for the boundaries of purchases from the Indians were at best vague and indefinite. Furthermore, Massachusetts Bay and Plymouth kept up a constant nagging at the colony which they had every reason to hate. They laid claim to its territory, and they annoyed its citizens. Roger Williams, Samuel Gorton, and others on the Bay colony's blacklist, had to have a safe-conduct from authorities in England to travel across Massachusetts without molestation. Troublemakers from Massachusetts and Plymouth sowed dissension in Rhode Island and did all in their power to discredit the democracy of Narragansett Bay. Rhode Islanders themselves were responsible for a state of disorder which existed at times within their borders and brought discredit upon the colony. Their individualism occasionally smacked of anarchy, and their bickerings gave color to the statement that "in the beginning Massachusetts had law but not liberty and Rhode Island liberty but not law." Nevertheless, Rhode Island stands out in the seventeenth century as a beacon light pointing to the freedom of later generations.

Heretics in search of liberty of conscience were not the only ones who swarmed from the Massachusetts hive to settle the neighboring lands. Even orthodox Puritans, irked by the success of rivals for power, made their way beyond the colony's borders. Traders and restless souls in search of better lands and opportunity also made up a portion of the migration away from Massachusetts. Boston was a great port of entry through which thousands funneled to all of New England.

Connecticut owed its settlement to numerous elements but chiefly to the overflow from Massachusetts. News of the fertility of the Connecticut River early attracted the interest of farmers who were having a tough time on hard-scrabble acres and were ready to brave the danger of the Indians for level land and deep soil. Rumors of profits from the fur trade on the Connecticut had also focussed attention on that region and brought from New Amsterdam inquiring Dutchmen who built a trading post in 1633 on the site of Hartford. Traders from the Pilgrim colony at Plymouth, competing with the Dutchmen, set up a palisaded station where the town of Windsor later developed. Ownership of the Connecticut lands was a matter of continuing dispute. The Pequot Indians were the aboriginal inhabitants of part of the territory; Massachusetts Bay claimed it as an extension of her grant; and a group of English noblemen headed by Lord Saye and Sele and Lord Brooke claimed it as a proprietary grant. In the end the frontiersmen who actually settled it became the possessors, but not without a deal of controversy. In 1635 the English proprietors sent over John Winthrop, Jr., as "governor of the river Connecticut" and places adjacent; with him came a small party who established a fort at the river's mouth and later expanded it into Saybrook plantation.

The Atlantic Frontier

Best known of the migrations to Connecticut was the exodus of the Reverend Thomas Hooker's congregation from Newtown (Cambridge), Massachusetts, in the summer of 1636. After making a somewhat complicated agreement with both Massachusetts Bay and John Winthrop, Jr., the congregation set out on foot, one hundred strong, driving their cattle before them; like the Israelites they went in search of the Promised Land. They were all Puritans, and they declared that their only reason for removal was a desire for better farm lands and more room for their cattle. But Hooker, and his colleagues, John Haynes, a former governor of Massachusetts Bay, and Roger Ludlow, an ex-magistrate, were not altogether satisfied with the leadership in the Bay; they had their own ideas of administration and looked forward to a freer hand in Connecticut. The migration of Hooker's congregation to the frontier was symbolic of a movement which would not end until the whole of the American continent was occupied. For more than two centuries after him, groups and communities would make the same sort of journey with the same gleam of hope in their eyes. Hooker's people settled near the Dutch fort and founded Hartford. Other congregations followed and established themselves at Wethersfield and Windsor.

In 1637, Windsor, Hartford, and Wethersfield united to form a self-governing colony of Connecticut with a general court, composed of six assistants and three representatives from each of the three towns. The system of government evolved in Connecticut grew out of the experience and practice in Massachusetts, but in several particulars it gave greater freedom to the people. On the last day of May 1638 Hooker himself preached a famous sermon which emphasized the mutual responsibilities of magistrates and people and declared that power in the state resides in the people. Some phrases suggest a similarity with the ideas of Roger Williams, whom Hooker had known, but Hooker did not go so far as Williams in the advocacy of anything approaching modern democratic doctrines. The platform of government was laid down in a document drawn up by the general court entitled the Fundamental Orders. The most distinctive difference from the laws of Massachusetts was the extension of the franchise, for church membership was not made a prerequisite for voting. Even with that improvement, Connecticut was not a democracy, for in the seventeenth century less than half the male inhabitants were admitted as freemen by the general court. Nevertheless, Hooker, Haynes, Ludlow, and their brethren did make a great advance over the theocracy whence they had come. Conservatives in Massachusetts Bay looked upon Hooker's experiment in government with more favor than upon Rhode Island's, but many shook their heads over the incipient democracy, which they detested.

More to the taste of the elders of Massachusetts was the colony of New Haven, established on Long Island Sound in 1638 under the leadership of John Davenport, a Puritan preacher of the extreme type, and Theophilus Eaton, a London merchant. New Haven from the first was a bulwark of conservatism, peopled by devout trading folk chiefly from London, who looked to the laws of Moses for their guidance. Modelling their polity on the practices in the Bay colony, they outdid that theocracy in strictness. As in Massachusetts only church members could vote. Theophilus Eaton became the first governor and retained that office until his death in 1658. Since the Scriptures made no mention of trial by jury, New Haven did not permit jury trials in either the town or colony courts. Instead the reverend magistrates dispensed justice. In this respect New Haven differed from the other New England colonies.

Connecticut in 1662 applied to Charles II for a royal charter to legalize its right to the territory which the colony claimed by occupation and possession. John Winthrop, Jr., a man of great personal charm and cultivation, who for many years had been the guiding spirit of Connecticut, was the agent who persuaded the king to confirm the colony's rights of self government as already established in the Fundamental

Orders. To New Haven's distress, the communities which made up that Old Testament commonwealth were included in the charter and New Haven was perforce absorbed into Connecticut.

In the meantime, immigrants from Massachusetts Bay, as well as traders and adventurers from England, had filtered into the region to the north. That shadowy organization known as the Council for New England, after vainly trying to establish plantations, granted to Sir Ferdinando Gorges and Captain John Mason the country north of Massachusetts. In a division of the territory in 1629, Gorges took over Maine and Mason the district which he named New Hampshire. Actual colonization, however, resulted less from the activities of the proprietors than from the enterprise of sundry immigrants in search of liberty, land, or beaver pelts.

John Wheelright, the Antinomian fugitive from Massachusetts, led a little flock of fellow believers into New Hampshire and settled Exeter. The town of Hampton was a trading post occupied by orthodox Puritans from the Bay. Other settlements were made up of Anglicans or plain sinners. In spite of Mason's claims, Massachusetts asserted a right to New Hampshire and during the Puritan Revolution in England spread her jurisdiction over its towns. At length in 1679, after many years of dispute, New Hampshire was declared a royal province. Maine had a similar history of development. Massachusetts also laid claim to this territory and succeeded in establishing her jurisdiction over Maine and maintaining it until 1820.

Danger from outside and quarrels within induced the Puritan colonies in 1643 to create an informal confederation called "the United Colonies of New England," composed of Massachusetts Bay, Connecticut, New Haven, and Plymouth. Because of Rhode Island's heterodoxy—and perhaps because of a desire of Massachusetts to absorb it—that colony was omitted from the league. Fear of the French to the north and the Dutch to the south made some union desirable, but a greater and more immediate danger at this time was the unrest of Indian tribes as the colonists encroached still further upon their lands. The Pequot War of 1637 had resulted in the annihilation of that tribe to the satisfaction of the Puritans, but other tribes were strong and threatening. In 1675, the Indians themselves united under a chief known as King Philip and made a devastating onslaught upon outlying settlements. By providing a certain measure of cooperation, the New England Confederation now proved its utility. When King Philip's War was over, many a settler lay dead, but the power of the Puritans had been established on the gradually expanding frontier. Defeated and captive Indians were retained as slaves in New England or sold to the sugar planters of the West Indies.

While Massachusetts Bay was extending its political influence in New England, it was growing apace at home and expanding its commerce with other American settlements. Ships from Boston, Salem, and other ports traded with the French in Acadia, the Dutch in New Netherlands, the English, French, and Spanish in the West Indies, and with neighboring English settlements. From the mid-seventeenth century onward, Massachusetts rapidly grew prosperous, and Boston became the greatest port in New England. From it went ships to Europe, Africa, and the West Indies bearing cargoes of New England products and returning with goods which the inhabitants required.

Making a virtue of her necessities, New England turned to trade and commerce instead of depending upon a single staple of agriculture in the way that Virginians looked to tobacco for their livelihood and prosperity. Farming in New England was a valuable complement to trade, but it was a varied type of agriculture, based on the needs of subsistence, with surplus food products swelling the exports carried by New England's ships to foreign ports. Wheat, corn, peas, pork, and beef, dried, cured, or pickled as each might require, went from New England farms to the European or West Indian market. And always there were fish—fish salted and dried stiff as oak boards, fish pickled in brine, fish reduced to train oil, fish fresh and fish rancid—eternally fish to bring prosperity to those who caught them and to those who transported them. Ship stores and wooden ware early became commodities of profitable export. The hardwood forests yielded staves and hoops for barrels to hold the sugar and molasses of the West Indies, or the wine of Madeira, the Canaries, Spain, and Portugal. Oak timbers for ships' hulls, tall pines for spars and masts, and rosin for the seams came from the forests of Massachusetts, New Hampshire, and Maine. Horses and live cattle, especially from the pasture lands of Rhode Island, were a profitable export. The forests swarmed with hogs that grew fat on autumn acorns and eventually found their way into the casks of salt pork which made up the sailor's staple of diet. The fur trade was also a constant source of profit in international commerce.

From the day in 1631 when John Winthrop launched his locust-ribbed ship of thirty tons, "The Blessing of the Bay," shipbuilding was an ever-growing industry in New England. By the middle of the seventeenth century, ocean-going craft were slipping down the ways in Boston, Dorchester, Salem, and Charlestown. When the 200-ton "Trial" was launched in 1642, a sermon by John Cotton was part of the christening; its initial voyage to the Canaries, thence to the West Indies, and home to Boston blazed a way later followed by hundreds of others. It brought home as part of its cargo wine, sugar, and molasses. Building their own ships, sailing them to the ports of the world, carrying freight as they went, the shipmasters of New England in the seventeenth century laid a foundation for a traffic which constantly grew in importance in the following years.

New England shippers discovered two commodities which enriched them and their ports: rum and slaves. The celebrated triangular traffic between New England, the African coast, and the West Indies had its beginning in the seventeenth and its fruition in the eighteenth century. With a cargo of rum, shipmasters sailed along the Guinea coast and traded it for a cargo of slaves whom they brought back to Barbados or some other West Indian port. There they sold them at a handsome profit and loaded sugar, molasses, and rum which they brought to New England. Early in the eighteenth century New Englanders perceived that they could distill fermented molasses into rum more efficiently than the West Indians; from that time onward, distilling was a major industry, and the rum of Boston or Newport became an important article of barter for ship captains in the Guinea trade, who brought back ever increasing cargoes of Negroes greedily bought up by sugar-growers in the islands. But not all of the Negro slaves were consigned to the West Indies. Gradually more and more went to the English colonies on the mainland—a few to New England, but most to the plantations of Virginia, Maryland, and the Carolinas. One of the richest importers of Africans in the eighteenth century, Peter Faneuil, a pious soul, thanked God that he had been the instrument for bringing so many heathen to salvation. His seventeenth-century forerunners were equally conscious of their divine mission.

Upon an ingenious, thrifty, and diligent people, God smiled and gave them the blessing of prosperity. Their religion, seeming so cheerless, was a strength and an asset in mundane affairs of trade and commerce. As religion was inextricably mingled with politics, so it was part of the web of business. The New England Puritan's code of ethics, with its everlasting insistence upon the prudential virtues of sobriety, thrift, and diligence provided an almost fool-proof guide to success.

From the time the child was old enough to toddle, he heard injunctions against waste of any kind, especially against wasting God's precious time, against extravagance, against any folly which tended to disperse one's substance. Poverty, which somehow smacked of begging friars and popery, found no favor in Puritan eyes. Protestant asceticism never suggested retirement from the world but rather an incessant devotion to one's calling. Acquisitiveness became an end in itself and prosperity was an evidence of the earnest and righteous pursuit of one's vocation.

The prudential code of New England was not exclusively Puritan; it was a part of the bourgeois ethics which had been preached for generations by middle-class Englishmen, but it received new emphasis and direction from the Puritans. God was infinitely closer to the Puritans than to most of human creatures, and adherence to this code was part of the covenant of works which the clergy so zealously supported.

The happy alliance between religion and trade did not deter the saints from evading the Navigation Acts when they could. Indeed, these laws, enacted to create a closed empire in which the colonies would supply the raw materials and the mother country the manufactured products, were often more honored in the breach than in the observance. Not only did American skippers carry on a legitimate trade with England and other English colonies, or with the ports of Southern Europe as permitted under the law, but they also smuggled extensively. Enumerated articles such as tobacco and dye-woods, which legally could be delivered only to English ports, found their way to France and Holland, while the manufactures of those countries instead of being imported by way of England and paying the duty there, came direct and duty free to American merchants.

As English commerce expanded in the later seventeenth century, the Stuarts and William III in turn attempted to discipline the colonies for failure to observe the Navigation Acts. The New England colonies' persistent disregard of these laws prompted both Charles II and James II to curb the self-governing powers of Massachusetts Bay and adjacent territories. After the accession of William III and the beginning of the struggle which he waged with the French, the necessity of guarding the northern frontier as well as the desirability of enforcing the maritime laws induced that monarch to strengthen the royal authority in New England. The golden age of Massachusetts Bay, when the saints dwelt in independent obscurity, was over before the end of the seventeenth century. Henceforth New England, as part of a growing empire, could not be neglected by the authorities in England.

To improve the administration of colonial affairs, Charles II, in 1674, vested control in the hands of the Privy Council, which set up a standing committee called the Lords of Trade. When this committee proved inefficient, William III, in 1696, reorganized colonial administration by creating the Board of Trade and Plantations.

The Lords of Trade in 1676 realized that all was not well in the conduct of affairs in New England. To discover the truth of conditions there, they sent over an inquisitive and persistent agent named Edward Randolph who immediately became a thorn in the flesh of the authorities governing Massachusetts Bay. For many years, bad-tempered Edward Randolph and the equally irascible magistrates of the Bay colony carried on a diplomatic vendetta in which each side tried to blacken the other's motives and character.

Randolph, a loyal servant of the King and a devoted communicant of the Church of England, could see nothing but fault in the independence of Massachusetts Bay. His reports were damaging. He pointed out that the Puritans had usurped authority by coining money, calling themselves a "Commonwealth," issuing a charter to Harvard College, and disobeying the Navigation Acts; he also condemned both Massachusetts and Connecticut for the harshness and severity of their Mosaic laws; invariably he accused the colonies of conspiring to evade and circumvent the King's authority. Biased as were Randolph's reports, they contained much truth and confirmed suspicions already held by the Lords of Trade. After several years of listening to accusations and denials, the Lords of Trade made up their minds and on October 23, 1684, the King declared the famous charter of Massachusetts Bay null and void. In the eyes of the conservative deputies and magistrates the worst had befallen the colony. Now the devil and all his hosts even to the surpliced priests of the Church of England might be expected on their sacred soil.

The old government, evolved under the charter, of elected governor, magistrates, and deputies was no longer legal, though for a time it continued to function. The English authorities, in 1686, as a temporary expedient chose Joseph Dudley president of a provisional government and sent over hated Edward Randolph to serve in various capacities, including that of secretary to the colony and collector of customs. Almost worse than the new government, in the eyes of die-hard Puritans, was the arrival at the same time of the Reverend Robert Ratcliffe, a parson of the Church of England, who organized the first Anglican congregation in Boston and conducted the orthodox ritual with surplice and prayer book. To add insult to injury, he presently obtained permission to hold his services in old South Church before the regular Congregational sermon. Grumbling Puritans waited outside for the last echo of the prayer book to die away before stalking in to their own service. Nothing more clearly symbolized the collapse of the Puritan Commonwealth than the Anglican prayers read from the pulpit of South Church.

Shortly before Christmas, 1686, Sir Edmund Andros, a former governor of New York, arrived in Boston with the new title of Governor-General. The authorities in England were determined to weld New England into a unified dominion and to that end Randolph had already served notice on Connecticut and Rhode Island to surrender their charters. Though Rhode Island complied, Connecticut delayed evasively. At length Connecticut was brought under the authority of the governor-general, but it maintained the fiction of independence by hiding its charter in a hollow tree.

Andros had come with authority to extend the dominion over all of New England. When the danger from the French threatened more acutely in 1688, he received a second commission extending his authority over New York and the Jerseys. Thus the Dominion of New England gave the appearance of a great unified front facing the Dominion of France in the north. Actually it was a paper realm. Andros had no adequate colonial service to govern his dominion, hardly more than a corporal's guard of regular troops, almost no military equipment, and few funds under his control. Nevertheless the experiment was significant of the future. It showed a new determination to incorporate the colonies into an imperial organization and it sounded the knell for the kind of isolated independence which the New England colonies particularly had cherished.

Though local government and the minor courts continued to operate as formerly, Andros as viceroy of the authoritarian Stuarts was commanded to rule without benefit of representative assemblies. New Englanders who had grown accustomed to self-government felt gloomy indeed over the arbitrary rule which the governor-general seemed destined to establish and they set about blocking his administration where they could.

When the report of the Glorious Revolution and the accession of William and Mary reached Boston in the early spring of 1689, the news precipitated a revolt against Andros and his party. By June Massachusetts had resumed its former way of government and the other colonies quickly wiped out all vestiges of Andros' brief regime.

But if New England expected the new rulers to look with favor upon their independence, they were mistaken. King William had a war to wage against France, with the rewards of empire at stake, and he was determined that the northern colonies should be ruled for the military, as well as for the economic, advantage of the home country. Although Increase Mather had gone to England to plead for the restoration of the charter and a legal return to the old way of the commonwealth, he was only partially successful. The new charter which he managed to procure in 1691 was at best a compromise which gave Massachusetts the general character of a crown colony and yet retained some features of self-government which the old charter had provided. For example, though the King appointed the governor, the legislative assembly chose the members of his council. The new charter divorced New Hampshire from Massachusetts, though later the same governor ruled over both. Massachusetts retained control of Maine. Under William and Mary, Rhode Island and Connecticut were permitted to resume their charters and rule themselves, with, however, somewhat more surveillance from overseas.

The threat of the French and their Indian allies on the northern and northwestern frontiers made even conservative isolationists in Massachusetts realize that there was virtue in unification. Men who had damned the Dominion of New England under Andros found reasons after 1689 to commend a united front—under the leadership of Massachusetts Bay. Finally in 1699 a nominal unity was achieved under Richard Coote, first Earl of Bellomont, who was commissioned governor of Massachusetts, New Hampshire, and New York, and military commander in time of war of Rhode Island, Connecticut, and New Jersey. Lord Bellomont's dominion was no bed of roses. Irreconcilables in Massachusetts still resented a royal governor and Bellomont found himself checked by hostile factions. Lacking any effective military power or adequate financial support, and without even the intelligent backing of the home government, Bellomont, like many royal governors who followed him in New England and elsewhere, discovered that the colonies were an unruly lot and governing them a thankless task.

The transition of the commonwealth of saints into a royal province was the work of years but the early eighteenth century saw its completion. As New England's prosperity increased, it became less austere. Boston and the larger towns lost their rustic simplicity. Sailors who had visited the four corners of the earth swaggered—and sometimes reeled—down their streets. Rich men rode in coaches and wore periwigs. Women, godly and ungodly, flaunted silk petticoats and took pride in gold brooches, earrings, and such baubles. Anglican clergymen were no longer as rare as the phoenix.

Piety and Commerce in New England

In politics, there was even a court party composed of supporters of the royal governor—rich merchants, members of the Anglican Church, wealthy and privileged folk in general, and especially those who distrusted the pious and provincial Puritans of the country and smaller towns. The old order was changing. The old isolation was gone. But Puritan traits, which had made a deep impression upon all of New England, would persist in religion, government, and society throughout the eighteenth century and later. The royal province of Massachusetts, which, because of her position and power exercised a considerable influence over the neighboring colonies, was royal with a difference.

The Puritans who came to Massachusetts Bay in the 1630's were convinced that they were a peculiar people chosen of God to establish his kingdom in the New World. The very title of Edward Johnson's historical narrative, the *Wonder-Working Providence of Sion's Savior in New England* (1654), is indicative of their sense of divine mission. Throughout the seventeenth century the idea that New England was the glorious culmination of a long cycle of development finds constant iteration among the preachers and historians, and the notion of New England's special destiny prevailed long after it had lost any religious connotation.

Because they were a people set apart as an example of God's elect, an obligation rested upon them to be fit vessels of the Lord. This sense of their responsibility to God accounts for the unusual zeal for education displayed in Massachusetts Bay and in other portions of New England from the days of the earliest settlements. "After God had carried us safe to New England—and we had builded our houses, provided necessaries for our livelihood, reared convenient places for God's worship, and settled the civil government —one of the next things we longed for, and looked after, was to advance learning and perpetuate it to posterity, dreading to leave an illiterate ministry to the churches when our present ministers shall lie in the dust," declared the author of *New England's First Fruits* (1643). When John Winthrop and the first contingent of Puritans sailed from England for the new Canaan across the seas, John Cotton advised in his farewell sermon that they provide teachers for their children lest they "degenerate as the Israelites did." The immigrants needed little urging on this score. The education of children and the training of ministers became a major concern soon after their settlement.

The citizens of Boston in the spring of 1635 held a mass meeting and elected "our brother Mr. Philemon Pormort" as schoolmaster and established a grammar school which was later known as the Boston Public Latin School. In 1642 the General Court passed a law requiring the selectmen of each town to inquire into the literacy of the children and to fine parents and masters who refused to render an account of their children's ability "to read and understand the principles of religion and the capital laws of the country." In 1647, the General Court, noting that "one chief project of that old deluder Satan [was] to keep men from the knowledge of the Scriptures," instructed each township of fifty householders to provide a schoolmaster to teach reading and writing.

Furthermore each township of one hundred households was required to provide a Latin grammar school. In 1648, the General Court again looked into the state of education and ordered the selectmen to maintain "a vigilant eye over their brethren and neighbors to see first that none of them shall suffer so much barbarism in any of their families as not to endeavor to teach, by themselves or others, their children and apprentices so much learning as may enable them perfectly to read the English tongue. . . . And further that all parents and masters do breed and bring up their children and apprentices in some honest and lawful calling, labor, or employment, . . . if they will not or can not train them up in learning to fit them for higher employments."

Connecticut and New Haven followed the example of Massachusetts Bay in providing for compulsory elementary education, and by 1671 only Rhode Island among the New England colonies had failed to enact such legislation.

Implicit in these early pieces of legislation were two ideas which became a part of the American tradition: first, that salvation in some fashion can be achieved through literacy, and second, that through education every individual has an opportunity of moving into some "higher employment." These beliefs, nurtured by the Puritans of New England, became articles of faith which most Americans to the present day accept and believe.

The Latin grammar schools set up in New England were modelled after the traditional schools of England. The basis of their curriculum was Latin grammar and literature, with some attention to Greek. To curriculum-makers of the present day, the course of study seems barren and arid, but the schoolmasters of the seventeenth century instilled, not merely the rudiments of grammar, but the wisdom of the ancients as revealed in the literature.

One of the most famous Latin teachers was Ezechiel Cheever, who became the master of the Ipswich Grammar School in 1650 and in 1670 moved on to the Boston Public Latin School, where he established a reputation for thoroughness. Stroking his long white beard, he was a figure as venerable as Moses, but when he snatched his birch rod his wrath blazed like Jehovah's rage. Cheever, the author of a Latin *Accidence*, turned out a long line of pupils well-drilled in correct grammar, good manners, and sound principles of religion. Surely New England fathers could ask for nothing better in a teacher. When Cheever died in 1708 at the age of ninety-four Cotton Mather, a former pupil, wrote in an elegy:

> *Do but name Cheever, and the echo straight*
> *Upon that name good Latin will repeat.*

Higher education had its beginning with the establishment in the autumn of 1636 of a college, soon to be called Harvard in honor of John Harvard, the first benefactor, who gave a sum of money and his library to further so promising an undertaking. The college was authorized on October 28 by the General Court which "agreed to give £400 towards a school or college, whereof £200 to be paid the next year and £200 when the work is finished. . . ." A year later the General Court ordered the college erected at Newtown, and one year after this, in 1638, the Court changed the name of Newtown to Cambridge as the proper name for a college town. The new institution got off to a bad start through the appointment of one Nathaniel Eaton as the first professor and head of the school. Though Eaton had come recommended for his knowledge of theology, he proved a rascal, starved the students, embezzled college funds, beat his assistant with a cudgel, and finally fled to Virginia where he succumbed to vice, "being usually drunken, as the custom is there," John Winthrop reported.

Despite this untoward beginning, the college at Cambridge soon became a nursery of learning and a training school for Puritan preachers. Influenced strongly by Emmanuel College, Cambridge, a great seminary of Puritanism, Harvard was designed to insure a continuous supply of ministers who would not be ashamed to measure their learning with the best graduates of the universities in England. Indeed, in the minds of the founders there was a distrust of the older universities and a suspicion that they were being corrupted by prelatical influences.

During the first half of the seventeenth century, Harvard teachers were fond of demonstrating the logic of Petrus Ramus, a French Protestant, who had challenged the authority of Aristotle and the old scholastic philosophy, but Aristotelian learning continued for many years to have an important place in the Harvard curriculum. Finally, the newer doctrines of Descartes found their way into Harvard, and according to the official historian, there was "the interplay of three distinct systems of logic at Harvard in the Puritan century: the Aristotelian, Ramean, and Cartesian."

Piety and Commerce in New England

Although Harvard in the seventeenth century was primarily theological in its purpose, its influence in maintaining intellectual standards is incalculable. During the middle of the century, strict Puritans of old England sent their sons to Harvard in the hope of finding a more religious influence, and Cotton Mather boasted that New England had sent back to England more preachers than it had ever obtained therefrom—a statement of doubtful statistical accuracy. By 1696, one hundred and seven preachers out of a total of one hundred and twenty-two in Massachusetts and Connecticut were graduates of Harvard.

Near the turn of the century, conservatives in New England were disturbed over allegations that Harvard had become a hotbed of latitudinarianism and worldliness. The Reverend Solomon Stoddard preached an election sermon in Boston in 1703 in which he criticized the college at Cambridge: "Places of learning should not be places of riot," he sourly remarked; "ways of profuseness and prodigality in such a society lay a foundation of a great deal of sorrow. . . . 'Tis not worth the while for persons to be sent to the College to learn to compliment men and court women; they should be sent thither to prepare them for public service and had need to be under the oversight of holy men."

To organize a college in which holy men would guide aspirants to knowledge along orthodox paths was the purpose behind the establishment of the institution which was presently called Yale. The new college was the creation of staunch Puritan preachers and conservative laymen like Judge Samuel Sewall who looked askance at the growing liberalism at Harvard. In the autumn of 1701 the Reverend James Pierpont, pastor of the New Haven church, with the help of some of his brother-ministers and of Isaac Addington and Judge Sewall of Boston, procured from the legislative assembly a charter for a "Collegiate School" in Connecticut. The school was first established at Saybrook under Mr. Pierson as rector, but in 1716 the trustees agreed to move to New Haven. Through the efforts of Jeremiah Dummer, agent for the colony of Connecticut in England, the school received gifts of books and money. Among the benefactors was Elihu Yale, a former official of the East India Company, who had been born in Boston. After a letter from Cotton Mather suggesting that the hopeful school might confer immortality upon him by taking his name, Yale in 1718 sent over three bales of goods from India, some books, and a portrait of George I. The sale of the goods brought over £500 in cash and the school at New Haven became Yale College. Throughout the eighteenth century it stood as a fortress against unpuritan heresy and was a bulwark protecting the steady habits of Connecticut.

Although Harvard and Yale and the grammar schools of the principal towns gave to the more settled regions of New England educational advantages similar to those which Englishmen could find at home, the outlying districts, the frontiers of New Hampshire and Maine, and the plantations of Rhode Island suffered for lack of schools. Furthermore, the increasing materialism of the commercial towns, the preoccupation of the frontier with the elemental struggle for existence, and the gradual weakening of religious incentives diminished the zeal for education at the end of the seventeenth century. The average literacy and the cultural level perceptibly decreased as time went on. This slump was inevitable as commercial activity and pioneering ventures absorbed more and more of the country's energy.

From the earliest days of settlement, books played an important part in the cultural development of New England. The first immigrants brought along their little libraries and continued to import books from London. Though the Puritans had an inordinate appetite for religious writings, they did not confine their reading to such works. Even the Pilgrims at Plymouth, far less bookish than their more erudite neighbors of the Bay colony, had substantial libraries. Miles Standish, for instance, had about fifty books, including histories, works of military science, Homer's *Iliad*, Calvin's *Institutes*, a handbook on farming, and an encyclopedia.

William Brewster had similar books with somewhat more emphasis on religion. He also owned such works as Machiavelli's *Prince*, Bacon's *Advancement of Learning*, and Sir Thomas Smith's *Commonwealth of England*.

In the Bay colony, the clergy and many of the better educated laymen gathered useful libraries. John Winthrop was constantly ordering books from London. His son, John Winthrop, Jr., had approximately one thousand volumes in 1640. The largest library in all New England was collected by Cotton Mather who, at the time of his death in 1728, owned nearly four thousand volumes. Only William Byrd's library in Virginia equalled Mather's collection in number and variety. Utilitarian works—schoolbooks and treatises on medicine, farming, horsemanship, housewifery, conduct, and all of the affairs of everyday life—works of classical literature, histories, treatises of statecraft, politics, law, philosophy, science, and learning, books of devotion, sermons, and religious controversies, theological works, and a sprinkling of belles-lettres were to be found on the bookshelves of New England. By the 1680's booksellers were doing a thriving business in Boston. Invoices of books shipped to John Usher, for example, show a wide variety of works ranging from Greek and Latin classics and theological and religious works to the interminable prose romances of the day. Apprentices, and perhaps their masters, were also buying from Mr. Usher less edifying works like *Scoggin's Jests* and *The Damnable Life and Deserved Death of Dr. John Faustus*.

In literary production, New England had an advantage over the other colonies through the establishment in 1639 of a printing press in Cambridge. A preacher, the Reverend Jose Glover, bound for New England, conceived the notion of bringing along a printing press to be an instrument of salvation. Unhappily the minister died on the voyage, but his colleague in the venture, Stephen Daye, a locksmith, survived to set up the press and operate it for the Widow Glover and her children. So far as known, the first imprints

[153]

were *The Oath of a Freeman* and *An Almanac for the Year 1639*, but the press's next work was *The Whole Book of Psalms* (1640), better known as the "Bay Psalm Book," edited by the learned Richard Mather, first of that name in America. This metrical translation of the Psalms, intoned by godly Puritans on the Sabbath, symbolized the religious output of the printing press in Massachusetts Bay for the next half century. Samuel Green, who took over the operation of the Cambridge press in 1649, was the progenitor of a line of printers, who carried the art in later years to Connecticut, Maryland, and Virginia. A press was established in Boston in 1674 by Marmaduke Johnson, who died before it had printed a sheet, but the work was continued by other hands.

Boston also saw an attempt in 1690 to establish a newspaper, but after the first issue, which offended the authorities, it was suppressed. Finally in 1704 the Scottish postmaster, John Campbell, managed to launch successfully the *Boston News-Letter* which survived despite—or perhaps because of—its dullness. Fifteen years later a new postmaster, William Brooker, established a rival sheet, the *Boston Gazette* which had for its first printer, James Franklin, half-brother of Benjamin Franklin. Neither the *Boston News-Letter* nor the *Boston Gazette* satisfied all tastes, and James Franklin, who had ceased to be the *Gazette's* printer by 1721 became the publisher of a third paper, the *New England Courant*, which deliberately chose to flout long-faced Puritans by announcing that its main design was "to entertain the town with the most comical and diverting incidents of human life, which in so large a place as Boston will not fail of a universal exemplification." Franklin's paper was soon thoroughly hated by the Mathers and others of the "best people" but it succeeded in entertaining the town for nearly five years. Boston, however, was not yet a safe haven for believers in the freedom of the press, as Franklin discovered when he was forced to spend a month in jail for offending the governor. Finally in 1727, he moved to Newport, Rhode Island, where a few years later he began the publication of another newspaper, the short-lived *Rhode Island Gazette*. Other newspapers and other printing presses, established in New England in the first third of the eighteenth century, increased the means of expression of a region already more articulate than other parts of English America.

The literary production of New England in the first century of settlement was characteristic of the religious preoccupations of the dominant classes. Of all forms of writing, sermons were by far the most numerous of the products of the printing press. The pulpit eloquence of the more popular preachers soon found its way into print. Regular sermons on the Sabbath, occasional homilies on the execution of a notorious criminal or the election of the magistrates, the week day lectures—in short, the wisdom of the clergy delivered on any occasion—were deemed worthy of publication for the instruction of the public. The high water mark for ecclesiastical production was reached in the person of the Reverend Cotton Mather who alone was the author of more than four hundred and fifty separate works. As befitted one so erudite, Mather felt himself equipped to discuss any question, from the iniquities of man to the mind of God. The crowning masterpiece of his career was the *Magnalia Christi Americana or, The Ecclesiastical History of New England* (1702), a work so huge, and so important in the author's eyes, that it had to be printed in London. In this monstrous folio, the whole pageant of New England's history is displayed as it appeared to the prejudiced eyes of its most prolific and pedantic writer.

The most popular single work in colonial New England was neither sermon nor history, but a long poem describing in terrifying and sulphurous terms the Last Judgment, Michael Wigglesworth's *The Day of Doom*, published at the Cambridge Press in 1662. The first edition of eighteen hundred copies was quickly bought up and it was immediately republished at Cambridge and in England. Thereafter it saw frequent reprintings. As a broadside it was sold by peddlers. Everybody read it, and nearly everybody owned a copy of the fearful epic of doom. Children, trembling with terror, were forced to memorize and recite its warnings. Until the nineteenth century it remained the best known poem in America.

What effect *The Day of Doom* had on New England psychology, no man can say with certainty, but the influence of this detailed and concrete description of man's condemnation and punishment for innate depravity, the result of Adam's sin, must have been stupendous. How much hysteria it induced in children and in adults is not recorded, but to it must be attributed some of the abnormal fears which produced the witchcraft hysteria culminating in 1692. When not even blameless infants who died at birth could escape the excoriations of the avenging Judge who sat on the Throne of God, sinful men and women could only tremble at the thought of the last day. Even the Elected Saints, certain of sitting at the right hand of God, must have been moved by vicarious fear. Not even the small mitigation vouchsafed infants was much comfort:

> *A crime it is; therefore in bliss*
> *You may not hope to dwell;*
> *But unto you I shall allow*
> *The easiest room in hell.*

Men, women, and children pondered the lines of this dreadful poem, written in mind-gripping ballad meter, and suffered relentless torment.

Supernaturalism, magnified by the Old Testament ideology of the Puritan religion, manifested itself in its grimmest form in the trials and punishment of witches. The belief in witchcraft was not peculiar to New England; for centuries it had been a popular delusion, and from time to time in all of the American colonies the charge of witchcraft had been brought against someone; but only in the Puritan commonwealths was witchcraft prosecuted vigorously, with the professional aid of the clergy, and only there were witches punished with terrifying severity. A wave of witchcraft

Piety and Commerce in New England

prosecutions had swept Massachusetts and Connecticut between the years 1647 and 1663, but it paled into insignificance beside the campaign against these minions of Satan from 1688 to 1693. To strengthen any faltering belief in supernatural interventions in the affairs of men, the Mathers, Increase and Cotton, did their best. Increase Mather published in 1684 *An Essay for the Recording of Illustrious Providences* which was so immediately popular that it had three printings within the year. With convincing detail the book described "things preternatural which have happened in New England," including a report on demons, possessed persons, and apparitions. Increase's son Cotton made even more telling contributions after the children of a Boston brickmason named Goodwin were reported bewitched; Cotton took one of the Goodwin girls into his house for observation of the case and published the result of his study as *Memorable Providences Relating to Witchcrafts and Possessions* (1689).

By this time the whole community was aflame with talk about witches and no eccentric old woman or man was safe from suspicion. The hysteria reached a crescendo in the year 1692 and centered at Salem, which seemed peculiarly afflicted with witches and their victims, but the terror was not confined to any neighborhood. Before the orgy of fear was over, more than two hundred persons had been accused, the jails were full, and a score of witches had been hanged. One man, old Giles Corey, for refusing to put himself on trial, had been pressed to death with weights in accordance with ancient English law. During the height of the terror not even social prominence was certain protection, and Cotton Mather began to have qualms over the summary justice which the courts handed out. Though he later expressed some doubts concerning the validity of the tests given the accused, he published a defense of the judge's work at Salem which he called *Wonders of the Invisible World* (1693).

The part played by the learned Mathers and other preachers in the witchcraft delusion helped to discredit the doctrine of the clergy's infallibility. Out of the trials and their after-math came a new appreciation of common sense and a new impetus toward rationalism. A Boston merchant, Thomas Brattle, had openly declared in 1692 that the furor over witches was a manifestation of ignorance and folly. Another enlightened merchant, Robert Calef, carried the fight for rationalism into the enemy's camp with a pamphlet attacking the Mathers and the conduct of the witchcraft trials. Although no Boston printer would bring out the attack, Calef published it in London in 1700 with the satirical title of *More Wonders of the Invisible World*. By this time many New Englanders felt remorse over their part in the hysterical persecution of harmless old men and women. Judge Samuel Sewall had already made public confession of his repentance.

Paradoxically, Cotton Mather's tremendous concern with witchcraft was evidence of his own scientific interest, for his investigations of witches were clinical in their methods even though his conclusions were erroneous. Both Mathers, father and son, exemplified an interest in natural science that was fairly widespread among educated colonists from the later seventeenth century onward. Cotton Mather was sufficiently advanced in his scientific views to accept Copernican astronomy and explain from his pulpit the apparent Scriptural contradictions of the new theories. Mather and other Puritans may have shared with the learned dissenter Charles Morton a religious prejudice in favor of the Copernican hypothesis which Galileo had proved, for Morton had noted that "only Papists were tender of declaring their mind too plainly in this matter because the Pope (forsooth out of a private peck to Galilaeus) had from St. Peter's chair condemned the opinion."

The two Mathers were both vitally concerned with scientific theory and observations. In 1682 Increase participated in the organization in Boston of a philosophical society which had for its major interest the discussion of scientific matters. Cotton was a careful observer of natural phenomena and made diligent reports to the Royal Society in London. For his efforts he was elected a member in 1713, an honor in which he took vast pride. From a Negro slave whom he had received as a gift he learned about an African practice of inoculation for smallpox and characteristically wrote a pamphlet on the subject. This tract is given credit for influencing the first experiments in America with smallpox inoculation, for it persuaded Zabdiel Boylston of Boston to attempt the treatment during an epidemic in 1721. A great furor broke out in Boston over Boylston's inoculations and the lives of both Mather and Boylston were threatened for advocating and practicing a treatment regarded as barbarous. But these pioneers of medical science stood their ground and defended themselves with a barrage of pamphlets which deserve a creditable place in the history of American medicine.

The observation of nature occupied the interest of a number of scientifically minded New Englanders, some of whom made such interesting reports to the Royal Society that they were elected Fellows. The first American Fellow of the Royal Society was John Winthrop, Jr., governor of Connecticut, whose interests in chemistry, medicine, metallurgy, and the will-o'-the-wisp alchemy were insatiable. While in England seeking a charter for his colony from Charles II, he met Sir Isaac Newton and many of the leading English scientists and in 1663 was formally elected one of the charter members of the Royal Society. For years he continued to correspond with his scientific associates. By the time of Cotton Mather's election, New England could boast five other members of the Royal Society.

By the end of the first quarter of the eighteenth century, the older settled regions of New England were centers of considerable cultivation and urbanity. The well-to-do lived in comfortable houses, furnished with the best which money could buy in the English market. Local craftsmen—turners, joiners, woodcarvers, and silversmiths—also helped to supply the demand for some of the amenities. An occasional limner painted the portraits of a few citizens who longed to see themselves in oils. The Puritan prejudice against instrumental music was gradually relaxing. Thomas Brattle brought the first organ to Boston and willed it to the Brattle Street Church when he died in 1713, but because the members of that congregation were not yet ready to risk damnation from so unholy an instrument, Brattle's executors gave it to the Episcopalians of King's Chapel. Booksellers continued to import not merely pious and useful volumes but some of the latest and most fashionable pieces of literature appearing in London. Owners of private collections of books often lent their books until they served the purpose of lending libraries. In a few places town libraries had already been established. Throughout urban New England, men were discussing matters of intellectual interest which concerned educated Englishmen at home. They were also learning to bring their minds to bear on problems peculiar to New England and to the New World. The intellectual and social development of the early eighteenth century made possible the intense activity of the later period which ended in the Revolution.

CHAPTER FOUR

Babel on the Hudson and the Delaware

WHILE Englishmen were duplicating in some fashion the civilization of their native land on the shores of Chesapeake Bay and its river systems and along the narrow coastline of New England, men of diverse tongues were establishing trading posts in the valleys of the Hudson and the Delaware. As if anticipating future characteristics, this region from the beginning received a polyglot assortment of immigrants from the continent of Europe. Dutchmen, Swedes, Finns, and Frenchmen predominated, but an occasional Dane, German, Spaniard, Portuguese, Italian, and Jew found his way to this new haven—the forerunners of millions more of their compatriots in the centuries to come. Their object was trade and they established a commercial civilization which again anticipated the characteristics of succeeding generations and left a permanent impression on the New World.

By some quirk of Fate, Englishmen in search of likely spots for colonies had missed the greatest river on the Atlantic seaboard, but in 1609, an English navigator, one Henry Hudson, employed by the Dutch East India Company to search out a sea route to Asia, sailed into Delaware Bay, made some soundings, and continued northward until he found the river which bears his name. Thinking that the great river might be the elusive Northwest Passage to Asia, Hudson cautiously pushed the "Half-Moon" upstream until he cast anchor on September 19 near the future site of Albany. Although the shallowness of the stream stopped him at this point, Hudson had already penetrated farther into the North American continent than any previous Englishman.

When Hudson retraced his route across the Atlantic in the late autumn, he put in at Dartmouth, where the English authorities arrested him for taking service under a foreign flag but eventually allowed him to forward a report to his employers in Holland. Stirred by Hudson's narrative of his expedition, Dutch merchants made up their minds to develop a trade with the Indians along the North River as they called the Hudson. Within the next five years, several vessels sailed from Holland to engage in the fur trade. To exploit this profitable business, a syndicate of merchants from Amsterdam and Hoorn in 1614 organized the New Netherland Company and received a concession from the States General of exclusive rights in the region between New France and Virginia. The Dutch regarded this territory as theirs by reason of Hudson's explorations under the Dutch flag, but England also had a claim based on the discoveries of John Cabot late in the fifteenth century. This English claim, which was never relinquished even though the Dutch occupied the Hudson Valley, was the excuse invoked by the Duke of York when he seized New Netherland in 1664.

The New Netherland Company made a handsome profit out of its expeditions, but though it established bases up the Hudson—first on an island below Albany, which was abandoned in favor of Fort Orange on the site of Albany—their High Mightinesses, the States General, refused to renew the Company's monopoly, and in 1618 the trade was thrown open to other merchants.

Issues more important to Dutchmen even than profits from sables and beaver pelts soon influenced the States General to adopt another policy toward the New World. Calvinistic citizens of the United Provinces hated Spain with a consuming bitterness and dreamed of ways of destroying the power of the Catholic colossus. A shrewd Calvinist refugee from Antwerp, Willem Usselinx, as early as 1606, had proposed the formation of a Dutch West India Company with the avowed purpose of ruining Spain's empire in the New World. As Usselinx explained it to his fellow Calvinists, such a corporation would get rich by serving God and country. Trading posts which the company would establish in the New World would make useful naval bases from which stout Dutch ships could operate against the treasure fleets of Spain. The gold and silver of the Spanish mines in America would be diverted to Dutch strongboxes, and Spain, cut off from its lifestream, would dwindle in power and lose its grip upon both the Old and New Worlds. Heathen destined to conversion by the Spanish friars would be translated into Calvinists and the Protestant Jehovah would reign supreme. As a reward for their virtue and enterprise, Dutch burghers would rejoice in overwhelming prosperity. Political expediency prevented the immediate adoption of Usselinx's program, but memories of it lingered in the back of many a Dutch patriot's mind. In 1620, when the end of the Twelve Years' Truce, made with Spain in 1609, was approaching, Usselinx and his friends revived plans for a West India Company and succeeded in having the company chartered in the following year, though final plans were not completed until 1623.

The principal objectives of the West India Company were war against the Spanish possessions in the New World, and trade. Less was said about colonization and peopling Dutch territory than might be supposed. Canny merchants who were realistic enough to know that warfare of any kind was an expensive business had the enterprise sweetened for them by the exclusive right to the salt trade with Punto Del Rey. Moreover the charter gave the West India Company a sweeping monopoly of all trade with the New World as well as the west coast of Africa from the Guinea coast to the Cape of Good Hope and the islands of the South Atlantic. The enterprise looked both profitable and patriotic. By the autumn of 1623, subscribers had invested more than seven million guilders in the company.

The early activities of the West India Company are not entirely clear because in 1821 the Dutch minister of colonies ordered the company's seventeenth-century records sold for wastepaper, but it is reasonably certain that by 1624 plans were matured for settlements on both the North (Hudson) River and the South (Delaware) River. The first contingent of colonists of whom there is definite record came over in the spring of 1624 in the ship "New Netherland" commanded by an experienced Atlantic skipper, Captain Cornelis Jacobsen May, who gave his name to Cape May, New Jersey. With Captain May came another skipper who was already familiar with the coastal waters, Captain Adriaen Jorissen Thienpont. The colonists consisted of about thirty families, mostly Walloons, French-speaking Protestants from the southern provinces of the Netherlands which remained under the heel of Spain.

Not much is known about the movements of the first colonists, but apparently a few men were put ashore on Manhattan Island to form a garrison there; a small group went to a post on the Delaware River; and the rest settled about Fort Orange on the upper Hudson. Captain May, who was the senior officer in New Netherland, did not tarry long to govern the colony but placed Thienpont in command of Fort Orange and returned to Holland.

During the next year, the West India Company sent out more colonists under the direction of Willem Verhulst; the company also sent over an engineer, Cryn Fredericksen, with instructions to erect a fort at the most suitable spot near the mouth of the Hudson River. Three vessels appropriately named the "Sheep," the "Cow," and the "Horse" brought over a supply of livestock. The grass and water on Manhattan looked good and the lower point of the island was suitable for defense. When Fredericksen had measured off a proper number of farms, he set to work on the fort which he completed before the autumn of 1626 and named Fort Amsterdam. The town which grew up in the shadow of the fort took the name of New Amsterdam. Within a few years New Amsterdam was the principal settlement in New Netherland. The outpost on the Delaware dwindled, and most of the colonists moved down the Hudson from Fort Orange leaving only a few soldiers and fur traders in that garrison.

Like the English colony in Virginia, New Netherland in the early stages suffered from the incompetence of its rulers and the disorderliness of its people. The laws for the colony were the laws of Holland, but the West India Company, through its Amsterdam branch or "chamber," appointed the governing body consisting of a director and council. The people had no voice in the government; at first they were simply employees and tenants of the company. They had to agree to live for six consecutive years on land allotted by the Company's officials. Though they were free to trade as they chose within the colony, all external trade had to be carried on through the Company. Handicrafts, even spinning, were permitted only for one's own household and the product of such skill could not be sold for profit. The Company officials at first dictated even the crops which should be planted.

Since the Netherlands were prosperous despite the eternal imminence of war with Spain, and the toleration of the homeland gave no impetus for emigration in search of religious freedom, the West India Company had trouble finding settlers. The Dutch colonists who were persuaded to go overseas were not of the best type, and the Company had to enlist foreign refugees in Holland, particularly Walloons and French Huguenots. A few adventurers from the various countries of northern Europe found employment with the West India Company. By the Company's orders all emigrants had to be of the Reformed religion, but this rule clearly was not strictly enforced, for Jewish traders soon reached New Amsterdam, and one wonders whether the handful of Spaniards, Portuguese, and Italians who arrived during the Dutch regime were all Protestants. The West India Company could not afford to be too particular if it hoped to find sufficient settlers. The official religion of the colony was the Dutch Reformed Church, a Calvinistic faith, supervised by the classis of Amsterdam. Although New Netherland nominally did not enjoy the toleration of the mother country, and the erection of other churches was at first forbidden, sectarians were not molested in their private worship.

The West India Company had as hard a time finding competent officials as it did colonists. The first director Willem Verhulst proved so incompetent that the council deposed him and early in 1626 appointed Peter Minuit in his place. Although a fortress now protected lower Manhattan, the colony was in a sorry state. In a letter to the Amsterdam Chamber of the West India Company on September 23, 1626, Isaac de Rasière, who had been sent out as secretary, reported: "As the people here have become quite lawless, owing to the bad government hitherto prevailing, it is necessary to administer some punishment with kindness in order to keep them in check, to break them of their bad habits, and to make them learn to understand their bounden duty and the respect they owe your Honors both in writing and speaking, which cannot easily be done unless your Honors provide some fine or other penalty in the matter." Conditions at Fort Orange were worse and the inhabitants there were in peril from Indian attacks. Though official instructions had counselled neutrality in feuds among the Indians, the garrison had taken sides with the Mohicans against the powerful Mohawks—and received a thorough licking.

To prevent disaster to outlying settlements Minuit called in the farmers at Fort Orange, and at Fort Nassau on the Delaware, and allotted them land on Manhattan under the guns of Fort Amsterdam. To keep peace with the local Indians, he made an agreement with them for the purchase of Manhattan Island for sixty guilders worth of trinkets or roughly twenty-four dollars, probably the most famous bargain in American history.

Although Minuit was courageous and shrewd, he lacked diplomacy and quarreled with members of his council. Worse still, he succeeded in making an enemy of his pastor, the Reverend Jonas Michaëlius, a stern and sour man, the first ordained minister sent by the classis of Amsterdam to rebuke the sinners of New Netherland. When Michaëlius arrived in 1628, the colony had no formal church organization; the preacher's first task was to persuade Minuit and his brother-in-law, Jan Huyghens, the colony's storekeeper, to serve as elders of the Dutch Reformed Church of New Amsterdam which he now established. But Michaëlius' pleasure in having the director as an elder soon cooled, and in 1630 he vented his hatred in a letter to a friend in Holland: "We have a governor," he declared, "who is entirely unworthy of his office, a slippery fellow who, under the painted mask of honesty, is a compound of all iniquity and wickedness. For he is accustomed to the telling of lies, in which he abounds, and to the use of horrible oaths and execrations. He is not free from fornication, he is a most cruel oppressor of the innocent, and deems no one worthy of his favor and protection who is not of the same kidney as himself." The violence of the parson, like that of other Calvinistic preachers, had its origins perhaps in Minuit's refusal to be dominated by ecclesiastical authority. The clergy sent to New Netherland would have liked to exert an influence similar to that of their brethren of the cloth in Massachusetts Bay, but they made small headway against the stolid opposition of the Dutch directors.

Though Peter Minuit encouraged peaceful trade with the Indians, made friends with the Pilgrim colony at Plymouth, and greatly improved conditions in New Netherland, his enemies brought about his downfall and he was recalled to Holland in 1631 to answer charges of maladministration. To the discomfiture of New Netherland, he turned up in 1638 as commander of an expedition sent out by Sweden to establish a colony on the Delaware.

To Jonas Michaëlius' propensity for writing letters, we are indebted for sidelights on conditions in New Netherland during the early stages of development. Soon after his arrival he sent to his sponsor, the Reverend Adrianus Smoutius of Amsterdam, a lengthy account of the progress of religion on the Hudson. At the first communion at least fifty souls, both Dutch and Walloons, appeared for the Sacrament. Though the Walloons understood some Dutch, Michaëlius read them a sermon in French and administered the Lord's supper in that language. Since the council of New Netherland was composed of men who were "for the most part simple," having "little experience in public affairs," Michaëlius declared himself ready "to serve them in any difficult or dubious affair with good advice"—and he hoped not to be considered a busy-body for his pains. But the West India Company took a glum view of preachers' sitting at the right hand of the civil authority. Later, after Michaëlius had returned to Holland, the classis of Amsterdam wanted to send him once more to New Netherland but the Company significantly vetoed the proposal. In the meanwhile, his correspondent Smoutius had meddled so arrogantly in the civil affairs of old Amsterdam that the burgomasters had exiled him from the city. Seventeenth-century Dutchmen, for all of their Calvinism, were vastly different from English Puritans.

The dream of the more pious promoters of the West India Company of converting the Indians to Protestant Christianity had small hope of realization, Michaëlius explained in his letter to Smoutius. "As to the natives of this country," he declared, "I find them entirely savage and wild, strangers to all decency, yea, uncivil and stupid as garden poles, proficient in all wickedness and godlessness, devilish men who serve nobody but the Devil. . . They have so much witchcraft, divination, sorcery, and wicked arts that they can hardly be held in any bands or locks. They are as thievish and treacherous as they are tall; and in cruelty, they are altogether inhuman, more than barbarous, far exceeding the Africans." In short, he saw no hope of saving the souls of any adult Indians and suggested that the only feasible method would be to persuade Indians to allow their children to be brought up in white schools. Meanwhile lands deserted by the Mohicans excited the parson's cupidity: "The Mohicans have fled and their lands are unoccupied and are very fertile and pleasant. It grieves us that there are no people, and there is no order from the Honorable Directors to occupy the same."

The scarcity of labor in New Netherland and the lack of industry on the part of the settlers paralleled conditions in early Virginia. Michaëlius, whose wife had died, had difficulty finding someone to take care of his children: "Maid servants are not here to be had, at least none whom they can advise me to take, and the Angola slave women are thievish, lazy, and useless trash." Since the African slave trade was a profitable enterprise of the Dutch in the seventeenth century, it is not surprising that New Netherland already had a number of black slaves.

When Michaëlius wrote his letter in 1628, the fur trade was dull on account of inter-tribal wars of the Indians, but despite occasional slumps, the traffic in furs and skins provided the one steady stream of revenue. There were other sources of profit, however, as the preacher pointed out: "Much timber is cut here to carry to the Fatherland, but the vessels are too few to take much of it. They are making a windmill to saw lumber, and we also have a gristmill. They bake brick here, but it is very poor. There is good material for burning lime, namely, oyster shells, in large quantities. The burning of potash has not succeeded. . . We are busy now in building a fort of good quarry stone, which is to be found not far from here in abundance. . . There is good opportunity for making salt." The wood and waters abound with game and fish, he asserts, and the soil produces well. "The harvest, God be praised, is in the barns, and is larger than ever before. . . Until now there has been distress because many people were not very industrious and also did not obtain proper sustenance for want of bread and other necessaries. But affairs are beginning to go better and to put on a different appearance, if only the Directors will send out good laborers and exercise all care that they be maintained as well as possible with what this country produces." Thus did the Reverend Jonas Michaëlius appraise conditions in New Netherland in the days of Peter Minuit.

During Minuit's regime, the West India Company relaxed its hold on the soil of New Netherland by issuing a "Charter of Freedom and Exemptions" (1629) whereby any promoter who would undertake to settle fifty adult inhabitants upon the land would be declared a "patroon," or lord of a manor, with the right of collecting rents and exacting many feudal dues. The patroon might occupy land extending four leagues along one bank of a navigable stream or two leagues along both banks and as far inland as desirable provided he did not encroach on other occupants. The Indian owners of the land had to be satisfied by purchase. Though the patroon system thus established was never very profitable, it proved just successful enough to persist until the English occupation, when the old patroonships were reestablished as manors in the English style and other manors were marked out along the Hudson. The landed aristocracy thus created had a profound influence upon New York's later history.

A thrifty and ambitious diamond and pearl merchant of Amsterdam, himself an influential member of the West India Company, one Kiliaen Van Rensselaer, apparently thought up the plan by which land-hungry Dutchmen might possess themselves of baronial estates in the New World. At any rate, Van Rensselaer hastened to send over a colony which eventually occupied a territory called Rensselaerswyck on both sides of the Hudson in the neighborhood of Fort Orange. Most of the area now comprising Albany, Rensselaer, and Columbia counties was included in Rensselaerswyck, surely acres enough to satisfy a merchant whose landed possessions hitherto had been circumscribed by the narrow grachts of Amsterdam.

But Kiliaen Van Rensselaer was pleased to contemplate his barony in New Netherland from the pleasant rooms of his counting house. Though no pioneering zeal prompted him to risk his comfort in the wilderness, he sent his agents to administer Rensselaerswyck and even took thought for the salvation of his tenants by sending over a learned pastor, the Reverend Johannes Megapolensis, who detested Lutherans and Quakers, but proved himself a shrewd missionary to the Indians. In 1643, a few years before John Eliot of Massachusetts Bay began his labors among the red men, Megapolensis was preaching to the Mohawks, and in the following year, a printer at Alkmaar brought out *Een kort Ontwerp vande Mahakvase Indiaenen* (*A Short Account of the Mohawk Indians*), written by the preacher, which gave a realistic and unflattering picture of the natives. But whatever were Megapolensis' private opinions of the Indians, his efforts to win their friendship helped to keep the peace on the upper Hudson.

Although Van Rensselaer was the most successful of the patroons, he was not the only merchant and capitalist interested in landed estates. By 1630 five patroons had registered territory in New Netherland and its environs, including land on the Delaware and Connecticut rivers. Michiel Pauw, for example, in addition to land in Connecticut, laid claim to a patroonship on the New Jersey shore and included with it the whole of Staten Island. This territory he called Pavonia, a Latinized form derived from his own name. For a venture on the Delaware River, Samuel Godyn had as partners Kiliaen Van Rensselaer, Samuel Blommaert, Johan de Laet, and David de Vries. They made a settlement in 1631 near the present site of Lewes, Delaware, and named it Swanendael, but the Indians quickly wiped it out.

The large patroonships were so unsuccessful that in 1640 the West India Company altered the charter to permit the settlement of smaller estates, but they too proved less attractive than the promoters had hoped. The truth was that in the New World tenantry in the medieval manner would not work. Tenants could not be induced for long to submit to feudal exactions which made them little better than serfs. When land could be acquired with relative ease free men would not settle contently upon some absentee landlord's estate. By the time of the English seizure of New Netherland, the West India Company had been obliged to buy in all except two patroonships. Under English rule a modified system of manors with more attractions for the inhabitants had greater success.

Among the more persistent patroons was an adventurous ship captain named David de Vries who had been in the service of the Dutch East India Company and could never cease comparing his former employers with the West India Company, to the latter's disparagement. To his vivid if unsympathetic pen we are indebted for descriptions of the rule of two director-generals who came after Minuit, Wouter Van Twiller and Willem Kieft.

Van Twiller, a nephew of Van Rensselaer, probably owed his appointment to his uncle, who may have regretted his choice. De Vries, who reached New Amsterdam on one of his voyages in April, 1633, shortly after the arrival of Van Twiller, describes the director as a foolish fellow usually drunk. For instance, when an English vessel sailed up the Hudson in the face of the Dutch at New Amsterdam, Van Twiller made a drunken bluster of defiance. "When Commander Wouter Van Twiller assembled all his forces before his door," says De Vries, "[he] had a cask of wine brought out, filled a bumper, and cried out for those who loved the Prince of Orange and him to do the same as he did, and protect him from the outrage of the Englishman, who was already out of sight sailing up the river. The people all began to laugh at him; for they understood well how to drink dry the cask of wine, as it was just the thing that suited them, even if there had been six casks, and [they] did not wish to trouble the Englishman, saying they were friends."

Babel on the Hudson and the Delaware

Van Twiller violated all of the most cherished principles of his bourgeois uncle Kiliaen, who admonished the errant director for being too often drunk, for displaying a proud spirit, for showing insufficient interest in religion, and, what may have offended the merchant most of all, for keeping books poorly. For all of his shortcomings, Van Twiller was not completely incompetent. He fostered the expansion of Dutch settlements on Long Island and thriftily acquired a goodly farm there for himself. He at first encouraged a building program in New Amsterdam so that the town rang with the sound of hammer and saw and presently could boast three new windmills, new dwelling houses of both brick and wood, a special stable for some goats sent to Van Twiller by the governor of Virginia, a brewery, and a church, which replaced the loft where the faithful had previously worshipped. Some citizens, however, grumbled at the expense of the new buildings and the director's own enthusiasm soon dwindled as he turned his attention to private gain. Before the end of his regime many buildings were dilapidated and the walls of the fort were in a sad state of repair. Van Twiller did order the completion of a fort on the Connecticut River on the site of the present city of Hartford and named it the House of Good Hope. With the Connecticut Indians he made treaties and bought titles to their soil. His reputation for honest dealings, and perhaps his generosity in dispensing strong drink, won the affection of the Indians who looked forward to his return years after his regime was ended.

But in the days of Wouter Van Twiller a movement gained strength which promised ultimate disaster to Dutch rule. The English began an infiltration of Dutch territory which Van Twiller was powerless to stop. Fur traders from Plymouth had sailed boldly past the House of Good Hope and established themselves at Windsor. Though Van Twiller protested and even sent a force of seventy men with drums beating, the Pilgrim traders stood their ground and Van Twiller's militia merely marched up the hill and down again. Elsewhere on the Connecticut Englishmen were encroaching upon preserves which the Dutch regarded as theirs, and soon they would be competing for the Delaware Valley and even for Long Island.

Complaints against Van Twiller's government induced the Company in 1637 to recall him and send in his place Willem Kieft, a soberer but scarcely a more competent man. Nevertheless events forced developments which advanced the colony. Land tenure was stabilized by the grant of patents to settlers, and it was symbolic of the polyglot nature of New Netherland that the first three patents issued in 1638 went to a Dane, an Englishman, and a Dutchman. Immigration increased, particularly the influx of Englishmen, some with the blessing of the authorities, others without it. Dissenters from the rule of the saints in Massachusetts Bay like Anne Hutchinson and her husband found a refuge in New Netherland, where the Dutch permitted them to worship as they pleased. A Dane, Jonas Bronck, whose name is preserved in the Bronx, developed a farm in what became lower Westchester County. A little later, Adriaen Van der Donck, who was honored with the title *jonker*, patented a farm north of the Harlem River; his title is remembered in the name Yonkers. Farms and villages began to flourish on Manhattan, on both sides of the Hudson River, and on Long Island. The West India Company's decision in 1638 to permit a greater freedom of trade between the inhabitants of New Netherland and all friendly people—provided that goods were transported in the Company's ships and paid certain duties—also stimulated commerce and encouraged adventurous youths to seek their fortunes on the Hudson.

If the Dutch had kept peace with the Indians, New Netherland might have had an era of prosperity despite the shortcomings of the director. But the friendly relations which Van Twiller had maintained with most of the Indians did not endure under the thin-lipped and bitter Kieft who hated the savages.

He antagonized the Indians along the lower Hudson by levying tribute upon them; he made revengeful enemies of the Raritans on Staten Island by sending soldiers who killed their tribesmen in punishment for deeds actually committed by white men; and he determined to wipe out the Indians on upper Manhattan to avenge the murder of a Dutch wheelwright.

The possibility of war with the Indians influenced Kieft to take the first step toward popular government in New Netherland. Because the people were complaining at the prospect of war and accusing him of personal cowardice, Kieft called an assembly of masters of households on August 23, 1641, and asked their advice. They promptly elected twelve representatives, called simply the "Twelve," headed by David de Vries, who urged caution and delay in attacking the Indians. If an attack should be made, they cunningly suggested that Kieft "ought to lead the van." Displeased, Kieft disbanded the Twelve and forbade public meetings without his approval. Biding his time, he planned in February 1643 to wipe out the Indians in the environs of Manhattan. Against the advice of de Vries, on February 25 he ordered his soldiers to cross the river to Pavonia and to destroy a group of harmless Indians who had themselves fled from the attack of another tribe. De Vries later put together a vivid description of the massacre—one of the worst blots on the Dutch record in the New World:

> I remained that night at the Governor's [Kieft's], sitting up. I went and sat by the kitchen fire, when about midnight I heard a great shrieking, and I ran to the ramparts of the fort, and looked over to Pavonia. Saw nothing but firing, and heard the shrieks of the savages murdered in their sleep . . . When it was day the soldiers returned to the fort, having massacred or murdered eighty Indians, and considering they had done a deed of Roman valor, in murdering so many in their sleep; where infants were torn from their mother's breasts and hacked to pieces in the presence of the parents, and the pieces thrown into the fire and in the water, and other sucklings, being bound to small boards, were cut, stuck, pierced, and miserably massacred in a manner to move a heart of stone. Some were thrown into the river, and when

the fathers and mothers endeavored to save them, the soldiers would not let them come on land but made both parents and children drown—children from five to six years of age, and also some old and decrepit persons. Those who fled from this onslaught and concealed themselves in the neighboring sedge, and when it was morning came out to beg a piece of bread, and to be permitted to warm themselves, were murdered in cold blood and tossed into the fire or the water . . . After this exploit, the soldiers were rewarded for their services, and Director Kieft thanked them by taking them by the hand and congratulating them. At another place, on the same night, on Corler's Hook near Corler's plantation, forty Indians were in the same manner attacked in their sleep, and massacred there in the same manner. Did the Duke of Alva in the Netherlands ever do anything more cruel? This is indeed a disgrace to our nation . . . As soon as the savages understood that the Swannekens [Indian for Dutch] had so treated them, all the men whom they could surprise on the farmlands they killed; but we have never heard that they ever permitted women or children to be killed. They burned all the houses, farms, barns, grain, haystacks, and destroyed everything they could get hold of. So there was an open destructive war begun.

Although de Vries oddly enough borrowed the horrible details of the massacre from an anonymous anti-Kieft pamphlet, the facts are borne out by other evidence. Before the end of the war which Kieft had so stupidly begun, all of New Netherland south of Rensselaerswyck had been laid waste and the war whoop of the Indians had frightened the inhabitants even of New Amsterdam. Anne Hutchinson's little group in Westchester was destroyed save for one child of eight; English and Dutch settlements on Long Island were laid waste; de Vries' houses at Pavonia were burned; and the farms and pastures of Manhattan were raided with impunity until Kieft ordered a palisade built along the boundary now commemorated by Wall Street to protect the few cattle left on Manhattan.

Culminating disasters forced the director to appeal once more to the people, who elected the Eight; the counsellors included two Englishmen, one of whom, Isaac Allerton, had come to Plymouth in the "Mayflower" and had later removed to New Netherland. Because Dutch freemen available for military service numbered only about two hundred, Allerton persuaded Captain John Underhill, a colorful dissident from Massachusetts Bay, to lead a company of English settlers recruited and hired for the campaign. In February 1644, Underhill and a Dutch colleague attacked a concentration of Indians in Westchester and slaughtered between five and seven hundred. But not until the end of the summer of 1645 was peace restored by treaties patched up with the local Indians, partly through the good offices of the Mohawks, with whom the Dutch at Fort Orange had made a treaty of friendship. The disasters of the war led to representations from the Eight of such force that the West India Company replaced Kieft in 1647 by Peter Stuyvesant, a doughty soldier and former governor of Curaçao.

While the Indians were proving an immediate threat to the very existence of the Dutch in New Netherland, another hazard to the West India Company's elusive monopoly appeared on the Delaware. In the spring of 1638, Peter Minuit, erstwhile director at New Amsterdam, sailed up the broad river in a Swedish man-of-war, the "Key of Kalmar," and, with a kettle and some trinkets, bought from the Indians two strips of land on the west side of the Delaware. Two years later Minuit's successor, another Dutchman named Peter Ridder, extended the Swedish holdings from Cape Henlopen to the falls at Trenton. As was usual in colonial purchases from the Indians, the boundaries were vague. The Swedish territory extended inland as far as the colonizers might desire.

Though the Dutch, in the person of Director Kieft, proclaimed against the invasion, Minuit went ahead unperturbed and established a trading post and fort on the site of the modern city of Wilmington, Delaware, which he named in honor of the youthful Queen of Sweden, Fort Christina. Gradually during the next decade, Swedish immigrants, with a few refugee Finns, began to build log cabins in the territory, which both the English and the Dutch regarded as theirs.

The competition of the three great Protestant nations for lands in this region brought to an ironical climax their common desire to check the power of Catholic Spain by establishing themselves in the New World. The same Willem Usselinx who had urged the formation of the Dutch West India Company to be a thorn in the side of Spain was influential in persuading the Swedish warrior-king, Gustavus Adolphus, of the advantages of American colonization. During a campaign in Germany against the forces of the Hapsburgs, Gustavus stopped at Nuremberg to make plans for an American colony which, he anticipated, would become "the jewel of his kingdom." Shortly after this hopeful beginning, the King of Sweden died on the battlefield of Lützen, but his colonial plans did not perish with him.

The rule of Sweden fell to a strong man, Count Axel Oxenstierna, who determined to create a New Sweden by the methods which the Dutch had employed in New Netherland. After considering various schemes—including a proposal for Swedish aggrandizement by attacking Spain in the West Indies, submitted by one Peter Stumpff, a German of Hamburg—Oxenstierna in 1637 issued a charter to the New Sweden Company and gave his blessing to a group of Swedes and Dutchmen for trade and settlement on the Delaware under the flag of Sweden. It was under this charter that Minuit built Fort Christina.

Sweden suffered the same difficulties which the Dutch had experienced in finding colonists. Few Swedes had any desire to emigrate to the New World. Sweden itself was a forest country with room for immigrants. Indeed, Finns had been invited to settle in Sweden and clear the forests in the North but had proved a nuisance because of their nomadic habits and their undiscriminating method of burning the woods. The fur trade of New Sweden, which at first proved reasonably profitable, did not induce large numbers of settlers to establish farms and homes in the wilderness. There was no religious compulsion, as in the case of the English Puritans, to induce Lutherans of Sweden to leave home. Ridder suggested to the authorities in Sweden that deserters from the army might be deported, along with their families, but the records do not make clear whether this was done. To some, the Finns looked like the best prospects for immigrants, and a few were induced to go as early as 1641, but despite the efforts of the Company's officials at home and abroad, the settlers who acknowledged allegiance to Sweden were just numerous enough to annoy the Dutch.

Few as were the Swedes, they were sufficient to establish the Lutheran Church on the Delaware. With Director Ridder—sent in 1640 to take Minuit's place when the latter was drowned on a voyage home—came the Reverend Reorus Torkillus, who conducted Lutheran services in the fort and procured the erection of a church. The Dutch, being of the Reformed faith and Calvinists, disliked the Lutheran minister and wrote abusive letters about him.

Both the Swedes and the Dutch—who retained their hold on the upper Delaware at Fort Nassau—were troubled by the increasing penetration of Englishmen into their lands. Interlopers from Plymouth and from the Connecticut settlements competed with the established traders for beaver skins and in the 1640's made settlements at Varkens Kill, or Salem Creek, and on the Schuylkill. Realizing that the English were a common threat, the Swedes and Dutch united against them and in the spring of 1642 burned the Schuylkill village. But a discerning observer on the Delaware or the Hudson might have realized that neither gunfire nor edicts would keep out the persistent trickle of Englishmen who would in time become an overwhelming stream. The only hope of either Swedish or Dutch survival lay in a tide of immigrants from the homeland—and that tide was not forthcoming.

Though success had eluded the directors of New Sweden, the Company in 1642 appointed a man who promised to make something of the backward colony. The new director was Johan Printz, a Gargantuan officer from Gustavus

Adolphus' army, who could out-eat, out-drink, and out-swear several ordinary mortals. For his tremendous size and huge girth, the Indians called him, not without respect, "Big Guts." Printz ruled New Sweden nearly eleven years and proved its most energetic governor. Soon after his arrival he began to bombard the Company at home with demands for more settlers, for artisans and farmers, for miners and metal workers, and for the varied trades necessary to the economic health of his colony. Printz, himself the first Swedish director of the colony, insisted upon Swedish settlers rather than Dutchmen or Englishmen whom his predecessors had been willing to accept, but he admitted Finns who had violated the laws of Sweden and might need a refuge in the New World, and he so impressed some of the English interlopers that they swore allegiance to Swedish authority.

Printz, a soldier, knew that New Sweden must dominate the Delaware River with military power and to that end he erected a fortress on the east bank of the river, south of Varkens Kill, and named it Fort Elfsborg. He moved the capital up the river to Tinicum Island and built another fortress nearby called Fort New Gothenburg. With that done he ordered built for himself a fine house, two stories high, lavishly supplied with glass windows. Farms were beginning to dot the countryside; crops of tobacco and grain were brought to maturity; the fur trade, despite competition, pleased the new director; and prosperity seemed to beckon.

Printz's instructions had commanded him to keep peace with the Indians, the English, and the Dutch. With the Indians, the Swedes had a good record for honest dealings, but troublemakers had been busy and Printz expected difficulties. With the English and the Dutch, much would depend upon diplomacy. Almost pathetically he wrote home for a secretary who could answer in good Latin the correspondence from his foreign neighbors. In that language, Printz pointed out, "I do not now find myself very competent, but when need so requires I must sit and laboriously collect together an epistle, and when it at last is accomplished it is only a patchwork, especially since I have more often for the last twenty-seven years had the musket and pistol in my hands than Tacitus and Cicero."

Though Printz might keep peace with his neighbors, he could not overcome the neglect of the colony which the wars in Europe caused. Ships from home were few and far between. Immigrants failed to keep up with the death rate in New Sweden and the population, which had not yet reached as many as two hundred souls, dwindled. Trading goods and trinkets, necessary for barter with the Indians, ran out and no new supply arrived. Even the grain crops failed and tobacco was not so good as expected. In the winter of 1645, the powder magazine on Tinicum Island blew up, the director's fine house burned down, and only a barn was left standing on the island. Though Printz rebuilt the house, his glory had departed and he longed to go home, but the Company would not send a new director to relieve him. The Indians, seeing the weakness of the Swedes, lost their respect for "Big Guts" and became unruly.

To make matters worse, Peter Stuyvesant, the director of New Netherland, now decided to reassert Dutch authority on the Delaware, and Printz was powerless to resist. In the summer of 1651, Stuyvesant moved two hundred men across the Delaware between Fort Elfsborg and Fort Christina and established a fortification of his own, Fort Casimir, which cancelled the strength of the Swedish strongholds. Printz's own people were in a rebellious state, and in 1652 twenty-two of his men openly defied his authority and demanded the release of a Finnish prisoner. In a towering rage, the director hanged the leader of the insurrection, but this revenge gave him small comfort. In the autumn of 1653, he shook the dust of the country from his feet and journeyed to New Amsterdam where he accepted the hospitality of his great rival, Stuyvesant, until he could get passage on a Dutch ship bound for Europe.

About the time Printz was leaving New Sweden, efforts

were being made at home to reinforce the colony in strength. The young queen, Christina, heard stories of the New World and encouraged the enterprise. Under the command of an impetuous director, Johan Rising, more than two hundred and fifty colonists embarked on the ship "Eagle" in January 1654 with high hopes of a new life on the Delaware. But misfortune rode the whirlwind and the "Eagle" took more than three months to make the passage. When she eventually reached the Delaware, more than a hundred of her crew and passengers were dead. Though his strength was depleted, Rising captured Fort Casimir from the Dutch, disembarked the immigrants, and began a trade for food and supplies with New England and the Indians. His antagonism of the Dutch, however, proved a fatal error, for Stuyvesant in the summer of the next year sent soldiers and sailors who plundered the Swedes and reduced them to subjection.

With this conquest, the authority of the Swedes on the Delaware ended, but both Swedes and Finns continued to live on both banks of the river and in time merged with the English and the Dutch. Some remnants of their culture persisted as Swedish families pushed into the interior of New Jersey and made small isolated settlements which lasted till late in the eighteenth century. Log cabins, notched at the corners in the style peculiar to Sweden, provided models widely adapted on the American frontier. Wood carving was taught by Swedish craftsmen who made furniture out of native woods. Folk tales which had entertained their ancestors passed into the American stream. The Finns, who were believed to have unusual traffic with witches and devils, became the subject of folk superstitions. More important than other cultural influences was the persistence of the Swedish Lutheran Church. From the days of Pastor Torkillus until the coming of German Lutherans in the eighteenth century, the Lutheran Church survived. After the German immigration, Lutheranism became an important element in the religious complex of the Delaware Valley.

While the Swedes were working out their destiny in competition with the English and Dutch, the latter people were reaching their greatest strength and prosperity under Peter Stuyvesant, a peg-legged soldier, who ruled with an iron will and much irascibility but with more efficiency, withal, than his predecessors had shown. By the end of his regime, the population numbered somewhere in the neighborhood of 8,000 souls, of whom the Dutch were the most numerous, with the English coming second. New Amsterdam was still a small town but it rivalled Boston as a trading port and had so many visitors that the West India Company erected a tavern for their entertainment. The town's population was approximately 2,500.

Despite the danger from the Indians, settlers steadily pushed outward from the tip of Manhattan; they reached across to the Jersey side and established farms; they made clearings along both sides of the Hudson River and raised cattle, grain, and tobacco. As immigration increased, farms were established even farther away. By 1658, Esopus, in what is now Ulster County, had between seventy and eighty inhabitants and was described by a contemporary as an "exceedingly beautiful land." Settlements had multiplied on Long Island where the Dutch and the English each boasted a group of five towns. Since the English had for years laid claim to Long Island, Stuyvesant was obliged in 1650 to journey to Hartford where he sat down with English commissioners from the New England colonies to arbitrate a boundary between their jurisdictions on Long Island and elsewhere. By agreement, the Dutch retained the land east of a line from Oyster Bay to the sea. Of the patroonships, only Rensselaerswyck showed promise. There the authorities had welcomed, in addition to Dutchmen and Walloons, Swedes, Norwegians, and Germans as well as various British elements: English, Scotch, Welsh, and Irish.

In the back country, prosperity depended upon farming and the fur trade, but New Amsterdam developed a diversified commerce, not only with Europe, but with the West Indies, Africa, and the other American colonies. Dutch skippers were inveterate slavers and were responsible for the early sale of Negroes in the colonies. Some of the slaves were retained in New Netherland but the majority were sold in the West Indies and in the tobacco colonies on the Chesapeake. Merchants of New Amsterdam imported an incredible quantity of liquor, chiefly brandies, wines, brewed ales, and beer. Some of this the Dutch sold to the Indians; some they shipped to neighboring colonies; but a great quantity they themselves consumed. When Stuyvesant arrived, New Amsterdam had seventeen taphouses; nearly one-fourth of the buildings of the town were dedicated to the dispensation of strong drink—and the one church was still not completed. One of Stuyvesant's first official acts was to issue a decree against drunkenness and the sale of liquor to the Indians.

Although Stuyvesant had the heart and disposition of a dictator, the people had grown too independent to be ruled like hirelings. The day was long past when the people of the colony were merely employees of the West India Company. Now men owned land and were free traders in their own right. The West India Company, it is true, continued its monopoly of shipping, collected duties at the port, and received other fees and rents, but to all intents and purposes the colony was peopled by freemen. Though they still had little or no voice in government, they were determined to remedy that fault. Because Stuyvesant required money for restoring the buildings burned by the Indians, for completing the church, and for establishing schools lest the colony lapse into ignorance and shame, he had to concede something to the people to gain their financial support. Accordingly he ordered the inhabitants to elect eighteen men from whom he and his council would select half of the number to serve as the board of the Nine. This board was established with clearly outlined responsibilities in the autumn of 1647.

The director soon had cause to storm and fume over the independence of the Nine, for in 1649 they prepared and sent to the States General in Holland a petition for the redress of grievances. Among the documents submitted was a long *Remonstrance of New Netherland*, the work of Adriaen Van der Donck. To bring pressure on the States General, the Nine procured the publication of the *Remonstrance*, a remarkable description of conditions in the colony with suggestions for its advancement and improvement. Among other things the petition criticized the arbitrary government of the director, the heavy duties and taxes, the frequency of war with the Indians, the numerousness of traders, the scarcity of good farmers, and the lack of essential supplies. The *Remonstrance* pleaded also for good public buildings, a public school with at least two good masters, and better rulers, men "who are not too indigent, or indeed are not too covetous." Shrewdly the author of this document observed that "in our opinion this country will never flourish under the government of the Honorable Company, but will pass away and come to an end of itself without benefiting thereby the Honorable Company . . ."

The States General, which had the power to force the West India Company to make reforms, received a committee report favoring the changes sought, but the Company objected; finally it made some concessions, which included the establishment of a municipal government of the burghers of New Amsterdam after the manner of town governments in Holland. Under stress of public danger, when a Rhode Island pirate in 1653 threatened to lay waste the towns of Long Island, Stuyvesant was constrained to call a general assembly representing the communities nearby. Again under threats from Indians and the English in 1663 and finally when the English were before New Amsterdam in 1664, the old dictator was obliged to call the representatives of the people together, but not until the colony came under English rule did it achieve a true legislative body.

The little city of New Amsterdam in 1657 took steps to make social and political distinctions among its citizens somewhat in the manner of the old country. An ordinance established two classes of citizens, the great and small burghers.

The right of being a great burgher could be obtained on payment of fifty guilders, the theory being that the substantial and well-off would purchase the *burger-recht* at this price. Only great burghers were eligible for municipal offices and dignities. Members of the government, past and present, preachers, and officers of the militia were granted this *burger-recht* without fee. The common or small *burger-recht* could be obtained on the payment of twenty guilders. Native-born citizens, husbands of native-born daughters of burghers, and others who had "resided and kept fire and light within the city one year and six weeks" were eligible to become small burghers without payment. The possession of the small *burger-recht* was a requirement for carrying on a trade or craft within the city. At first only twenty citizens qualified as great burghers, but the small burgher class numbered about two hundred at the start. Efforts to maintain artificial distinctions in a new country proved useless, however, and the difference between the two burgher classes was abolished sometime after the English took possession. Nevertheless, the concern of the Dutch for control by the wealthier merchant class helped to encourage the evolution of the mercantile aristocracy characteristic of the city in later periods.

As New Amsterdam and other settlements lost a little of the crudeness of the earliest frontier days, the demand for churches and schools increased. The charter of the West India Company had required that ministers and schoolmasters be supplied to the colony. When an ordained minister could not be found, a sort of lay preacher, known as a "comforter of the sick," served instead. Though a few of the early ministers of the Dutch Reformed Church—the established religion and the only one officially permitted—were scholarly and pious persons, not all proved worthy of the cloth.

The second ordained minister to serve in New Amsterdam, for example, the Reverend Everardus Bogardus, was a violent man who quarreled, first with Director Van Twiller

Babel on the Hudson and the Delaware

whom he described as "a child of the devil" and "an incarnate villain," and later with Director Kieft whom he characterized publicly as one of the "fountains of evil." Bogardus himself was charged with the habitual use of abusive language and with being drunk in his own pulpit. The bitter enemies, Bogardus and Kieft, called to Holland to answer complaints, sailed in the same ship and were lost at sea. Other ministers made more favorable records. Johannes Megapolensis at Rensselaerswyck and his son Samuel, who studied three years at Harvard, helped to advance both religion and culture in the colony. Domine Hermanus Blom, who settled on the frontier at Esopus, proved a faithful pastor. During the last decade of Dutch rule, the communities on Long Island and new settlements on the Hudson procured capable preachers. From the Dutch colony in Brazil came Johannes Polhemus who divided his time between Flatbush and Brooklyn until the latter congregation obtained a pastor of its own in the person of Henricus Selyns.

Other Dutch Reformed ministers arrived until the faithful in New Netherland were in no danger of lapsing into either barbarism or heresy. Of the two disasters, the ministers appeared to fear heresy most. For instance, in 1653, they bitterly opposed the request of a group of Lutherans for permission to organize a congregation openly and applauded when Stuyvesant jailed Lutherans for worshipping contrary to law. Of the other religions in their midst, they approved only of the English Presbyterians whose Calvinism seemed sufficiently orthodox. The intolerance of the Reformed preachers in New Netherland was exceedingly displeasing to the officers of the West India Company in Holland, who commanded Stuyvesant to let variations in religion "pass in silence and permit them [the Lutherans] their free worship in their houses."

Schools scarcely existed in the Hudson Valley before the advent of Stuyvesant, though a schoolmaster or two had earlier found a place in New Netherland. Because of the high degree of literacy in seventeenth-century Holland, a few romantic historians have imagined that the Dutch in America were zealous to introduce public schools. Actually, the *Remonstrance* of 1649 complained that "the plate had been going around a long time for the purpose of erecting a common school but as yet the first stone is not laid."

Stuyvesant offered to dig down in his own pocket for a contribution toward the school and to appropriate some of the Company's money, but since the public of New Amsterdam had more use for seventeen taphouses than for one school, nothing was immediately done. Of the two or three schoolmasters who received appointment in the next few years, none proved satisfactory. At last however, between 1557 and 1664, the Dutch managed to set up schools of a sort in more than a half-dozen communities. Some well-to-do parents hired tutors as did the planters of Virginia and Maryland. For instance Stuyvesant himself employed as a teacher for his own children a young candidate for the ministry named Aegidius Luyck, proficient in both Latin and Greek, who later conducted a Latin school in New Amsterdam where he had two students from as far away as Virginia. Two other Latin schools had preceded Luyck's but the first had failed and the second, taught by Alexander Carolus Curtius—who claimed to have been a professor in Lithuania—proved a disappointment because the professor could not keep his students from fighting and tearing "the clothes from each other's bodies." Poor as were the schools, the children of New Netherland managed somehow to learn a little reading and arithmetic.

Of reading matter there was practically nothing yet beyond the Bible and a few pious books. No printing press was dreamed of and few books appear to have reached New Netherland in the cargoes of Dutch ships. The preachers sometimes had small libraries, mostly of a professional or utilitarian sort. By no stretch of the imagination can one legitimately ascribe a literary interest to the New Netherlanders. The learned lawyer, Adriaen Van der Donck, whose pen had composed the *Remonstrance* of 1649, was the author of the colony's most impressive piece of literature, a *Descrip-tion of New Netherland*, printed in Amsterdam in 1655, with a second edition a year later.

The primary interest of the Dutch was in trade, especially the fur trade with the Indians, and to that end every effort was made to keep peace with the frontier tribes. Although the colony suffered in Kieft's administration from wars with the Manhattan and river Indians, and in Stuyvesant's time from three Indian attacks—one of which practically wiped out the settlement at Esopus—the Dutch maintained peaceful relations with the powerful Iroquois and their allies in the north and west. Through the Iroquois, they pushed their trade on the western frontiers in beaver, mink, and other skins. Their friendship with the Iroquois, who were the traditional enemies of the Algonquins (the Indian allies of the French), also gave the Dutch a shield against French invasion from the St. Lawrence and the lake region.

The British in America owed more to Dutch possession of the Hudson Valley in the critical years of the seventeenth century than they realized. Had the French instead of the Dutch managed to occupy that strategic territory, British America would have been split by the power which exerted the greatest military strength in North America, and the English might have been driven back into the sea. As it turned out, the Dutch served as a bulwark against France until the English colonies were strong enough to resist the northern enemy. Throughout the dynastic wars with the French in the eighteenth century, the New York frontier was the most critical zone for the British colonies. It was the good fortune of the English that Dutch traders pursued a policy of peace on that frontier in the preceding generations when the English settlements were too weak to protect themselves from the French.

Peter Stuyvesant was a forceful administrator and a brave soldier, but he could not overcome the destiny which translated his colony from New Netherland to New York. From the rapidly growing English colonies of New England trespassers constantly filtered into the Dutch domain. Any semblance of Dutch control of the Connecticut River had long since vanished, though Dutchmen were still engaged in the fur trade there. On the Delaware, Englishmen were becoming more numerous than either the Dutch or the Swedes. The proprietor of Maryland laid claim to land in that region which the Dutch had once hoped to possess. Between the English pincers, the Dutch had small hope of ultimate survival as a political power.

The impetus for the final conquest of New Netherland by Englishmen came, however, as a result of a renewed spirit of colonial enterprise which was developing in England itself. Merchants and nobility alike, eager to replenish fortunes depleted during the Civil Wars, turned to the plantations overseas. Trade and development of new sources of profit became the preoccupation of influential merchants of London and Bristol and of powerful courtiers surrounding the merry monarch, Charles II, who showed himself ever ready to confer a favor—if it cost him no more than the stroke of the royal pen, by which he granted princely domains in the New World. Within a few months after Charles' restoration to the throne, he granted a charter to the Company of Royal Adventurers to Africa, a name later changed to the Royal African Company, to monopolize the slave trade between Africa and America. Heading this company was James Duke of York, the king's brother and heir apparent to the throne. This company's most powerful rival was the Dutch West India Company, which controlled New Netherland. The dimmest wit could see that a stroke which would weaken the Dutch company and increase the wealth of Englishmen was a patriotic act for God and king—or, at the very least, for the king's brother. This was the constant argument of Sir George Downing, English minister at The Hague, the son of Emmanuel Downing of Boston and a graduate of Harvard, who made it his business to urge the reduction of New Netherland to English authority.

By a fortunate coincidence, the Duke of York was also

the Lord High Admiral, with full control of his Majesty's navy. The duke, with the aid of such loyal servants as Samuel Pepys, the diarist, conducted his office with energy and zeal. The king's ships were soon put in repair and stood ready for any adventure. If they should be used to aid the Royal African Company, or to further the ends of any of the duke's financial friends in the city, few in the navy office would think it amiss.

A technique familiar in the modern world was employed to create an issue against the Dutch which would warrant the seizure of coveted possessions. England, it must be remembered, had never conceded that the Dutch had any legal rights in the valleys of the Hudson and the Delaware. With the tightening of the Navigation Acts after 1660, the admiralty kept a sharp eye on Dutch merchantmen in an effort to maintain a closed empire of trade. The merchants of London and the speculators at court began to complain loudly of insults from the Dutch on the coast of Guinea, in America, and as far away as India, where for two generations the English and Dutch East India Companies had carried on a bitter rivalry which sometimes reached the proportions of war. From The Hague, Sir George Downing kept up a stream of reports about the insolence of the Dutch and the need to avenge outrages and damage to English interests overseas. In April 1664, the House of Commons passed a resolution deploring the injuries to Englishmen at the hands of Dutchmen in the far corners of the earth. Already a fleet was ready and a commission was appointed to go to New England to investigate reports of violations of the acts of trade and of course to proceed against New Netherland. The king named his brother, the Duke of York, lord proprietor over territory in North America occupied by the Dutch and over a curious assortment of other neighboring lands, including a part of Maine to the St. Lawrence River, Long Island, Nantucket, Martha's Vineyard, and the west bank of the Delaware, which Lord Baltimore claimed. The boundaries of this proprietary grant were vague and indefinite, and others, including a few English proprietors as well as the French, had prior claims to portions of it, but Charles II and his advisers were more than careless about such matters. With an easy pen, the king was ready to reward his favorites with land in the New World, and if the grants overlapped, that would merely make work for hungry lawyers.

The Duke of York lost no time in asserting his authority. At the end of August 1664, an English fleet cast anchor off New Amsterdam, and the commander, Colonel Richard Nicolls, whom the duke had named his deputy governor, sent word to Peter Stuyvesant to surrender. England and the Netherlands were not at this time at war, but the English maintained that this was not an act of war against a friendly power: the rightful owner was merely recovering his own from the Dutch West India Company! Storm as he might and breathe threats of vengeance and death as he would, Stuyvesant was helpless. As he later declared to the States General, his chief gunner reported that the gunpowder at Fort Amsterdam was so damaged and scanty that "were I to commence firing in the morning, I should have [it] all used up by noon."

Sure of the outcome, Nicolls waited while Governor John Winthrop of Connecticut headed a delegation of mediators who persuaded Stuyvesant of the hopelessness of his situation. When his own council and the burghers of the town joined the plea for surrender, the old man, on September 8, grouchily gave up. The terms of capitulation were exceptionally generous. The citizens of New Amsterdam, now changed to New York, received a guarantee of "free voices in all public affairs" and were confirmed in their property rights in accordance with Dutch law. Liberty of conscience was assured and the right of trade with the Netherlands was allowed. The shift in ownership from the West India Company to the Duke of York seemed to promise little change in the colony except a new name. Although for a brief interval, from July 30, 1673, to November 10, 1674, the Dutch reoccupied New York, the English had come to stay.

Though the Dutch were through as a political force in the Hudson and Delaware valleys, they would remain a social influence for generations to come. The sharp gabled roofs which they introduced became a permanent part of the New York landscape and spread to other regions. Dutch merchants gave to New York a commercial atmosphere which became the most characteristic quality of that city. New York, which in time would surpass both Boston and Philadelphia as a port, owed much of its commerce and industry to the shrewdness and thrift of Dutch burghers.

The habits bequeathed by the Dutch also gave New York a greater concern with the pleasures to be found in everyday life than one could discern in the more austere atmosphere of Puritan Boston. Though the Puritans were no mean trenchermen, they never equalled the Dutch for belly cheer; and Boston, for all of the complaints of the preachers about its wickedness, never placed as much emphasis as New York upon the pleasures associated with the beer pot, tobacco pipe, and convivial board. If the Dutch were not gay in the volatile fashion of French city dwellers, they at least took solid comfort from the pleasures of this world. Their holidays were occasions of feasting and merry-making. Many customs associated with New Year's Day—like the habit of calling on one's neighbors and friends and sharing their drinks—with May Day, and with the holiday after Whitsunday known as Pinkster (Pentecost) Day were Dutch contributions to the festivities of New York. Pinkster Day soon became the special holiday of the Negro slaves. The introduction of the jovial Saint Nicholas—corrupted perhaps after the colonial period to Santa Klaus—was also a Dutch innovation whose significance needs no commentary. From the Dutch era down to the present time, New York's business and its pleasures have never been far apart in American consciousness.

The administrator whom the Duke of York had chosen to manage his affairs in New York was one of the wisest officials any of the colonies had seen. Richard Nicolls, a loyal adherent of the Stuarts, set about remodelling the legal structure of New York to fit English traditions, but he did his work so gradually and with so much tact that he won the friendship and respect of Dutch and English alike. A code of laws, known as the Duke's Laws, based on those in effect in New England, was promulgated in March 1665, effective at once in the English settlements on Long Island and more slowly, as adjustments could be made, in the Dutch portion of the colony. Though no provision was yet made for a general legislative assembly, town governments had much of the autonomy characteristic of New England. Despite Nicolls' autocratic powers, his administration proved just and beneficent. When he resigned and went home in August 1668, he had achieved a reasonably workable fusion between residual Dutch law and customs and English procedures and practice.

The scattered territory which Nicolls took over in 1664 was reduced within a few months by the Duke of York's conveyance of the land between the Hudson and the Delaware to two courtiers, John Lord Berkeley and Sir George Carteret, who were already among the eight who had received the proprietary grant of the Carolinas. As a tribute to Carteret for his defense of the island of Jersey against Parliamentary forces during the Puritan Revolution, the grant was named New Jersey. New York also returned to Connecticut the land west of the Connecticut River which New Netherland had claimed. Territory on the western bank of the Delaware River remained in dispute between New York and Maryland.

The Duke of York's grant of New Jersey to Berkeley and Carteret raised vexing legal questions: Were the new owners subservient to the ducal proprietor of New York, or were they lords proprietors in their own right as if they had received their grant directly from the king? They assumed that they were proprietors independent of New York and set about establishing their authority after the fashion of the Carolina proprietors. Their domain was sparsely inhabited and contained within its borders, besides Indians, a few Swedes, Finns, Dutch, and English families in tiny scattered settlements. If they were to wring a profit out of the grant, they had to make it attractive to immigrants. This they tried to do by issuing a body of "Concessions" which guaranteed liberty of conscience and a representative assembly for the purpose of making laws and levying taxes, provided that the settlers swore allegiance to the king and the proprietors and agreed to pay quitrents. Procurement of land was made easy and the prospect looked attractive.

To be governor of New Jersey, the proprietors sent over Sir George's cousin, Philip Carteret, an inexperienced youth in his twenties.

If the proprietors dreamed of quick profits they were doomed to disappointment. From the first, their province was beset by disputes over land, the most characteristic element in New Jersey's history for generations to come. Some individual grants had already been made by Richard Nicolls of New York before the news of the transfer to Carteret and Berkeley reached him. Controversy over these patents was only the beginning of trouble, for Carteret and Berkeley divided New Jersey between them, and from that division and the eventual disposition of their respective territories came confusion worse confounded. Berkeley held the western portion, known as West Jersey, and Carteret the portion nearest New York, known as East Jersey. The boundary at first was indefinite but in 1676 a diagonal line from Little Egg Harbor to Pensauken Creek a little above the site of Camden separated the two Jerseys.

Despairing of making any money out of West Jersey, Berkeley, for a thousand pounds, had already sold his proprietary right to two Quakers, John Fenwick and Edward Byllinge, who soon quarreled in most unquakerlike fashion over the division of their purchase and called in William

Penn as mediator. Thus Penn got his first acquaintance with America and the possibility of a Quaker haven in the New World. Both Fenwick and Byllinge ran into debt and had to dispose of West Jersey, a large portion of which came eventually under the control of three trustees, Penn, Gawen Lawrie, a London merchant, and Nicholas Lucas, a Hartford brewer. Through the activities of these men, West Jersey attracted Quaker immigrants and became predominantly Quaker before Pennsylvania was settled. But because of the rapid transfers of land titles and the uncertainty of the proprietary rights, if any, of the various owners, the legal status of lands held in West Jersey became ever more complex and subject to litigation.

East Jersey fared little better. In 1680, Carteret died leaving a will which placed the American possessions in the hands of his widow and a board of trustees, who were instructed to sell the East Jersey proprietary lands to satisfy his obligations. After vainly trying to dispose of East Jersey privately, the executors sold it at public auction for £3,400 and a peppercorn of quitrent, to a syndicate of twelve men, among whom were Penn, Byllinge, and Lawrie. Later these twelve added twelve others to help them share the responsibilities. Though some of the twenty-four were Quakers, the proprietors included Presbyterians and Roman Catholics as well, and both Scots and Englishmen. Their only common interest was hope of profits from East Jersey. Since the individual proprietors could sell and bequeath their shares, the land problem in East Jersey quickly became more confused, if anything, than that in West Jersey.

In both Jerseys the ownership of land, the right to vote, which went with the possession of land, and the right of proprietors to meddle in the political affairs of the colony were often in dispute. The confusion which began in this period transmitted a heritage of litigation to later generations and made necessary the persistence of boards of proprietors down to the present age. Their function in recent times has been to provide quitclaims to land purchased in the two portions of New Jersey.

Despite the confusion of control in East and West Jersey, the region attracted settlers and developed both agriculture and commerce. Prosperous Quakers by the hundreds came to West Jersey and settled the towns of Salem, Burlington, and Greenwich. Most of these were refugees from persecution in England: squires, merchants, tradesmen, and artisans of one kind or another. They made peaceful bargains for land with the Indians and set diligently to work. From the pine and cedar forests, which then covered the land, they sawed lumber and hewed ship timbers; they built sea-going vessels and engaged in trade and fishing; their plantations grew in area and produced grain, corn, livestock, and a little tobacco.

Some of the Quakers—who for all of their love of their fellow-men, were not above owning slaves—developed an economy not unlike the agrarian life in Virginia and Maryland. New Englanders also migrated to West Jersey, especially to the region around Cape May. There they found prosperity in the fisheries. Whaling for many years was the occupation of Cape May seamen, and from Cape May came supplies of whale oil and bone. East Jersey attracted Quakers too, but men of other beliefs were more numerous. Migrants from Connecticut crossed over from New York and settled around Newark Bay, bringing with them Congregational doctrines and Puritan strictness. Scotch Presbyterians, persecuted at home, sought a refuge in East Jersey, and after 1685, French Huguenots added to the complexity of the groups already there.

Both East and West Jersey experienced much unrest, partly because of the disparate nationalities and religions which made up the population, but more acutely because of the uncertainty of their political rights. While the Duke of York was proprietor of New York, and after he became king of England, the governors of New York continued to meddle in the affairs of New Jersey, especially East Jersey, a condition which from time to time caused rioting and rebellious disorder. Finally, in 1702, the two Jerseys were united into one colony under a royal governor. The proprietors still had their rights in the land, with the quitrents which ownership of the soil implied.

The government established by the ducal proprietor over New York, oddly enough, pleased the Dutch better than the English inhabitants. The English settlements on Long Island, for example, had long enjoyed virtual independence and had grown accustomed to governing themselves. When the Duke of York's governors sought to tax them and to impose ready-made laws, they objected with vehemence and abuse of the duke's agents. The Dutch, who had no tradition of self-government, found English governors better, or at least no worse, than the directors formerly sent over by the West India Company. So long as the duke's representatives did not interfere too much with trade, which was food and drink to a Dutchman, the burghers were reasonably satisfied. The Long Island Puritans, on the other hand, held far different views, and raised a clamor against taxation without representation.

The governors who succeeded Nicolls found the Long Islanders a stiff-backed and contentious group. In Governor Francis Lovelace's administration some of the towns refused to pay taxes to "an arbitrary power" which held them "enslaved," and the towns on the eastern end of Long Island even petitioned the Privy Council—in vain—to annex them to Connecticut. Major Edmund Andros, who succeeded Lovelace in 1674, was an aristocrat of the British Army who was certain he knew how to deal with such recalcitrants. He simply declared them rebels and wrote a stern letter to the governor of Connecticut commanding him to quit giving aid and comfort to such rascals. But Andros' measures had no better success. The Long Islanders continued to raise an uproar and to demand a popular legislature, upon which the duke looked with ill-favor. Of assemblies, he declared that he could not "but suspect they would be of dangerous consequence, nothing being more known than the aptness of such bodies to assume to themselves many privileges which prove destructive to, or very oft disturb, the peace of the government wherein they are allowed." Nevertheless the duke finally consented to create a representative assembly chosen by the landed class, as was customary in other colonies, and instructed his next governor, Colonel Thomas Dongan, to call an assembly which first met in New York on October 17, 1683. This body drew up a "Charter of Liberties and Privileges," which was sent to England and received the duke's approval.

But before the charter was returned to New York, the Duke of York had become King James II, and the document was left in England to gather dust. The new king had other ideas now about the disposition of New York and its government. In 1688 he established the Dominion of New England, which included New York and New Jersey, and appointed Andros governor-general, with Francis Nicholson as his deputy in New York. Government by legislative assembly was over for a time, and the old discontents, along with certain new grievances, were rife again.

The strength of the political discontent with which the early governors had to contend was in a measure indicative of the growth of the colony in population and economic importance. After 1664, immigration increased, both from Europe and adjacent colonies. By 1698, the colony contained more than eighteen thousand souls, of whom over two thousand were Negro slaves, and in the succeeding quarter of a century the population increased to approximately forty thousand. The proprietor having sought to encourage immigration to New York was not inquisitive about nationality or religion. Though James II was a Catholic, his province was glad to welcome French Huguenots, who soon made New Rochelle a French Protestant center. Since the Huguenots were noted for their thrift and diligence, neither Governor Dongan, himself an Irish Catholic, nor the King found fault with the new immigrants. A decade after James II's expulsion from the throne of England, when the Earl of Bellomont was royal governor of New York, swarms of Palatine Germans were induced to come to New York to work in the pine forests and make ship stores. Constantly the colony was drawing on England, Scotland, Ireland, the Continent, and other parts of America for population.

Land was easy to obtain in the rich valleys of the Hudson, Mohawk, and other streams. Though many great manors were established by the English governors, the lords of these manors needed tenants, or were willing to give freehold rights to their soil on generous terms. Hence land, which to a European meant prestige and prosperity, lay within the grasp even of poor immigrants. Extensive manors and small independent farms both contributed to the increasing prosperity of New York.

Side by side, an aristocracy of rich merchants and landholders—frequently combined in the same individuals—and a small farmer and craftsman class developed. The aristocrats were represented by such men as Stephanus Van Cortlandt, Frederick Philipse, Peter Schuyler (the first mayor of Albany), Robert Livingston, Jeremias Van Rensselaer, Nicholas Bayard (nephew of Peter Stuyvesant), and, a few years later, Caleb Heathcote, who in 1711 was mayor of New York while his brother Gilbert was Lord Mayor of London. David Jamison, a poor Scot, who reached New York as an indentured servant in 1686, became the owner of vast tracts of land in Westchester and Dutchess counties; by 1711 he was chief justice of New Jersey and, by 1720, attorney-general of New York. The landed aristocracy was confined to no group or caste; as elsewhere in the New World, thrift, diligence, enterprise, and often ruthlessness helped men up the social ladder. The smaller folk—the craftsmen, the workingmen, and the yeomen-farmers—did not always dwell in halcyon peace with their great neighbors, and they soon found a leader in Jacob Leisler, a German, who had arrived in 1660 as a soldier of the West India Company.

Babel on the Hudson and the Delaware

Leisler, who had married the well-to-do widow of Pieter Van der Veen, had himself grown rich in the fur, tobacco, and wine trade, and had become a captain of the militia and a deacon in the Dutch Reformed Church. As a zealous Calvinist he hated popery and all its works which, in his mind, included the Church of England. Therefore he bitterly opposed the appointment of Nicholas Van Rensselaer as a minister of the Dutch Reformed Church, because Van Rensselaer was reputedly an Anglican. Furthermore, he joined with others who hated Governor-General Andros and his deputy in New York, Francis Nicholson, because it was whispered that they were secretly Catholics intent upon fastening popery upon New York to please their royal master, King James. English Puritans and Dutch members of the Reformed Church were mightily disturbed by these rumors in the later months of 1688. The agitators for a legislative assembly were also making a new outcry against government by executive order. Many of the more violent were small farmers, artisans, craftsmen, and petty traders.

When news of the Glorious Revolution of 1688 and the accession of William and Mary reached the colonies early in 1689, the reaction in New England and New York was explosive. In Boston, Andros was deposed and jailed; in New York, six weeks later, on May 31, Jacob Leisler led a company of militia against Nicholson and occupied the fort but allowed Nicholson to sail for England. Leisler set himself at the head of a revolutionary government and proclaimed William and Mary the rightful sovereigns. As the self-appointed defender of the Protestant faith and the liberties of common men, he should have won widespread support, but unhappily he was obstinate and arrogant; he also started with the bitter enmity of the aristocratic landlords, with some of whom he was connected by marriage.

Although Leisler professed loyalty to William and Mary, he showed no disposition to abdicate gracefully when the new sovereigns appointed as governor, Henry Sloughter, who did not reach New York until March 19, 1691. In the

[201]

meantime, Leisler had defied Major Richard Ingoldesby and a regiment of their Majesties' troops, and Leisler's men had killed two and wounded seven of the soldiers. When Leisler finally yielded the fort to Sloughter, he was arrested for treason.

His adherents thought that he ought to have been thanked for saving the province from "the treachery of Papists and Jacobites" and from the French to the north. Instead, he and seven of his chief followers were tried for their lives and sentenced to death. While fuddled in drink, it was later charged, Sloughter signed the death warrants of Leisler and his son-in-law, Jacob Milborne, who were hanged on May 16, 1691. The six others convicted with them were reprieved. The rich landowning class, who feared and hated Leisler, openly gloated, while a few loyal followers secretly swore vengeance. For a generation and more, the issues raised by Leisler's faction split New York into rival political groups. In 1695 the English Parliament reversed the attainder against him and thus declared him innocent of treason, and in 1702 the province of New York gave his heirs £2,700 indemnity —paltry amends for the execution of a citizen whose chief offense was narrow-minded stubbornness and demagogic agitation against his enemies among the landed aristocracy.

If Sloughter was no better governor than the worst of King James' appointees, he at least brought with him instructions from the crown for calling general assemblies of the "free-holders within your government, according to the usage of our other plantations in America." The first assembly under these instructions met in April, 1691, and though it was composed of vengeful enemies of the Leislerians, the mere fact of something approaching representative government was important for the future. In the years to come, the assembly slowly and painfully gained power, particularly the power of the purse. The political history of the province in the early decades of the eighteenth century is the story of the conflict between the legislative assembly and the royal governors over revenues and taxes.

Babel on the Hudson and the Delaware

New York's governors in this period were singularly inept, incompetent, or corrupt. Soon after Leisler's execution Sloughter died—of delirium tremens, some said. His successor Benjamin Fletcher was notable chiefly for his friendliness to pirates who made New York harbor their rendezvous and saw that some of their Guinea gold reached the governor's pockets. Richard Coote, the Earl of Bellomont, the next governor, was more ornamental than useful, but he was far better than Edward Hyde, Lord Cornbury, who became governor of New York and New Jersey in 1702.

Of all the fatuous rascals who tried to rule the American colonies, Cornbury was one of the least attractive and most avaricious. As a cousin of Queen Anne, he was arrogant and dictatorial. Given to drink and debaucheries, his conduct was as foolish as it was disgraceful. One of his pleasures was to dress in women's clothing and carouse in the dives of New York with his boon companions. Not above thievery, he embezzled £1,500 of public funds appropriated by the assembly and ran through all the money he could borrow. When at last he was recalled in 1708, his creditors had him arrested for debt and placed in the custody of the sheriff. This was the creature who went slinking back to England to inherit the title of the Earl of Clarendon. His successor, Lord Lovelace, seemed a better character but he caught a cold on landing and died within a few months. Finally Robert Hunter, a Scot, with more ability than his predecessors, became governor in 1710 and set about the Herculean task of bringing order into the administration. If his success was limited, his effort was at least sincere and honest.

One acute problem which the accession of King William brought to New York was the imminence of war with the French in Canada. And war with the French meant Indian wars on the frontier between the respective allies of the French and English. The Dutch had been remarkably successful in keeping peace with the Iroquois and their allies, or the Five Nations as they were called. The English inherited this friendly relationship and used the alliance to protect the back country against the incursion of the French and their Algonquin cohorts.

If the French could detach the Five Nations from the English, the British colonies would be in dire peril. Since the 1670's this had been the dream of the ablest French strategists, notably the Comte de Frontenac, governor-general of Canada. French missionaries penetrated the country of the Iroquois and tried to lure the savages into the French sphere of influence. Adroitly Frontenac combined force with persuasion. The Iroquois saw that their hated rivals, the Algonquins, were well armed and supplied by the French, while they, the allies of the English, received few or no guns except at an extortionate rate. If they should come under the protection of France, Frontenac's agents suggested, they too would have powder, lead, and guns, and the great father would also assure them protection from his other children, the Algonquins. Had not France recalled Frontenac at a crucial moment in 1682 and replaced him with two rash and inexperienced governors in succession, his strategy might have been successful. When Frontenac returned to Canada in 1689, he found his earlier work undone and the Iroquois on the warpath. War between France and England had broken out, and frontiersmen, French and British, would pay with their blood for political feuds in the chancelleries of Europe.

French and Indians, sweeping out of the forest at midnight on February 9, 1690, fell on the sleeping village of Schenectady and murdered the inhabitants, men, women, and children. One man, half dead, crawled from the burning huts, and, riding a crippled horse, reached Albany to tell his tale of horror. During the winter, villages on the borders of Maine, New Hampshire, Massachusetts, and Connecticut also lived in terror of the savage onslaught. The English fought back, but with divided strength and counsels. New York and New England tried without success to unite. A joint expedition from Connecticut and New York, commanded by Fitz-John Winthrop of Connecticut, was so unsuccessful that Jacob Leisler, then acting as governor of New York, arrested Winthrop for cowardice. From Boston, Sir William Phips led an expedition by sea against Acadia and on May 11, 1690, captured Port Royal. Gleefully his Puritans plundered the Catholic church and Phips himself robbed the French governor of all his possessions down to his spare drawers and nightcaps. Encouraged by this success, Phips commanded another expedition in the autumn against Quebec but he was no match for the veteran Frontenac; unable to take or even to threaten Quebec, his fleet, bedraggled and beaten, limped back to Boston. John Schuyler, brother of Peter Schuyler, the mayor of Albany, headed an expedition against Montreal and succeeded in killing a few French *habitants* and some Indians. Thus the indecisive war dragged on until the Peace of Ryswick in 1697 made a short and uneasy truce.

King William's War, as this first general conflict between France and England in North America is called, was characteristic of the struggles which drenched the frontier settlements in blood until the Peace of Paris in 1763. New York's frontier became a critical area for all of British America. Though New England's borders were exposed and easily attacked, the capture of the waterways of New York promised more of strategic importance. Frontenac dreamed of taking Albany and sending his soldiers down the Hudson to divide the British. The facts of geography made this strategy obvious. Later, in the Revolution, General Burgoyne hoped to win the war against the colonies by the same tactics. Upon New York, therefore, depended the destiny of the British in America, and this critical position gave peculiar point to her requests for aid from the other colonies in the wars which followed in grim succession during the eighteenth century.

Though French and Indian enemies might threaten her borders, and incompetent governors might bring chaos to the government, nevertheless New York flourished. Farmers constantly extended their holdings and brought more land under cultivation; the forests themselves yielded timber and lumber for export; the sea provided an income from fisheries and whaling. While some industries developed—such as the weaving of coarse cloth, part linen and part wool, known as linsey-woolsey—New York almost perfectly exemplified the ideal of the mercantilists. Her raw products supplied the needs of England, and she was so rich in natural resources that her exports enabled the inhabitants to accumulate enough exchange to buy abundantly of the mother country's manufactures.

The largest proportion of New York's population consisted of farmers. The small yeoman, cultivating a few acres with the help of his family, and the great landlord, farming his estates with tenants and bondservants, both managed to make a living and profit. Unlike the Chesapeake Bay colonies, New York was not tied to one crop and therefore did not suffer the extreme depressions which the fall in the price of tobacco brought with painful regularity to Virginia and Maryland. New Yorkers practiced subsistence farming plus. The fertile soil produced abundant crops of grains, especially wheat; and for most of the year, the grasslands and woods supplied provender for cattle, sheep, horses, and pigs with little effort on the farmer's part; indeed, pigs lived and fattened on acorns in the oak forests until their numbers made them a pest requiring the constant attention of local governments; droves of rooting and grunting pigs were a common affliction of New York City's streets well into the eighteenth century. Tobacco and flax grew with sufficient ease to make them profitable. Fruits, especially apples, were abundant. Every farm had its cider press, and cider, either sweet or hard, was a common beverage. Bee-keeping provided honey and wax. From his fields, pastures, and orchards, the New Yorker obtained almost every article required for comfortable living, with a surplus for export.

The varied national groups in New York's population help to account for the enterprise of the inhabitants. Dutchmen, for example, brought with them a knowledge of intensive farming unknown in seventeenth-century England, and other Europeans contributed special knowledge and skills. Although the pioneers in New York exploited the soil and forests with the reckless abandon common on the frontier everywhere, they tried so many profit-making activities that they could not exhaust all of their resources.

Great as was the value of farm products, they were not the one source of New York's prosperity; they were rather ancillary and complementary to a trade which was making New York City and Albany towns of consequence in the American colonies. Although the fur trade, originally the mainstay of the Dutch, gradually diminished in relative importance, it remained throughout the seventeenth and early eighteenth centuries a business worth fighting for. Albany was the center of this traffic. There the Iroquois brought loads of beaver pelts and other skins, some of which they had obtained from the western Indians, for the Iroquois were traders and brokers between far distant tribes and the white men at Albany. From Albany, the Hudson made a convenient waterway for the shipment of furs and the products of northern farms to the port of New York.

New York was a busy port with its own ships going out to England, southern Europe, the West Indies, Africa, or wherever the acts of trade allowed—and often where these acts did not permit. Like the shippers of Boston, New Yorkers had flexible consciences in matters of smuggling. The cargoes exported from New York were wondrously varied: wheat, beans, peas, oats, corn, salt pork, hams, bacon, dried venison, beef tongues, butter, cheese, ships' biscuits, flour, flax and flaxseed, tobacco, furs, deer hides, pitch, tar, ships' spars, barrel staves, beeswax, live horses, and cattle found their way to overseas markets. From the West Indies, vessels brought back molasses and sugar for rum, logwood, mahogany, lime juice, indigo, cotton, and various other tropical products; from the Azores and Madeira came wine and grape brandy in astonishing quantities; from Africa, slaves, elephants' tusks, ebony, and pure gold; from Europe, all of the manufactures and luxuries which made life pleasant and easy.

The Atlantic Frontier

The pirates who haunted the coast of Madagascar and found a welcome in New York, surreptitious or otherwise, disposed of vast quantities of East Indian loot: rugs and tapestries, jewelry, gems, and gold ornaments, bullion, and coins. New York merchants and shippers learned the way to wealth in the seventeenth century and have never forgotten it.

As wealth accumulated, the richer merchants grew prouder and more aristocratic in their living and their bearing. About the autocratic royal governors and their officials there developed a "court party" which included some but not all of the wealthier citizens of New York City and outlying territory. Whatever may have been the qualities of the nascent aristocracy of New York, a contempt for trade was unknown. The market place, the counting house, and the country place were early found mutually compatible by the great men of New York.

Too busy with material progress to pay much attention to cultural matters, seventeenth-century New Yorkers lagged far behind both Virginians and New Englanders, and not until well into the eighteenth century was even New York City much better than an intellectual desert. Schools were notoriously poor. Well-to-do citizens were obliged to continue the habit of hiring tutors; poorer citizens had a few makeshift schools where their children might acquire the rudiments of learning; but no adequate public school system was evolved for generations. Dutch schools, sometimes taught by the pastor of the Reformed Church, continued for many years to teach elementary subjects in the Dutch language. Only spasmodic and half-hearted efforts were made by the royal government to provide education for the children of common people. A grammar school was finally established by act of the assembly in 1732 in New York City where Scottish schoolmasters taught mathematics, Latin, and Greek. Most of New York's schools were private schools which only the well-to-do could afford. As late as 1741, the six English schools open in New York City at that date were

NEW YORK IN THE EARLY EIGHTEENTH CENTURY

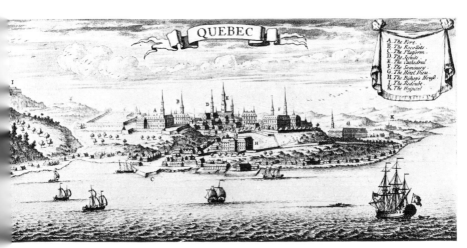

QUEBEC IN THE EARLY EIGHTEENTH CENTURY

From the Huntington Library copy of Henry Popple, *Atlas* (1733).

THE BUSY PORT OF PHILADELPHIA IN 1761

(1) Christ Church (2) State House (3) Academy (4) Presbyterian Church (5) Dutch Calvinist Church (6) Court House

From a contemporary engraving in the Huntington Library collection.

Babel on the Hudson and the Delaware

all privately conducted. Twenty years later, of one French, one Hebrew, two Dutch, and ten English schools, all were private. No institution of higher learning developed until the founding of King's College under charter from King George II in 1754. Books and libraries were scarcer in New York than in Virginia and New England, and those which existed in the seventeenth century were chiefly religious and theological works owned by the clergy. Of a library at Rensselaerswyck in 1642 consisting of seventeen titles, one was an eight-volume set of John Calvin's *Works*. Like other colonies in North America, New York owed its first public library to that devoted Anglican, Dr. Thomas Bray, who about 1698 sent over a collection of books to be used by both clergy and laymen. Inventories of the earlier period list a few scattered collections of books, but the development of libraries of significance came after the mid-eighteenth century. The New York Society Library was founded in 1754, the year which saw the beginning of King's College. On some of the New Jersey plantations, inventories reveal better collections of books in the seventeenth century than could be found in New York in the same period. For example, John Allen of Woodbridge had a library in 1684 of 252 volumes; John Skeene of Peachfield in Burlington County left in 1695 a library valued at more than £24; and Elizabeth Tatham of Burlington, widow of John Tatham, gentleman, in 1702 listed 552 books which her husband had collected in his mansion house.

Small as was the interest in books in New York, it had the advantage of printing presses from 1693, when William Bradford came from Philadelphia and set up a press which specialized in printing laws and proclamations, pious works, and hymn books. Bradford was also the founder of the colony's first newspaper, the *New York Gazette*, issued from 1725 to 1744. More famous was the *New York Weekly Journal*, begun in 1733 by John Peter Zenger, who had learned his trade as an apprentice of Bradford's. Zenger was a Palatine German whose paper became the mouthpiece of those who opposed the governor's or "court" party. When Governor William Cosby could tolerate Zenger's satirical barbs no longer, he had him thrown into prison charged with libel. For nine months the hardy editor conducted his paper from the jail and his trial on August 4, 1735, excited the interest of lovers of liberty throughout the colonies. To his defense came a great lawyer, eighty-year-old Andrew Hamilton of Philadelphia, whose plea in defense of freedom of speech and the press deserves to be better known. The jury returned a verdict of not guilty and Zenger went free. Though the Zenger trial of course did not immediately establish the freedom of the press in the American colonies, as writers sometimes loosely state, it was an important landmark in the development of that principle.

Religious freedom also owed much to another famous trial in New York, that of the Reverend Francis Makemie, a Scotch Presbyterian, whom Governor Cornbury had arrested in January 1707 for preaching without a license and kept in jail six weeks. The court freed him and the assembly passed legislation designed to prevent religious persecution. Freedom of worship was essential in a colony like New York if violent unrest was to be avoided, for the faiths of the people were as various as their backgrounds. Calvinistic Dutchmen, Puritans and Anglicans of English derivation, Huguenot Frenchmen, Lutheran Swedes and Germans, Quakers and other pietists, a miscellaneous sprinkling of Catholics, and a congregation of Jews were among the diverse religious groups who found asylum in the borders of the province. The Anglicans, who had been increasing since 1664, pushed through the assembly the Church Act of 1693, which had the effect of establishing their religion in lower New York. Trinity Church, in time the richest and most fashionable congregation in New York City, was established by charter in 1697.

Although the churches helped to mitigate in some degree the crass materialism of the province of New York, the cultivation of the mind and spirit had to wait for later generations. Not until well along in the eighteenth century could New Yorkers boast of a professional class who enjoyed the prestige which goes with learning. Cadwallader Colden, physician, scientist, political figure, and merchant, was one of the first intellectuals to attract attention outside of the province. His treatise on the Indians, published in 1727 as the *History of the Five Nations*, is one of the few important literary works produced in New York before the midcentury. New York's genius in the earlier period lay not in learning and literature but in trade.

CHAPTER FIVE

The "Holy Experiment" in Pennsylvania

A S no other American colony, Pennsylvania enjoyed from the beginning remarkable prosperity and freedom, and it owed this initial success to the dreams of a visionary Quaker, William Penn. With less self-interest than Lord Baltimore had shown in obtaining Maryland, Penn conceived of his proprietary grant, received at the hands of Charles II in 1681, as a refuge of oppressed peoples—Quakers in particular—and only secondarily as a means of aggrandizing himself and his family. Deliberately, in his first Frame of Government, he cut himself off from rich fees which he might have claimed as proprietor, and though in later years when he was deep in debt he pleaded anxiously for the collection of quitrents, it should not be forgotten that he impoverished himself by paying the administrative expenses of the colony out of revenue from his English and Irish estates. If Penn's propensity for making mistakes, especially in the choice of officials, was phenomenal, he was also responsible for policies which gave the citizens of Pennsylvania personal liberty unknown in the other colonies, which freed them from the fear of Indian wars, and which allowed them to penetrate the fertile valleys of the territory and enrich themselves from the produce of the land. The early history of

The "Holy Experiment" in Pennsylvania

Pennsylvania is so much a part of William Penn's plans that it cannot be separated from his biography.

Penn was a complex character with qualities so seemingly contradictory that he could be an honest Quaker preacher and at the same time a successful courtier of two of the least exemplary of English kings, Charles II and James II. His critics have made much of his devotion to the House of Stuart and his apologists have gone to great lengths to explain away his apparent blindness to the corruption of his royal patrons. The truth is that Penn was unusually susceptible to the emotion of gratitude and extraordinarily unmindful of shortcomings in men who professed a friendship for him, as he later demonstrated in his appointments. His father, Admiral Sir William Penn, a self-made man with habits more suited to the quarter-deck than the drawing room, had served the Stuarts loyally—and with great profit to himself. As an official of the navy office, in the manner of the times, he had enriched himself, but he had proved competent and faithful to the interests of his royal masters, who requited him with their trust and favor. From Charles and James, the admiral obtained a promise that they would befriend his son despite the inexplicable perversity which made that youth a Quaker. Throughout their reigns, Charles II and James II bestowed favors upon the wayward son of the old admiral, and William Penn himself never forgot his own loyalty to them. Because of his affection for his father's and his own patrons, he later detested the successor to the Stuarts, William III, whose moral virtues alone were not sufficient to endear him to Penn.

As a young man in his early twenties Penn became a Quaker after being arrested and imprisoned for attending a Quaker meeting. For several years he had shown an interest in the Quakers, and as a consequence of his first imprisonment in 1667, he developed a profound concern for the persecuted of all sects. When he was lodged in the Tower of London in 1669 for bringing out a tract attacking conventional ideas held by many Christians, notably that of original sin and the atonement, he wrote *No Cross, No Crown* (1669), best known of Penn's religious works, which emphasized that Quaker spirituality—the inner light—was essential to the correction of the sins and abuses of the day. Released and again arrested in August 1670 for preaching before a meeting house in London, he and a fellow-Quaker, William Mead, were brought before a court in the Old Bailey. Their trial is famous in the annals of English jurisprudence because it helped to establish the integrity of the jury against browbeating judges. When Penn was finally free again, he went on a missionary journey through Holland and the Rhine country of Germany. This experience brought him into contact, not only with Continental Quakers, but with other sects having kindred ideas. On a second missionary journey in 1677, he extended his acquaintance with the Dutch and German Pietists and paved the way for an advertising campaign which he later carried on to persuade them to seek greater freedom in America.

The violence of the persecution of sectarians in England so oppressed Penn that he determined to establish in America a colony of his own which would be a refuge for all Christians who could not live in peace under the existing laws of their countries. This commonwealth of the pious would become, as he said, a "holy experiment" in living an uncorrupted life in the fresh environment of the New World.

Quakers had already established homes in the wilderness of the Atlantic seaboard; and in nearly every colony except the Puritan commonwealths of New England, where they were violently persecuted, they had found greater freedom than in England. Penn had interested himself in the Quaker settlements of the Jerseys and had familiarized himself with the possibilities of expansion in that region. To give form to his dream of a Quaker commonwealth, he applied to his friend, King Charles II, in 1680 for a grant of land in America. The king referred the petition to the Privy Council and the Lords of Trade, who by now were growing reluctant to favor any more proprietary grants. At length, however, in the spring of 1681, Penn received a favorable answer to his petition and was awarded a princely domain between the Duke of York's territory on the north and Lord Baltimore's Maryland on the south, with access to deep-water harbors on the Delaware and the Susquehanna rivers. As was unhappily the case in most colonial grants, the boundaries were not precise and gave rise to an interminable controversy with Lord Baltimore. The principality was called Pennsylvania, not after the proprietor as is generally believed today, but because, as Penn himself states, it was "a name the king would have given it in honor of my father."

Penn's charter made him and his heirs the owners of the soil of Pennsylvania, subject only to fealty to the king of England and the annual payment of two beaver skins at his Majesty's palace at Windsor. The charter also gave him customary proprietary rights in the government of Pennsylvania, with somewhat less feudal power than had been conferred upon Lord Baltimore. Some of Penn's biographers have assumed that he himself restricted his power, but the Lords of Trade in his time were in no mood to set up absolute rulers in America, for they were busily trying to extend and unify their own authority over the colonies. At their insistence, Penn was required by charter to enforce the Navigation Acts, to submit to the Privy Council of England all laws passed in the colony, to permit the appeal of cases heard in Pennsylvania to the king's courts, and to allow the establishment of Anglican churches whenever as many as twenty people organized a congregation and requested a preacher.

The method of ruling Pennsylvania was prescribed by Penn in his famous first Frame of Government and various subsidiary concessions and laws. The proprietor of course was supreme head of the state and governor but might appoint a deputy to serve in his absence from the colony. The governor had a council, which, unlike other colonial councils, was elected by the freeholders. Ultimately the council consisted of eighteen members. The governor and council initiated laws which were submitted to a house of representatives, also elected by the freeholders, for approval. This popular assembly, reduced in 1683 from two hundred to thirty-two members, at first had no right to initiate legislation and could only register approval or disapproval, but by 1696 it had already assumed the right of proposing laws and of amending laws submitted by the governor and council. Although Penn has been romanticized as a great democrat, his notions of popular liberty, in the opinion of the most acute of modern historians of his settlement, was "distinctly circumscribed. He believed not in the divine right of kings but in the divine right of government." Nevertheless, under Penn the citizenry of Pennsylvania claimed many democratic privileges; they were free to quarrel with the proprietor and even to flout his decrees. Penn's later years were full of controversy with the people of Pennsylvania over his rights as proprietor.

The colony of Pennsylvania in 1681 was not a virgin land untouched as yet by settlers. For nearly fifty years, parts of it had been exploited by fur traders and a few farmers. Scattered Dutchmen, Swedes, and Finns lived on the lower reaches of the Delaware, and sparse settlements of Englishmen were to be found here and there along the waterways of Penn's domain. Especially conglomerate was the population of the so-called "Three Lower Counties"—later the state of Delaware—which Penn obtained from the Duke of York in August 1682. Instead of sending pioneers to make a beginning in a barren land, Penn's first task was to establish his authority over a diverse people who already looked upon Pennsylvania as home. Accordingly, in April 1681, he sent over his cousin, William Markham, to serve as his deputy governor and to take possession of his vast property. A year later Penn himself sailed up the broad reaches of the Delaware in the ship "Welcome" and accepted tokens of fealty from his subjects. In accordance with Penn's instructions a popular assembly was called on December 4, 1682, at Upland, a town whose name was presently changed to Chester, and the "Great Law" was passed which, among other provisions, affirmed the rights of all Christians to liberty of conscience.

When Penn made his first personal contacts with the Indians is not known, but he was much interested in them and was determined that Pennsylvania should set an example of fair and honest dealings with the savages. As Francis Daniel Pastorius, leader of the German Pietists who came to Pennsylvania in 1683, observed, "William Penn did not drive forth the naked native inhabitants of the land with military authority, but brought with him upon his arrival especial clothing and hats for the principal Indians, and thereby secured their goodwill and purchased their land (and territory) to the extent of twenty leagues, and they, thereupon, withdrew that much farther back into the wild forest."

The principle of acquisition of Indian land by purchase had already been established by the Dutch, Swedes, and English who had preceded Penn, but the difference between Penn and his predecessors lay in his sincere determination to treat the savages like brothers and to avoid any semblance of sharp practice. One of the most cherished traditions of colonial Pennsylvania perpetuates the legend of a "great treaty" drawn up by Penn and the Indians under an ancient elm at Kensington, as portrayed in a scene painted in 1773 by Benjamin West at the request of the Penn family. A speech purported to have been made by Penn on this occasion is sometimes quoted. But the speech unfortunately was delivered twenty years after this supposed event, and no record exists of one formal treaty. Instead Penn is known to have held several pow-wows with the Indians and to have exchanged affirmations of eternal friendship. Though the purchases of land and the "treaties" were necessarily extended and marked by the formalities characteristic of Indian negotiations, West's painting is merely the idealization of Penn's success in treating with the Indians, a success in which Pennsylvanians take a justified pride. Both Penn and the Indians religiously observed their agreements, and peace reigned in the wilderness of Pennsylvania for many years. The fame of Pennsylvania's happy relations with the Indians spread afar in the early eighteenth century and induced Voltaire's ironic statement that Penn's first step "was to enter into an alliance with his American neighbors; and this is the only treaty between those people and the Christians that was not ratified by an oath and was never infringed." No serious trouble involved whites and Indians until the arrival of stern Scotch-Irish Presbyterians who justified the slaughter of Indians and the appropriation of their lands by quoting texts from the Old Testament.

Pennsylvania's growth in the first few years was unusual, both for the number of immigrants and the ease with which they adapted themselves to the new land. No other colony, not even Massachusetts Bay during the "great migration," had seen settlers pour in with such rapidity. For the flood of immigrants, William Penn could take the credit. Impractical as he was in many respects, he proved a shrewd master of propaganda, and the first-comers soon spread the news that Penn's glowing reports of his province were justified. To many a persecuted Quaker or harassed Mennonite, Pennsylvania, with its rich fields and valuable forests, seemed indeed the earthly paradise. Within a year after Penn's own arrival in the colony, fifty vessels cast anchor in the Delaware or the Schuylkill and at least three thousand new citizens came ashore.

Before he himself embarked for Pennsylvania, the proprietor sent ahead a surveyor-general, Thomas Holme, with instructions to find a spot on high ground near deep water navigable to ships and to plan a city which would be his metropolis. Holme selected a site on the Schuylkill a little above where it empties into the Delaware and Penn named it Philadelphia, the "city of brotherly love," after one of the seven cities in Asia Minor where primitive Christianity had flourished. Holme laid out the town in squares like a checkerboard with an avenue running along the Delaware side. From the trees which furnished shade Penn chose street names like Walnut, Chestnut, and Pine. Within a year the city had eighty houses and busy docks by the waterside; nearby approximately three hundred farms were surveyed and assigned.

The city grew so rapidly that by the end of the colonial period it numbered forty thousand inhabitants and was the largest and most prosperous city in America. More than that, it became the second city in the British Empire, exceeded only by London, for Bristol, the next largest city, had in 1776 something less than 36,000 inhabitants.

Penn devoted his attention to the art of advertising the province; his pamphlets soliciting immigrants are persuasive documents which might still teach Chambers of Commerce something in the technique of promotion. Unlike many another piece of promotional literature, these tracts gave the impression of complete honesty and sincerity. By skillful understatement he conveyed the idea that Pennsylvania held greater potentialities for riches and happiness than an honest Quaker would let himself promise. The descriptions of the woods and waters and wild inhabitants made the documents readable and exciting. Penn's first advertising pamphlet, *Some Account of the Province of Pennsylvania*, appeared in London in April, 1681, and before the end of the year had been issued at Rotterdam in Dutch and at Amsterdam in German. Shrewdly Penn emphasized the improvement and prosperity certain to follow removal to Pennsylvania. "Such as could not only not marry here, but hardly live and allow themselves clothes, do marry there and bestow thrice more in all necessaries and conveniences (and not a little in ornamental things too) for themselves, their wives, and children, both as to apparel and household stuff," he pointed out. In Pennsylvania, men and women alike may be freed from servile occupations and gain a new self-respect as they pursue honest and gainful vocations certain to bring them prosperity and independence. The situation of Pennsylvania in itself is an inducement to emigration, for the new land "lies

600 miles nearer the sun than England" and its climate favors nearly every good thing which grows. After mentioning the beneficent laws which he intends for his colony, the proprietor closes in a fatherly vein: "To conclude, I desire all my dear country folks who may be inclined to go into those parts to consider seriously the premises, as well the present inconveniencies as future ease and plenty, that so none may move rashly or from a fickle but solid mind, having above all things, an eye to the providence of God in the disposal of themselves. And I would further advise all such at least to have the permission, if not the good liking, of their near relations . . . In all which I beseech Almighty God to direct us that his blessing may attend our honest endeavour, and then the consequence of all our undertaking will turn to the glory of his great name and the true happiness of us and our posterity. Amen." Thus with a hope and a prayer Penn concluded an effective advertisement but added a practical "postscript" which advised interested persons to see his agents in Cheapside or Lombard Street.

The foregoing tract was the first of several descriptions of Pennsylvania in which Penn informed an eager world of the virtues of the promised land. From first-hand observation he wrote an enticing account of the province, published in 1683 as *A Letter from William Penn, Proprietary and Governor of Pennsylvania in America to the Committee of the Free Society of Traders of That Province Residing in London.* To this corporation, organized as a land and trading company, Penn addressed his remarks but all of Europe was his intended audience. The letter had two editions immediately in England and in 1684 it appeared on the Continent in French, German, and Dutch. Readers learned that in Pennsylvania "the air is sweet and clear, the heavens serene, like the south parts of France"; that the fields and woods are infinitely fruitful; that the sweet wild grapes will make "as good wine as any European countries of the same latitude do yield"; that creatures of profit and pleasure, fish, fowl, and fur-bearing animals, abound in the woods; that among the plants and shrubs are many herbs having great curative value; that "the woods are adorned with lovely flowers" of varieties which might improve even the beautiful gardens of London; that the Indians are essentially virtuous though lately contaminated by so-called Christians and that they are possibly of "the Jewish race . . . of the stock of the Ten [Lost] Tribes"; that the Dutch and Swedes resident in Pennsylvania have grown prosperous and have houses full of fine and healthy children, "some six, seven, and eight sons"; that the land is intersected by many navigable rivers and creeks "any one of which have room to lay up the royal navy of England"; and finally that the new city of Philadelphia is building apace to the satisfaction of the inhabitants and promises to be a thriving mart of trade.

Within a few years, news of Pennsylvania made a great noise in the world and inquiries were so numerous that he could not keep up with his correspondence, Penn asserts in *A Further Account of the Province of Pennsylvania and Its Improvements, for the Satisfaction of Those That Are Adventurers and Inclined to Be So*, which in 1685 was published twice in English and once in Dutch. This pamphlet is even more glowing than previous tracts. In language anticipating thousands of later real estate advertisements, Penn boasted of the profits which purchasers of lots in Philadelphia had already made: "The improvement of the place is best measured by the advance of value upon every man's lot. I will venture to say that the worst lot in the town, without any improvement upon it, is worth four times more than it was when it was laid out, and the best forty." As a testimonial of his own accuracy in the description of the increasing prosperity, Penn added "one of the many letters that have come to my hand"—a message written by Robert Turner, well-to-do merchant of Philadelphia. Because of Penn's feud with Lord Baltimore over his southern boundary, he could not have thought amiss Turner's statement that "we are generally very well and healthy here but abundance dead in Maryland this summer."

Penn's advertising pamphlets carried conviction and received confirmation from other writers who gave Pennsylvania a good name. More substantial than predictions of future prosperity was the immediate opportunity which Penn offered of fertile land at a reasonable price. Purchasers with £100 pounds sterling could obtain five thousand acres of land. This land became the permanent possession of the buyer, subject only to an annual quitrent of a shilling per hundred acres. Smaller tracts were also available, and for those unable to buy land, the proprietor stood ready to rent farms of two hundred acres or less for a shilling an acre. Land, the key to prosperity and prestige—good land which would grow the best of God's fruits and crops—was available in plenty. Any man with a stout will and strong arm could make his way in the paradise which Penn was developing.

The proprietor chose a spot for himself twenty miles up the Delaware River from Philadelphia and began the erection of the manor house of Pennsbury which cost at least £5,000. Quaker though he was, the proprietor's life at Pennsbury represented a degree of splendor rarely equalled at this time in America. The house, two and a half stories high, built of red brick, and surrounded by beautiful gardens, was comfortably if not ostentatiously furnished. The orchards were filled with fruit and nut trees; the flower and vegetable gardens were a model for other Pennsylvanians to imitate. Among the twelve horses in his stables one favorite thoroughbred bore the warlike name of Tamerlane. Though he rode a great deal, Penn's preferred mode of travel was by a six-oared barge in which the great man was rowed ceremoniously between Pennsbury and Philadelphia. Penn dreamed of spending the rest of his life in his province, at his town house in Philadelphia or on his broad acres at Pennsbury, but fate commanded him to return to England.

Readers of Penn's descriptive pamphlets, warmed with hope of freedom and plenty, came in swarms to Pennsylvania during the last two decades of the seventeenth century.

The "Holy Experiment" in Pennsylvania

Substantial English businessmen and craftsmen, country gentlemen of Wales, English Quakers who had found Ireland inhospitable, Scots and Ulstermen, German and Dutch Pietists and Quakers—a great stream of folk of high and low degree, representing many languages, creeds, and trades—found a safe haven on the Delaware and the Schuylkill. A considerable number of immigrants came from other American colonies where they had failed to find liberty of conscience or the good things of this earth.

Immigrants of British stock were the most numerous. Oppressed sectarians of various persuasions heard Penn's message of hope and left the British Isles in droves. Quickly they occupied the eastern counties of Philadelphia, Chester, and Bucks and scattered elsewhere in Pennsylvania. Into the interior counties where Germans later predominated, appreciable numbers of Englishmen and Scots found their way. The English and the Welsh were responsible for the pattern of civilization established in eastern Pennsylvania and for the cultural development of Philadelphia. Between 1682 and 1700 a group of Welsh immigrants acquired a large tract on the Schuylkill River, near Philadelphia, where they attempted to erect a semi-independent barony and succeeded in giving to the region a few of the more pronounceable Welsh names like Merion and Radnor. Several thousand Welshmen—many of them substantial citizens, lawyers, farmers, and artisans—founded homes in this tract and made useful contributions to the progress of the colony. Fiercely independent, hating tyranny from church or state, the Welsh contingent provided some of the colony's most zealous protagonists of liberty.

The Scotch-Irish also heard Penn's message and looked upon Pennsylvania with longing. Although their great migration began about 1728 and continued until the American Revolution, some of them reached Pennsylvania before the end of the seventeenth century. These Scots were descendants of colonists who, from the reign of Elizabeth onward, had been induced to leave the hills and dales of Scotland to occupy the confiscated lands of Catholics in the north of Ireland. They had pushed the Catholic Irish out of Ulster and become a numerous company themselves, but they had found neither peace nor prosperity in Ireland. Fanatically Presbyterian in religion, they hated Church of England folk and the English government which attempted to force Anglicanism upon them. Though they despised the pacificism of the Quakers and were of no mind to conform to Penn's fantastic notions of quietism, they could not resist the lure of his rich land. When they began to arrive in Philadelphia, they found the older coastal region already in possession of Englishmen whom they detested and they pushed on to the backwoods counties.

From the seventeenth century onward, the Scotch-Irish were vigorous frontiersmen, taking land where they wanted it, defending their assumed rights with rifles and interminable texts from the Scriptures. From John Calvin as interpreted by John Knox, they took with fervent seriousness the doctrine of foreordination, which they somehow translated into the notion that God had called them to take their land from the Indians and smite these Amalekites hip and thigh. Often lawless and obstreperous, they proved a sore affliction to the godly Quakers of the eastern counties. But their very shortcomings made them a force of incalculable importance in later history. Believing in both religion and learning, these hardy Scots were the spearhead of civilization as Americans pushed ever farther into the wilderness. Whatever they lacked in sweet reasonableness, they made up in strength of character and vigor of mind. From their numbers came some of the great figures of American history. Pennsylvania, from the 1690's to 1776, was the principal gateway through which the Scotch-Irish entered America, and from Pennsylvania they spread to all the adjacent territory.

Pennsylvania was likewise the center of German immigration in the late seventeenth and early eighteenth centuries. Many German settlers who later drifted into the valleys of Maryland, Virginia, and even the Carolinas, got their first pioneering experience in Penn's colony. Second only to the British stock were the Germanic peoples who heard of Penn's holy commonwealth and came by the thousands to take up land to the west of the English settlements. The Germans were of various groups but prevailingly they belonged to Pietist sects from the Rhineland. Some were Quakers and all were sympathetic to the Quaker point of view. Pietism, which placed the emphasis in religion upon the inner or spiritual life and denied the virtues of formal ecclesiasticism, had spread throughout the Rhine country as orthodox Lutheranism had become encrusted with formality and ritual. Orthodox Lutheranism, moreover, had grown corrupt in the German Protestant states, and the Lutheran clergy were more eager to please aristocratic landlords than to minister to the needs of the poor majority. As schism developed, the Lutheran clergy called upon civil governments to enforce conformity, and the sectarians found themselves persecuted severely in German states which had formerly been tolerant. Many non-German Protestant sectarians, indeed, who had previously sought refuge in the Rhine country now found themselves the victims of fresh persecutions. Walloons from Flanders, Mennonites from Switzerland, Huguenots from France, and Pietists of sundry sorts from many German localities sorrowfully contemplated their plight.

Combined with the religious unrest was severe economic distress caused by recurrent wars. The Thirty Years' War which ended in 1648 left the Rhine Valley devastated and ruined. Before the country had recovered from this disaster, the dynastic wars, which began in the late seventeenth and continued through the eighteenth century, again made this region a battleground. The area known as the Palatinate on the upper Rhine was particularly hard hit. Grasping landlords, who themselves felt the pinch of need, ground down their tenants until farmers and vinegrowers even in fertile Baden were close to starvation. To these people, the pamphlets describing Pennsylvania, printed in their own language and distributed by Penn's agents, came as a message from heaven. They had learned to hate war as the destroyer of men's bodies and souls and most of them were ardent pacifists. Accustomed to hard work, skilled in many trades and crafts as well as in agriculture, these refugees now had a vision of a country where they might be free to worship as they pleased, where the fruit of their labor would not be snatched from them by greedy landlords or destroyed by marauding armies, and where their sons would not be dragged away to serve as cannon fodder.

The first Germans to reach Pennsylvania as a group had as their leader, Francis Daniel Pastorius, a learned lawyer of Frankfort, who served as business agent for certain Pietists in his home city who were negotiating with Penn for the purchase of land. He arrived at Philadelphia in August 1683 and arranged with Penn for the new immigrants to settle a few miles north of the center of Philadelphia. This community, occupied in October 1683 by Frankfort Pietists and a number of Quakers of Swiss Mennonite background from Crefeld on the lower Rhine, was soon named Germantown.

Pastorius was a man of broad education and an ornament to the colony. A skillful administrator, well versed in science, agriculture, theology, history, and other branches of learning, he guided the destinies of the early German immigrants and helped them gain a foothold in the new country. After he had ceased to take an active part as immigration agent, he served as schoolmaster in Germantown and Philadelphia and was the author of several tracts which induced many other Germans to come to America.

In describing his own voyage to America, Pastorius suggests the diversity of trades and beliefs among the immigrants pouring into Pennsylvania: "My company consisted of many sorts of people: There was a doctor of medicine with his wife and eight children, a French captain, a Low Dutch cake-baker, an apothecary, a glass blower, a mason, a smith, a wheelwright, a cabinetmaker, a cooper, a hatmaker, a cobbler, a tailor, a gardener, farmers, seamstresses, etc., in all about eighty persons besides the crew. They were not only different . . . in respect to their occupations, as I have mentioned, but were also of such different religions and behaviors that I might not unfittingly compare the ship that bore them hither with Noah's Ark. . . . In my household I have those who hold to the Roman, to the Lutheran, to the Calvinistic, to the Anabaptist, and to the Anglican church, and only one Quaker."

The inhabitants, Pastorius found, were not perfect, and he classified the Pennsylvanians, not as savages and Christians, lest he "do great injustice to many of both varieties," but as "the native and the engrafted." The latter occasionally were something less than exemplary. "The Lutheran preacher," he observes with scorn, "who ought as a *statua Mercurialis* to show the Swedes the way to heaven, is, in one word, a drunkard. Also there are coiners of false money and other vicious persons here whom nevertheless, it may be hoped, the wind of God's vengeance will in his own time drive away like chaff. On the other hand there is no lack of pious, God-fearing people, and I can with truth affirm that I have nowhere in Europe seen the notice posted up, as here in our Philadelphia, that such an one has found this or that, and that the loser may call for it at his house." Honest Philadelphians, who made up the majority of the inhabitants, were about to erect a house of correction, Pastorius wrote, because they had discovered that they were likely to suffer more from spoiled Christians than from heathen Indians.

Though the rich lands of Pennsylvania produced abundantly, Pastorius warned that no idlers need come to the province expecting manna to fall from heaven. "Certainly the penance with which God punished the disobedience of Adam, that he should eat his bread in the sweat of his brow, extends also to his posterity in these lands, and those who think to spare their hands may remain where they are," he counselled. "*Hic opus, hic labor est*, and it is not enough to bring money hither, without the inclination to work, for it slips out of one's hands, and I may well say with Solomon: It has wings. . . . Working people and husbandmen are in the greatest demand here, and I certainly wish that I had a dozen strong Tyrolese to cut down the thick oak trees." Among the old inhabitants of the colony Pastorius reported a few Germans and Swiss who had made a place for themselves: Silesians, Brandenburgers, Holsteiners, and one Nuremberger. Many others were on the way, hardworking folk, who asked only that they might, indeed, eat the bread which they earned by the sweat of their brows, as they had not been able to eat it in their war-ravaged land.

For two decades after Pastorius blazed the way in 1683, the Germans who came to Pennsylvania belonged, for the most part, to one of the numerous pietistic sects. Quakers were more numerous in the first wave, but about 1700 larger numbers of Mennonites—scarcely distinguishable in belief from Quakers—came over and settled in Lancaster County where their descendants are still to be found. A little later German Baptist Brethren, commonly called Dunkers, joined the Mennonites in Lancaster County, or took up farms in the neighborhood of Germantown. More than twenty separate varieties of sectarians have been counted among these early immigrants, most of whom were tinged with mysticism and some of whom bore strange names, like the New Mooners, the members of the Society of the Woman in the Wilderness, the Mountain Men, and the River Brethren. Almost without exception they were pacifist in doctrine and believed in living apart from the rest of the world.

These tendencies made the Germans stick together in compact communities where they could maintain their local customs and enforce their religious rules on the younger generation. As they grew in numbers their communities spread out from Lancaster County until German settlements stretched in a great arc from the Delaware at Easton to the borders of Maryland across the lower Susquehanna.

These early Germans were known in Pennsylvania as members of the sects to distinguish them from an even more numerous migration from Germany of "church people," which began early in the eighteenth century. The sectarians were often well-educated and many of them were skilled in the arts and crafts. The church people—mainly Lutherans and members of the German Reformed Church—were largely of peasant stock. Since many Germans came from the Palatinate, English colonists gradually came to apply the name "Palatines" to Pennsylvania Germans in general. The sectarians had usually been able to buy land and set up for themselves on arrival. The later church people generally came as "redemptioners"—that is, indentured servants who sold themselves into bondage for five years or more to pay their passage. By their labor they redeemed themselves and frequently acquired land. Though many of these redemptioners drifted into the German communities, others became pioneers and pushed ever farther afield in search of land and independence until all the neighboring colonies felt their influence.

A third group of German immigrants, the Moravians, led by Count Zinzendorf, who revived the sect in Saxony, reached Pennsylvania in 1740. They settled the towns of Bethlehem, Nazareth, and Lititz, where at first they practiced a communism of labor. Like other pietistic groups they were opposed to war. The Moravians were never very numerous, numbering at the Revolution hardly more than 2500, but their cultural influence was considerable. They were especially diligent and successful as missionaries to the Indians; they developed church music to high art; and they emphasized education as did no other German group. In 1749 Moravians founded a boarding school for girls at Lititz and a seminary for young ladies at Bethlehem. Ten years later they established a boys' boarding school at Nazareth.

As a group, however, the Germans made their major con-tribution to the growth of colonial Pennsylvania by dili-gence and hard work. They were the province's most skillful farmers, and they brought with them the knowledge of important cottage industries: weaving, shoe-making, wood-carving, cabinet-making, the moulding of pottery, and the practice of other crafts. From German farms came great quantities of wheat, barley, rye, beef and pork, ham and bacon—food for export as well as for home consumption. German cattle produced a surplus of hides, tanned to be used in the making of leather goods, or exported raw to the European market, along with tan bark from Pennsylvania oaks. The Germans were frugal, thrifty, and home-loving. They lived a patriarchal existence surrounded by the good things which the earth would produce, asking little of the outside world except peace. Their contacts with the Germany they had left rapidly dwindled until they became self-sufficient Pennsylvanians, provincial even by colonial standards. But they had contentment beyond the dreams even of Pastorius and the pioneers. Unlike the Scotch-Irish, the Welsh, and the English, the Germans displayed almost no political interest or activity. They were content to let the Quakers in Philadelphia run the colony, for they had neither knowledge of politics nor experience in government.

A considerable group of French Huguenots also found relief from persecution in Pennsylvania, but they were assimilated with other national groups. Some French farmers joined the Germans and were completely absorbed in the German communities. Others, Huguenots chiefly, the educated and those possessing special trades and crafts, settled in Philadelphia with the English and became a part of the cosmopolitan life of that expanding center of commerce.

Sanguine as William Penn was, he hardly expected that his colony would grow with such phenomenal speed. He certainly had no conception of the problems which a complex state, containing an infinite variety of people, would create. By nature something of a patriarch himself, he thought he could live in idyllic peace at Pennsbury, or at one of his other houses, and let his province run along on the Frames of Government which he provided. Perhaps had Penn been permitted to remain in the colony, his personality and his sense of justice and fairness would have solved many of the difficulties which arose. But Penn had to return to England in

The "Holy Experiment" in Pennsylvania

August 1684 to argue his case concerning the boundary between Pennsylvania and Maryland.

When he departed, with an almost inspired impracticality Penn delegated his power as governor to the eighteen members of the provincial council, which, in effect, gave the colony eighteen governors, though the president of the council, Thomas Lloyd, served as executive officer. Soon the assembly and the council were at loggerheads because the assembly demanded the right to originate legislation and was prone to reject such laws as the council proposed. Since the assembly declined to approve the body of laws for more than one year at a time, the province stood in annual jeopardy of having no acceptable laws—a situation which vexed Penn and his friends extremely. When the council of eighteen clearly proved that it was too unwieldy to exercise administrative authority, Penn appointed five of the councillors to serve as commissioners of state, but they were scarcely more successful than the larger group had been.

With bland complacence the provincial government sent Penn the bills for administrative expense and refused to impose necessary taxes. Even money from quitrents was not forthcoming and the proprietor complained that he had spent £5,000 more than he had received in compensation. What boded ill for the future was the lack of zeal displayed by the authorities in Philadelphia for the enforcement of the Navigation Acts, as Penn's charter required. Merchants were getting rich and no one saw any particular reason why Pennsylvanians should be too scrupulous about enforcing laws which they did not approve, for the benefit of England.

Harassed at home by contentions over his boundaries and worried by reports from Pennsylvania, Penn with the rashness of inexperience decided to settle governmental problems in his colony by fiat. He instructed his commissioners of state to call the assembly together and announce the abrogation of previous laws; they were then to promulgate such laws as seemed advisable and send the assembly home. Whether Penn had this power under his charter is doubtful;

fortunately his commissioners were discreet enough to do nothing and not to put the proprietor's rights to the test, for they understood the independent and stubborn quality of the citizens of Pennsylvania.

To bring some order out of administrative chaos, Penn appointed, of all people, a Puritan soldier who had served in Cromwell's army, Captain John Blackwell, and sent him late in 1688 to take charge of the colony as deputy governor. Blackwell, like Markham, Penn's first deputy, was a cousin of the proprietor. Quakers naturally resented a non-Quaker and a soldier being placed over them, and they made Blackwell's life miserable. His most persistent opponents were two Welshmen, Thomas and David Lloyd, possibly cousins. Thomas Lloyd, a learned physician of Jesus College, Oxford, who had served as president of the council, was now keeper of the great seal. He contemptuously refused to affix the seal to some of Blackwell's commissions and otherwise annoyed the deputy governor. David Lloyd, a lawyer whom Penn commissioned as attorney-general in 1686, would not deliver certain records to the council at Blackwell's command. Two members of the council also expressed their disapproval of the new governor by refusing to serve. The furor of argument and debate in the council reached such a pitch that passers in the street noted it as a scandal and Penn wrote to his steward at Pennsbury that he was "sorry at heart for your animosities . . . for the love of God, me, and the poor country, be not so governmentish, so noisy, and open in your dissatisfactions." After a little over a year among the contentious Quakers, Blackwell begged to be relieved and left Pennsylvania with thanksgiving, observing at parting that each Philadelphian "prays for his neighbor on First Days and then preys upon him the other six."

When Penn recalled Blackwell early in 1690, he wrote to the council urging them to make peace among themselves and empowering them to elect their own executive officer, or president. They chose Thomas Lloyd, who remained in office until April 1693, after Penn himself had lost his proprietary rights and the colony had become temporarily a royal province under another ex-soldier, the none-too-competent governor of New York, Benjamin Fletcher. Because of Penn's long friendship for the House of Stuart —and the visible favors which he had received from them— he found himself under a cloud after the Revolution of 1688. He had been arrested and brought before the Privy Council in December 1688, but had managed to satisfy King William of his loyalty, but when James tried to regain his throne in 1690 by invading Ireland, Penn, along with other known adherents, was thrown into prison and there he remained for several months. Released at the end of the year, he proposed to return to Pennsylvania, but before he could take ship, he was forced to flee to escape arrest again. For three years he remained in hiding, where, nobody knows.

The king's appointment, in the spring of 1692, of Fletcher as governor of Pennsylvania transformed the colony from a proprietary to a royal government. The Privy Council and the Lords of Trade had regretted the grant to Penn and were glad to work the change. They had looked with glum disapproval upon the "holy experiment" and the reports of frequent violations of the Navigation Acts had done nothing to sweeten their attitude. Lately the stubborn Quakers had also refused to come to the aid of New York in the war with the French which had broken out in 1689. The grudging decision of the Philadelphians to supply a certain amount of food and raiment to distressed Indians, allied with the English, was so hedged about with conditions that it served to irritate their lordships even more than outright refusal.

Fletcher came in person to Philadelphia in 1693 and tried to reason with the assembly. To aid him in his efforts, he chose a council consisting of a few Quakers and other old hands in the colony, including Penn's former deputy, William Markham. But the assembly bargained, argued, and stood on its privileges, until Fletcher, never a patient man, was worn out with long-winded eloquence. Most ardent of the defenders of the rights of the assembly was David Lloyd, who presented a remonstrance to Fletcher soon after his arrival, and presently was chosen speaker of the house. The chief contention between Fletcher and the assembly was over the latter's refusal to appropriate money for supplies to the Indians until grievances complained of in Lloyd's remonstrances had first been redressed. Fletcher in his wrath finally complained that the assembly had wasted time searching for fresh grievances while the security of the province was threatened; and he refused to approve certain of the laws passed. The quarrel between the assembly and the royal governor over the prerogatives of each was characteristic of struggles in other colonies between the people and the crown, a conflict which would grow in intensity in the years to come.

At this juncture, in the late summer of 1694, the king recalled Fletcher and, miraculously, restored the colony to Penn, against whom charges of treason had collapsed. To regain his proprietary rights, Penn had to affirm his allegiance to William III, and to promise, among other things, to preside in person over Pennsylvania. Moreover he agreed to furnish eighty soldiers to New York for warfare against the French. As a concession, because Penn could not leave England immediately, the king permitted him to appoint William Markham as his deputy governor.

Markham's struggles with the assembly began about where Fletcher's had left off. The assembly sought to abridge the powers granted to the proprietor and resisted Markham's efforts to reissue the former Charter of Privileges in the name of the proprietor. Instead, they argued that the colony's rights should be set forth in a bill enacted by the assembly itself. Since this procedure would be an acknowledgement of the legislature's supremacy over the proprietor, Markham opposed it. Finally in the autumn of 1696 he reached a compromise by devising a constitution known as "Markham's Frame of Government" which he permitted the assembly to draw up in the form of a bill. Although this action tacitly acknowledged the power of the assembly, Mark-

The "Holy Experiment" in Pennsylvania

ham stipulated that the new charter of privileges would require the proprietor's acceptance. Actually Penn never formally gave his approval but Markham's Frame, which permitted the assembly to initiate legislation and had other liberalizing provisions, served the colony until 1701, when the assembly and council hammered out a more satisfactory constitution, which Penn accepted.

To the joy of the majority of the Quakers Penn himself returned to the colony on the last day of November, 1699. A few Pennsylvanians were displeased to see the proprietor in person. Most of these were members of an anti-proprietary group in the assembly, led for many years by David Lloyd. Others who shouted no welcome were principally Church of England people who preferred a royal government. Leaders of these were Edward Randolph, surveyor-general of his Majesty's customs, and Colonel Robert Quarry, judge of the court of vice-admiralty, which had been established in 1697 to try to force the recalcitrant Quakers to obey the acts of trade.

Penn, who this time had brought along his family, established himself in a house in Philadelphia and set about making peace with quarreling factions. He succeeded so well that for the next two years even Quarry, who could find little good to say of Pennsylvanians, was reasonably quiescent. With Penn had come a competent secretary, James Logan, destined to become one of Pennsylvania's most learned citizens and benefactors, and a loyal supporter of the proprietary authority.

After hearing endless arguments about the state of the government, Penn at last conceded that the elected representatives of the colony should have authority to decide upon laws which should govern them. Impatient with endless complaints, he ordered the council and assembly to alter laws which displeased them and to draft new laws which suited them. The charter of privileges, or constitution, of 1701 was the result. This document, which Penn approved, made the assembly virtually the supreme authority. The law-making power of the council was gone. Pennsylvania had established a unicameral legislative body—the only one in the colonies—and the proprietor's own governing privileges were so drastically curtailed that little was left.

Penn later regretted the loss of his power, and his representatives, led by Logan and various deputy-governors appointed by the proprietors, fought many a weary battle with the assembly—usually in vain. This struggle can hardly be called a contest between feudal overlords and lovers of democratic liberty, as romanticists are inclined to view it. The franchise was so narrowly limited that the assembly was elected by a small group of rich and privileged citizens. The majority of Pennsylvanians had little or no voice in government. As Charles M. Andrews has observed, the proprietors' long contest "was not with 'the people' but with an assembly elected on a limited franchise and controlled by an oligarchy of Quaker leaders who dominated Pennsylvania politics until the outbreak of the Seven Years' War." Regardless of whether Penn and his successors liked the charter of 1701, it was the constitutional basis of government until the Revolution.

Not all of the varied people over whom Penn claimed proprietary authority accepted the rule of the Philadelphia Quakers with docile contentment. Least satisfied were the citizens of the Three Lower Counties, which after the Revolution took the name of Delaware. Penn's title to "the territories," as he called this region, depended upon a doubtful grant from James, Duke of York. The territorial citizens, abetted by Robert Quarry, called Penn's title into question and demanded their separation from Pennsylvania. The Philadelphians themselves had no brotherly love for their neighbors dwelling in what one Quaker described as "that Frenchified, Scotchified, Dutchified place," and the Calvinists and Anglicans there returned the unfavorable view fourfold.

After several years of wrangling and complaints to the Board of Trade in London, the Privy Council agreed in 1703 that Penn and his successors might be allowed to appoint the governor of both Pennsylvania and the territories, subject to the English sovereign's approval and a declaration by the proprietor that he recognized the royal claim to the territories embraced in the Three Lower Counties. A separate legislative assembly which met in November 1704 gave final proof of the separation from Pennsylvania. Thereafter until the Revolution the future state of Delaware lived its own life, in effect independent, safe in its rustic obscurity from serious interference.

Before the end of the year 1701, Penn was obliged to return to England to combat a growing movement to transform all proprietary grants into royal colonies. Colonial experts in the English government were becoming more insistent upon tightening their control throughout English possessions overseas. As something like a consistent colonial policy slowly evolved in the Board of Trade, the shadowy outlines of an integrated empire began to be discernible. To the planners in Whitehall, personal domains like Penn's vast territory were obnoxious, and they determined to bring such governments under the royal authority.

The truth was that the Board of Trade in London was not alone in objecting to the proprietary colony of Pennsylvania. In America Pennsylvania had proved unpopular with neighboring commonwealths and Penn's own preaching journeys into Maryland, New Jersey, and New York had not increased the liking of non-Quakers for their neighbor. Perhaps much of the dislike of Pennsylvania had its origin in envy of that colony's prosperity and the detestation of authoritarians for the religious and personal liberty which flourished there. Whatever the motives, American critics accused Pennsylvania of harboring pirates, of violating the Navigation Acts, of refusing to aid in colonial defence, and of encouraging runaway debtors and servants to take refuge within its borders.

William Byrd of Virginia, for example, in a report to the Board of Trade in 1699 declared that "Pennsylvania has little trade with England but pretty much with the West

Indies, and are not precise in consulting what trade is lawful and what is not." Moreover, even with the increasing threat of French invasion, Pennsylvania would take no responsibility for defence, an attitude which irritated Byrd. "In Pennsylvania," he reported, "the Quakers under the management of Mr. Penn can't find in their conscience to gird on the carnal sword so they are very liable to become a prey to any invader, and New Jersey by reason of the multitude of Quakers is pretty near in the same condition."

An anonymous Virginian, who reflected Byrd's views, in 1701 brought out in London *An Essay upon the Government of the English Plantations on the Continent of America*, which asserted, among other criticisms of proprietary colonies, that "we in the king's governments look upon pirates and privateers to be robbers and thieves, but the good people of Pennsylvania esteem them very honest men for bringing money into their country and encouraging trade." And he reported the case of Giles Shelley, master of the ship "Nassau," who, in the summer of 1699, brought "about sixty pirates (passengers) with great quantities of goods from those parts [India and Madagascar] and lay at anchor off Cape May, at the mouth of the Delaware, till he had dispersed most of them into Pennsylvania, the Jerseys, and other neighboring colonies." Even if the Quakers will not "swear and be drunk so publicly as is usual in some other places, . . . their morals are no better than those of their neighbors, perhaps not so good. . . . Whence hath proceeded the great opposition they have made to the court of admiralty lately erected by his Majesty's authority, whence their pretense of making laws for the management of their trade without regard to the acts of Parliament, and whence their esteem of pirates . . ." In short this Virginian insisted that Pennsylvania, along with other proprietary colonies, should be placed in the king's hands to insure decency, order, and obedience to the laws enacted by Parliament.

The outlook for the retention of his province was far from bright when Penn sailed from Philadelphia in October

1701, but, with characteristic optimism, he had faith in his powers of persuasion. So confident was Penn of success and a quick return that he would have left his family in Philadelphia had they been willing to stay. His faith was justified, for he did contrive to hold Pennsylvania as a proprietary grant, but Fate decreed that he should never return to the country which he loved so well.

If Pennsylvania had contributed to the proprietor's pleasure and satisfaction, he had paid dearly for his joy. On his departure, he estimated that his losses by reason of the payment of officials' salaries and other expenses, which he had taken out of his own pocket, then amounted to £20,000. Though many of his Quaker brethren in the colony might feel a genuine affection for him, they were careful not to let their emotions betray them into the prodigal voting of taxes so long as the proprietor could be induced to foot administrative expenses. Nevertheless just before Penn left the colony, the assembly finally appropriated £2,000 as reimbursement for some of his expenses, but his quitrents and revenues from the sale of lands had dwindled and he was facing bankruptcy. In his financial distress, he even offered to sell his political rights in Pennsylvania to the crown, an idea which he played with for the rest of his active life.

Political wrangles in Pennsylvania and hostility to the proprietor reached a new intensity in the decade after Penn's departure. For much of the trouble, the proprietor had only himself to blame. His worst choice of a deputy came in 1704 with the appointment of John Evans. This Welshman, then only twenty-six years old, had neither administrative ability nor moral virtue, but Penn thought so well of him that he placed his dissolute son, William, in the deputy's charge and sent the precious pair to America. Evans at once became involved in an endless quarrel with the assembly and antagonized the whole governing class in Philadelphia; young Penn set about spending his father's money and making a fool of himself. Governor and proprietor's son proved birds of a feather and boon companions. Their conviviality reached a dramatic climax one night in a Philadelphia public house. When they drunkenly tried to beat the constables, someone thoughtfully put out the lights, and bystanders, who claimed not to recognize them in the darkness, gave them both a sound drubbing; Penn, who tried to declare his identity, received a second beating on the grounds that he was a liar claiming to be the proprietor's heir. The behavior of Evans and young Penn provided ammunition for the anti-proprietary party now ably led by David Lloyd, whose bitter invectives rang in the halls of the assembly. Lloyd went so far as to try to impeach James Logan, an honest and competent man, whom Penn had appointed provincial secretary and clerk of the council. Finally, after the assembly had remonstrated against the evil behavior of his governor, Penn reluctantly recalled Evans and in 1709 appointed in his place an abler man, Charles Gookin. For several years Gookin and the assembly got on with reasonable harmony, but he too at length made so many enemies among the Philadelphia Quakers that the proprietary authorities in 1717 replaced him with Sir William Keith.

In the meantime, Penn had almost lost his province through the knavery of the steward of his English and Irish estates, a brazen scoundrel named Philip Ford whom Penn trusted implicitly. Of all the rascals who deceived Penn, Ford was the most colossal. By systematically altering and forging accounts, he made it appear that Penn owed him thousands of pounds, and with amazing effrontery induced Penn to secure the "debt" by signing a paper, which Penn perhaps thought a mortgage, but which actually proved to be a deed to the province of Pennsylvania. The fact that Penn was so unbusinesslike as to sign such a document provides an interesting sidelight on his trusting nature. The matter remained a secret between Penn and Ford until the latter's death when his wife and son pressed for a settlement. They even went so far as to petition the crown to declare them proprietors. Fortunately Penn still had powerful friends, among them Sarah Churchill, Duchess of Marlborough, and

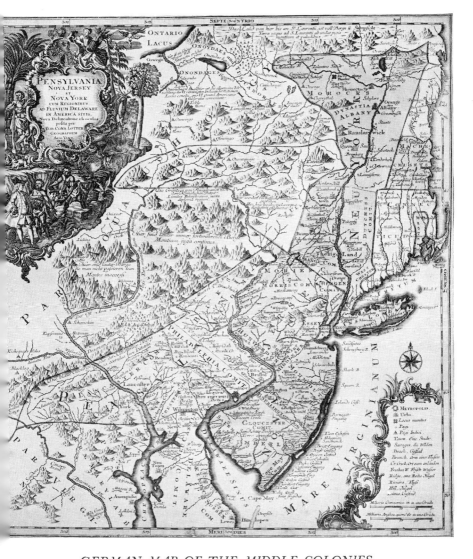

GERMAN MAP OF THE MIDDLE COLONIES

om a map engraved by Conrad Lotter, 174?, in the Huntington Library map collection.

THE MORAVIAN SETTLEMENT AT BETHLEHEM, PENNSYLVANIA

From Thomas Pownall, in the Huntington Library copy of *Six Remarkable Views . . .* (London, 1761),

the Fords' petition was rejected. But they did succeed in getting a judgment in the courts requiring Penn to pay the alleged debt, and when Penn was unable to raise the money, in January 1708, they had him thrown into Fleet Prison, where he remained for nine months—suffering no great hardship, however, for he had comfortable rooms and could entertain friends and occasionally preach to visiting Quakers. Through the effort of his father-in-law and friends, including some of the less tightfisted Quakers of Pennsylvania, Penn raised £7,600 which enabled him to buy off the Fords and retain his province.

For the next three years Penn busied himself about the court of Queen Anne—the greatest Quaker in England, the intermediary with her Majesty when any fellow member of his faith needed the influence of a courtier in a broad-brimmed hat. He also had business of his own with the politicians, for he was still planning to sell the government of Pennsylvania to the crown when he could wheedle the Board of Trade and the Privy Council into offering enough and guaranteeing all the privileges which he had given his colony. But before he could make the final arrangements for the transfer, Fate intervened. On October 4, 1712 he suffered a mild stroke of apoplexy. Though his body recovered, his mind was too impaired to permit his carrying out the plan to sell Pennsylvania. Six years more he lived, a bland and placid smile lighting his face, but he was mercifully immune at last to the invectives of David Lloyd and other troublemakers. The proprietary office was conducted with good sense and skill by Penn's second wife, Hannah Callowhill, whose children ultimately succeeded to the proprietorship. The renegade son William, child of his first marriage, received no part of the American property when Penn died on July 30, 1718.

With all the errors of judgment which William Penn sometimes displayed, he had succeeded beyond the wildest imagination of dreamers in establishing a colony of almost Utopian freedom. The relaxation of many feudal privileges which the proprietor might have retained gave an opportunity for the development of representative government. By the definition of the twentieth century the Quaker oligarchy who assumed control in Pennsylvania was anything but democratic, but the long struggle of the assembly to establish the prerogatives of the legislative body provided a training school in self-government. Out of incessant bickering and squabbling came the statement of fundamental principles of liberty important for the future. In the American colonies, only Rhode Island equalled Pennsylvania in the positive assertion of the liberty of the individual conscience. By the standards of the eighteenth century, Pennsylvania's laws were liberal. While England still retained on the statute books more than two hundred offenses punishable by death, Pennsylvania permitted capital punishment for only two, treason and murder.

Like the ethical code of the Puritans, Quaker ethics were conducive to the growth of the capitalistic spirit and to the increasing commercial prosperity of Pennsylvania. The Puritan preachers of Boston never emphasized the virtues of thrift, diligence, and sobriety with greater earnestness than the Quaker merchants of Philadelphia. Mystics as they were, they never let the illumination of inward revelation blind them to the good things of this earth. Few traders had sharper eyes for a sixpence or showed greater care for the conservation of money than the Friends displayed. Though they rejected ostentation and extravagance, they loved no ascetic retirement from the world and made good use of their money.

If the great houses looking out upon the docks at Philadelphia were plain, they were also built with an eye to comfort. Their tables groaned with excellent food, often selected in person by the master of the house in the well-stocked markets of the town. The grim visage of prohibition was unknown in Philadelphia. With becoming gravity, well-to-do Quakers drank deeply of old Madeira and discussed the state of politics and finance. Decorously they damned the

War of Spanish Succession, which seriously interrupted the movement of ships from the Delaware to the ports of Europe in the years between 1701 and 1713. If the war for a time caused a glut of the natural products of Pennsylvania, it could not ruin the country as it might have ruined a less thrifty and careful commonwealth. The Quakers invested prudently in land, buildings, ships, and stores of goods. When one market failed, they tried another. They learned the value of legitimate interest compounded regularly. They feared as the devil bankruptcy and insolvency. When currency was scarce in Governor Keith's time, the assembly approved the issuance of paper money secured by silver plate or land owned in the colony. So great was the care and moderation of the Quaker assembly that Pennsylvania's paper currency circulated at face value and no one doubted its value. When a prodigal planter of Maryland found himself in need of money, he was certain that the merchants of Philadelphia could relieve his needs—provided his security was gilt-edged and he could afford Quaker interest.

Shrewd, careful of their credit and their reputations, eternally diligent in the pursuit of business, the Quakers of Pennsylvania created the greatest center of wealth in the American colonies. With such merchants, drawing upon a back country productive beyond belief, Philadelphia could not help becoming a thriving city, which forged ahead of Boston before the middle of the eighteenth century and became the metropolis of colonial America.

Although the Quaker ruling class, unlike the theocracy of Massachusetts Bay, distrusted punitive laws as a means of making good Christians, they shared with the Puritans something of their moral strictness and never confused liberty of conscience with license to behave as one might wish. Indeed, the Quakers were often annoyingly censorious and some of their laws restricted artistic and cultural development. For example, they were unutterably opposed to stage plays and similar follies and provided in the laws of 1682 penalties of hard labor for anyone who should introduce "into this province or frequent such rude and riotous sports and practices as prizes [prize-fights], stage plays, [and] masques."

Although a theatre was finally erected just outside the limits of Philadelphia and stage plays were popular in the eighteenth century, the Quakers, the Presbyterians, and other pious folk continued to make war upon the devil's schoolhouse. Although no laws forbade, the Quakers sought to discourage by moral suasion "the reading of plays, romances, novels, and other pernicious books." Upon their own members, Quaker discipline was strict; the monthly meetings sought to regulate by admonition any erring brother who showed a disposition to extravagant behavior, ostentatious dress, or wasteful frivolity. Nevertheless, as wealth increased, Philadelphia, like Boston, relaxed and cultivated the pleasure of living. The gayer sort—many of them Quakers, to the scandal of their reverend elders—went to horse races, made up parties for fox hunting, and attended fashionable balls. Although a monthly meeting might appoint a committee to investigate a report "that two Friends have allowed fiddling, dancing, and playing at cards in their houses," the older Quakers were waging a losing battle. Under the influence of ease and luxury, the younger Friends would not remain a people apart.

The peculiar religious structure of Pennsylvania determined its early educational development. Both the English speaking Quakers and the Germans emphasized secondary education rather than higher learning and both groups showed immense concern that their children be trained in some useful knowledge. Not for them were the frills of learning, though the assertion sometimes made that the Quakers were opposed to classical culture is only a half truth. Quaker grammar schools followed the traditional curriculum which stressed Latin and included Greek, but they also gave a prominent place to mathematics and "useful arts."

In his educational theory, William Penn was a rebel against slavish adherence to the dry bones of grammar and rhetoric, the conventional framework of education in his age. In words which sound like a premonition of Rousseau's *Émile* he declared that the living world ought to be the proper study of youth. "We are in pain to make them scholars but not men," he complained, "to talk rather than to know, which is true canting. . . . We press their memory too soon, and puzzle, strain, and load them with words and rules to know grammar and rhetoric, and a strange tongue or two that is ten to one may never be useful to them, leaving their natural genius to mechanical, physical, or natural knowledge uncultivated and neglected. . . . To be sure languages are not to be despised or neglected; but things are still to be preferred. . . . It were happy if we studied nature more in natural things, and acted according to nature, whose rules are few, plain, and most reasonable. . . . It is pity, therefore, that books have not been composed for youth by some curious and careful naturalists, and also mechanics, in the Latin tongue, to be used in schools, that they might learn things with words: things obvious and familiar to them, and which would make the tongue easier to be obtained by them."

Penn's first Frame of Government provided that the governor and council should "erect and order all public schools and encourage and reward the authors of useful sciences and laudable inventions in the said province." Furthermore it specified that "all children within this province of the age of twelve years shall be taught some useful trade or skill, to the end that none may be idle, but the poor may work to live, and the rich, if they become poor, may not want."

Although in practice, the colony fell short of Penn's dream of government schools which would provide utilitarian education for everybody, his theories, which reflected the ideas of other Quakers, influenced the quality of the schools for generations. In some fashion, every Quaker community provided for the elementary teaching of the children in reading, writing, and arithmetic so that an illiterate Quaker was almost unheard of, and Quaker youths were in demand as bookkeepers and clerks in business houses.

The first school after Penn acquired the colony was established at Philadelphia in 1683 under Enoch Flower, an English schoolmaster of long experience, who was employed to teach reading, writing, and the keeping of accounts. From that time onward numerous schools of this type provided elementary education. For more advanced training, the Friends Public School was established in 1689 at Philadelphia with George Keith, later the leader of a schism against orthodox Friends, as its first master. This institution, which still exists under the name of the William Penn Charter School, was free to the poor, though parents whose financial ability permitted were required to pay tuition for their children. Gradually the Friends Free School became an aggregate of various schools with the so-called "Latin School" at the top of the educational hierarchy. Here Pennsylvania boys could learn the rudiments of the classical languages and gain some acquaintance with classical literature and history.

A school established in 1702 at Germantown had for its teacher the learned Pastorius, who later taught the classical languages at the Friends Free School in Philadelphia. For all of his pacifistic religion, Pastorius enforced discipline with the severity of a drill sergeant and never spared the rod. One of his pupils, Israel Pemberton, wrote down his testimony that the teacher beat him about the head and shoulders with a stout stick until his "flesh was bruised [so] that it turned black and yellow and green."

Although some learned men like Pastorius came with the early German immigrants, the German sects as a whole were interested only in schools which taught the fundamentals of reading, writing, and arithmetic. Most of the sects were opposed to higher learning on religious grounds, though the Lutherans and Reformed Church people gave lip service to the classical curriculum of the conventional grammar schools of the age. Notwithstanding, since most of the Lutheran and Reformed Church Germans were peasants, they did nothing to advance education in the colony but rather developed a stolid opposition to schooling which would violate an axiom with them that children should not be more learned than their parents. Among the Germans as a national group, only the Moravians actively exerted themselves in the interest of education.

Although most of the religious groups who found asylum in Pennsylvania contributed in some fashion to the educational development of the colony, private schools having no religious affiliations played a great part in the education of its citizenry from the early years of the eighteenth century onward. Schoolmasters of infinite variety flourished in Pennsylvania. The subjects which they taught covered most of human knowledge, and the claims of some of them in their advertisements made Pennsylvania sound like a Utopia of wise men. The private teachers sometimes made boastful claims for the efficiency of their instruction. Charles Phipps, for example, in 1729 advertised that he taught "after an easy method," and Thomas Ball in the same year announced newly invented methods of improving the memory and intensifying the process of learning. Private schools were most numerous, of course, in Philadelphia. There instructions in almost any language could be had—English, German, French, Spanish, Portuguese, Latin, Greek, Hebrew, and even Arabic. The schools making the widest appeal, however, were those which stressed "useful" subjects, especially mathematics, surveying, navigation, and what we would call natural science, speculative and applied. Andrew Lamb, a London instrument maker, who set up a school in Philadelphia in 1733, offered instruction in surveying, navigation, Italian bookkeeping, writing, and arithmetic. Lamb's long career as a teacher of utilitarian subjects suffered no taint because he had arrived in America as a convict whose sentence of hanging had been commuted to transportation. Even more famous than Lamb was Theophilus Grew of Maryland, almanac-maker and teacher of the mathematical sciences, who in 1734 opened a school of navigation, surveying, and mathematics in Philadelphia. From 1731 onward night schools flourished in Philadelphia and provided the means for artisans and working men to improve their status. In that

year John Lloyd advertised "a night-school in Water Street
. . . where writing, arithmetic vulgar and decimal, with
some parts of mathematics are taught." Theophilus Grew at
first conducted his school at night for the benefit of apprentices and other workers.

The prominence which the early teachers gave to mathematics and scientific subjects made the outburst of scientific
interest in Philadelphia in the mid-eighteenth century no
mere accident. Benjamin Franklin could have chosen no
more congenial environment for the development of his
genius than Philadelphia, where he arrived as a boy of seventeen in 1723. The city teemed with bright young apprentices,
eager and ambitious, bent upon self-improvement. Private
teachers of almost any desirable subject were available to
every thrifty youth who could save enough money to pay
the fees. Scientific learning increased until Philadelphia by
the middle of the century was the center of scientific activity
in America.

The education of women was not overlooked by private
teachers. In 1722 a certain Mrs. Rhoades advertised that she
had lately arrived in Philadelphia and stood ready to "teach
young ladies or gentlewomen to read and write French to
perfection." She added that she also taught the art of fancy-
work in muslin and drew patterns for lace and the embroi-
dery of petticoats. "And those who have a mind to learn,"
the advertisement concluded, "she will teach very reasonable." Other teachers of schools for girls stressed music,
dancing, painting, singing, grammar, and even so useful a
subject as bookkeeping. Though solemn Quakers might look
askance at the frivolity of so much ornamental education,
Philadelphia had many prosperous daughters who sought the
social graces through private tutors and schools. Music occupied a high place in the subjects advertised by the schools
for young ladies, some of which offered easy lessons on the
flute, the viol, the dulcimer, the spinet, and other instru-
ments.

Despite Quaker skepticism about its value, music reached

a higher development in Pennsylvania than in the other colonies. Among the German sectarians, the Moravians and the Seventh Day Baptists at Ephrata stressed religious music and did much to teach its principles.

Because the Quakers and many of the German sects both distrusted a hireling ministry and eschewed a professional clergy, they had no incentive to found colleges for the training of an educated ministry. The failure of the Quakers—so long the political leaders in Pennsylvania—to provide for higher education in the end proved disastrous for their intellectual leadership.

On the frontiers the hardy and tough-minded Scotch-Irish Presbyterians held to contrary views. Though they might live in primitive cabins and defend themselves with their long rifles, they did not intend to become uneducated barbarians. This country has had no more convinced devotees of learning than the Scotch-Irish Calvinists who planned for a constant supply of learned ministers wherever they found themselves and believed implicitly that laymen likewise should cultivate all the mental talents with which the Lord endowed them.

Earliest of the Presbyterian academies of higher learning in Pennsylvania was the Reverend William Tennent's school at Neshaminy, which lasted from 1726 to 1742. Commonly called the "Log College," its major purpose was to instruct candidates for the Presbyterian ministry but lay students were permitted to attend the classes. Tennent—described by a contemporary as "skilled in the Latin language so as to speak it and write it almost as well as his mother tongue, a good proficient also in the other learned languages and well-read in divinity"—taught all of the classes himself and preached on Sunday as well. George Whitefield, the evangelist, recorded in his *Journal* that from Tennent's school "seven or eight worthy ministers of Jesus have lately been sent forth; more are almost ready to be sent, and a foundation is now laying for the instruction of many others." Though the Reverend Mr. Tennent gave his students a competent knowledge of Latin and classical learning, the examining synod complained that his candidates for the ministry were in some cases deficient in theology and certain branches of college learning.

More famous than the "Log College" was the Presbyterian Latin Grammar School at New London, Pennsylvania, founded in 1743 and directed by the Reverend Francis Allison, a classical scholar of eminence. This school attracted the sons of the Philadelphia gentry who were concerned lest their children grow up without the benefit of traditional learning. In similar academies and schools, the Scotch Presbyterians upheld the classics and stressed the discipline of grammar and rhetoric and the cultural values to be found in the great writers of the past. In consequence of their emphasis on mental training and higher education, the Scotch Presbyterians in time outdistanced the complacent Quakers and wrested from them both intellectual and political leadership in the colony.

The intellectual and cultural development of Pennsylvania in the first half of the eighteenth century owed much of its direction and impetus to a few vigorous personalities. Foremost of these in the period before the ascendancy of Benjamin Franklin was James Logan, Penn's confidential agent and secretary of the colony. A Quaker of Scottish parentage, Logan had a fine classical training and possessed the versatility and breadth of interest which made him at home in many fields of learning. He lived in aristocratic luxury at Stenton and gathered the finest library in Pennsylvania. There the young Franklin found the latest scientific works, as well as treatises on classical science by Ptolemy, Euclid, and other ancient writers.

Logan's library, one of the best in the colonies, was open to serious students during the owner's lifetime. In 1745, Logan erected a brick building for his collection at Sixth and Walnut Streets in Philadelphia, and bequeathed building and books to the city, along with a modest endowment.

Other Pennsylvanians collected books and had useful libraries, but Logan's served the greatest utility.

Logan was a leader as well as a book collector, a doer as well as a student. He became a proficient botanist and encouraged the study of botany. John Bartram owed his start in botany to Logan's interest and aid. Logan's scientific interest was broad. When a young glazier named Thomas Godfrey came to his house to borrow a copy of Newton's *Principia,* Logan recognized a man of promise and helped him in studies and experiments which resulted in the perfection of a new kind of mariner's quadrant, for which Godfrey later received a prize from the Royal Society. Logan was also a classical scholar of distinction. His *Cato's Moral Distichs Englished in Couplets* was printed in Philadelphia in 1735. In 1744 he brought out an edition of Cicero's *Cato Major* and he left at his death in 1751 an unpublished essay, a "Defense of Aristotle and the Ancient Philosophers." His scientific observations were written in Latin and published in Europe. Possessed of a working knowledge of Greek, Latin, Hebrew, and Arabic, Logan showed even greater zeal for classical learning than his contemporary, William Byrd of Virginia, who shared some of his scholarly and scientific interests.

Benjamin Franklin, who combined in his character the best of the Puritan tradition modified by eighteenth-century rationalism, probably contributed more than any other single citizen to the stimulation of intellectual activity in Philadelphia. In Franklin's own development the liberal spirit of Philadelphia was a profound influence.

When the seventeen-year old boy ran away from his apprenticeship to his half-brother in Boston, he went first to New York, where he sought out William Bradford, who had established the first printing press in Philadelphia and had later removed to New York. Bradford advised him to apply to his son Andrew Bradford, who four years before, in 1719, had started in Philadelphia the *American Weekly Mercury,* the third continuous paper in the colonies. Since Andrew Bradford could not find employment for young Ben, he advised him to apply to one of the three other Philadelphia printers, Samuel Keimer, a long-bearded prophet with the ambition of becoming a religious poet, who gave the boy his first job in Philadelphia. By 1729 Franklin was able to buy out Keimer's curious paper, *The Universal Instructor in all Arts and Sciences and Pennsylvania Gazette*. Probably only a religious enthusiast in utilitarian Philadelphia would have set out as Keimer did to benefit mankind by devoting his newspaper to the serial reprinting of Ephraim Chambers' *Cyclopedia, or an Universal Dictionary of the Arts and Sciences*. Ben Franklin was too good a journalist to follow this plan, laudable as it may have been. He threw out the encyclopedic articles, brightened up the paper, and short-ened its title to *Pennsylvania Gazette*. With this venture he began a long and prosperous career as printer and publisher. In 1732 Franklin undertook to publish a German language newspaper but the venture failed. Two German language periodicals, both religious in purpose, did eventually succeed: Christopher Sower's *Zeitung*, founded at Germantown in 1739, and Heinrich Miller's *Wöchentliche Staatsbote*, first published in Philadelphia in 1762.

From Franklin's day, Philadelphia became increasingly important as a printing center. Franklin's own printing house was one of the best, and his famous *Poor Richard's Almanac* was widely read. The influence of its homely and pragmatic philosophy has continued from that day to this. In 1741, Franklin attempted to establish a literary periodical, the *General Magazine*, but it failed after six issues.

Philadelphia, which attracted many of the ablest crafts-men of the day and freed them from shackling inhibitions imposed by theocratic authority, developed a vigorous intel-lectual atmosphere. When the brightest young men of the town were led by a personality possessing Benjamin Frank-lin's creative imagination and practical judgment, the intel-lectual force of the community was not likely to be dissipated in futile speculation. Franklin was instrumental in creating organizations and institutions which had a permanent value in the improvement of the cultural and intellectual opportunities, not only of Philadelphia, but of all the colonies. A club known as the Junto, formed by Franklin in 1727, was the embryo from which the American Philosophical Society grew. Franklin's own statement in the *Autobiography* suggests his purpose and throws light on the quality of the youthful tradesmen of Philadelphia. Franklin, it should be remembered, was twenty-one at the time. "I had formed most of my ingenious acquaintances into a club of mutual improvement which we called the Junto," he explains; "we met on Friday evenings. The rules that I drew up required that every member in his turn should produce one or more queries on any point of Morals, Politics, or Natural Philosophy, to be discussed by the company; and once in three months produce and read an essay of his own writing on any subject he pleased. Our debates were . . . to be conducted in the sincere spirit of inquiry after truth, without fondness for dispute or desire for victory."

Among the first members were Thomas Godfrey, glazier and self-taught mathematician; Joseph Breitnal, scrivener, a "middle-aged man, a great lover of poetry, reading all he could meet with and writing some that was tolerable, very ingenious in many little nicknackeries, and of sensible conversation," says Franklin; Nicholas Scull, surveyor, "who loved books and sometimes made a few verses"; William Parsons, shoemaker and astrologer, who loved reading and "had acquired a considerable share of mathematics"; William Maugridge, joiner, "a most exquisite mechanic and a solid, sensible man"; William Coleman, merchant's clerk and later a great business man; Robert Grace, a witty young gentleman; and three of Franklin's fellow printers. This club, bent upon self-improvement and the search for truth, was symbolic of the best of American cultural aspirations in the years to come.

The experience with the Junto influenced Franklin to

widen the scope of his activities. In 1743 he sent to his friends a circular letter the title of which is self-explanatory, *A Proposal for Promoting Useful Knowledge Among the British Plantations in America.* The result of his suggestions was the establishment the next year of the American Philosophical Society, the first important scientific society in America, which has had a distinguished record from that day to this.

Formal education in Pennsylvania also owes a debt to Franklin. At the time that he was planning the Philosophical Society he was also proposing a scheme for the "complete education of youth" by the establishment of a college but was obliged to "let the scheme lie a while dormant." Franklin, however, was not one to be discouraged in so worthy an endeavor, and he published in 1749 *Proposals Relating to the Education of Youth in Pennsylvania* which advocated an institution of higher learning. The colony had drawn many educated and professional men from Europe. By this time two generations of youths born in the colony had experienced the need of college training which Pennsylvania could not supply. Some had gone to Oxford and Cambridge. A few had gone to Harvard but the Puritan atmosphere of that community was still uncongenial to Pennsylvanians. Though the College of New Jersey, founded in 1746, offered opportunities reasonably near, Franklin believed that Pennsylvania needed its own school of higher learning.

As a result of his agitation, he was named in 1749 president of a board of trustees empowered to found "a Public Academy in the City of Philadelphia." The Philadelphia Academy opened in 1751 in the building of the Charity School which had been erected in 1740, but the Academy was still not sufficient, and in 1755 its trustees requested and received from the proprietary government a charter creating both academy and college. The College of Philadelphia, as it was called, later became the University of Pennsylvania. The first provost was an Anglican parson, the Reverend William Smith, whose book, the *General Idea of a College of Mirania,* published in New York in 1753, pleased Franklin so much that he urged the appointment and soon regretted the decision, for Smith, a vigorous and calculating person, brought the college under the dominance of the Anglican Church, which was increasing in numbers and social influence. He also helped to give a greater emphasis to classical studies than Franklin wished.

Franklin's efforts in behalf of learning resulted in the most effective subscription library in the American colonies. Because the members of the Junto were handicapped in their search after truth by the lack of books, they had in 1731 agreed to solicit fifty subscribers who would give forty shillings each and ten shillings per year thereafter for the purchase of books. This organization, chartered in 1742 as the Library Company of Philadelphia, collected the books most useful and instructive to its membership, which was soon increased to one hundred subscribers. Its first order of books—nearly fifty items—showed careful selection and covered a broad field of knowledge; included were the works of Homer, Plutarch, Xenophon, and Tacitus; recent histories, grammars, dictionaries, and encyclopedias; treatises on mathematics, chemistry, physics, astronomy, botany, natural history, architecture, farming, and surveying; works of Dryden, Addison, and Steele; and finally, *The Complete Tradesman*. Franklin was greatly pleased at the success of his library undertaking and boasted in the *Autobiography* that "this was the mother of all the North American subscription libraries, now so numerous. It is become a great thing itself, and continually increasing. These libraries have improved the general conversation of the Americans, made the common tradesmen and farmers as intelligent as most gentlemen from other countries, and perhaps have contributed in some degree to the stand so generally made throughout the colonies in defense of their privileges."

Since nearly every printer was also a bookseller, and other tradesmen sold books, Philadelphia became a book market of importance. Its printers not only published such American writers as came their way but they also turned out reprints of European authors. Its merchants imported books from England and the Continent and made Philadelphia a distribution point for works of the mind as well as the hand.

The growth of Philadelphia's trade, which by 1740 made it the greatest city in the American colonies, had enormous implications for the future of Pennsylvania and the rest of British America. Despite the desire of some of its Quaker citizens to remain apart from the rest of the world, Philadelphia became a cosmopolitan city. Its merchants had contacts with the four corners of the earth, and its learned men corresponded with their kind abroad. Franklin's letters to Peter Collinson in England, for example, revealed in 1751 the Philadelphian's notable experiments in electricity and made him famous overnight.

The commercial interests of Pennsylvania's great port resulted in the development of characteristic middle-class attitudes which reached their ultimate expression in Franklin's pragmatic philosophy. *The Way to Wealth*, that epitome of Franklin's sententious wisdom gathered out of *Poor Richard's Almanac* and published in 1757, has influenced America more profoundly than any other gospel message. The important thing to remember, however, is that *The Way to Wealth*—the very essence of middle-class ethics—was not struck fire-new from Franklin's brain. It reflected the commercial civilization of his milieu and betokened the trend of American thought.

Important as Philadelphia was, however, it was not characteristic of all of Pennsylvania. Since the colony under Penn's shaping hand had become the refuge of the persecuted peoples of the world, its population was almost as polyglot as that of New York and within its borders were unassimilated groups, notably the German sects, who had little in common with the citizens of Philadelphia or of the other port towns. German farming communities carried on many local traditions of the old world and developed some new provincialities of their own. On the frontier, the Scotch-Irish were hewing their way through the woods, killing In-

dians when it suited them, and developing a righteous indig-
nation against the restraining orders which came from the
government at Philadelphia. By the mid-eighteenth century
Pennsylvania was a colony in ferment, but Philadelphia was
only one of many places where the yeast was at work. A
diverse people with ideologies more varied than their national origins made Pennsylvania one of the most complex
and difficult areas in the period of unrest which culminated
in the Revolution.

CHAPTER SIX

Southern Spearheads of Trade and Imperial Expansion

THE earliest dreams of English empire in the New World concerned the region of the present South Atlantic states where Elizabethan expansionists believed that England might make a successful stand against the northward thrust of Spain. When Richard Hakluyt presented to Queen Elizabeth his *Discourse of Western Planting* in 1584, just as Sir Walter Raleigh was sending out his first expedition to Virginia, he made his principal argument the necessity of establishing English bases north of Florida as a check to Spanish domination of the Atlantic coast. Raleigh's colony failed; but the imperial plan which it symbolized remained alive and became in the seventeenth century a cardinal point of English policy. The penetration of the interior from the Carolinas, and later from Georgia, by indomitable and ruthless English and Scottish traders, challenged both the declining power of Spain and the rising might of France in the whole South Atlantic and Gulf region. The settlement of the Carolinas successfully prevented Spain, by that time becoming moribund, from pushing any farther to the north; the British infiltration of the hinterland checked the completion of the encirclement by which Louis XIV's imperial schemers hoped to contain the English within the narrow limits of the Atlantic coast line.

Southern Spearheads of Trade

Hakluyt and many another Elizabethan had insisted that England's destiny required the seizure of islands and naval bases in the Caribbean—outposts at the very gateway to the Spanish empire—partly as a safeguard of English sea lanes and partly as a protection for the English on the North American mainland. As Spanish enterprise and vigor weakened in the seventeenth century, that English aspiration was realized. The development of island centers of English trade and population in the West Indies had a tremendous influence upon the settlements on the southern mainland as well as upon the trade of all of British America.

The first island outpost to the south was the settlement, made in 1612, in the Bermudas, a base which proved a stepping stone to the Caribbean. Until that time, declared one of the preachers who took part in the enterprise, God in his wisdom had reserved those fine harbors especially for the English and had "terrified and kept all people of the world from coming into these islands to inhabit them." The earliest Englishmen to effect a permanent settlement in the Caribbean landed on St. Christopher's in 1624. They were led by Thomas Warner, a friend and former neighbor of John Winthrop's. Three years later, in 1627, English settlers sent out by a London promoter, Sir William Courteen, occupied the island of Barbados, at the southeastern end of the Caribbean Sea, a few hundred miles north of the mouth of the Orinoco River. Sir Walter Raleigh, dead since 1618, would have approved the seizure of that base. It could threaten the Spanish Main and serve as a point of departure for the realms of gold which he thought he had discerned in the valley of the Orinoco. From this time forward, expansion in the West Indies was accepted by the English as a part of their commercial and imperial destiny. Other small islands, occupied by English settlers, prospered. Finally Oliver Cromwell and his advisers, prompted by the need of money and the urging of merchants of London, organized an expedition under Admiral William Penn and General Robert Venables which in

1655 captured and held Jamaica, a large island in the very heart of the Spanish possessions.

The occupation of Jamaica was part of a large "western design" for the consolidation of the English colonies in the New World but Cromwell's government ended before these plans matured. With the restoration of Charles II, a group of promoters, chiefly merchants and traders of London and Bristol, allied themselves with some of the king's money-seeking courtiers for the purpose of advancing commerce, colonization, and their own interests.

The experience of planters in the West Indies had whetted their appetites for American profits. Barbados particularly was a shining example of the way to wealth. Indigent royalists who had fled to that tropical refuge during Oliver's iron rule had grown rich from the profits of the sugar plantations. Jamaica had not yet realized its economic possibilities but already apparent were its advantages as a rendezvous for privateers and other enterprising sea captains whose consciences were not too nice. The West India islands also offered an insatiable market for Negro slaves, a source of profit which the Duke of York and his colleagues of the Royal African Company would soon realize with acute relish. The pleasurable anticipation of quick riches from participation in some scheme of overseas enterprise, especially in the undeveloped American plantations, quickened the blood of greedy nobles and commoners alike in the early years of Charles II's reign and led, among other efforts, to the settlement of the Carolinas.

During the winter and spring of 1663, a group of courtiers —friends of the King and of his brother, that active promoter of money-making ventures, the Duke of York—were busily projecting a scheme to enrich themselves by means of a grant of vast territories in North America. The Duke of York already had his heart set on New York and part of New Jersey, which he would take when it suited him. Eight others, gentlemen and nobles, united by greed and an interest in American opportunities, looked upon the map and selected a domain between Virginia and Spanish Florida which the King on March 24, 1663, granted them as lords proprietors. The eight who received this imperial gift were Edward Hyde, later Earl of Clarendon, George Monck, later Duke of Albemarle, William Lord Craven, John Lord Berkeley, Anthony Ashley Cooper, later Earl of Shaftesbury, Sir George Carteret, Sir John Colleton, and Sir William Berkeley. Back of the proprietors were enterprising business men—merchants, traders, and creditors of their lordships—who scented profits in the new endeavor. Colonization and exploitation of the American wilderness had become big business which enlisted capitalists of all varieties.

Long before Charles II's grant of Carolina to the eight proprietors, his father, Charles I, in 1629, had given a charter to the same territory to his attorney-general, Sir Robert Heath. The king had named the land in honor of himself "Carolana" and had specified that it should extend from sea to sea between the parallels of 31 and 26 degrees north latitude. Heath's grant resulted from an effort to find an overseas home for Huguenot refugees in London, and in 1630 the "Mayflower" sailed with a group of French settlers destined for Carolana. By some mischance, the ship landed its passengers in Virginia and nothing came of Heath's project, though the name of his territory, slightly changed in spelling, was retained.

The eight proprietors of Carolina received a second charter on June 30, 1665 which extended their land from 36 degrees 30 minutes on the north to 29 degrees on the south, or from Currituck Inlet to sixty-five miles south of the Spanish stronghold of St. Augustine in Florida. They became the absolute owners of the soil and lords of the land, with authority to make the laws and administer justice.

The instrument of government which they drew up was one of the most remarkable yet seen in the American colonies. Called the Fundamental Constitutions, this piece of legal ingenuity is believed to represent the handiwork of Shaftesbury and his distinguished secretary, John Locke.

Only a philosopher and a politician could have achieved a document so elaborately impractical. A medley of feudal doctrine and seventeenth-century social theory, it drew heavily on James Harrington's Utopian treatise, *Oceana*, first published in 1656.

The Fundamental Constitutions provided for a social hierarchy with fanciful gradations in rank. This aristocracy was based on the possession of land. At the top were the lords proprietors, the senior member being the lord palatine. Each proprietor had a right to at least twelve thousand acres in each county of Carolina. Next to the proprietors were the landgraves who were expected to own not less than forty-eight thousand acres. The caciques, a title taken from the name for Indian chiefs, came next with twenty-four thousand acres. These three ranks made up the nobility. After them came gentlemen commoners and yeomen. The gentlemen commoners were to be lords of manors of at least three thousand but not more than twelve thousand acres. Yeomen were required to have a minimum of fifty acres to qualify them to vote. Although this aristocratic system was too grandiose ever to come to full flower in the wilds of Carolina, the proprietors managed to create some twenty-six landgraves and thirteen caciques before abandoning the scheme.

The plan of government was equally elaborate with provisions for sundry officials bearing resounding titles such as chamberlain, lord steward, and chancellor. The proprietors intended to appoint a governor of the colony but if any proprietor should emigrate he would automatically supersede an appointed governor. Each proprietor had a deputy in the colony to look after his interests. The governor, proprietary deputies, and the resident nobility soon became the upper house of the legislative assembly. The lower house, or commons, consisted of representatives elected by the people—at least those people who owned fifty acres or more of land. Since the Fundamental Constitutions, for all of the feudal authoritarianism implicit therein, required acceptance by the people of the colony, the document never became an effective constitution because the proprietors could not gain the people's approval. For many years the proprietors tinkered with their unwieldly instrument and revised it to no avail. The immigrants in Carolina would have none of it. Though an aristocratic society did indeed develop, the influence of the Fundamental Constitutions was indirect if not negligible in that evolution.

The province of Carolina had a few white inhabitants when the proprietors took over in 1663. How many runaway servants from Virginia had already reached the borders of what is now North Carolina cannot be known, but some had certainly found refuge there. A trickle of legitimate settlers had also crossed the border from Virginia and a few New Englanders had made an unauthorized settlement at the mouth of the Cape Fear River about 1662. So many squatters had taken up their residence in the region of Albemarle Sound that the proprietors instructed one of their number, Sir William Berkeley, when he returned to Virginia as governor in 1664, to look after their interests across the border. Accordingly Berkeley appointed a certain William Drummond to be governor over the "province of Albemarle"—a territory which after 1719 would be known as North Carolina.

If the proprietors and their business associates were to make any money out of Carolina, they had to find settlers in large numbers. They took pains therefore to encourage the publication of favorable publicity about their domain. One of the earliest of the promotion tracts was *A Relation of a Discovery* (1664) by William Hilton, a ship captain who had explored the Carolina coast line as the agent of a group of Barbadians who proposed to move to the mainland in search of more abundant acres. Although this particular group tried to drive too hard a bargain to suit the proprietors, the publication of Hilton's descriptive pamphlet gave the enterprise a good report in Barbados and induced later settlers to emigrate from the island to Carolina.

Because some of the New England interlopers had damned

the Cape Fear country as unfit for human beings, Hilton and two of his associates were careful to correct that libel. "Whereas there was a writing left in a post at the point of Cape Fair [Fear] River by those New England men that left cattle with the Indians there," Hilton and his colleagues solemnly testified, "the contents whereof tended not only to the disparagement of the land about the said river, but also to the great discouragement of all those that should hereafter come into those parts to settle: in answer to that scandalous writing we whose names are underwritten do affirm that we have seen facing on both sides of the river and branches of Cape Fair aforesaid as good land and as well timbered as any we have seen in any other part of the world, sufficient to accommodate thousands of our English nation, lying commodiously by the said river." Other pamphlets soon corroborated Hilton's good words about Carolina and added many special attractions. Robert Horne, the bookseller, in 1666, brought out *A Brief Description of the Province of Carolina*, an inspired piece of propaganda, which announced on the title page that it would "set forth the healthfulness of the air, the fertility of the earth and waters, and the great pleasure and profit [which] will accrue to those that shall go thither to enjoy the same." Horne concludes with a suggestion to women: "If any maid or single woman have a desire to go over, they will think themselves in the Golden Age when men paid a dowry for their wives, for if they be but civil and under fifty years of age, some honest man or other will purchase them for their wives."

Year in and year out the proprietors saw to it that a stream of advertising pamphlets described the wonders of Carolina. Thomas Ashe in 1682 prepared one of the more extravagant bits of advertising entitled *Carolina . . . and the Natural Excellencies Thereof, viz., the Healthfulness of the Air, Pleasantness of the Place, Advantage and Usefulness of Those Rich Commodities There Plentifully Abounding, Which Much Increase and Flourish by the Industry of the Planters That Daily Enlarge That Colony*. Among many beneficial commodities, Ashe reveals that Carolina produces a marvelous drug, "the famous cassiny," which "boiled in water as we do tea [will] wonderfully enliven and invigorate the heart with genuine easy sweats and transpirations, preserving the mind free and serene, keeping the body brisk, active, and lively." Furthermore, the fat from Carolina bears has "great virtue and efficacy in causing the hair to grow." These benefits were of course mere incidentals in the long catalogue of the colony's assets.

All of this good news could not help impressing thousands of prospective emigrants, eager for a better opportunity abroad. The publicity was especially effective in Barbados, which was already over-crowded. By the year 1684 that small island had a population of twenty thousand white settlers and forty-six thousand black slaves. Late-coming planters who had expected to get rich growing sugar cane, saw little prospect of acquiring sufficient land on the island and were easily persuaded to move to the mainland. Huguenots in England and in France heard the message and set out for Carolina; they had been especially impressed by stories of the prospects for vine, olive, and silkworm culture—illusions which persisted in South Carolina down to recent times.

During the summer of 1665, agents for the proprietors re cruited in the West Indies, chiefly in Barbados, about ninety settlers, intending them for Port Royal near where the Huguenots under Jean Ribaut in 1562 had made their ill-fated settlement, but wind and weather determined otherwise. They landed at the mouth of the Cape Fear River and named their settlement Charles Town. Quarrels and misfortunes rent the colony and it did not prosper. After two years the colonists scattered to other regions and the name Charles Town was left to be used for the later metropolis of South Carolina.

A new and more successful effort in 1670 resulted in a permanent settlement in South Carolina. An expedition organized in England came by way of Barbados where Sir John Yeamans was instructed to fill in the blank commission of governor of the new colony with his own or some other name. He chose to give the honor to William Sayle, then nearly eighty years old, whose only qualification was that he had formerly governed Bermuda. The colonists in April settled at a point about twenty-five miles from the sea on the Ashley River. A few years later they moved down the river to a neck of land which South Carolinians proudly describe as the point where "the Ashley and the Cooper rivers come together to form the Atlantic Ocean." There they finally established Charles Town, which after 1680 was the seat of government. The first settlement is generally called Old Town to distinguish it from the later capital.

The two settlements in Carolina under the authority of the proprietors—the scattered plantations around Albemarle Sound and the little group on the Ashley River—would remain widely separated for generations and develop entirely different ways of life. The Albemarle plantations were among the most isolated of American colonies. Their principal business consisted in the sale of tobacco, corn, and cattle to traders from Virginia, New England, and occasionally Bermuda. Shut off from contacts with the world, the Albemarle people became increasingly provincial. Charles Town, on the other hand, within a generation, had acquired the characteristics of a potential metropolis. Up the rivers and creeks lay plantations of incredible fertility. These same waterways provided access to Indian trading posts and to the beginnings of trails which led far back into the wilderness to tribes whose furs and deer skins eventually found their way to Charles Town merchants.

Charles Town was for years the most southerly outpost against Spain. Though England and Spain in 1670 had made a treaty recognizing the legality of each other's actual settlements in the New World, Spain had no intention of letting the English encroach upon Florida, as the grant to the proprietors specified. Spanish missions had reached as far north as St. Helena Island and Spanish friars had made contacts with many of the South Carolina Indians. After the settlement of Charles Town, the mission on St. Catherine's Island, off the coast of Georgia, was the Spaniards' most northern post. Their operating base was the fort at St. Augustine which about this time was rebuilt in stone. From St. Catherine's Island, the Spaniards had a line of missions reaching from Georgia across northern Florida to the Alabama Gulf coast. Weak as the Spaniards were at this time, they were not too weak to make trouble for the English, and until well into the eighteenth century, they were a threat to the peace of South Carolina and a hindrance to expansion south and southwestward.

Although the growth of South Carolina in the first few years was slow, the colony never underwent the sufferings of some of the earlier settlements. The English had learned something about colonization in the years since they had landed at Jamestown. Despite malarial fever and the scarcity of supplies, the first years saw the gradual strengthening of the settlement. When old Governor Sayle died in 1671, the settlers elected Joseph West to serve in his place. To West's skill and intelligence, the colony owed much of its early success. His fortification of Old Town with a stout palisade gave the people a sense of security against Indians and Spaniards. He encouraged the clearing of land and the planting of food crops, including oranges, lemons, pomegranates, figs, and bananas, for the Carolinians believed the country to be warm enough for tropical fruits—an illusion which the frosts of the second winter dispelled. West also welcomed two shiploads of Barbadian settlers and saw to it that vessels returning to the West Indies took cargoes of cedar and cypress timber, much in demand for building there. The growing numbers of Barbadians and the trade which they developed with the West Indies were a forecast of much future interchange between mainland and islands.

Land was easy to obtain, for the supply seemed limited only by the ever-receding horizon. At first each settler could expect to obtain one hundred and fifty acres for himself and each adult in his household, but this headright was later reduced to fifty acres, the practice in some of the other colonies. As a promotional tract of 1682 explained to prospective settlers, this land would "be enjoyed by them and their heirs forever, they paying a penny an acre quitrent to the lords proprietors, the rent to commence in two years after their taking up the land." Land at once became the basis of wealth and prestige but land was not the only asset of the colony. Situated strategically for trade, the settlers quickly learned to combine agriculture and commerce. As in no other colony, South Carolina developed a ruling class which represented a fusion of commercial and agrarian interests. The colonial aristocracy of South Carolina owed much of its prosperity to the market place.

The dense forests of pine, cypress, live-oak, and cedar, growing to the very edge of salt water, provided the first profitable revenue. So busy were the early settlers in cutting timber and sawing lumber that they neglected to plant sufficient food crops. Tar and rosin from the long leaf pine soon came to rival the best of the ship stores from the Baltic.

Cutting timber, sawing lumber, burning tar kilns, and collecting rosin are laborious procedures. Such work requires little skill but stout muscles. A very little experimentation showed that African slaves could be used profitably in the woods and on the plantations of South Carolina. If Africans were not available, then Indians might do, though they were less tractable and could more easily escape to their own kind. The proprietors and their associates in England were pleased that the South Carolinians recognized so quickly the utility of African slavery, for most of the proprietors also had a finger in the slave trade.

To hard-eyed Barbadian settlers, accustomed as were all West Indians to Indian slavery, the opportunities for a profitable slave trade awaiting at the very borders of the colony were not to be resisted. Indians, it was true, would not make good slaves in South Carolina, but in Bermuda, Barbados, or Jamaica they would fetch a good price. The once populous tribes of the West Indies had long since been depleted by the slavers, and African Negroes were still not abundant enough to supply the demand for labor there.

Since South Carolina was populated by numerous Indian tribes, some of whom were allied with the Spaniards, the English settlers had no difficulty reconciling their consciences to the capture and sale of the savages. During dull times of peace, a tribal war could be easily provoked and the tribes friendly to the English were ever-ready to bring in their captives for a small price. For settlers engaged in it, the Indian slave trade was a profitable venture during the first few decades of South Carolina's history. The West Indies provided only one of the markets for Indians. Ships returning to New England frequently carried a few Indian slaves, for New Englanders, who had long since learned that the red man could be induced to labor as a bond servant, preferred Indians from a distance. Though the proprietors frowned on the Indian slave trade, partly because the colonists' zeal sometimes led them to capture friendly Indians and thus endanger peace and profits, and partly because Indian slavery competed with the Royal African Company's monopoly, they were not able to stop the traffic.

Negro slaves, introduced in the first year of settlement, soon proved by far the most satisfactory form of labor on the larger plantations. Early in the growth of the colony, the typical pattern of life in the Low Country evolved. Well-to-do landowners who could afford to buy Negroes gained control of the best plantations on the rivers near Charles Town. Poorer whites had to seek farms farther back in the hinterland or work as craftsmen or small tradesmen in Charles Town. A class of slave owners and planters who assumed the prerogatives and position of an aristocracy became the ruling class.

The importation of Negroes furnished one of the most lucrative enterprises of Charles Town, for all the slaves destined for the plantations had to pass through that port.

Middlemen who dealt in slaves got rich, invested in plantations of their own, and bequeathed to their sons patrimonies which occasionally made them elegant aristocrats.

About 1685 a New England ship captain named John Thurber brought from Madagascar a little bag of rice seed which eventually transformed the agricultural economy of the tidewater country, for rice, the planters discovered, produced abundantly in the rich alluvial soil of the coast. By a system of dikes and canals, rice-growers utilized the innumerable rivers and creeks to flood their fields with fresh water during the growing season. Under the benign influence of hot weather, plenty of water, and fertile soil, rice planted in March was ready for the harvest in late August. Only when a hurricane off the coast drove corrosive salt water up the rivers and over the dikes was this money crop spoiled. By the end of the seventeenth century Carolina rice was an important staple of food in the West Indies and rice was becoming a profitable commodity in trans-Atlantic commerce.

Since the rice plantations in the summer were mosquito infested, only Negro slaves, who were relatively immune to malaria, could live inland. The white owners soon learned to move to the coast where the sea breezes gave them relief from mosquitoes and heat alike. Charles Town therefore developed a social season in the summer. During the winter, planters lived on their river estates and superintended the improvement of their property but during the torrid months, from late May to late September, all who could escaped to their town houses. The rising curve of the temperature—and the hum of the mosquito—were responsible for a closely knit society which came in time to have an influence out of all proportion to its size.

Unlike Virginia's bondage to tobacco, South Carolina was not beholden to a single crop for its prosperity. By the year 1718, it had a thriving commerce with England and with other colonies in British America. In addition to 9,106 barrels of rice, it exported in that year quantities of corn, peas, beef, butter, pork, leather, hides, deer skins, furs, and naval stores. From its pine forests in the single year of 1718 went 22,601 barrels of pitch and 33,337 barrels of tar, useful to the shipbuilders of Old and New England. From the American colonies in the North, South Carolina imported dried fish, flour, rum, beer, and cider; from the West Indies, slaves, molasses, more rum, sugar, and cotton, for cotton was not yet a profitable commodity of local growth; from England all kinds of manufactured products; from the Mediterranean ports and the Madeira Islands, wines for throats already phenomenally thirsty. The port of Charles Town was alive with ships and agog with the talk of sailing men. Only the most naïve observer could have failed to see that certain shipmasters were not overly scrupulous about observing Great Britain's acts of trade and that a few of the skippers who guzzled rum in dockside taverns were clearly rascals not above a little piracy when it suited them.

The population of the province of South Carolina by 1718 had grown to about six thousand white people and probably about ten thousand Negro slaves. By 1750 the population was estimated at 25,000 whites and 39,000 Negroes. In 1718 North Carolina had approximately 7,500 whites and 10,500 Negroes. By 1750, the province had something like 50,000 whites and 30,000 Negro slaves. In North Carolina the population was scattered over a wider area than in South Carolina and consisted of innumerable small farms in addition to large plantations near the coast. From the first, poor farmers found North Carolina a more congenial region than the colony to the south, where the great planters continued to monopolize the best land. In North Carolina poor whites found the competition with Negro slaves less acute and oppressive than in South Carolina.

North Carolina's principal growth in the early years of the eighteenth century came from other colonies, principally Virginia. This migration over the border was regarded as something of a scandal by the ruling class in Virginia who complained that North Carolina was the refuge of runaway servants, debtors, criminals, and ne'er-do-wells of every description. Certainly the poor and the underprivileged found land easy to obtain in the North Carolina backcountry and established themselves on hundreds of farms where they lived in primitive simplicity. Most of these backwoodsmen were dissenters of British stock, though religion was not one of their preoccupations. "One thing may be said for the inhabitants of that province, that they are not troubled with any religious fumes," William Byrd of Virginia sarcastically observed in 1727, "and they have the least superstition of any people living. They do not know Sunday from any other day, any more than Robinson Crusoe did, which would give them a great advantage were they given to be industrious." North Carolina attracted considerable numbers of Quakers, who objected strenuously whenever the more well-to-do Anglicans of the coastal settlements tried to establish the authority of the Church of England.

As early as 1691 a few French Huguenots left Virginia for North Carolina, and increments of Huguenots came at later times until the province had two or three settlements of French Protestants. About 1710 a Swiss nobleman, the Baron de Graffenried, who obtained a large grant of land and the title of landgrave, attempted to settle his territory with Germans from the Palatinate but only a few survived the Atlantic voyage and the diseases of the country. In the same year de Graffenried brought over a company of Swiss and settled the town of New Bern on the Neuse River. Other Swiss, who followed de Graffenried's group, took up land in the same region. Scotch-Irish, Welsh, and Highland Scots added variety to the North Carolina population. A few Highlanders came to North and South Carolina after the abortive Jacobite rebellion of 1715, and after the rebellion of 1745 a great flood of these clansmen poured into the country until whole counties were populated by Scots.

Like North Carolina, South Carolina attracted settlers from other British colonies, especially from the West Indies. Unlike the immigrants into North Carolina, colonials who

SAVANNAH, GEORGIA, AS IT APPEARED IN 1734

From a contemporary engraving in the Huntington Library collection.

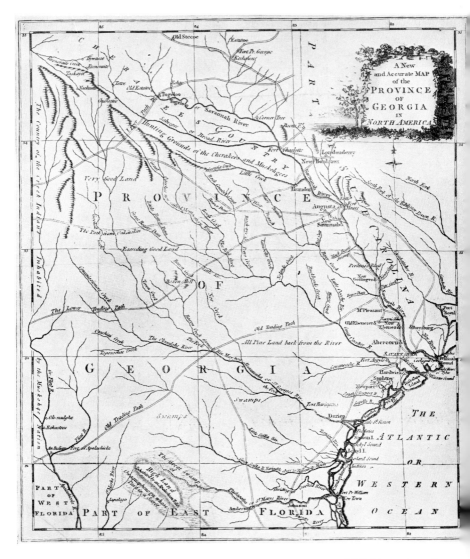

MAP OF GEORGIA SHOWING INDIAN TRADING PATHS
From an eighteenth century map in the Huntington Library map collection.

came to South Carolina were in general substantial citizens. The Barbadians, for example, constituted a well-to-do and cultivated addition to the colony. For the most part they were adherents of the Church of England. One of the most important additions to South Carolina's population began in 1680 with the arrival from England of forty-five Huguenots. England had furnished an asylum for French Protestant refugees since the reign of Elizabeth, but English workmen did not relish the competition of interloping French craftsmen, whatever their religion. Consequently the government of Charles II encouraged Huguenots in England to move to America. After the Revocation of the Edict of Nantes, many more Huguenots emigrated from France. While various colonies received groups of these fleeing Frenchmen, South Carolina proved particularly attractive to them, partly because the climate was mild and partly because the proprietors guaranteed them freedom to worship as they chose. Although the Huguenots probably never amounted to more than one-tenth of the total population, they attained a power and an influence far in excess of their numbers. Their skill in business and various crafts, their diligence, and their thrift, as well as their intellectual and moral qualities, soon gave them particular prominence in the life of the colony.

The freedom and opportunities of South Carolina induced even New Englanders to seek their fortunes in the South. For example, a congregation of Puritans in 1695 settled Dorchester, named after the town of their origin in Massachusetts. To maintain their morale under the softening influence of the South Carolina sun, Cotton Mather supplied them with pamphlets and tracts from his pen. A certain morbid gloom helped them keep their fear of the Puritan Jehovah. Elder William Pratt, for instance, kept a journal in which he enumerated the ills likely to befall saints and sinners alike. "A little after this," he sadly notes on January 3, 1698, "there was many died with the smallpox, that distemper growing more mortal than before, and the 24th day of February following there was a great fire in Charles Town which burnt down a great part of the town, and a few days before the fire there was an earthquake in Charles Town." Though Elder Pratt noted that God in his goodness had answered the prayers of the exiles on the Ashley River and sent "great showers of rain" which "revived the corn," their joy was presently dashed by a great "haurricane."

Like other colonies, South Carolina after about 1715 came to the attention of the Scotch-Irish of Ulster as well as Scots from Scotland. A substantial group of Scotch-Irish in 1732 settled in Williamsburg township, an area on the Black River, with a port of entry on Winyah Bay. These Scots, forerunners of thousands who arrived in the next forty years, helped to push South Carolina settlements inland from the coast. As in Pennsylvania and other colonies they became typical frontiersmen, hardy and determined, who led the vanguard of white conquerors of the great interior wilderness.

French and German Swiss, recruited by Jean Pierre Purry of Neufchatel, an eloquent promoter of emigration to South Carolina, arrived in the autumn of 1732. Purry selected a site on the Savannah River, more than twenty miles from the mouth, and established a township there. Within a year, nearly three hundred Switzers had found a home in this unhealthy locality and were attempting to introduce the growing of silkworms. New recruits took the places of the immigrants who died of malaria and, though the settlement never flourished, it persisted as a southern outpost of the colony. For years it struggled to produce silk and as late as 1772 Purrysburgh exported 445 pounds of raw silk.

Switzers, chiefly German, continued to look to South Carolina as a haven in the 1730's. They were responsible for the settlement of Amelia and Orangeburg townships in the central interior where the upland was better drained and the climate more conducive to health than in the swamplands of the coast. Most of the Germans who came to South Carolina before 1750 were German Swiss, though a few Germans from the Palatinate and the lower Rhineland boarded the immigrant ships which sailed ordinarily from Rotterdam. These German Swiss mingled with English and Scottish pioneers who gradually pushed inland and made the Up Country something more than an Indian hunting ground. Cattle raising and the growing of grain and corn brought a moderate prosperity to the newcomers. The movement toward the Up Country which began in the 1730's gained momentum with increasing immigration until the Piedmont region—the country of rolling hills and red clay subsoil—was dotted with frontier settlements. During the early years, the impenetrable swamps and the hostility of the Indians had served to confine the settlers to the coastal region around Charles Town, but wars of attrition had gradually broken the resistance of the unfriendly tribes and exploration had shown that good land lay beyond the swamps and pine barrens.

The expansion of South Carolina was closely connected with the colony's Indian policy. At first, the Charles Town settlers had been content to maintain a defensive position against the Spaniards and their savage allies, but before long the Carolinians became more active. Within a few years they were competing with the Spaniards and the French for Indian trade in the backcountry of upper South Carolina and what is now Georgia, and English traders soon pushed all the way to the Mississippi and Gulf coast of Alabama.

The pioneer explorer was a surgeon, Dr. Henry Woodward, who had chosen in 1666 to leave Captain Robert Sandford's ship at Port Royal and remain with the Indians to learn their language. He later joined the Charles Town colonists and became an Indian agent for the proprietors and a trader on his own account. Woodward's own interests sometimes conflicted with the colonists', as in 1680 when the Carolinians annihilated or enslaved the Westo Indians, with whom Woodward had a profitable trade. Woodward performed a service of immense importance to South Carolina in opening the eyes of the colonists to the possibilities of traffic with the Indians of the whole southwest.

The Atlantic Frontier

The great rivals of the English traders in the eighteenth century were the French who had established themselves on the lower Mississippi and the Gulf of Mexico. Pierre Le Moyne, Sieur d'Iberville, in 1699 built a fort at Biloxi. In 1702 Jean Baptiste Le Moyne, Sieur de Bienville, founded Mobile and in 1718, New Orleans. Meanwhile other French explorers had come down the Mississippi from the French outposts in the north. From their various bases French *coureurs de bois* pushed up the streams and displayed great talents in making friends with the Indians. Though the Spaniards were not the equal of the French in enterprise, they too remained formidable rivals of the British on the southern frontier, for, despite their evil name in the West Indies, they were fairly easy-going in Florida and made loyal allies of some of the savages.

Though the British were ruthless in their exploitation and showed small talents for diplomacy, they had one great advantage in trade: their blankets, their cloth, their guns, and their powder and shot were more desired by the Indians than anything the French had to offer—and their rum was cheaper than French brandy. The shrewdest of the Indians, however, soon perceived that they could play one nationality against another in the race for trade and empire—a game which the Creeks continued on the Georgia frontier until well after the Revolution. A constant struggle took place for the favor of the powerful tribes and various shifts in alliances occurred in the course of the years. In general the Choctaws remained allies of the French while the Chickasaws were usually in alliance with the British. The Cherokee nation in the mountains and foothills early came into the area of British domination and the Creeks for the most part favored the British.

But at best Indian relations were tricky and uncertain and the trade required courage and skill if the traders were to preserve their business and their lives. From two to three hundred men, many of them hardbitten Scots, were constantly employed by the merchants of Charles Town in the

Indian traffic. During the spring the traders made a rendez-vous in Charles Town. Then the cobblestones echoed with the tramp of their packhorses and the riverside was crowded with their dugouts. They came to receive the annual renewal of their licenses and to obtain a stock of trading goods. In some cases they went out as independent traders; more often they were agents of local merchants. Many of these men stood in some jeopardy of the law and came into Charles Town only upon sufferance. Fearing neither God nor the devil, they were as lawless as they were ruthless and greedy. For many years they brought back strings of Indian captives for the slave markets, along with their packs of deerskins, and the only scruple which they knew was that of prudence in not offending powerful tribes who might seek vengeful retaliation.

Before the end of the seventeenth century, the Charles Town traders had established two great trails to the interior. One ran northwesterly from Charles Town until it reached the mountains and tapped the Cherokee country; another went much farther to the west, beginning near where the modern city of Augusta, Georgia, now stands and stretching to the country of the Chickasaws on the Mississippi. In time other trails, or "paths" as they were called, pushed still farther into the back country until Carolina traders had grown familiar with a vast territory from the southern Appalachian Mountains to the Gulf of Mexico. As the eighteenth century wore on, British tentacles, which reached out from South Carolina in the southwest as they also reached from New York to the northwest, grappled tenaciously with the French in the bitter rivalry for commerce and empire. South Carolina and New York, by their geographical position and their commercial enterprise, were the two colonies with the greatest stake in the outcome of the recurring struggles with France.

Indian warfare, sometimes stirred by savage resentment against white encroachments and cruelty, sometimes fanned by French or Spanish intrigue, frequently flared on the

Carolina borders. During the War of Spanish Succession South Carolinians made several forays against the savage allies of the enemy. Under the leadership of Colonel James Moore, they fell on the Apalache Indians of northern Florida in January 1704 and won a decisive victory over these Spanish Indians. The slaves and plunder from this campaign more than paid the cost. The dream of the Carolinians was to wipe out the French base at Mobile, but in this they never succeeded. A disastrous uprising of the Tuscaroras in 1711 resulted in the massacre of hundreds of North Carolinians and required aid from South Carolina to prevent an even worse debacle.

The most calamitous struggle with the Indians occurred between 1715 and 1718 and is known in South Carolina history as the Yemassee War, after the tribe which bore the brunt of the war with the whites. Many other tribes, however, including the Creeks, and to a small degree, the Cherokees, were involved in this outburst of long smouldering resentment against the lawlessness, the tyranny, and the general knavery of the Carolina traders. Softened by use of the white man's goods, the Indians had given up their traditional crafts and had come to depend upon the traders for weapons, clothing, blankets, and rum. As the red men grew less self-sufficient, the traders became more arrogant and avaricious. Moreover they freely violated the customs and mores of the tribesmen and even made jests of their prowess in debauching the wives of the Indian hunters.

The first fury of Indian vengeance broke out on Good Friday, April 15, 1715, with the slaughter of traders and the destruction of settlements all along the border. Special tortures were visited upon a few. For instance, Captain Thomas Nairne, one of the most active of the Indian agents and a former leader of bands of Yemassee against the Spaniards, was taken at Pocotaligo Town and broiled for several days in a slow fire.

The white inhabitants on many lonely plantations were destroyed in the ensuing warfare and the very life of the colony was threatened. The story ran through the Carolina settlements that the campaign was being cunningly directed by French and Spanish emissaries with the ultimate design of driving the English out of America. Women and children fleeing from the interior flocked into Charles Town. In the crisis Governor Charles Craven proved a vigorous leader and mustered sufficient militia to ward off the danger. To New England he sent fast ships for guns and ammunition and he asked North Carolina and Virginia for immediate reinforcements. The slowness of Virginia's governor, Alexander Spotswood, in responding led to charges that the Virginians were taking advantage of South Carolina's distress to cement a friendship with the Cherokees and other hill country tribes with a view to stealing the business of the Carolina traders. At length the Carolinians won the Cherokees back to their allegiance and succeeded in restoring peace on the borders. The Yemassees and some of the lower Creeks, however, fled for protection to Florida and so augmented the Spanish Indians that they now became a permanent hazard to the peace of the southern frontier. This outbreak of the southern Indians, which temporarily weakened South Carolina, served one constructive purpose. It demonstrated to the Board of Trade in London—and to the other colonies—that relations with the Indians on the frontier constituted an intercolonial and an imperial problem.

During the later years of the seventeenth and the early years of the eighteenth century, when North and South Carolina were gaining in population and economic strength, they enjoyed something less than political peace. Proprietary government, which had never been popular, continued to lose favor in the eyes of the people. Always there was the suspicion that the proprietary governor was intent upon exploiting the populace in the interest of his masters. As the original board of eight proprietors passed from the scene, their places were taken by heirs who had little knowledge of colonial affairs, or their shares were purchased by speculators concerned entirely with quitrents and other emoluments. The proprietors were soon a diverse lot of gentry, businessmen, and adventurers, some of whom used their prerogatives as proprietors to serve as governors.

North Carolina was especially turbulent and restive under proprietary rule. To a frontier population without much respect for law at best, any special diligence in the collection of customs and quitrents or the enforcement of the Navigation Acts looked like tyranny and was liable to evoke a storm of disapproval and complaint. An open rebellion occurred in 1677, shortly after Virginia had been rent by the Bacon Rebellion. The North Carolinians refused to accept a governor and officials appointed by the proprietors and set up a revolutionary government under an old settler named George Durant. When the tangled controversy finally reached the Privy Council in London, the proprietors admitted their mistakes and promised to do better next time.

Their idea of improvement was the appointment as governor of one Seth Sothell, who had bought the Earl of Clarendon's proprietary interest. Though Sothell was captured by Algerine pirates on his way to take office, he at length was ransomed and reached Albemarle in 1683. The only skill he displayed was in lining his own pockets. Finally in 1689 when revolts were sweeping other colonies, a group of rebels seized Sothell on his plantation, jailed him in a convenient log house, and exacted an oath that he would depart the colony. He transferred his operations to South Carolina where he ruled as governor for about a year, when the proprietary office in London appointed Colonel Philip Ludwell of Virginia as governor of both North and South Carolina. Ludwell had the advantage of first-hand knowledge of the colonies. He was also the husband of the widow of Sir William Berkeley, one of the original proprietors, whose share of Carolina, however, had been purchased by a Quaker, John Archdale. Though Ludwell as an aristocratic Virginian had small respect for his North Carolina constituents, he at least managed to keep them at peace. But it was too much to expect that a Virginian of Ludwell's ineptness would long please the contentious Carolinians, North or South. When Ludwell resigned in 1693, Landgrave Thomas Smith tried his hand at governing, with no greater success. Finally the proprietors decided once more to appoint one of their own number, this time the Quaker John Archdale, who assumed the governorship in August 1695. Archdale demonstrated what a man of character and intelligence could do. He approved a more favorable land law which helped to settle complicated questions concerning tenure and quitrents; he called for a new election for members of the legislative assembly and approved many laws which the people had been demanding. When after a year in office he thought he had "settled" the government, he resigned in favor of Joseph Blake, who about this time acquired a proprietorship.

Blake, who ruled four years (1696–1700), had a greater vision than his predecessors of South Carolina's destiny as part of the nascent British Empire and was intent upon pushing the Indian trade and thwarting the Spaniards and the French. His successors, James Moore (1700–1703) and Sir Nathaniel Johnson (1703–1708) were equally interested in trade and fighting the country's enemies. But they and successive proprietary governors managed to become embroiled in bitter internal quarrels and feuds.

Religion, as everywhere in colonial America, was an issue richly productive of political confusion. The two Carolinas because of the many sects who had been induced to settle within their borders, could not escape religious rows. Though the proprietors had promised religious toleration, they had left a loophole for the establishment of the Church of England. In both North and South Carolina, church parties became active in the early eighteenth century, Anglicans in North Carolina, despite the bitter animosity of Quakers and other dissenting folk, pushed an act through the assembly in 1701 for the appointment of vestrymen and the organization of Anglican churches, but not until 1715 did they succeed in having the Church of England established officially with support from public funds. In South

Carolina, the Anglicans, who constituted a scant half of the population, contrived to pass an act in 1704 excluding all except communicants of the Church of England from the legislative assembly, but this law was disallowed by the proprietors on complaint of the Board of Trade. In 1706, however, the Anglicans managed to enact a law, which was approved, establishing the Church of England.

Surprisingly the South Carolina Anglicans won over the Calvinistic Huguenots, who might have been expected to join the most numerous dissenting sect in the colony, the Presbyterians. But the French saw the advantage of joining the church supported by public taxation; furthermore, the Anglicans in the Charles Town region, among whom most of the Huguenots had settled, made more of an effort to win their friendship and support than did the stiff-backed Presbyterians, many of whom were Scotch-Irish with an inherent dislike of the French. In time the Huguenots lost their religious identity and many of South Carolina's more distinguished Episcopal ministers were French in origin. The Established Church in South Carolina achieved great political and social influence, an influence which lasted long past the colonial period.

The establishment of a state church, however, was not accomplished without a tremendous amount of ill feeling. On the frontiers, the Presbyterians, the Baptists, and a scattering of New England Congregationalists made up a strong element suspicious of the Anglicans and always hostile to their political control. In the long years ahead, the Up Country dissenters, representing small farmers and artisans, would exert a powerful lever against the Low Country aristocracy of Episcopalians, who counted among their members most of the great planters, wealthy merchants, and professional men.

The Anglicans in North Carolina were less successful. Though the law of 1701 had theoretically provided for the erection of parishes and churches, little or nothing was actually accomplished, even after the official establishment of the

Church of England in 1715. The Reverend John Blair, who was sent to the province in 1704 by the Society for the Propagation of the Gospel, found no support and departed. "The country," he reported, "may be divided into four sorts of people: first, the Quakers, who are the most powerful enemies to Church government, but a people very ignorant of what they profess. The second sort are a great many who have no religion, but would be Quakers, if by that they were not obliged to lead a more moral life than they are willing to comply to. A third sort are something like Presbyterians, which sort is upheld by some idle fellows who have left their lawful employment and preach and baptize through the country, without any manner of orders from any sect or pretended Church. A fourth sort, who are really zealous for the interest of the Church, are the fewest in number but the better sort of people and would do very much for the settlement of the Church government there if not opposed by these three precedent sects; and although they be all three of different pretensions, yet they all concur together in one common cause to prevent anything that will be chargeable to them, as they allege Church government will be, if once established by law." Though jaundiced by his own unfavorable experience among the North Carolinians, Blair's description was essentially correct and was confirmed by other observers. Not until after 1732 was there a regular minister of the Church of England in the province of North Carolina. "They account it among their greatest advantages that they are not priest-ridden," William Byrd commented in 1728, "not remembering that the clergy is rarely guilty of bestriding such as have the misfortune to be poor." And of Edenton, the capital of the colony, Byrd observed: "I believe this is the only metropolis in the Christian or Mahometan world where there is neither church, chapel, mosque, synagogue, or any other place of public worship of any sect of religion whatsoever."

The sentiment against the proprietary authority received a new impetus as a result of the machinations to bring about the establishment of the Church of England in both North and South Carolina, but the religious issue was only one of many grievances against the proprietors. They were charged with encouraging the monopoly of trade by privileged favorites, with oppressive exactions of rents and duties, with general neglect of the colonies, and particularly with failure to provide adequate protection against external enemies. The South Carolinians were the first to rebel.

A report of an impending invasion of Spaniards from Havana disturbed South Carolina in the autumn of 1719. Already angry because of a wrangle with the proprietors over various complicated legal rights, the South Carolinians in November declared themselves independent of the proprietary authority; a convention meeting on December 21 then chose James Moore temporary governor and invited the English government to take possession. The Board of Trade, which for years had looked forward to the elimination of the proprietors, was delighted, and on its recommendation, the crown appointed Francis Nicholson, sometime governor of New York, Maryland, and Virginia, as the first royal governor of South Carolina. Nicholson reached Charles Town on May 29, 1721 and was acclaimed with a great fanfare.

North Carolina remained under proprietary rule several years longer, though the royal government began to tighten its controls. Finally in 1729, the charter under which the proprietors had ruled the two Carolinas was annulled and North Carolina also became a crown colony. Although the annulment of the charter eliminated the proprietary right to the government of the Carolinas, the proprietors still held title to the land but the British government took steps to cancel this too. For seven of the original eight shares the treasury paid £2,500 each; Lord Carteret, however, declined to sell his share and continued a vain struggle to collect an eighth of the quitrents.

By the time South Carolina became a royal province, it had developed a stable society in the tidewater country with

Charles Town as its social and political center. Before 1750 Charles Town would take its place with Boston, New York, and Philadelphia as one of the greatest ports in the colonies. Among its inhabitants were to be found a variety of skilled craftsmen equalled in few other towns; its leaders were the great merchants and planters who composed an aristocracy already beginning to display a modest glitter.

The South Carolina aristocracy of the early eighteenth century, like the aristocracy of Virginia, was generally self-made and was based upon created wealth and recently acquired land rather than upon inherited position. A few South Carolina families claimed the coat armor of established English families, but most such claims were tenuous at best. Many South Carolina families got off to a good start because their ancestors brought enough initial capital from Barbados or elsewhere to buy substantial tracts of land or to set up as merchants.

The early aristocracy had no reason to despise the market place, and there is little evidence that it did. The contempt for trade, which characterized the later landed gentry, was most noticeable in the nineteenth century when the planter class was becoming decadent. Such an attitude would have provoked surprise and scorn among the ruling class in Charles Town in the early eighteenth century. The ancestors of the nineteenth century grandees were an enterprising group troubled by few scruples to check their acquisitive instincts. The traffic in slaves, Indian or Negro, the selling of rum and guns to the Indians, the employment of known criminals as Indian traders—all these practices were a part of the normal business life of Charles Town. As merchants got rich they invested their profits in plantations until the landed and commercial "gentry" were usually indistinguishable. With the acquisition of wealth, families assumed coats of arms, or bought them from the College of Heralds in London, and developed the characteristics and manners of an aristocracy.

The rise of the Manigaults to positions of eminence provides an instructive example of the evolution of the South Carolina aristocracy. About 1695 two Huguenot refugees, Pierre and Gabriel Manigault, arrived in Charles Town. They had a little money and Gabriel even had a Negro slave named Sambo. While plying his trade of carpenter Gabriel fell off a scaffold and died of his injury. Pierre had better luck. He tried farming on the Santee but found the keeping of a victualing house in town more to his liking. In 1699 he married Judith Giton, widow of Noe Royer, herself a heroic soul who had helped her first husband work in the fields, fell trees, and saw lumber. Pierre and Judith prospered. Presently Pierre branched out and erected a distillery and a woodshop for the making of barrels. Before long he had a second distillery and was building a warehouse and store on the docks of Charles Town. At his death in 1729 he was a well-to-do merchant, the owner of slaves and land as well as stores and warehouses. His son Gabriel added lustre to the name and became the wealthiest man in South Carolina, a planter, a merchant, a money-lender, a slave-trader—and an aristocrat and a patron of the arts. His son Peter, born in 1731, received a classical education, acquired legal knowledge in London at the Inner Temple, made the grand tour of Europe, and came back to South Carolina to practice law. As a matter of course he took his place in the legislative assembly, became Speaker of the House, and otherwise served the commonwealth as a loyal patriot. Pierre and Judith Manigault, the founders of the dynasty, succeeded beyond their dreams, for by diligence, thrift, shrewdness, and sheer character they established a family which intermarried with the best names in South Carolina and contributed for many generations to the advancement of the colony and state.

Prosperous families from the West Indies were an important element in the development of the South Carolina aristocracy. Few individuals contributed more than Eliza Lucas, the daughter of George Lucas, the well-to-do governor of Antigua, who brought his family to South Carolina in 1738 and became the possessor of three plantations. When duty called her father away in 1739, Eliza at the age of seventeen was left to manage the South Carolina estates from the home plantation, "Wappoo," near Charles Town. To the efforts and experiments of this girl, South Carolina owed the advancement of indigo culture. Soon after the colony was settled, indigo was planted but it did not become a profitable commodity until its cultivation was revived by Eliza Lucas. From 1750 until the Revolution it was second only to rice as a money crop in the Low Country. In the eyes of South Carolinians, however, Eliza Lucas performed a still greater service to the commonwealth, for she married Charles Pinckney, later chief justice of the colony, and became the mother of Charles Cotesworth and Thomas Pinckney who played such conspicuous parts in the Revolution.

As Charles Town grew richer in the eighteenth century, it became more nearly a replica-in-little of Augustan London than any other American city. Though by 1742, its population amounted to only 6,800, half of whom were slaves, it was the fourth largest city in the colonies and the per capita wealth of its citizens was the greatest in North America. Like Paris, Charles Town dominated the country of which it was the capital and set the fashions for aristocratic imitation elsewhere in the South. So prosperous and so extravagant had the citizens of the metropolis become by 1749 that Governor James Glen in that year expressed the fear to the Board of Trade that their love of luxury, like that of the ancient Romans, would be their ruin.

The Charlestonians, however, made good use of their wealth. Taking the *beau monde* of London as their model, they imitated English fashions and manners with the zeal of all self-conscious social aspirants. Like provincial society-on-the-make everywhere, the Charlestonians outdid their models and developed a greater punctiliousness in manners than London society in the same period could boast. By the mid-century, the Low Country aristocracy was beginning to take on the gloss of an established gentility and could display as much polish and cultivation as Englishmen anywhere. Within another decade or two, South Carolina planters were already making a profession of being genteel in the manner of the English upper class. Indeed, many of them had been "finished" in English schools or the Inns of Court.

The planter-aristocrats of Virginia and South Carolina have been often compared and the pride of both became a byword. The description of lowly North Carolina as the valley of humiliation between two mountains of conceit, Virginia and South Carolina, is traditional. But the two aristocracies were significantly different. The Virginia planters, living in relative isolation, were more nearly imitative of the English county families. Furthermore, their inheritance of ideology from the early seventeenth century gave them a traceable connection with the great tradition of the English Renaissance that was less apparent in South Carolina. The South Carolina planter-aristocrats were a far more compact society than their counterparts in Virginia. They also were more urban in characteristics. Though they might live during most of the winter months on their river plantations, they gathered together in Charles Town for definite social seasons and enjoyed the benefits of a cultivated city life. Instead of Renaissance thought, South Carolinians found the essays and admonitions of Addison and Steele congenial to their tastes. Instead of reflecting old-fashioned notions of the obligations and responsibilities of the country gentleman as revealed in the seventeenth-century treatises of Peacham and Brathwaite, South Carolinians imitated the urbane life of Pope's London.

Education in South Carolina during the colonial period remained a problem which the individual family had to solve as best it could. The well-to-do depended upon governesses and tutors; the poor did without much schooling, or learned the rudiments of reading, writing, and arithmetic from their parents or in makeshift schools taught by preachers and itinerant school teachers. No serious effort was made to establish a college or other institution of higher learning.

Wealthy families sometimes went to England or the Continent for long periods while their children attended school.

In some fashion, the majority of white South Carolinians escaped complete illiteracy, though the missionaries of the Society for the Propagation of the Gospel reported shocking ignorance. The Society's efforts resulted in aid to several schools; in 1711 it sent over a master to conduct a school at Goose Creek, and it had general supervision for many years of the Charles Town Free School, founded early in the eighteenth century. This institution provided the traditional grammar school education with a strong infusion of Anglican religion which was distasteful to Presbyterians and other dissenters. Though a so-called Free School Act had passed the assembly in 1712, it provided for the training of only a dozen pupils at public expense. A few bequests sought to remedy the lack of schools. Richard Berresford, a planter, left £6,500 to the vestry of the parish of St. Denis and St. Thomas for the education of poor children—a foundation which has remained in existence. An Anglican minister, the Reverend Richard Ludlam, left a smaller estate in 1728 for a similar purpose. When James Childs in 1733 left £600 for a school at Childsbury, the inhabitants subscribed enough to make the sum £2,200. The citizens of Dorchester procured the passage of an act in 1733 establishing an elementary school with a further provision for the teaching of Latin and Greek since they found it inconvenient to send their children to the Charles Town Free School.

Although the back country was without formal schools of any consequence the stubborn Scotch-Irish and other dissenters managed to transmit to their children the elements of learning. Not even on the rawest frontier was literacy completely forgotten.

Educational opportunities in North Carolina were even more limited than in South Carolina. An occasional missionary of the Society for the Propagation of the Gospel, an earnest Scotch Presbyterian minister, or some private teacher tried to instruct the children of his community, but organized schools had to wait until after the mid-eighteenth century. Governor Gabriel Johnson, himself a graduate of St. Andrews, exhorted the assembly in 1734 and again in 1736 to do something for education, but all he obtained was pious agreement about "the general neglect in point of education." Finally, in 1749, the assembly passed an act providing for the erection of a schoolhouse in Edenton.

Dr. Thomas Bray's efforts to provide books for the Anglican clergy resulted in the first public libraries in the Carolinas. In 1698 he sent to Charles Town a shipment of books which became the nucleus of a provincial library designed for the use of both clergy and laymen. The assembly in 1700 passed an act "for securing the provincial library at Charles Town" and three years later Dr. Bray supplemented the collection with another gift of books. Chief Justice Nicholas Trott, himself a learned man, interested himself in the library as did other Charlestonians, but by 1724 it seems to have disappeared. Bray established smaller parochial libraries in South Carolina and sent one collection of books to Bath, North Carolina, but since that community lacked a regular clergyman, the library was neglected. Edward Moseley, a North Carolinian, in 1725, gave his personal library of more than sixty titles to the Society for the Propagation of the Gospel to found a provincial library at Edenton.

The first library to remain in existence was the Charles Town Library Society, founded in 1748 with seventeen members. Within two years its membership had grown to one hundred and thirty subscribers and it had begun a long and useful career as the focus of intellectual activity in the community. Charlestonians showed considerable interest in the collection of books and brought together substantial private libraries. They imported books directly from London or bought them from local booksellers, several of whom had opened shops before 1750.

The first newspaper in the Carolinas was the *South Carolina Gazette* founded in 1732 by Thomas Whitmarsh, who had learned his craft from Benjamin Franklin. When Whitmarsh died a year later, Louis Timothée, or Lewis Timothy as he Anglicized his name, continued the printing business and newspaper. Timothy was another of Franklin's apprentices. The *Gazette* not only printed news but provided an outlet for the literary efforts of local writers. Essays in imitation of the *Spectator*, verses in heroic couplets inspired by Pope, and serious articles on indigo, silkworms, or the yellow fever found a place in its pages. South Carolinians produced no great literature but they proved themselves intelligently interested in letters.

Music and painting had their patrons in early Charles Town. Although the St. Cecilia Society—the oldest musical society in British America—was not founded until 1762, long before this time Charles Town was accustomed to concerts of instrumental and vocal music. Musicians and teachers of music were numerous. Portrait painters found the wealthy planters and merchants of Charles Town worthy subjects of their craft. The first artist of whom there is definite record was Henrietta Johnson, who painted the portraits of many Charlestonians between 1708 and 1729. Best known of the early painters was Jeremiah Theus, a German artist, who advertised in 1740 that he was ready to do portraits and landscapes of all sizes, as well as "crests and coats of arms for coaches and chaises."

Next to balls and cotillions the theater was the favorite amusement of fashionable Charles Town. A wandering English actor, Tony Aston, appeared as early as 1703, but the theater proper dates from 1735. In that year, after witnessing a successful performance of Otway's *The Orphan*, a group of gentlemen underwrote the building of a theater in Queen's Street, which opened the following year with Farquhar's *The Recruiting Officer*. After this time stage players regarded Charles Town with special affection, for they were certain of a more cordial welcome than in other colonial cities. Pleasure-loving Charlestonians, less strict than Bostonians and less thrifty than Philadelphians, accorded special favors to all those who practiced the arts of entertainment.

The Atlantic Frontier

By the middle of the eighteenth century, Charles Town had become a sophisticated city with many of the attributes, good and bad, of London which it imitated. For generations this cultivation continued to be the monopoly of the Low Country aristocracy. The plain people of the hinterland went their own way, developed their own customs and mores, and in time developed a proud dislike of the coastal region's dandified society. The Low Country retorted with an axiom of its own authorship that "no gentleman was ever born above tidewater." As the years went on, the Piedmont acquired more schooling and cultivation, but the chasm which separated the Up Country from the Low Country was wider than the swamps and pine barrens which physically divided them.

Though South Carolina had grown rich and prosperous by the 1730's, it had not succeeded in protecting its southern flank against the Spaniards. Always the threat of invasion from St. Augustine disturbed the sleep of wealthy planters of the South Carolina coast. For that reason, the South Carolinians had welcomed various projects for settling the frontier region west of the Savannah River.

For nearly fifty years the border country had appealed to the imaginations of promoters and dreamers, many of them Scots. As early as 1684 Henry Lord Cardross had actually begun a refuge for Scotch Covenanters at Port Royal, but his settlement, which he had named Stuart's Town, was destroyed by the Spaniards two years later.

Wider in scope was the project of Sir Robert Montgomery of Skelmorly who hatched in his fertile mind a scheme for restoring the earthly paradise in the Margravate of Azilia, a territory between the Savannah and the Altamaha rivers, which the proprietors of Carolina actually granted him in 1717. As associates this visionary Scot had a poet and dramatist, Aaron Hill, and a politician, Amos Kettleby.

Montgomery—probably with the help of the poet Hill—outdid himself in advertising Azilia, later to be known as Georgia. In a pamphlet entitled a *Discourse Concerning the*

Southern Spearheads of Trade

Designed Establishment of a New Colony to the South of Carolina in the Most Delightful Country of the Universe, the noble author boldly declared of Azilia that "Paradise with all her virgin beauties may be modestly supposed at most but equal to its native excellencies." In this celestial land he proposed to set up a feudal aristocracy who would enrich themselves and the British state with the produce of their semitropical plantations: dates, figs, olives, currants, almonds, coffee, silk, and sundry other exotic commodities. When rhetoric failed to enlist enough settlers, the Scot sold out to the poet and the project died.

Still another Scot contrived a plan for the protection and population of the Carolina frontier. He was Sir Alexander Cuming of Coulter, an erratic baronet, who reached Charles Town in 1729 and in the following year went on a self-appointed mission to pledge the Cherokee Indians to allegiance to the Great King, George II. He also conceived a project to settle three hundred thousand Jews in the Cherokee country, but the Indians did not grasp the full significance of his plans when they met him at Keowee and swore allegiance to King George. Cuming succeeded in persuading six Cherokees to go to England with him, and on his way back to Charles Town, he picked up a seventh Indian. Cuming and his Cherokee "chiefs" reached London in the summer of 1730 and created a sensation, but nothing came of his projects.

The ultimate settlement of Georgia was the result of several movements, philanthropic, commercial, and political, which converged about 1730. The scheme for this border colony was a curious medley of utopian idealism, hardheaded mercantilism, and resurgent imperialism.

As a part of a new spirit of humanitarianism sweeping England, influential philanthropists had become interested in the relief of thousands of debtors who through misfortune had gone to prison and seemed destined to languish there. If these debtors could be released and given an opportunity for honest work, they might reclaim themselves, pay their

[293]

creditors, and become a national asset. Among those who interested themselves in the debtors' plight were Viscount Percival, afterward the Earl of Egmont, and General James Oglethorpe, a veteran of the War of Spanish Succession and a member of Parliament. An organization known as the Associates of the late Dr. Bray—named in honor of that notable doer of good works, Dr. Thomas Bray, who died in 1730—was also eager to do something for the debtors.

A discussion between Oglethorpe and his friend, Viscount Percival, one of the Bray Associates, resulted in a plan to send distressed debtors to a colony in America. Probably remembering Sir Robert Montgomery's grandiloquent description of the earthly paradise of Azilia, the Bray Associates petitioned the crown for this territory, and on June 9, 1732 they received a charter granting their wish. A little later Parliament appropriated money for the enterprise with a generosity which would have startled the founding fathers of the older colonies.

The charter differed from any ever given an American colony. It placed in the hands of twenty-one named Trustees the entire management of a colony situated between the Savannah and the Altamaha rivers to their headwaters and stretching from there to the Great South Sea—that is to say, to the Pacific Ocean. The charter provided that after twenty-one years, or in 1753, the colony should revert to the crown. Any laws made by the Trustees, who were given complete authority, had to be approved by the British government. In practice the Trustees got around this single curb by making only three laws during their regime and ruling instead by "regulations." From their number the Trustees appointed a smaller executive committee who carried out their policies. No one bore the title of governor.

News of the impending settlement of Georgia, named in honor of the sovereign, aroused enormous interest among all classes. The clergy took Georgia to its heart. Their sermons extolled the enterprise and their collections of money, goods, and pious books were designed to further the colony's material and spiritual welfare. No American colony was ever supplied with such vast quantities of uplifting reading matter. The merchants of London and promoters began to talk of the commercial possibilities of the new country. Here at last would be the happy home, not only of the indigent unemployed, but also of the silkworm, which had hitherto resisted naturalization in the British colonies. Silk from Georgia would serve to keep within the empire £500,000 a year, the average annual bill for silk which Britain paid to foreign countries. According to the economics of that day, such a drain upon the nation ought to be stopped. Georgia would perform that service to the joy of all mercantilists. The planting of mulberry trees to feed silkworms, therefore, was enjoined upon all who received land from the Trustees. The empire builders within the government also looked upon Georgia with special favor, for it constituted one more outpost against Spain and France.

Since Georgia would be a military district on the very borders of Spanish Florida, the Trustees persuaded General Oglethorpe, one of their number, to take personal charge of the colony and to accompany the first shipload of settlers, who reached Charles Town in January 1733. Governor William Bull of South Carolina gave them a cordial welcome and accompanied them on the remainder of their voyage to Georgia. Oglethorpe sailed about eighteen miles up the Savannah River and chose a bluff as the site of his town, which he called Savannah. To honor South Carolina's hospitable governor, he named a principal thoroughfare Bull Street.

By good fortune Oglethorpe won the friendship of the Creek Indians and, like William Penn, made satisfactory agreements with them for the purchase of land needed by the settlers. He also obtained from the Creeks a pledge of their alliance in case of war.

Within a few years Georgia had become a haven of distressed people and of others who came simply because they were attracted by the good reports of this promised land. Among the early arrivals were German Lutherans from

Salzburg in Austria, fleeing from religious persecutions. They finally settled in 1736 at Red Bluff on the Savannah River and called their town Ebenezer. Moravians who arrived the next year added to the German population, but since they were pacifists and were disturbed by the troubled relations with the Spanish, they migrated to Pennsylvania in 1740. More useful as potential soldiers were Scotch Highlanders who began coming to Georgia in 1735. Oglethorpe saw to it that they settled close to the Florida border where they would be serviceable when war broke out. A few Italians from Piedmont, as well as a few Swiss, were brought over to teach the art of silk culture. In 1733, about forty Jews arrived, somewhat to the embarrassment of the Trustees, who had intended their paradise to be free of Jews and Catholics. But the Jews were permitted to remain, and before long Georgia even had a sprinkling of Catholics. No one was persecuted for his religion and anyone could obtain as much as fifty acres of land.

The original plan of the Trustees provided that each indigent person coming to Georgia on the bounty of the Trust should receive fifty acres of land for a life tenure. The tenant was required to clear ten acres and to plant at least one hundred mulberry trees. After ten years he would pay to the Trustees a quitrent of two shillings an acre. A modification of the regulations permitted the eldest son to inherit the fifty acre tract, but land left without a male heir reverted to the Trustees, who paid the family for buildings and other improvements. Persons who came to Georgia at their own expense might also receive land at the rate of fifty acres for each white adult in the household, but the total grant could not exceed five hundred acres. These "adventurers," as they were called, had to undertake to plant one thousand mulberry trees on each one hundred acres and to pay twenty shillings quitrent per hundred acres after ten years.

Lest the inhabitants settle in haphazard fashion, the Trustees provided for carefully planned villages within which each family should have its town lot and garden with the main farm nearby. This traditional plan, inherited from the Middle Ages, which New Englanders had already adopted, insured compact communities adapted for defense, for Georgia was frankly designed as a defensive outpost and not even the most ardent humanitarians among the Trustees were allowed to forget that.

As a means of helping the debtors regain their economic independence and self-respect, the Trustees insured them against unfair competition by forbidding Negro slavery. Oglethorpe, who was a director of the Royal African Company, of course had no humanitarian objections to slavery but he thought slaveholding incompatible with the Georgia experiment in the rehabilitation of white indigents. The Trustees also forbade the importation or manufacture of rum and brandy. Both of these regulations quickly became exceedingly unpopular, for the Georgians demanded the right to drink what they pleased and to own Negro slaves as did their neighbors in South Carolina.

The Georgian Utopia attracted reformers and idealists, some of whom soon lost their illusions. Among the preachers who came as missionaries to the colony were John Wesley, the founder of Methodism, and his brother Charles, who had accepted a post as secretary to Oglethorpe. They reached Savannah in February, 1736, but within a week Charles had quarreled with his employer and with other Georgians, and had declared himself unwilling to stay longer in the swampy paradise. In less than three months he departed. John Wesley stayed long enough to become involved in a love affair with Sophia Hopkey, an adoring parishioner. Troubled in spirit, he sought the counsel of friendly Moravians, who advised him to give up the girl. She promptly married William Williamson. When Wesley was so unwise as to reprove her for behavior which he did not condone, her husband sued him for defamation of his wife's character, and Wesley in December 1737 was obliged to flee to Charles Town. From there he too returned to London.

[297]

The Atlantic Frontier

George Whitefield, one of Wesley's followers and a magnetic preacher, set out for Georgia just as Wesley arrived in England. His mission was more successful than the Wesleys'. With the cooperation of a successful merchant, James Habersham, he founded a school and orphanage at Bethesda, near Savannah. For years afterward Whitefield preached throughout the American colonies and took up collections for his beloved orphanage, which he sought unsuccessfully in 1764 to convert into a college. A part of the support for the orphanage came from a South Carolina plantation which Whitefield owned and operated profitably with slave labor.

While various preachers were trying to mold Georgia into a godly commonwealth, a strange German from Saxony, one Christian Gottlieb Priber, sought to establish among the Cherokees on the headwaters of the Tennessee River another kind of Utopia modelled in part after Plato's *Republic*. A precursor of Rousseau, Priber evolved a scheme representing a fusion of classical theory, the current doctrines of humanitarianism, and ideas of the noble savage which were already in the air. Arriving in Charles Town in 1735, he sold most of his personal possessions and made his way into the Cherokee country on the South Carolina-Georgia border. There he won the friendship of the Cherokees, adopted Indian dress, and set about organizing the tribesmen into a communistic state which would resist the inroads of white interlopers and protect its citizens against the knavery of traders. When news of this revolutionary procedure reached Charles Town and Savannah, the authorities of both colonies determined to extirpate his heresy, which was likely to impair their trade with the Indians. The Georgians finally succeeded in 1743 in arresting Priber whom they kept as a political prisoner in the fortress of Frederica on St. Simon's Island until his death a few years later. When captured, Priber had with him a manuscript dictionary of the Cherokee language and another manuscript in which he described his projected Utopian state, the "Kingdom of Paradise." This latter book, in the opinion of his examiners, was "extremely wicked" because "he enumerates many whimsical privileges and natural rights, as he calls them, which his citizens are to be entitled to, particularly dissolving marriages and allowing community of women, and all kinds of licentiousness." His greatest sin, however, lay in his success in winning the friendship of the Indians and developing an organization which threatened the imperialistic expansion of the British.

The long threatened war with the Spaniards in Florida broke out in 1739. The immediate cause, which gave to the conflict the whimsical name of the War of Jenkins' Ear, was the capture by the Spaniards off the coast of Florida of a British smuggler named Thomas Jenkins. When the Spaniards cut off his ears and told him to take them home to his masters, public opinion in Great Britain and the colonies flamed against Spain. General Oglethorpe led a joint expedition of Georgians and South Carolinians in an unsuccessful siege of St. Augustine, which produced nothing more tangible than a controversy between the two colonies over the conduct of the campaign. When Oglethorpe withdrew from Florida, the Spaniards threatened for a time the destruction of Georgia, but Oglethorpe managed to rally sufficient forces to defeat the enemy in a bloody ambush on St. Simon's Island in July 1742. The Spaniards retired to St. Augustine and refused to come out and fight when Oglethorpe went pounding at their doors the next year. The War of Jenkins' Ear thus came to an end without deciding anything. The Spaniards, however, were no longer belligerent.

Soon after his last foray against St. Augustine, Oglethorpe, in 1743, returned to England and left Georgia in charge of one William Horton. Although he had not borne the title of governor, as the local representative of the Trustees, he had exercised the power of a governor. The Trustees, as the supreme authority, had made no provision for representative government of the people. Presumably the Trustees' wishes would be conveyed to the inhabitants through a court comprised of three bailiffs and a recorder. Their patriarchal commonwealth was without any law-making machinery and was intended to remain "free from that pest and scourge of mankind called lawyers." The Georgians were far from happy over this arrangement and some of them made bitter complaints against Oglethorpe and certain other officials, particularly the bailiff Thomas Causton, who was charged with tyranny and with exacting exorbitant prices for goods furnished by the Trustees.

Dissatisfaction with Oglethorpe and his *de facto* regime was responsible for one of the few pieces of urbane literature produced in colonial Georgia. From the press of Peter Timothy in Charles Town appeared in 1741 *A True and Historical Narrative of the Colony of Georgia in America*, written by Patrick Tailfer, M.D., Hugh Anderson, M.A., David Douglas, "and others, land-holders in Georgia, at present in Charles Town in South Carolina." The authors were malcontents who had fled to the neighboring colony to escape the wrath of the Trustees' agents. Their book bore a long mock dedication to Oglethorpe in the satirical spirit of Jonathan Swift. After mentioning the privileges and prosperity of other colonies, the authors observed that "your Excellency's concern for our perpetual welfare could never permit you to propose such transitory advantages for us. You considered riches like a divine and philosopher as the *irritamenta malorum* and knew that they were disposed to inflate weak minds with pride, to pamper the body with luxury, and introduce a long variety of evils. Thus have you 'protected us from ourselves' as Mr. Waller says, by keeping all earthly comforts from us. You have afforded us the opportunity of arriving at the integrity of the primitive times by entailing a more than primitive poverty on us."

Most Georgians agreed that the prohibition against slavery and the restriction preventing the outright ownership of land were grievous injustices which retarded the colony's growth. Only a few Germans and Scottish Highlanders approved the Trustees' injunction against slavery. When Whitefield and the leaders of the Germans recommended that slavery be permitted, the Trustees in 1749 finally weakened and allowed the introduction of African labor. A year later the Trustees also approved the ownership of land in fee simple. The rule forbidding rum had long been disregarded and the Trustees in 1742 had legalized its importation.

With rum to qualify their drinking water, with African slaves to do their work, and with land to own and pass on to their children, such Georgians as remained in the colony by 1750 had only their peculiar government—or the lack of one —to complain of. That too would soon change. Under the charter the colony would automatically revert to the King in 1753, but a year before that time the Trustees voluntarily relinquished their rights. For three years longer, however, they had to govern the remnants of the colony until the British government finally took control in 1755 with the appointment of a naval captain, John Reynolds, as the first royal governor. As in the other colonies, a legislative assembly was established and was soon busy making laws and quarreling with the King's authorities.

As an experiment in achieving a Utopia for distressed debtors, Georgia had proved a rank failure, but as an outpost of empire it had at least survived. Only about fifteen hundred English debtors sought asylum in Georgia on the charity of the Trustees. Many of these eventually departed. When the colony became a royal province the population numbered about 2,000 whites and 1,000 Negro slaves. The hopeful silk industry, despite the best efforts of the Germans and the Swiss, had failed, as had all the other schemes for exotic products. Henceforth Georgia would develop in the manner of South Carolina by growing rice in the swamp lands, producing naval stores, and stimulating the Indian trade. As the southernmost border colony, Georgia occupied a position whose strategic importance to the British Empire increased during the conflicts of the mid-eighteenth century.

CHAPTER SEVEN

The Colonies Come of Age

THE seventeenth century was an era of experimentation, of trial and error, in the settlement of British America. An infinite variety of motives had inspired the promoters of colonial schemes as well as the venturesome souls who made up the emigrants to the New World. Neither in England nor in America did anyone worry about unity of purpose or objectives. "The settlement of our colonies was never pursued upon any regular plan," Edmund Burke observed in 1757, "but they were formed, grew, and flourished as accidents, the nature of the climate, or the dispositions of private men happened to operate." Like a house to which successive owners of varying tastes had added rooms and turrets, an empire of odd-shaped parts had simply grown by accretion. By the early years of the eighteenth century, Great Britain had become, almost unconsciously, an imperial power in America with a loose and broken string of colonies along the Atlantic coast from French Canada to Barbados in the Caribbean.

Except for a confirmed mercantilist view that colonies should supply the mother country with raw materials and must not compete in manufacturing, Great Britain had as yet formulated no consistent theory or policy of empire, nor had the colonies come to think of themselves as parts of a unified whole. But new ideas were germinating on both sides of the Atlantic as the seventeenth century drew to a close, and speculation concerning the relations between the colonies

The Colonies Come of Age

and the parent nation would occupy the attention of many thinkers in the succeeding decades.

The War of the League of Augsburg, known in America as King William's War, which ended with the Peace of Ryswick in 1697—the first of the dynastic wars which involved Europe and America—opened the eyes of the British colonies to the need for mutual protection. This struggle also gave Englishmen a perception of a new role in world politics in which their American possessions would play an important part. Upon the anvil of successive wars in the eighteenth century, Great Britain hammered out an imperial policy. The American colonies also shaped themselves—or were shaped by Britain—into some semblance of a related group. Although in the early eighteenth century the colonies thought of themselves as individual governments having only a modest obligation to the authorities in London, some faint stirrings in the direction of unity were already discernible. In London, the Board of Trade set out to organize the colonies more coherently and to strengthen Whitehall's control in America.

The several British colonies in 1700 differed vastly in population, economic development, and cultural attainments. Virginia and Massachusetts were the oldest and the most populous colonies, with long years of self-government behind them. They were assured and prosperous. Virginia with its wealthy tobacco planters and Massachusetts with a growing body of thrifty merchants who traded with the ends of the earth had well-established family dynasties who by this time had attained a vested interest in governing their respective commonwealths. In similar fashion all the older colonies —Maryland, Connecticut, Rhode Island, and New York— had attained stability and a certain degree of maturity. New Hampshire, Maine, the Carolinas, Pennsylvania, Delaware, and New Jersey were still sparsely settled but were beginning to show signs of the rapid development which would take place before 1750. At the opening of the century, the total population of the British colonies in what would later become the United States was probably about 250,000, distributed as follows: New England, 90,000; New York, New Jersey, Pennsylvania, Delaware, and Maryland, 80,000; Virginia and the Carolinas, 80,000. Fifty years later these colonies had slightly more than a million white inhabitants and approximately 220,000 Negro slaves. By 1760 the white population had grown to 1,385,000 and the black slaves to 310,000.

The implications of this growth in population were far greater than the mere numerical increase would indicate. The eighteenth century saw a new impetus to colonial expansion from the influx of immigrants from Europe. Since the best land near the seacoast had already been occupied by the end of the seventeenth century, late comers had to push inland beyond the fall line of the rivers. The early eighteenth century witnessed the first penetration of the mountain barrier and the beginning of the push westward. Close on the heels of adventurers like Governor Spotswood's party of explorers, who in 1716 crossed the Blue Ridge into the Valley of Virginia, came Indian traders and then farmers. Traders explored the backcountry and brought back tales of rich valleys which induced courageous farmers in search of better or cheaper land to take their families into the wilderness and establish isolated homes in the clearings. Some died under the scalping knives of the Indians but settlers kept coming until the inland valleys were peopled with self-reliant pioneers.

Of the immigrant stocks who came in the eighteenth century the most numerous and important were the Scots and the Germans. The Scots—at first from North Ireland and later from the Highlands—composed the vanguard of pioneers who pushed to the backcountry in every colony and fought the Indians or any other enemies who disputed their possession of coveted land. The Germans also made their way to the hinterland, but since many of them adhered to some religious belief which had pacifism as one of its tenets, they preferred to leave warfare with the Indians to the tough

THE CAPTURE OF QUEBEC

"A View of the Taking of Quebeck by the English Forces Commanded by Genl Wolfe Sep: 13th 1759." Engraved for the *London Magazine*, 1760; from the Huntington Library collection.

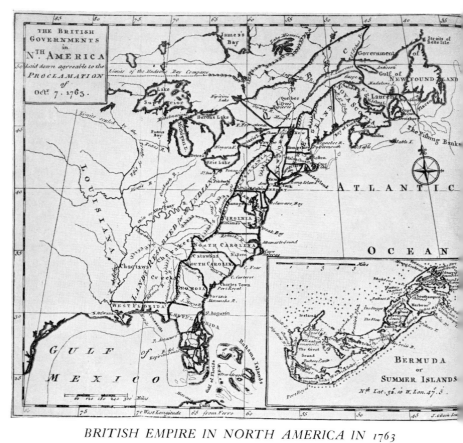

BRITISH EMPIRE IN NORTH AMERICA IN *1763*
From the Huntington Library copy of *The Gentleman's Magazine* (October, 1763).

The Colonies Come of Age

Scotch Presbyterians who felt no peaceful inhibitions. The Germans were the best farmers the country had seen, and they contributed more than any other group to the development of a balanced agriculture. The majority of the Scots and the Germans entered America through the gateway of Philadelphia, but many also came directly to ports in other colonies, especially to the Carolinas and Georgia. Although these Scottish and German settlers led hard lives on the frontier, their lot was better than it would have been had they not crossed the Atlantic. They had liberty and land and a chance to rise by their own diligence—opportunities which every colonial American had a right to expect.

From Cumberland County and adjacent territory on the Pennsylvania frontier which the Scotch-Irish occupied between 1720 and 1750 settlers pushed still further westward. A few of the more daring crossed the Alleghenies in this period but most of them moved into the unoccupied areas of western Maryland, Virginia, and the Carolinas. By the third decade of the eighteenth century frontiersmen and their families were pouring down the Shenandoah Valley and following other watercourses into yet more distant territory. The Scotch-Irish and Germans, drifting into the Piedmont region of the Carolinas, met other settlers moving inland from the Atlantic coast. Lumbering wagons were taking the place of packhorses as families moved with their little household goods to the "west." A movement which would not end until Americans had occupied the land all the way to the Pacific Ocean had begun. Each of the colonies felt the stir of migration to the frontier, but Pennsylvania was the great hive which provided the largest swarms of settlers.

Farmers in search of new homes were not the only ones attracted by "western" land in the period before 1750. Possession of land had been the key to wealth since the first settlers landed on these shores. Great promoters like the proprietors of Maryland, Pennsylvania, and the Carolinas had sought wealth in the huge grants which they obtained from the crown. Lesser speculators had soon discerned that cheap land in the backcountry might be the way to wealth. William Byrd of Westover, for example, obtained a great tract on the Dan River between Virginia and North Carolina, which he attempted to sell to Swiss immigrants. The speculative attraction of land to the west became a characteristic of American life which has remained constant from that day to this. The greed for western land displayed by the wealthy landed proprietors in the older settled regions had repercussions in both domestic and foreign politics. The titular claims of land companies and individual proprietors often ran afoul of squatters already on the soil and created animosity between the actual settlers and the technical owners.

The competition for western land also brought English claimants into conflict with the French in the trans-Allegheny country. For example, in 1748 a group of wealthy planters from Virginia and Maryland organized the Ohio Company under the presidency of Thomas Lee and acquired title to vast holdings across the mountains. The stockholders included Lawrence Washington, who passed on his interest to his brother George Washington. A report made by Christopher Gist, an explorer employed by the Ohio Company to survey the country as far as the site of Louisville, convinced the speculators that this western empire would make them even richer than they were. The chief hindrance to the exploitation of land across the mountains lay in the activities of the French in that region.

Every settler and land speculator in the British colonies looked forward to the time when the French would be driven out of North America. Since King William's War, many a colonial citizen had believed that a fight to the finish with France for possession of Canada and the backcountry was inevitable. The War of Spanish Succession—or Queen Anne's War—in 1701 brought Great Britain into conflict with the combined powers of France and Spain. For a time, hopeful South Carolinians and New Englanders believed that both of these traditional enemies on their borders might be eliminated, but the struggle resulted in only a partial victory.

The Colonies Come of Age

Though South Carolinians and Spaniards raided back and forth, the war ended about where it had begun except for some shifts in the alignment of the border Indians. In the North, after several abortive attempts to invade Canada, Colonel Francis Nicholson finally led a joint expedition of New England militia and British marines which captured Port Royal in French Acadia (Nova Scotia) and renamed the town in honor of the English queen Annapolis Royal. By the Treaty of Utrecht in 1713 France ceded Acadia to the British and gave up her claims to Newfoundland and certain poorly defined territory around Hudson Bay. Along with important European concessions—including Gibraltar and Minorca—Great Britain wrote into the treaty a clause granting her slave-traders the exclusive right to supply the Spanish-American colonies with Negroes for thirty years.

France was left in possession of the whole backcountry of America: the St. Lawrence Valley, the Great Lakes region, and Louisiana. Borders of course were ill-defined and the western slope of the Appalachian Mountains, the Ohio Valley, and the eastern bank of the Mississippi to West Florida remained a no-man's-land where the French and the British would still contend for possession. France was left in possession of Cape Breton Island, just north of Nova Scotia, and there she set to work to create a great fortification at Louisbourg. Both sides looked forward to future wars.

The two wars which had already involved British and French America—King William's War and Queen Anne's War—drove home to many a colonist the need for some kind of unified front against the common enemy. A few thoughtful colonials were also wondering whether the mother country ought not exert more positive efforts to bring the disparate colonies into a better integrated empire.

William Penn in 1697 submitted to the Board of Trade a plan for a union of the colonies with a congress composed of an equal number of representatives from each of the colonies, meeting in New York. Four years later an anonymous Virginian suggested another plan in *An Essay upon the Gov-*

ernment of the English Plantations on the Continent of America (London, 1701). This author proposed that representation be roughly in proportion to population, with meetings of the congress held in one of the five districts into which he would group the colonies. In these two proposals the debate over the method of representation, which was resolved with such difficulty in the Constitutional Convention of 1787, was plainly forecast. Writing just before the outbreak of Queen Anne's War, the author of the *Essay* pointed out that danger from Spain and France made a common front against these enemies essential. He also called upon England to display greater intelligence in the management of the colonies and to remove some of the official ignorance of conditions in America. Though neither Americans nor the Board of Trade were unmindful of the critical issues discussed by this Virginian, not even the fear of the French was sufficient to overcome political inertia in London or in America.

Although farmers and fur traders from the British colonies pushed ever farther into western territory in the quarter of a century of relative peace after the Treaty of Utrecht, everyone expected trouble sooner or later with France and Spain. British Protestants were certain that French Catholic missionaries in the Northwest and Spanish Catholic missionaries in the Southwest were spending more time arousing the Indians against the Protestants than they were in saving heathen souls. At best the frontier had achieved an armed truce; at worst it suffered from sporadic Indian outbreaks.

Not until 1739, however, when England attacked Spain in what is known as the War of Jenkins' Ear, were the colonies again officially engaged with a European power. When this conflict expanded into the greater War of Austrian Succession, or King George's War, the northern colonists once more saw a chance to cripple France. Led by Massachusetts' imperialist governor, the lawyer William Shirley, New England organized a citizen army which laid siege to the French fortress of Louisbourg. Under the command of William

The Colonies Come of Age

Pepperrell, a fish and lumber merchant of Kittery, Maine, farmers and fishermen from New England, supported by an English squadron from the West Indies, captured the stronghold on June 17, 1744. This exploit—half luck and half sheer audacity, which one participant described as something like a boisterous commencement at Harvard—so impressed the authorities in London that they made the fish merchant of Maine a baronet. But the colonies soon learned a lesson in imperial politics and suffered a cruel disappointment when Great Britain at the Treaty of Aachen in 1748 returned Louisbourg to France in exchange for Madras in India.

King George's War, like the previous wars, settled nothing in North America. The French remained entrenched in the vast interior at the back of the British colonies. There they set to work fortifying their positions and tightening their alliances with the Indians. Trade rivalry became more acute as the British pushed into the Great Lakes region. Their trading post at Oswego on Lake Ontario was regarded by the French as a threat and an affront to their authority. Even more intense was the rivalry for farm lands and trading posts in the Ohio Valley and adjacent territory. Since late in the seventeenth century, the French had been in possession of farms along the Illinois River and had established forts and trading posts on the eastern bank of the Mississippi a short distance below St. Louis. The country between the Illinois and the Ohio river systems now took on greater importance. So long as the French controlled this network of rivers, their communications from Canada via Lake Erie and the Ohio to the Mississippi and thence to New Orleans were safe. To the British, French control in this area meant ultimate disaster, for it limited the British colonies to the eastern slope of the Alleghenies. No compromise was possible. The two powers girded for a decisive struggle while farmers and traders waited grimly for the warcry and the burning cabins which would proclaim once more that the frontier was aflame.

The French took no chances that their claim to the Ohio

Valley would be misunderstood. Under instructions from the governor of Canada, Céloron de Bienville in 1749 set out from Lake Erie with an expedition which traced the main tributaries of the Ohio and at strategic points sank leaden plates once more declaring France's possession of that portion of the earth. Next came a new governor of Canada in person, the Marquis Duquesne, who in 1753 erected a series of block houses on the Ohio and Allegheny rivers, which challenged further British expansion in that direction.

The Virginians particularly resented this incursion of the French, for it placed them upon land which Virginians regarded as rightfully theirs. Furthermore a wave of speculation in western lands, just beginning, made the Ohio Valley an especially desirable territory. Governor Dinwiddie of Virginia therefore determined to do what he could to discourage the French. He first sent young George Washington in 1753 with a diplomatic protest to the French military commander on the Ohio; when that had no effect, he sent Washington back with a company of militia, but the French were already established at Fort Duquesne on the site of modern Pittsburgh and had no mind to leave. Encountering a force of Frenchmen near Great Meadows, Washington rashly opened fire and killed the French commanding officer and twenty men. Washington's success was short-lived, for the French trapped him in a temporary log stronghold, fittingly named Fort Necessity, and on July 4, 1754 forced him to surrender. He and his men were allowed to retain their arms on their promise to go back to Virginia.

The French had asserted their determination to stay in the Ohio Valley. Washington unwittingly had fired the first round in a new war, the greatest of all the colonial conflicts, the French and Indian War, known in Europe as the Seven Years' War.

Never had there been greater need of unity in the British colonies. France occupied a more powerful position in the New World than ever before. The governments of Canada and Louisiana had increased in strength and had risen in

The Colonies Come of Age

prestige with the Indians. From the St. Lawrence to Mobile, Frenchmen travelled the waterways and portages with new assurance. French missionaries and French *coureurs de bois* had succeeded with the Indians beyond their own hopes. Even the Iroquois, the traditional allies of the British, were being won away from their old friends. With a new war imminent, every British American who was wise in Indian matters knew that drastic measures were needed to ward off disaster. At this juncture, the Board of Trade in London, which had been hearing reports of the deteriorating relations with the Indians, ordered the governor of New York to call a meeting of Iroquois chiefs and commissioners from the other colonies to frame a treaty to which all the colonies would be a party. Heretofore every colony had made its own deals or treaties with the Indians.

The famous Albany Congress of 1754, which transcended the original purpose of an Indian conference, was the result. Governor James de Lancey of New York took the lead in calling this meeting which soon made its major purpose the consideration of a scheme for unified action. Benjamin Franklin set forth his famous Plan of Union and argued earnestly for its acceptance. Before Franklin left for Albany, he had printed in his *Pennsylvania Gazette* for May 9 an article pointing out that the French were confident of success because the separate British colonies would never "agree to any speedy and effectual measures for our common defense and security." He also printed for the first time a famous cartoon, used later in the Revolution, the picture of a snake cut into segments with the legend, "Join or Die."

The Albany Congress gave an opportunity for the airing of many grievances. Not least were the complaints of the Indians. For instance, Chief Hendrick of the Mohawks charged that greedy land speculators in New York—Philip Livingston among others—had procured "writings for all our lands" and intended to leave the Indians only "the very spot we live upon and hardly that." Furthermore, this chieftain continued, the Albany traders had supplied the Mohawks' enemies in Canada with powder, lead, guns, and other goods—all for the immediate profit which these merchants got from Canadian beaver pelts. This was a telling shot, for New York had a bad record for trading with the enemy. Governor de Lancey himself had been involved; and in Queen Anne's War, New York had contributed little to the efforts against the French because her merchants did not want their trade with Montreal disturbed. Chief Hendrick's rebuke made clear why an alliance with the English no longer aroused enthusiasm among the Six Nations—the name by which the Iroquoian tribes were known after the Tuscaroras, fleeing North Carolina in 1711, had joined their northern brethren.

After much debate, the commissioners at Albany accepted a proposal for union which provided for a Congress representing the several colonies in accordance with their size and importance. But the commissioners—with the exception of the representatives from Massachusetts—had no authority to enter into a confederation. Furthermore Virginia had declined to send delegates to the Albany Congress because Governor Dinwiddie in May, 1754, had called a powwow of his own at Winchester with chiefs of the Six Nations and the Southern Indians. The New Jersey assembly, despite the scolding of Governor Belcher, had also disregarded the Albany Congress because the colony had never been a party to any treaty with the Iroquois and felt that this affair did not concern New Jersey. When finally the question of joining in an effective confederation was laid before the several colonies, not one would agree to sacrifice a jot of its individual sovereignty in the interest of union. Unity would have to wait until the colonies had gained further maturity and experience. Benjamin Franklin, however, had not wasted his words. The seed which he sowed at Albany remained alive and grew into the Articles of Confederation when the colonies a little later came to grips with the mother country.

Before the war broke out in Europe, Great Britain sought to strengthen her position in America by sending over two regiments of regulars and a professional soldier, General James Braddock, to serve as commander-in-chief. He added to his staff George Washington, who wanted to learn what he could from professionals in the art of war. Washington found himself going to school to a poor master. Braddock, an opinionated and obstinate man, failed to put into practice the best tactics of European warfare, much less to adapt those tactics to wilderness conditions. When he led an expedition against Fort Duquesne, the gateway to the West, the French and their Indian allies fell on his troops at the Monongahela River on July 9, 1755, and sent them reeling back in complete rout. Braddock himself was mortally wounded. The latest historian to analyze the defeat concludes from fresh evidence that the traditional story of Braddock's incompetence is correct. Nevertheless the disaster provided object lessons not lost upon General John Forbes, leader of the troops who occupied on November 25, 1758, the smoking ruins of Fort Duquesne which the French had at last abandoned.

Braddock's defeat left the frontier of Virginia and adjacent regions exposed to hostile Indians who were less inclined than ever to make common cause with the British, whom they despised now for their weakness. To guard the borders in this crisis, Governor Dinwiddie made Washington, at the age of twenty-three, commander-in-chief of the Virginia militia. The protection of more than three hundred miles of exposed frontier was his responsibility—a task which he performed as well as his small army permitted; rarely could he muster more than fifteen hundred indifferently trained men. Though he was not able to keep the Indians from scalping settlers and burning farmhouses and trading posts, he fought a holding campaign on the border —and he gained experience which would be useful at a later time.

For all of the fine talk at Albany about unity, the war against the French and Indians began without any consistent plan or systematic cooperation. Colonial governments squabbled about quotas of militia, appropriations for military expenses, leadership of expeditions, and general objectives. Colonial militia disliked British regulars, and British professional officers and soldiers despised what they considered yokels-in-arms. Insofar as there was agreement, it lay in a determination to contain the French on the New York frontier.

The most valuable leader who emerged in the early years of war was William Johnson, a great landowner in the Mohawk Valley, a cunning negotiator with the Indians, and the one white man who retained an influence over the Six Nations. Johnson managed to hold enough Indians in alliance with the British to defeat a French force on Lake George in September 1755. This victory—the only one of any importance in that year—saved New York for a time from disaster. As a reward King George made the leader a baronet; henceforth Sir William Johnson was an even greater man with the Indians, and before his death he had accumulated a vast acreage of their land—one of the largest landed estates in America.

All the other military efforts in 1755 were fumbling and ineffective. Governor William Shirley of Massachusetts led an unsuccessful attack on Fort Niagara which did nothing to increase English prestige with the Indians. Though the French were unable to invade New York in force, they retained their old positions and added a few others. Even Johnson had been unable to take Crown Point on Lake Champlain, and he could not prevent the French from building another stronghold at Fort Ticonderoga.

Hysterical fear, prompted by Indian massacres and reports of growing unrest among the Indians from Maine to Georgia, ran through all the colonies. The danger was indeed great and seaport towns no less than frontier villages worried about their defenses. Scalping parties raided within fifty miles of Philadelphia and murdered defenseless farmers in their sleep. Not far from the Moravian town of Bethlehem, Indians fell on the village of Gnadenhütten and massacred the inhabitants. Though the Pennsylvania assembly appropriated £55,000 for the relief of distress on the frontier and "for other purposes," the Quaker-controlled government refused to take effective military measures. When finally the governor and council of Pennsylvania declared war on the Indians, so many Quakers resigned from the assembly that they lost control of the government, which they never entirely regained. Conditions on the Pennsylvania frontier were duplicated in New York, Maryland, Virginia, and elsewhere. In the far South, the Indians remained at peace for a time, but the Cherokees, lukewarm in their alliance with the English, attacked the South Carolinians before the war was over.

Since the Treaty of Utrecht, the British had controlled a population of Frenchmen, the Acadians in Nova Scotia. Though these farmers and fishermen had been British subjects for more than forty years, they had remained French in language and customs and Catholic in religion. The chilling thought of what some fifteen thousand Frenchmen might do if they chose to rebel caused the British to plan their expulsion. Beginning in the autumn of 1755, more than six thousand Acadians, men, women, and children, were loaded on ships and scattered up and down the Atlantic Coast. Other Acadians fled to French territory in Canada. Families were separated never to meet again. Ships were overloaded and ill-supplied with food and bedding. Many of these miserable displaced persons, whose only fault was that they were French, died at sea or in makeshift quarters in the Atlantic ports where they were dumped.

When more than a thousand were landed at Charleston, South Carolina, a wild rumor spread through the town that the Frenchmen were plotting a slave insurrection. This excitement soon passed but the plight of the Acadian refugees was unrelieved. Public and private charity finally eased the worst suffering. Many of the desperate people sold themselves, or were sold by the authorities, into temporary servitude. The same tragedy was enacted in most of the colonial ports as the exiles tried to find some means of existence.

Within a few years many of them made their way to Louisiana where their descendants have preserved their language and traditions to the present day. A few of the exiles remained in the British colonies. A descendant of one of the Acadians who stayed in South Carolina was the brilliant classical scholar, Basil Lanneau Gildersleeve. The dispersal of the Acadians, believed by the British to be a military necessity, was a grim illustration of the hysterical fear which gripped the whole of British America in 1755.

At the beginning of the year 1756, the outlook for the British was anything but bright. The war which had begun in the American backwoods, by the spring of the year spread to the rest of the world. Britain, in alliance with Prussia, faced France, Austria, and Russia. Before the war was over, Spain would throw in her lot with France. From Madras to the Mississippi, the world was an armed camp.

To improve the military situation in America, the British government appointed another professional soldier to be commander-in-chief, John Campbell, the Scottish Earl of Loudoun. The choice, as so often happened, was unfortunate. Loudoun blustered and swore at the colonials and damned them for their lack of discipline, their failure to provide quarters for his regulars, their slowness in finding recruits, money, and supplies. Officials of the colonial governments heard him with sour resentment, and their dispositions were not sweetened when he won no victories. The French, who had sent over a brilliant and scholarly general, the Marquis de Montcalm, marched down and took Fort Oswego on the south shore of Lake Ontario, the most important of the English out-posts. Montcalm a year later destroyed Fort William Henry at the south end of Lake George and his Indian allies slaughtered the New Englanders whom they captured. Loudoun's plans to take Louisbourg came to naught and he was recalled at the end of 1757.

A worse defeat was in store for the British and colonial troops. In July 1758, Major General James Abercromby, an-

The Colonies Come of Age

other professional soldier, led an army of nearly fifteen thousand British regulars and colonial militia against Montcalm at Ticonderoga. This was the best equipped army that had yet marched to battle in America and it outnumbered Montcalm's garrison four to one. Without waiting for artillery to blast out the trees which the French had cut and sharpened in front of the fort, Abercromby ordered his men to attack. The French fire slaughtered the attackers as they crawled through the log barricades. Two thousand fell before Ticonderoga on July 5 and the rest withdrew the next day leaving Montcalm undisturbed in his stronghold. When the French commander erected a cross on the battlefield with an inscription giving credit to God for the victory, colonial Americans grumbled that Abercromby had had a hand in it too.

But the slaughter at Ticonderoga marked the last of the great French victories. After disasters in every part of the world, the British government in June 1757 made William Pitt secretary of state for war with the responsibility for the conduct of the war in all theaters. Pitt at once began to shake the incompetents out of commands in the army and navy and to tighten the coördination between the services. He made Jeffrey Amherst, just forty years old, commander-in-chief of troops in America and gave him for his second in command a serious and literary young man of thirty named James Wolfe. Reaching an obvious conclusion that he could never get enough trained soldiers from the disputing and jealous colonial governments, Pitt sent over an adequate number of regulars. Before the end of July 1758, the British had captured the great fortress at Louisbourg. Young General Wolfe at that siege proved himself a leader of courage and intelligence. The English also captured Fort Frontenac, which had given the French control of Lake Ontario, and the occupation of Fort Duquesne before the end of the year at last removed the French from control of frontier gateways.

The greatest victory came in 1759 with the capture of

Quebec. From the 26th of June to the 13th of September a British fleet and army had besieged the powerful fortress which Montcalm defended with skill and courage. But Wolfe, who commanded the British troops, combined in a high degree military wisdom and audacity. Before dawn on the morning of September 13, he surreptitiously led his troops up a steep path above Quebec and deployed them on the Plains of Abraham opposite the weakest bastions in Quebec's walls. When Montcalm discovered the stratagem, he realized that attack was the best defense, but he was unable to concentrate enough men to overwhelm his opponents. At Wolfe's command each British soldier had loaded his musket with two balls; their first murderous volley followed by a bayonet attack sent the surviving French flying back to the protection of their walls. When the smoke cleared both Wolfe and Montcalm lay dying. The Marquis de Vaudreuil, governor of Canada, whose conflicting orders had handicapped Montcalm's defense, ordered the remnants of the French army to abandon Quebec and fall back to Montreal.

The capture of Quebec was a decisive victory. Though the French held out at Montreal for another year and in fact tried to retake Quebec, their cause was lost. On September 7, 1760, General Amherst, who had brought an overpowering army to Montreal, received the Marquis de Vaudreuil's unconditional surrender. Because the French had not restrained their Indian allies from the cruelest atrocities, the British refused their foes the usual courtesies accorded defeated enemies.

From defeat that seemed overwhelming in 1755–56, Great Britain had climbed to victory. In Europe, in India, and in America France had now suffered humiliating reverses. In recompense for Spanish help—too little and too late—France in 1762 ceded Louisiana to Spain. By the Treaty of Paris in 1763, France was forced to cede to Great Britain the rest of her North American territory except the minute islands of St. Pierre and Miquelon off Newfoundland, which the British, in contemptuous generosity, left to France so that her

fishermen might dry their nets on French soil. In the shuffle
of territory Great Britain also received Spanish Florida.

The very success of the Seven Years' War, however, carried with it the germs of disintegration of the British Empire
in America. So long as France had threatened the existence
of the colonies along the Atlantic seaboard, they had looked
to the mother country for support and leadership and they
had been willing to contribute, however grudgingly, to the
common defense. With the removal of France as a threat,
the colonies determined to go their individual ways, each
comfortable in its own sovereignty. Though they accepted
the idea of being part of an imperial system in trade and
commerce, they were far less amenable than before to dictation from London.

Despite the long series of wars which had devastated the
frontiers, the colonies had grown in population and general
prosperity. New generations of Americans had been born
who knew not the charm of England. They were Americans
and they took unkindly to any air of superiority assumed
by Englishmen. The great increments of Scotch-Irish and
Germans who had come to America in the eighteenth century were either actively anti-English or oblivious to any
appeal of British ties. Frontiersmen who had rarely experienced any favorable contact with Englishmen or received
any aid from British troops had a new spirit of self-reliance
and independence. Great Britain would need to walk wisely
if she expected to avoid overturning the applecart of empire.
That skill was not found among her politicians after 1763.

Observing the inability of the colonies to cooperate successfully, English politicians argued logically that the imperial government must show a stronger hand in the management of American affairs. In this view, many Americans
concurred. Much depended, however, on the manner and
the wisdom of imperial interference in American affairs. As
long before as 1701, the author of *An Essay upon the Government of the English Plantations on the Continent of
America* had complained of the ignorance in London con-

cerning the colonies: "But the last and greatest unhappiness the plantations labor under is that the king and the court of England are altogether strangers to the true state of affairs in America, for that is the true cause why grievances have not been long since redressed." To remedy this situation, the author suggested that each colony keep a representative in London to inform the government about his colony's affairs, and that the English government maintain an efficient commissioner to travel through all the colonies systematically as an observer of their economic and political conditions. "By these means it is probable," this author asserted, "the king and court of England may be made thoroughly sensible of the true state of affairs in this remote part of the world, which, it is presumed, will be the first and greatest step towards remedying any former mismanagements." Despite this hopeful conclusion, the English government never succeeded in gaining more than a partial comprehension of American affairs, and decisions predicated on half-truths, arrived at from inadequate or biased information, sped the empire on its way to ruin.

The Indian problem was one of the most vexing which faced the colonies after 1763. The English had become the nominal masters of tribes which for more than a century had regarded the French as their natural allies. Encouraged by French malcontents and chiefs disgruntled at the highhanded treatment accorded them by English officers and English traders, the Indians rebelled in a violent war which flared along the whole western frontier during 1763–64. Since Francis Parkman's romantic history of the rebellion, this war has been known as the Conspiracy of Pontiac after the Ottawa chief who is traditionally but perhaps erroneously supposed to have organized the Indians. Before it was over all except three of the western outposts—Fort Niagara, Fort Pitt, and Detroit—had fallen to the savages and hundreds of frontiersmen had lost their homes and their lives in the fray. When British regulars finally put down the outbreak, Sir William Johnson in 1765 negotiated a peace at Oswego.

Since the colonies had developed no unified policy in dealing with the Indians and had failed to defend even their own borders, the government in London thought up a simple plan for the future to eliminate zones of friction. With a map of North America spread out before them, members of the Board of Trade in October 1763 drew a long line along the crest of the Alleghenies and declared that the territory west of the "Proclamation Line" would be an Indian reservation. White settlers might not move into this region and those who had already settled west of the mountains were ordered to move out. At some later time, when the imperial authorities should approve, agents appointed by London might buy land from the Indians in the West and permit westward emigration. But for the time being, London had sealed the west against expansion. By this logical expedient, the fur trade, in which many English financiers had a deep interest, would be protected, Indian lands would be saved from trespassing squatters, and foolhardy frontiersmen, who had previously risked their scalps in utter recklessness, would be protected from their own folly. The Board of Trade was pleased with its day's work.

The difficulty with the Proclamation Line of 1763 was that it violated the vested interests of the older colonies who claimed land to the west by charter rights. It also antagonized both the capitalistic land speculators, who were organizing companies for the exploitation of western land, and the independent frontiersmen, who had already settled in the West. Furthermore, the Indians themselves knew little or nothing about London's authority to make a reservation for them west of the Alleghenies. The Proclamation of 1763 succeeded merely in providing one more grievance of the colonies against the home government.

Wars invariably produce social upheavals, strains and tensions among the people, and a backwash of reaction when

[321]

peace comes. Since the end of the Seven Years' War in 1763 marked the culmination, not of one war, but of a long sequence of wars which had involved the colonies since the late years of the seventeenth century, the reaction throughout colonial America was acute. Within each colony, tensions which had been accumulating for years, found expression in violence and turbulence on the frontiers, dissatisfaction with established government, ill-will between classes, and the loud expression of grievances among political factions. As the rich had grown richer and more entrenched in their vested interests, the poor had grown more independent and violent in their objection to domination by the wealthy ruling cliques. Not a colony was free from this gathering cloud of unrest. By the whim of Fate and the ineptitude of British politicians, a majority of colonial Americans found a focus in "British tyranny" after 1763 to polarize their hate and discharge it against a common enemy rather than against one another. The passage by Parliament of the Revenue Act of 1764 and the Stamp Act of 1765 drew the lightning of revolution and poised the thunderbolts over the luckless heads of royal governors and imperial officers instead of the representatives of the privileged orders sitting in local assemblies. In the end King George became the scapegoat upon whose thick German head American politicians eagerly placed the blame for all their troubles.

The social conflicts characteristic in greater or lesser degree of all the colonies were the logical consequence of the opportunities offered by an expanding society in a new country. While the colonists had naturally enough imitated the broad outlines of the English social system, they had not reproduced many of the details of that system, sometimes to the distress and unhappiness of the well-to-do gentry, who complained of the impudence of the "lower classes." As the colonists had acquired land and property, they had of course assumed where they could the prerogatives of an aristocracy —in Boston, in Philadelphia, on the Virginia rivers, or in Charleston—and they had displayed some of the arrogance which invariably goes with new riches. Although by the mid-eighteenth century most of the colonies had developed a semblance of class stratification, society as a whole simply refused to harden into the precise patterns of England or Europe.

Easily possessed land was the key, then as later, to the free flow of American society. While capitalists with money to invest could get the best land in the older settled regions, the farmer with enough courage and enterprise could always procure land just beyond the point of convenient transportation or safety. What is more, he could own this land in fee simple, something impossible for him in England or on the Continent. And while he might not get rich from his own labor, he could subsist in greater comfort than most of the immigrants had previously known, and he was free from countless restrictions of law and custom. This farmer, who frequently combined with agriculture a little trading or the practice of some craft, developed into an independent fellow not overly impressed by wealthy merchants in the towns or pretentious planters who owned great estates.

During the eighteenth century, the commercial centers of Boston, New York, Philadelphia, Charleston, and lesser ports as well, developed substantial middle-class groups of tradesmen and craftsmen. Benjamin Franklin, himself a skilled craftsman, gives a clear impression in his *Autobiography* of the alertness, intelligence, and independence of the middle-class in the thriving town of Philadelphia. New England had a large population of seafaring people, fishermen and deep water sailors, many of whom owned in whole or in part the vessels they took to sea. This middle-class was generally characterized, whether in Puritan New England, Quaker Philadelphia, polyglot New York, or in any of the other trading communities, by ambition and hope for the future, as well as by diligence and thrift. The virtue of "push," a quality enormously glorified by Americans of a later day, was praised with equal fervor by eighteenth-century colonials who read with complete approval Franklin's *Way to*

[323]

Wealth and set to work to put into practice injunctions which clearly led to self-improvement and material prosperity.

The advancement in material wealth, and the attributes of civilization which wealth makes possible, had changed the face of the older communities in the first fifty years of the eighteenth century. Merchants and planters of the wealthier sort built more commodious houses, and filled them with imported furniture and luxuries. Peter Kalm, a Swedish scientist who visited the middle colonies in 1748–51 was impressed with the fine homes, churches, and public buildings which he observed in the larger towns. Of Philadelphia he remarked that the streets were "regular, pretty, and most of them fifty feet, English measure, broad. . . . The houses make a good appearance, are frequently several stories high, and built either of bricks or of stone; but the former are more commonly used, since they are made near the town and are of good quality." Of New York's streets, Kalm observed that they did "not run so straight as those of Philadelphia and sometimes are quite crooked; however, they are very spacious and well-built." Even in Albany—still an outpost of civilization—he found that the houses were "very neat and partly built of stones covered with shingles of white pine." But of the people of Albany, whom he described as all Dutchmen, he gave an ill report: "The avarice, selfishness, and immeasurable love of money of the inhabitants of Albany are very well known throughout all North America. . . . If a real Jew, who understands the art of getting forward perfectly well, should settle amongst them, they would not fail to ruin him."

A young English candidate for holy orders, Andrew Burnaby, who travelled through the colonies in 1759–60 registered his impressions of both the material and spiritual state of the localities visited. The capital of Virginia, Williamsburg—which he described as "far from being a place of any consequence" with only two hundred houses and a thousand inhabitants, white and black—was "regularly laid out in parallel streets, intersected by others at right angles," and it had "a handsome square in the center through which runs the principal street, one of the most spacious in North America, three quarters of a mile in length and above a hundred feet wide. At the opposite ends of this street are two public buildings, the college and the capitol; and although the houses [dwellings] are of wood covered with shingles, and but indifferently built, the whole makes a handsome appearance. . . . The governor's palace is tolerably good, one of the best upon the continent, but the church, the prison, and the other buildings are all of them extremely indifferent."

Burnaby like others from his country was disappointed that North America did not duplicate England to perfection. The inhabitants, like the buildings, merited a modest commendation though they were scarcely equal to native English types. Of Virginia women, for example, he commented that they were "generally speaking handsome though not to be compared with our fair country-women of England." He thought that they lacked accomplishments and were immoderately fond of dancing, including jigs, "a practice originally borrowed, I am informed, from the Negroes." He also thought it worthy of note that Virginians were addicted to eating ham: "Even at Williamsburg, it is the custom to have a plate of cold ham upon the table, and there is scarcely a Virginian lady who breakfasts without it."

As Burnaby travelled northward his enthusiasm for colonial civilization increased. "Can the mind have a greater pleasure than in contemplating the rise and progress of cities and kingdoms?" he asked rhetorically as he approached Philadelphia through the neat farms and villages of Pennsylvania; "than in perceiving a rich and opulent state arising out of a small settlement or colony?" The trade of Philadelphia, which had received a great impetus from the development of the backcountry, stirred Burnaby to excitement:

The trade of Pennsylvania is surprising extensive, carried on to Great Britain, the West Indies, every part of North

America, the Madeiras, Lisbon, Cadiz, Holland, Africa, the Spanish Main, and several other places, exclusive of what is illicitly carried on to Cape François, and Monte Cristo. Their exports are provisions of all kinds, lumber, hemp, flax, flaxseed, iron, furs, and deer-skins. Their imports, English manufactures, with the superfluities and luxuries of life. By their flag-of-truce trade, they also get sugar, which they refine and send to Europe. Their manufactures are considerable. The Germantown thread-stockings are in high estimation, and the year before last, I have been credibly informed, there were manufactured in that town alone above 60,000 dozen pair. Their common retail price is a dollar per pair. The Irish settlers make very good linens. Some woolens have also been fabricated, but not, I believe, to any amount. There are several other manufactures, viz. of beaver hats, which are superior in goodness to any in Europe, of cordage, linseed-oil, starch, myrtle-wax, and spermaceti candles, soap, earthen ware and other commodities.

Reading between these lines it is plain that Americans were getting rich, and that their methods were not altogether pleasing to the strict mercantilists of the Board of Trade in London. The manufactures which Burnaby mentions, as well as the illicit trade with the French West Indies and with countries of Europe, were growing in Pennsylvania, and also in New England. A tightening of imperial restrictions against manufacture and commerce which violated the acts of trade would become a major cause of disagreement between the colonies and the mother country.

The commercial zeal of Americans and their willingness to flout the laws of England to enrich themselves continued to draw Burnaby's notice. Of the Rhode Islanders, whose commerce with the West Indies was one source of their prosperity, he comments: "The private people are cunning, deceitful, and selfish; they live almost entirely by unfair and illicit trading. Their magistrates are partial and corrupt, and it is folly to expect justice in their courts of judicature, for he who has the greatest influence is generally found to have the fairest cause. Were the governor to interpose his authority, were he to refuse to grant flags of truce or not to wink at abuses, he would at the expiration of the year be excluded from his office, the only thing perhaps which he has to subsist upon." After mentioning the prosperous trade of New Hampshire in ships and ships' stores, including fine masts for the King's navy, Burnaby adds the comment that "the province of New Hampshire, I was informed at Portsmouth, has grown rich during the war by the loss of its own vessels, they having been commonly insured above value."

After discounting Burnaby's natural prejudice, one is forced to conclude that his observations about the sharp practice of colonial traders was not unfounded. Americans had tasted the material rewards of this world and they wanted more.

Although in every level of society, colonial citizens kept uppermost in their minds the concern with getting ahead materially, they did not neglect intellectual and spiritual advancement. Schools, colleges, and libraries multiplied. The number, the variety, and handsomeness of the churches in the major cities and even in some of the smaller towns astonished travellers. Newspapers and a few magazines flourished as Americans began to develop an interest in letters and the arts.

Burnaby observed that the arts and sciences were yet in their infancy, but he saw many signs of progress. In Philadelphia—the city where Benjamin West was developing his talents as a painter—he discerned "some few persons who have discovered a taste for music and painting; and philosophy [science] seems not only to have made a considerable progress already but to be daily gaining ground." If he had inquired he might have made the acquaintance of a physical scientist named Benjamin Franklin already famous, a distinguished botanist, John Bartram, and his botanist-son William, a young astronomer, David Rittenhouse, soon to add lustre to the American Philosophical Society, and many other alert young men of a scientific bent. Burnaby praised the Library Company as "an excellent institution for propagating a taste for literature" and he found the College of Philadelphia, under the leadership of Dr. William Smith, "well calculated to form and cultivate it."

If Burnaby's observations about the cultural achievements in the colonies were superficial, they nevertheless suggest a progress that was gathering momentum. He kept an eye open for evidences of the advancement in learning and literature. New Jersey, for instance, had the promise of improvement through the recent founding of the College of New Jersey (1746), later Princeton. King's College (1754), later Columbia, in New York impressed the traveller with its prospects and its location, "the most beautifully situated of any college, I believe, in the world." The Redwood Library in Newport, chartered in 1747 by Abraham Redwood, a Quaker merchant of the city, received a reserved commendation for its architectural beauty, for it was "built in the form of a Grecian temple, by no means inelegant." He might have added that the architect was Peter Harrison, who displayed professional skill and taste. Boston and Cambridge— the oldest of colonial cultural centers—brought forth the observation that the "arts and sciences seem to have made a greater progress here than in any other part of America. Harvard College has been founded above a hundred years; and although it is not upon a perfect plan, yet it has produced a very good effect. The arts are undeniably forwarder in Massachusetts Bay than either in Pennsylvania or New York. The public buildings are more elegant, and there is a more general turn for music, painting, and the belles lettres." And Burnaby, an Anglican, adds as an afterthought: "The character of the inhabitants of this province is much improved in comparison of what it was, but Puritanism and a spirit of persecution is not yet totally extinguished."

Though the Anglican parson considered Boston still too much under the thumb of the Puritans, religious conditions in New England and in the other colonies had undergone great changes during the eighteenth century. For one thing, the Episcopal Church had become the church of the wealthy and the fashionable, even in such a stronghold of Puritanism as Boston or such a Quaker haven as Philadelphia. King's Chapel in Boston, that city's first Episcopal congregation, had flourished since the later years of the seventeenth century; the church edifice especially pleased Burnaby because it was "exceedingly elegant and fitted up in the Corinthian taste."

Since the rich, the privileged, and the fashionable groups in all the colonies naturally drifted to the Episcopal Church —the church of the royal governors and other imperial officials—it became a bulwark of conservatism in the period of controversy leading up to the Revolution. And even though many Episcopalians became ardent advocates of independence, the Episcopal Church and most of its ministers took a firm stand against radical propaganda. Even after the Revolution began, many of the clergy and their parishioners remained loyal to King George.

A religious revival, which began about 1734, swept the colonies and helped to drive conservative elements into the Episcopal Church. Under the curiously contrasting influences of Jonathan Edwards, an eloquent Calvinist of Northampton, Massachusetts, and George Whitefield, a follower of John Wesley, an evangelical wave struck every town and hamlet along the Atlantic seaboard and rocked frontier communities with an outburst of prayer meetings, confessions, repentances, amateur preaching, and hysterical conversions. This religious upheaval disturbed and alarmed many a conservative who forthwith deserted his over-wrought Congregational or Presbyterian congregation and joined the Episcopal Church, which was emotionally tidier. The revival, known as the Great Awakening, caused a split in the Presbyterian Church which led to still further schism. The Baptists, who found no objection to emotionalism, and the followers of Whitefield, who would eventually be known as Methodists, grew in numbers, particularly in backwoods communities. Among these groups, radical political ideas, as well as emotional religion, developed apace.

[329]

The Atlantic Frontier

In keeping alive revivalistic fervor, George Whitefield was the greatest influence of his age. For many years after his arrival in Georgia in 1738, Whitefield travelled the length of the Atlantic colonies. His sermons held vast congregations hypnotized. Such was the power of his eloquence that David Garrick, the greatest English actor of the eighteenth century, once sighed that he would give a hundred guineas if he could only say "Oh!" with Whitefield's emotional effect, and Benjamin Franklin, in a famous passage in the *Autobiography*, tells how Whitefield's eloquence moved him, against his better judgment, to empty his pockets into the collection plate.

Although the Great Awakening aroused considerable hysteria, its general effect was beneficial: it served to spread liberal ideas in theology and in politics; it aroused a new spirit of compassion and humanitarianism; and it helped to advance ideas of toleration. The colonies by the very nature of the divergent elements in the mass immigration of the eighteenth century had already relaxed many of the older restrictions against particular sectarians who had not been acceptable earlier. For example, most of the colonies now had Jewish and Catholic citizens who exercised their religion without interference. Peter Kalm reported that "besides the different sects of Christians, many Jews have settled in New York, who possess great privileges. They have a synagogue [in which he attended a service], own their dwelling-houses, possess large country-seats, and are allowed to keep shops in town. They have likewise several ships, which they load and send out with their own goods. In fine, they enjoy all the privileges common to the other inhabitants of this town and province." Andrew Burnaby thought the Jewish synagogue in Newport the finest house of worship in the town.

The diversity of religion and variety of sectarian preachers made the pulpit in the eighteenth century, as in previous generations, a forum of incalculable influence. Many a citizen who read little himself heard from his preacher, not only religious, philosophical, and ethical homilies, but also discussions of social, political, and even scientific problems.

The rising power of the press, which would receive a clamorous demonstration in the approaching era of controversy, was apparent by the middle years of the eighteenth century. By 1763 every colony had a printing press of sorts, and Boston, New York, Philadelphia, and Charleston had newspapers and presses of considerable influence. Boston and Philadelphia had a long established book trade and the printers of those cities were also experienced in book publishing. The great mass of books read in America, however, continued to be imported from London. With the spread of education, the reading public had grown in importance and in its capacity for articulate expression, as Englishmen would learn from colonial propagandists protesting against imperial regulations.

Eighteenth-century newspapers provided an outlet for an increasing amount of literary expression, sometimes merely the uninspired imitation of English writers, but more often the expression of vigorous opinions on contemporary affairs, especially political events which aroused the authors' anger. A reader of colonial newspapers is soon impressed with the alertness and the contentiousness of Americans, who already seemed to have a chip on their shoulders.

A social factor of considerable significance was the great increase in the number of lawyers as commerce broadened and society became more complex. Some of the brightest boys in New England, who would have become preachers in the seventeenth century, in the eighteenth trained themselves for the practice of law. Similarly in the South, and even among the Pennsylvania Quakers, who distrusted legal quibbling, lawyers multiplied and flourished in a litigious age. Since this was the one learned profession which promised social prestige, influence, and wealth, it drew many of the best brains in the colonies. The quality of their minds became apparent in the political and legal controversies with the British government.

The Atlantic Frontier

To the casual observer in 1763, the British colonies in North America would have seemed too disparate and separate ever to achieve anything like unity of purpose. Their commercial and social interests were so different that it would have seemed easy for the imperial government to control them, however obstreperous they might become, by the simple formula of "divide and rule." Commenting on his travels in 1759–60, Andrew Burnaby declared that "America is formed for happiness, but not for empire. In the course of 1,200 miles I did not see a single object that solicited charity; but I saw insuperable causes of weakness, which will necessarily prevent its being a potent state."

The weaknesses and the natural divisions in the colonies received detailed elaboration as Burnaby analyzed the conditions which he had observed. The Southern colonies were victims of indolence and ease induced by an enervating climate, he believed. "I myself have been a spectator," he remarked, "and it is not an uncommon sight, of a man in the vigor of life, lying upon a couch, and a female slave standing over him, wafting off the flies, and fanning him, while he took his repose." The lure of easy land in the West, which Burnaby accurately appraised, also served, he thought, to draw off the population and keep the eastern colonies thinly settled, for "men sooner than apply themselves to laborious occupations . . . will gradually retire westward and settle upon fresh lands, where, by the service of a Negro or two, they may enjoy all the satisfaction of an easy and indolent independency."

Although the northern colonies were of "stronger stamina," they had, in Burnaby's opinion, "still more positive and real disadvantages to contend with. They are composed of people of different nations, different manners, different religions, and different languages. They have a mutual jealousy of each other, fomented by considerations of interest, power, and ascendency."

The tendency of the colonies to divide each from the other seemed so clear to Burnaby that he thought it "a very doubtful point, even supposing all the colonies of America to be united under one head, whether it would be possible to keep in due order and government so wide and extended an empire, the difficulties of communication, of intercourse, of correspondence, and all other circumstances considered."

But Burnaby, like many of George III's advisers, was unaware of subtle changes taking place in the colonies. The eighteenth century had brought maturity and a new realization on the part of individual colonials that they were "Americans." From the first years of the century, colonial citizens with self-conscious pride and increasing frequency, began to describe themselves by that term. Although the wealthy classes showed more and more imitativeness of English manners and social externals, they did not let their Anglophilia betray their political or commercial interests—a fundamental fact which British officialdom, then as now, was prone to forget.

For all of the bickerings which colonial wars had occasioned between the various provincial governments, these conflicts had drawn the colonies closer together. Cut off at times from their normal commerce across the Atlantic, the colonies had learned to depend more upon one another. Intercolonial shipping and commerce had expanded, and communication had improved between the cities and towns of the Atlantic seaboard. The rice planter of Charleston discovered that he shared many of the views of society and government held by the prosperous merchant of Boston or Newport. They both agreed that the insolence and growing independence of mechanics and yokels endangered decent and orderly government; and they both insisted that government was the prerogative of those whom God and good luck had particularly endowed for that function, namely the privileged and the well-to-do.

With the coming of peace in 1763, communication between the colonies, especially for members of the upper classes, instead of dwindling, began to increase. More frequent trips between New York and Philadelphia, Boston and

Newport, and even between Charleston and the northern ports, brought business and professional men, and even a few bent on pleasure, into closer contact.

Newspapers were also potent carriers of intercolonial ideas. The printers in the various capitals were often connected by business ties or family interest. Newspapers, circulating between printshops, from colony to colony, carried news of their particular localities, editorial commentary, satirical or indignant essays and poems by subscribers, and other manifestations of regional interest or excitement. From this material the local printer felt free to clip what he wanted and publish it for the benefit of his patrons.

When Great Britain, with singular ineptness, united the most articulate groups in America—the merchants, the lawyers, the planters, and the printers—by trying to enforce the Stamp Act, the representatives from the several colonies who assembled in New York in October 1765 to shape the developing protest against "taxation without representation" did not meet as utter strangers. Though old jealousies and rivalries persisted, as they would persist for generations to come, the delegates to the Stamp Act Congress, some of whom knew each other personally, felt a new surge of common interest. It was Great Britain's misfortune that her politicians—and her king—continued to provide the stimulus which eventually united the colonies.

Christopher Gadsden of South Carolina, who had been a delegate to the Stamp Act Congress, reported on his return to Charleston that "the friends of liberty here are all as sensible as our brethren to the northward that nothing will save us but acting together. That province that endeavors to act separately will certainly gain nothing by it; she must fall with the rest, and not only so, but be deservedly branded besides with everlasting infamy." And Gadsden added a statement which was not original in idea but was new in the force with which it was uttered and the enthusiasm with which it was received: "For my part, I have ever been of the opinion that we should all endeavor to stand upon the broad and common ground of those natural and inherent rights that we all feel and know, as men and as descendants of Englishmen, we have a right to . . . I wish that the charters . . . being different in different colonies may not be the political trap that will ensnare us at last by drawing different colonies upon that account to act differently in this great and common cause . . . There ought to be no New England men, no New Yorker, &c., known on the continent, but all of us Americans; a confirmation of our essential and common rights as Englishmen may be pleaded from the charters safely enough, but any farther dependence on them may be fatal." The colonies had come a long way since the Congress at Albany in 1754. They had come of age, and their citizens had indeed become Americans.

BIBLIOGRAPHICAL NOTES

THE literature of the subjects treated in this volume is voluminous, and much of it has been repeatedly listed in bibliographies, textbooks, and guides to historical reading. The limitations of space prevent the repetition here of extensive bibliographies. An effort has been made only to suggest books which will serve as further guides to the subject, books which contain useful bibliographies, and works of special value for themes and points of view peculiar to this volume.

CHAPTER I

Most of the recent surveys of colonial American history provide material on the historical background of Europe and the movements leading to exploration and colonization overseas. Concise and useful, especially for its bibliographical notes, is Curtis P. Nettels, *The Roots of American Civilization* (New York, 1938). In the same category are Oliver P. Chitwood, *A History of Colonial America* (New York, 1931), and Max Savelle, *The Foundations of American Civilization* (New York, 1942). Still one of the most informative and provocative of the briefer discussions is Carl Becker, *The Beginnings of the American People* (Boston, 1915). An excellent survey, with classified bibliographies, is Herbert I. Priestley, *The Coming of the White Man, 1492–1848*, A History of American Life Series, Vol. I (New York, 1929).

Brief and readable narratives of events mentioned in this chapter are to be found in the following volumes from the Yale Chronicles of America Series: Irving B. Richman, *The Spanish Conquerors* (New Haven, 1919); William Wood, *Elizabethan Sea-Dogs* (New Haven, 1918); William B. Munro, *Crusaders of New France* (New Haven, 1918); and Mary Johnston, *Pioneers of the Old South* (New Haven, 1918). The early chapters of Carl Wittke, *We Who Built America* (New York, 1940), and Marcus Lee Hansen, *The Atlantic Migration* (Cambridge, Mass., 1940), provide information on causes and effects of Continental immigration to America in the colonial period. See also Thomas J. Wertenbaker, *The Founding of American Civilization: The Middle Colonies* (New York, 1938).

The most recent extensive study of colonial settlements in America—and one of the best balanced treatments—is Charles M. Andrews' great work, *The Colonial Period of American History*

(4 vols., New Haven, 1934–38). H. L. Osgood, *American Colonies in the Seventeenth Century* (3 vols., New York, 1926–30), will still prove useful as a supplement to Andrews.

Valuable for the general background of English colonial activity, and especially useful for its detailed bibliographies, is *The Cambridge History of the British Empire*, Vol. I, *The Old Empire from the Beginnings to 1783* (Cambridge, 1929). The most compact and readable of the single-volume histories of England, emphasizing social and economic factors, is George M. Trevelyan, *History of England* (London, 1926). See also Trevelyan, *England Under the Stuarts* (London, 1920), and *English Social History* (London, 1942). Helpful also is Godfrey Davies, *The Early Stuarts, 1603–1660* (Oxford, 1937).

Economic problems discussed may be studied at greater length in Ephraim Lipson, *The Economic History of England* (3 vols., London, 1929–31); Mildred Campbell, *The English Yeoman* (New Haven, 1942); William R. Scott, *The Constitution and Finance of English, Scottish, and Irish Joint Stock Companies to 1720* (3 vols., Cambridge, 1910–12); David Hannay, *The Great Chartered Companies* (London, 1926); George Cawston and A. H. Keane, *The Early Chartered Companies* (London, 1896); Edward P. Cheyney, *Social Changes in England in the Sixteenth Century as Reflected in Contemporary Literature* (Boston, 1893), and *European Background of American History, 1300–1600* (London, 1904). See also Julian S. Corbett, *Drake and the Tudor Navy* (2 vols., London, 1898).

The relations between intellectual and social history, of significance to the development of ideas in America, are treated in Louis B. Wright, *Middle-Class Culture in Elizabethan England* (Chapel Hill, N. C., 1935), and *Religion and Empire: The Alliance between Piety and Commerce in English Expansion, 1558–1625* (Chapel Hill, N. C., 1942). Valuable for its discussion and analytical bibliographies is Merle Curti, *The Growth of American Thought* (New York, 1943). Background material with classified bibliographies may be found in Preserved Smith, *A History of Modern Culture* (2 vols., New York, 1930–34).

CHAPTER II

Charles M. Andrews, *The Colonial Period in American History* (4 vols., New Haven, 1934–38), a fundamental work for the history of all the colonies in this period, is particularly sane and helpful in controversial questions concerning the early history of Virginia and Maryland. Three chapters in his volume of lectures, *Our Earliest Colonial Settlements* (New York, 1933), treat these colonies. The involved history of the Virginia Company is lucidly discussed in

Bibliographical Notes

Wesley F. Craven, *Dissolution of the Virginia Company of London*: *The Failure of a Colonial Experiment* (New York, 1932).

Thomas J. Wertenbaker, *Patrician and Plebeian in Virginia* (Charlottesville, Va., 1910), *Virginia under the Stuarts* (Princeton, 1914), and *The Planters of Colonial Virginia* (Princeton, 1922), provide interpretative studies revising somewhat the conclusions of Philip A. Bruce in *Economic History of Virginia in the Seventeenth Century* (2 vols., New York, 1907), *Institutional History of Virginia in the Seventeenth Century* (2 vols., New York, 1910), and *Social Life in the Seventeenth Century* (Lynchburg, Va., 1927). Wertenbaker, *The First Americans, 1607–1690*, A History of American Life Series, Vol. II (New York, 1927), is particularly useful for both its interpretation and classified bibliographies. The most extensive of the modern histories of Virginia is Matthew Page Andrews, *Virginia, the Old Dominion* (New York, 1927). A discussion of the development and qualities of the ruling class will be found in Louis B. Wright, *The First Gentlemen of Virginia* (San Marino, Calif., 1940). A considerable amount of interesting detail is given in Mary Newton Stanard, *Colonial Virginia, Its People and Customs* (Philadelphia, 1917), and *The Story of Virginia's First Century* (Philadelphia, 1928). John Esten Cooke, *Virginia, a History of the People* (Boston, 1895), is a romantic but readable narrative.

Matthew Page Andrews, *The Founding of Maryland* (New York, 1933), and *History of Maryland: Province and State* (New York, 1929), are the most extensive of the modern histories of Maryland. An excellent work providing more material on the early eighteenth century than the title might indicate is Charles A. Barker, *The Background of the Revolution in Maryland* (New Haven, 1940). Among earlier books on Maryland, Newton D. Mereness, *Maryland as a Proprietary Province* (New York, 1901), supplies a great amount of documented material, while William H. Browne, *Maryland, the History of a Palatinate* (Boston, 1890), gives a brisk narrative account.

CHAPTER III

Works of special importance for New England have already been mentioned in the previous chapters or in the definite references which follow. Among other works not specifically referred to here, the following are especially helpful: William B. Weeden, *Economic and Social History of New England, 1620–1789* (2 vols., Boston, 1890); E. A. J. Johnson, *American Economic Thought in the Seventeenth Century* (London, 1932); Samuel E. Morison, *Builders of the Bay Colony* (Boston, 1930); James Truslow Adams, *Provincial Society, 1690–1763*, A History of American Life Series, Vol. III (New York, 1927); Carl Bridenbaugh, *Cities in the Wilderness* (New

York, 1938); John Winthrop Platner et al, *The Religious History of New England* (Cambridge, Mass., 1917); Joseph Haroutunian, *Piety Versus Moralism: The Passing of the New England Theology* (New York, 1932); Perry Miller, *Orthodoxy in Massachusetts, 1630–1650* (Cambridge, Mass., 1933); Thomas Cuming Hall, *The Religious Background of American Culture* (Boston, 1930); George F. Dow, *The Arts and Crafts in New England, 1704–1775* (Topsfield, Mass., 1927); George F. Dow, *Every Day Life in the Massachusetts Bay Colony* (Boston, 1935); George F. Dow, *Domestic Life in New England in the Seventeenth Century* (Topsfield, Mass., 1925); Franklin B. Dexter, *Documentary History of Yale University* (New Haven, 1916); Samuel H. Brockunier, *The Irrepressible Democrat, Roger Williams* (New York, 1940); Edward Channing, *The Narragansett Planters*, Johns Hopkins University Studies in History and Political Science, 4th Series, Vol. III (1886); Irving B. Richman, *Rhode Island, Its Making and Its Meaning* (New York, 1908); Howard M. Chapin, *Documentary History of Rhode Island* (2 vols., New York, 1908); Alexander Johnson, *Connecticut, A Study of a Commonwealth-Democracy* (2 vols., New York, 1898); George L. Clark, *A History of Connecticut* (New York, 1914); Florence S. M. Crofut, *Guide to the History and the Historic Sites of Connecticut* (2 vols., New Haven, 1937); Isabel MacBeath Calder, *The New Haven Colony* (New Haven, 1934); and Henry S. Burrage, *The Beginnings of Colonial Maine, 1602–1658* (Portland, Me., 1914).

CHAPTER IV

The colonial history of the Hudson and Delaware valleys has been explored in painstaking detail for the past century, and in consequence a vast quantity of material is available in local histories, historical society publications, and public documents now in print. The work of some of the older antiquarians and historians is still useful. Among the more valuable of these are J. R. Brodhead, *History of the State of New York* (2 vols., New York, 1853–71); E. B. O'Callaghan, *History of New Netherland* (2 vols., New York, 1846–48); J. R. Brodhead, E. B. O'Callaghan, and others, *Documents Relative to the Colonial History of the State of New York* (15 vols., Albany, 1853–87).

The most valuable recent synthesis is the ten-volume *History of the State of New York*, ed. Alexander C. Flick (New York, 1933–37). Individual chapters, written by specialists, deal with the varied aspects of social, intellectual, and political development. Adequate bibliographies accompany the separate chapters. The most astute summary of the early political history of New York and New Jersey is to be found in Charles M. Andrews, *The Colonial Period of American History*, Vol. III (New Haven, 1937). Convenient and readable are Maud Wilder Goodwin, *Dutch and English on the Hudson*, and Sydney G. Fisher, *The Quaker Colonies*, both in the Chronicles of America Series (New Haven, 1919). A detailed study of the patroonships is S. G. Nissenson, *The Patroon's Domain* (New York, 1937). The definitive work on New Sweden is Amandus Johnson, *The Swedish Settlements on the Delaware* (2 vols., Philadelphia, 1911). Also useful is *The Swedes and Finns in New Jersey*, American Guide Series (Bayonne, N. J., 1938). The preliminary chapters of Donald L. Kemmerer, *Path to Freedom: The Struggle for Self-Government in Colonial New Jersey, 1703–1776* (Princeton, 1940), are useful for the earlier period. Miscellaneous information of varying value will be found in Francis B. Lee, *New Jersey as a Colony and as a State* (4 vols., New York, 1902). Some information in a semi-popular narrative concerning Indian relations has been collected by Francis W. Halsey, *The Old New York Frontier* (New York, 1901). Pioneer work on the cultural aspects of New York and New Jersey will be found in Thomas J. Wertenbaker, *The Founding of American Civilization: The Middle Colonies* (New York, 1938). Also valuable is Carl Bridenbaugh, *Cities in the Wilderness* (New York, 1938). Considerable information about social and cultural conditions has been brought together in Ellis L. Raesly, *Portrait of New Netherland* (New York, 1945). Readable and suggestive is Dixon Ryan Fox, *Yankees and Yorkers* (New York, 1940). Interesting sidelights on social customs will be found in Alice Morse Earle, *Colonial Days in Old New York* (New York, 1896). An excellent picture of the development of the New York manorial gentry is Dixon Ryan Fox, *Caleb Heathcote, Gentleman Colonist* (New York, 1926). Other bibliographical items will be found below.

CHAPTER V

General works on colonial America already cited devote considerable space to Pennsylvania. For the early political history, the most valuable of these is Charles M. Andrews, *The Colonial Period of American History*, Vol. III (New Haven, 1937). Much new material describing social conditions and cultural developments will be found in Thomas J. Wertenbaker, *The Founding of American Civilization: The Middle Colonies* (New York, 1938). A mine of information about the Quakers in Pennsylvania, as well as elsewhere, may be found in Rufus M. Jones, *The Quakers in the American Colonies* (New York, 1923). Sydney G. Fisher, *The Quaker Colonies*, Chronicles of America Series, Vol. 8 (New Haven, 1919), is a brief and readable account of settlements on the Delaware. A convenient and recent history devoted to the colony and state of Pennsylvania is Wayland F. Dunaway, *A History of Pennsylvania* (New York, 1935), which has well-selected bibliographies at the end of each chapter. A brief analysis of the population of Pennsylvania will be found in Sydney G. Fisher, *The Making of Pennsylvania* (Philadelphia, 1908), and a short narrative of political development is provided by the same author's *Pennsylvania, Colony and Commonwealth* (Philadelphia, 1907). Wayland F. Dunaway, *The Scotch-Irish of Colonial Pennsylvania* (Chapel Hill, N. C., 1944), provides a well-documented study with an excellent bibliography of monographs dealing with the history of the colony. Considerable out-of-the-way information about the Germans will be found in James O. Knauss, Jr., *Social Conditions Among the Pennsylvania Germans in the Eighteenth Century as Revealed in the German Newspapers Published in America* (Lancaster, Pa., 1922). Invaluable for the great amount of detailed information about the cultural development of Philadelphia is Carl and Jessica Bridenbaugh, *Rebels and Gentlemen: Philadelphia in the Age of Franklin* (New York, 1942). Also useful is Carl Bridenbaugh, *Cities in the Wilderness* (New York, 1938). James Mulhern, *A History of Secondary Education in Pennsylvania* (Philadelphia, 1933), and James P. Wickersham, *A History of Education in Pennsylvania* (Lancaster, Pa., 1886), are adequate treatments of that subject. Mulhern includes a detailed bibliography.

Of the numerous biographies of William Penn, Sydney G. Fisher, *The True William Penn,* first published in 1899 and reprinted as *William Penn, A Biography* (Philadelphia, 1932), is still the most useful for the light it throws on the Pennsylvania colony. Bonamy Dobrée, *William Penn, Quaker and Pioneer* (London, 1932), and C. E. Vulliamy, *William Penn* (London, 1933), are suggestive.

The most interesting travel narrative describing conditions in Pennsylvania in the mid-eighteenth century is *The America of 1750: Peter Kalm's Travels in North America. The English Version of 1770,* ed. Adolph B. Benson (2 vols., New York, 1937).

CHAPTER VI

The relevant chapters in Charles M. Andrews, *The Colonial Period of American History,* Vol. III (New Haven, 1937), present a concise discussion of the political development of the Carolinas. Frank W. Pitman, *The Development of the British West Indies, 1700–1763* (New Haven, 1917), contains much useful information throwing light on the relations of the West Indies with the colonies of the mainland. David Duncan Wallace, *The History of South Carolina* (3 vols., New York, 1934), is the most recent detailed history of South Carolina. Still valuable are Edward McCrady, *The History of South Carolina Under the Proprietary Government, 1670–1719* (New York, 1901), and *The History of South Carolina Under the Royal Government, 1719–1776* (New York, 1901). Samuel A. Ashe,

Bibliographical Notes

History of North Carolina (2 vols., Greensboro, N. C., 1925), provides useful information about that colony. On the development of the South Carolina backcountry, Robert L. Meriwether, *The Expansion of South Carolina, 1729–1765* (Kingsport, Tenn., 1940), supplies a great deal of information from contemporary documents, journals, letters, and newspapers. The significance of the border regions of South Carolina and Georgia in the struggle for empire is best treated in Verner W. Crane, *The Southern Frontier, 1670–1732* (Durham, N. C., 1928), and Lawrence H. Gipson, *The British Empire Before the American Revolution*: Vol. II, *The Southern Plantations* (Caldwell, Idaho, 1936). The best brief treatment of Georgia is E. Merton Coulter, *A Short History of Georgia* (Chapel Hill, N. C., 1933). The significance of Charleston as a center of Southern colonial civilization is concisely treated by Frederick P. Bowes, *The Culture of Early Charleston* (Chapel Hill, N. C., 1942). Also valuable is Mrs. St. Julien Ravenel, *Charleston: The Place and the People* (New York, 1929). The contributions of French immigrants are ably discussed by Arthur H. Hirsch, *The Huguenots of Colonial South Carolina* (Durham, 1928).

CHAPTER VII

A vast store of information about the American colonies in the eighteenth century, and their relation to the other elements of the British Empire is to be found in Lawrence Henry Gipson, *The British Empire Before the American Revolution*, Vols. I–III (Caldwell, Idaho, 1936); Vols. IV–VI (New York, 1939–46). Still useful is *The Cambridge History of the British Empire*: Vol. I, *The Old Empire from the Beginnings to 1783* (Cambridge, 1929). Among the many brief treatments of this period, one of the most satisfactory is that by Samuel Eliot Morison and Henry Steele Commager, *The Growth of the American Republic*, Vol. I (New York, 1942). A convenient single volume work is Oliver P. Chitwood, *A History of Colonial America* (New York, 1931). A volume of special excellence, dealing with a single colony, is Charles A. Barker, *The Background of the Revolution in Maryland* (New Haven, 1940). The most readable brief account of the colonial wars is George M. Wrong, *The Conquest of New France*, Chronicles of America Series, Vol. 10 (New Haven, 1918). The cultural history of the period is treated in volumes by Bridenbaugh and others, cited in previous chapters. Merle Curti, *The Growth of American Thought* (New York, 1945), is especially useful and has convenient bibliographies. A small volume filled with valuable side lights on the history and culture of the mid-eighteenth century is one by Lawrence C. Wroth, *An American Bookshelf, 1755* (Philadelphia, 1934). Useful information concerning cultural relations between the colonies will be found in Michael Kraus, *Intercolonial Aspects of American Culture on the Eve of the Revolution* (New York, 1928). Two detailed and shrewd appraisals of the colonies by contemporary travellers are to be found in *The America of 1750: Peter Kalm's Travels in North America* (2 vols., New York, 1937), and *Burnaby's Travels Through North America*, ed. Rufus R. Wilson (New York, 1904). The most succinct account of the rise and influence of the press is to be found in Frank L. Mott, *American Journalism* (New York, 1941).

REFERENCES

CHAPTER I

PAGE 7. New Amsterdam's population: Carl F. Wittke, *We Who Built America*, p. 15.

PAGE 15. Lord Spencer's origins: Campbell, *The English Yeoman*, p. 43.

PAGE 31. William Cecil: Douglas Bush, *The Renaissance and English Humanism*, p. 79. Billingsley quoted: Louis B. Wright, *Middle-Class Culture in Elizabethan England*, p. 398.

PAGE 42. LaHontan quoted: Louis de LaHontan, *New Voyages to North America*, preface.

CHAPTER II

PAGES 50–1. Attitude toward colonization: Louis B. Wright, *Religion and Empire: The Alliance between Piety and Commerce, 1558–1625*, pp. 84ff.

PAGE 52. Raleigh's charter: Henry Steele Commager (ed.), *Documents of American History*, pp. 6–7.

PAGE 55. Newport's Report to Lord Salisbury: Alexander Brown, *The Genesis of the United States*, I, p. 105. Letter from council: *Ibid.*, p. 108.

PAGES 60–1. Virginia Company: Wesley F. Craven, *Dissolution of the Virginia Company*, pp. 47–60, 67–8, *et passim*; Charles M. Andrews, *The Colonial Period*, I, pp. 180–2.

PAGE 64. Sardonic historian: Marcus W. Jernegan, *Laboring and Dependent Classes in Colonial America, 1607–1783*, p. 49. Number of indentured servants: Thomas J. Wertenbaker, *Patrician and Plebeian*, p. 159.

PAGES 66–7. Calvert's instructions: Clayton C. Hall (ed.), *Narratives of Early Maryland*, p. 16.

PAGES 67–8. Calvert's privileges: Charles M. Andrews, *Our Earliest Colonial Settlements*, pp. 148–50.

PAGE 71. Account of Matthews: *A Perfect Description of Virginia* in Peter Force's *Tracts*, II, pp. 14–15; quoted by Louis B. Wright, *The First Gentlemen of Virginia*, p. 50.

PAGES 75–6. Governor Harvey: Thomas J. Wertenbaker, *Virginia Under the Stuarts*, pp. 74–80.

PAGES 78–9. Reasons for trouble in Maryland: Andrews, *Colonial Period*, II, pp. 313–23.

PAGE 82. Poem on Bacon: Charles M. Andrews (ed.), *Narratives of the Insurrections, 1675–1690*, p. 76.

PAGES 83–4. Fendall and Coode: *Colonial Period*, II, pp. 345ff.

PAGES 84–5. Changes after 1688: Wertenbaker, *Virginia Under the Stuarts*, pp. 256–7.

PAGES 85–6. *Essay*: Louis B. Wright (ed.), *An Essay Upon the Government of the English Plantations on the Continent of America.*

PAGES 86–7. William and Mary College: Wright, *The First Gentlemen of Virginia*, pp. 106–8.

PAGES 87–9. William Fitzhugh: *Ibid.*, pp. 170–3.

PAGE 90. Qualities of Lee: *Ibid.*, pp. 213–16.

PAGES 90–2. Robert Carter: Louis B. Wright (ed.), *Letters of Robert Carter, 1720–1727*, p. 25.

PAGES 92–3. Byrd's Diary: Louis B. Wright and Marion Tinling (eds.), *The Secret Diary of William Byrd of Westover, 1709–1712*, p. 183.

PAGE 94. Spotswood's expedition: Wright, *The First Gentlemen*, pp. 88–90.

CHAPTER III

PAGES 101–2. Gorges's settlement in 1607: James Phinney Baxter, *Sir Ferdinando Gorges and His Province of Maine*, Prince Society, I, pp. 74–90; James Truslow Adams, *The Founding of New England*, pp. 50–2. Map of New England: The Church copy in the Huntington Library, No. 3409, has the map and table of names.

PAGE 103. Smith's views of New England: John Smith, *A Description of New England*, pp. 10–11, 31. Council for New England: Andrews, *The Colonial Period of American History*, I, pp. 321–3. New France: William B. Munro, *Crusaders of New France*, Chronicles of America Series, 4, pp. 33–52.

PAGES 105–6. Bradford: William Bradford, *History of Plymouth Plantation 1620–1647*, Massachusetts History Society, I, p. 55.

PAGE 106. Terms of partnership: Andrews, *Colonial Period*, I, 264–7. Mayflower's voyage: *Ibid.*, I, pp. 270–2. "Firm element": Bradford, *History*, I, p. 155. Mayflower compact: *Ibid.*, pp. 189–91.

PAGE 108. First Thanksgiving: George F. Willison, *Saints and Strangers*, p. 191. Adams on Plymouth: Adams, *Founding of New England*, p. 102.

PAGE 109. Andrews on New England: Charles M. Andrews, *The Fathers of New England*. Chronicles of America Series, VI, pp. 19–20; see also Andrews, *Colonial Period*, I, pp. 274–8.

PAGE 110. Morton's May-pole: Bradford, *History*, II, pp. 48–58.

PAGE 112. "Lord Brethren": Quoted by Andrews, *Colonial Period*, I, p. 340.

PAGES 114–15. Charter of Massachusetts Bay: Andrews, *Fathers of New England*, p. 26. Quality of immigrants: Andrews, *Colonial Period*, I, p. 383.

References

PAGE 117. Sixty-five preachers: William Warren Sweet, *Religion in Colonial America*, p. 87.

PAGE 118. Quotation from Schneider: Herbert W. Schneider, *The Puritan Mind*, p. 23. Clergy a supreme court: Sweet, *Religion in Colonial America*, p. 88. Clergy's influence on the courts: William Hubbard, *General History of New England*, quoted by Moses Coit Tyler, *A History of American Literature During the Colonial Period, 1607–1675*, I, p. 213. Williams on Cotton: *Narragansett Club Publications*, IV, p. 42, quoted by Tyler, p. 213.

PAGE 119. Cotton's death foretold: Nathaniel Morton, *New England's Memorial*, quoted by Tyler, p. 214. Massachusetts Laws: Max Farrand (ed.), *The Laws and Liberties of Massachusetts*, v–ix; see also William H. Whitmore, *A Bibliographical Sketch of the Laws of the Massachusetts Colony*, pp. 6, 9. System of government: Andrews, *Colonial Period*, I, pp. 434–5.

PAGES 121–2. Question of veto: *Ibid.*, I, p. 451.

PAGE 124. Slaughter at Mystic: Bradford, *History*, II, pp. 251–2. Downing letter: *Collections of the Massachusetts Historical Society*, 4th Series, VI, p. 65.

PAGE 127. Hutchinson trial: Andrews, *Colonial Period*, I, pp. 485–6.

PAGES 129–30. Persecution of Quakers: Adams, *Founding of New England*, pp. 264–72; Sweet, *Religion in Colonial America*, pp. 145–7.

PAGES 131–2. Williams' simile of ship: *Narragansett Club Publications*, VI, 278–9.

PAGES 134–5. "Liberty but not law": Andrews, *Colonial Period*, II, p. 61.

PAGE 137. Fundamental Orders of Connecticut: *Ibid.*, II, pp. 100–10; also Andrews, *Fathers of New England*, p. 64.

PAGE 142. Bourgeois ethics: Wright, *Middle-Class Culture*, pp. 121–296.

PAGES 147–8. *New England's First Fruits*: Quotation from reprint in Samuel E. Morison, *The Founding of Harvard College*, p. 432. Quotation from Cotton: *Ibid.*, p. 151.

PAGES 148–9. Founding Boston Latin School: Pauline Holmes, *A Tercentenary History of the Boston Public Latin School, 1635–1935*, p. 3. Laws concerning education: *Ibid.*, pp. 6–8; Morison, *Founding of Harvard College*, p. 158.

PAGE 149. Elegy on Cheever: *Dictionary of American Biography*, sub Cheever.

PAGES 149–51. Harvard: Morison, *Founding of Harvard College*, p. 168. Winthrop: *Ibid.*, p. 239. Official historian: Samuel E. Morison, *Harvard College in the Seventeenth Century*, Part I, p. 193. For a refutation of Morison's claims for Harvard, see Winthrop S. Hudson, "The Morison Myth Concerning the Founding of Harvard College," *Church History*, VIII (1939), pp. 148–59. An elaborate discussion of Ramean influences on learning in Massachusetts Bay Colony is that by Perry Miller, *The New England Mind*. One hundred and seven preachers: Wertenbaker, *The First Americans, 1607–1690*. A History of American Life Series, II, p. 248. Solomon Stoddard: Morison, *Harvard College in the Seventeenth Century*, Part II, p. 547.

PAGES 151–2. Founding of Yale: Franklin B. Dexter, *Sketch of the History of Yale University*, pp. 1–15.

PAGES 152–3. New England books: Thomas G. Wright, *Literary Culture in Early New England, 1620–1730;* Louis B. Wright, "The Purposeful Reading of Our Colonial Ancestors," *ELH, A Journal of English Literary History*, IV (1937), pp. 85–111.

PAGES 153–5. Printing presses: Lawrence C. Wroth, "Book Production and Distribution from the Beginnings to the War Between the States," in *The Book in America*, ed. Hellmut Lehman-Haupt, pp. 7–42. Purpose of Courant: Frank L. Mott, *American Journalism*, p. 16.

PAGE 158. Charles Morton: Morison, *Harvard College in the Seventeenth Century*, Part I, p. 219.

PAGES 158–9. Royal Society: Frederick E. Brasch, "The Royal Society of London and its Influence upon Scientific Thought in the American Colonies," *The Scientific Monthly*, XXXIII (1931), pp. 336–55, 448–69.

CHAPTER IV

PAGES 163–4. Objectives of West India Company: A. J. F. Van Laer (ed.), *Documents Relating to New Netherland in the Henry E. Huntington Library*, p. xi.

PAGE 165. Early government: *History of the State of New York*, I, pp. 232–3.

PAGE 166. Rasière quoted: Van Laer, *Documents*, p. 187.

PAGE 167. Michaëlius quoted: *History of the State of New York*, I, p. 255.

PAGES 168–9. Michaëlius to Smoutius: J. Franklin Jameson (ed.), *Narratives of New Netherland, 1609–1664*, Original Narratives Series, pp. 122–33.

PAGE 171. Megapolensis: *Ibid.*, pp. 165–7.

PAGE 171–2. Patroonships: *History of the State of New York*, I, pp. 263–5.

PAGE 172. De Vries on Van Twiller: Jameson, *Narratives*, p. 188.

PAGE 174. Land grants: *History of the State of New York*, I, p. 283. Kieft advised to lead: J. R. Brodhead, *History of the State of New York, First Period, 1609–1664*, p. 318.

PAGES 175–6. De Vries on the massacre: Jameson, *Narratives*, pp. 227–9.

References

PAGES 176–7. End of war: *History of the State of New York*, I, pp. 292–3.

PAGE 178. "Jewel of kingdom": Brodhead, *History*, p. 280. Oxenstierna: *Ibid.*, p. 281.

PAGES 178–9. New Sweden Company: Johnson, *Swedish Settlements*, I, pp. 100–1, 107.

PAGES 180–1. Printz quoted: *The Swedes and Finns in New Jersey*, p. 41.

PAGE 182. Log cabins: H. R. Shurtleff, *The Log Cabin Myth*, passim.

PAGES 183–4. Population: *History of the State of New York*, I, pp. 313–17, 325–33. Esopus: *Ibid.*, I, p. 314; Brodhead, *History*, p. 536. Taphouses: *History of the State of New York*, I, p. 298.

PAGE 185. Remonstrance quoted: *Ibid.*, I, pp. 311–12.

PAGES 185–6. Burgher rights: *Ibid.*, I, pp. 309–10.

PAGES 186–8. Preachers: *Ibid.*, II, pp. 5–12. Company's attitude toward toleration: *Ibid.*, II, p. 15. Quotation concerning school: *Ibid.*, II, p. 24. Curtius' school: *Ibid.*, II, p. 28.

PAGES 190–1. Royal African Company; Downing: Andrews, *Colonial Period*, III, pp. 52ff.

PAGES 191–3. Duke of York's proprietary grant: *Ibid.*, III, pp. 55–7. Stuyvesant's report: Jameson, *Narratives*, p. 460. Capitulation: *History of the State of New York*, II, pp. 79–80.

PAGE 193. Dutch social influence: Wertenbaker, *Founding of American Civilization: The Middle Colonies*, pp. 29ff. Holidays and pleasures: Alice M. Earle, *Colonial Days in Old New York*, pp. 184–226. Saint Nicholas: H. L. Mencken, *The American Language, Supplement I*, pp. 186–7.

PAGE 194. New Jersey grants: Andrews, *Colonial Period*, III, pp. 102–3, 139ff.

PAGES 194–5. Land troubles: *Ibid.*, III, pp. 138ff. On modern boards of proprietors, see *ibid.*, Note 1, p. 179.

PAGES 198–9. Duke quoted: *Ibid.*, III, p. 113.

PAGES 199–200. Assembly and charter: *Ibid.*, III, pp. 115–17. Population increase: *History of the State of New York*, II, p. 263. Manors and small farms: *Ibid.*, III, pp. 285–91. See also, Joel N. Eno, "The English Manors in New York," *The Journal of American History*, XV (1922), pp. 361–77; Martha I. Lamb, "Van Cortlandt Manor-House," *Magazine of American History*, XV (1886), pp. 217–36; E. B. O'Callaghan, "David Jamison, Attorney-General of New York, 1710," *Magazine of American History*, I (1877), pp. 21–4; Fox, *Caleb Heathcote*, p. 130.

PAGE 202. "Treachery of Papists": Andrews, *Colonial Period*, III, p. 133. "Free-holders within your government": *Ibid.*, III, p. 137.

PAGES 208–9. School statistics: *History of the State of New York*, III, pp. 70–4. See also Carl Bridenbaugh, *Cities in the Wilderness*, pp. 286–9. Libraries: *History of the State of New York*, IX, pp. 47–51. Bridenbaugh, *Cities*, pp. 133, 294. New Jersey books: William Nelson (ed.), *Documents Relating to the Colonial History of the State of New Jersey*, 1st Series, XXIII (1901), pp. 10, 422, 452.

PAGE 210. Zenger trial: Mott, *American Journalism*, pp. 31–8.

CHAPTER V

PAGE 214. "Holy Experiment": Andrews, *Colonial Period*, III, p. 275.

PAGE 215. Name Pennsylvania: *Ibid.*, p. 281. Penn's Laws: *Ibid.*, pp. 286–8.

PAGE 216. "Divine Right of government": *Ibid.*, p. 288.

PAGE 217. Pastorius on Penn: Albert Cook Myers, *Narratives of Early Pennsylvania, West New Jersey, and Delaware*, Original Narratives Series, p. 374.

PAGES 217–18. Penn's "treaty": Sydney G. Fisher, *William Penn*, pp. 242–3. Voltaire on Penn: Voltaire, *Letters Concerning the English Nation*, p. 22.

PAGES 218–19. Philadelphia founded: Fisher, *William Penn*, pp. 213, 234–5.

PAGE 219. Population of Philadelphia: Carl and Jessica Bridenbaugh, *Rebels and Gentlemen*, pp. 3–4; see also Fisher, *Quaker Colonies*, pp. 19–20.

PAGES 219–20. Quotations from Penn: Myers, *Narratives*, pp. 203–6, 215.

PAGE 220–1. Quotations from *Letter*: *Ibid.*, pp. 224–44. Quotations from *Further Account*: *Ibid.*, pp. 262, 272.

PAGE 222. Price of land: Fisher, *William Penn*, p. 209. Pennsbury: *Ibid.*, pp. 352–5.

PAGES 225–6. Conditions in Palatinate: Wertenbaker, *Founding of American Civilization*, pp. 267ff.

PAGES 226–7. Pastorius' comment: Quotation from Pastorius' *Nachricht auss America* in Myers, *Narratives*, pp. 395–6. Pastorius on Lutheran preacher: *Ibid.*, pp. 299–400.

PAGES 227–8. On penance of Adam's seed: *Ibid.*, p. 397.

PAGE 232. Penn and Blackwell: Andrews, *Colonial Period*, III, p. 310.

PAGES 234–5. Markham's Frame: *Ibid.*, p. 317.

PAGE 236. Andrews' comment: *Ibid.*, p. 321. Quaker's comment: *Ibid.*, p. 322, note 1.

PAGES 237–8. Byrd's comment: Quoted from the appendix to *An Essay Upon the Government of the English Plantations on the Continent of America*, Louis B. Wright (ed.), pp. 58–63. Anonymous Virginian: *Ibid.*, pp. 25–6, 32.

PAGE 240. Sarah Churchill: Letter of Isaac Norris to Joseph Pike, January 25, 1708, in the *Correspondence between William Penn*

References

and James Logan . . . and Others, printed in the *Publications of the Historical Society of Pennsylvania,* X (1872), p. 267.

PAGE 242. Punishment for treason and murder: Fisher, *The Making of Pennsylvania,* p. 209.

PAGE 244. Opposition to plays: Wertenbaker, *Founding of American Civilization,* p. 203. Reading romances: *Ibid.,* p. 197. Fiddling Friends: Rufus M. Jones, *Quakers in the American Colonies,* p. 47, note 1.

PAGES 244-5. Penn's comment on education: Quotation from Penn's "Reflections and Maxims," reprinted in James P. Wickersham, *A History of Education in Pennsylvania,* pp. 35-6. Penn's First Frame quoted: *Ibid.,* p. 33.

PAGES 246-7. Pemberton's comment: James Mulhern, *A History of Secondary Education in Pennsylvania,* pp. 61-2. Private schools: *Ibid.,* p. 101. Andrew Lamb: Carl and Jessica Bridenbaugh, *Rebels and Gentlemen,* p. 38.

PAGE 248. John Lloyd's school: Mulhern, *History,* p. 102. Education of women: *Ibid.,* pp. 103-5.

PAGES 249-50. "Log College": *Ibid.,* pp. 65-6. Francis Allison: Carl and Jessica Bridenbaugh, *Rebels and Gentlemen,* p. 42.

PAGES 250-1. James Logan: *Ibid.,* pp. 89-90, 101, 306-8.

PAGE 253. Franklin on the Junto: *The Autobiography of Benjamin Franklin,* John Bigelow (ed.), pp. 153-4.

PAGE 254. Franklin on the college plan: *Ibid.,* p. 267.

PAGES 254-5. William Smith: Carl and Jessica Bridenbaugh, *Rebels and Gentlemen,* pp. 56-8.

PAGE 255. Franklin on the library: *Autobiography,* pp. 171-2.

PAGE 256. *Way to Wealth*: Louis B. Wright, "Franklin's Legacy to the Gilded Age," *The Virginia Quarterly Review,* XXII (1946), pp. 268-79.

CHAPTER VI

PAGES 258-9. Hakluyt: Louis B. Wright, *Religion and Empire: The Alliance between Piety and Commerce in English Expansion, 1558-1625,* pp. 44-9.

PAGE 259. Bermudas reserved by God: *Ibid.,* pp. 113-14.

PAGE 262. Fundamental Constitutions: Andrews, *The Colonial Period,* III, pp. 213ff.

PAGES 264-5. Hilton's testimony: A. S. Salley (ed.), *Narratives of Early Carolina,* Original Narratives Series, p. 53. Horne's comment: *Ibid.,* pp. 66, 73. Ashe's comment: *Ibid.,* pp. 138, 147, 150.

PAGE 266. Albemarle's trade: Andrews, *The Colonial Period,* III, pp. 248-9.

PAGES 267-8. Joseph West's contributions: Wallace, *History of South Carolina,* I, pp. 80-1. Land tenure: *Ibid.,* p. 81; see also Salley, *Narratives,* p. 173.

The Atlantic Frontier

PAGES 268–9. Indian slave trade: Wallace, *History of South Carolina*, I, pp. 97–8.

PAGE 270. Rice culture: *Ibid.*, pp. 121–2. See also Duncan C. Heyward, *Seed from Madagascar*, pp. 3–44.

PAGES 270–1. Trade in 1718: Wallace, *History of South Carolina*, I, p. 251.

PAGES 271–2. Population of South Carolina: *Ibid.*, p. 251. Population of North Carolina: E. B. Greene and Virginia D. Harrington, *American Population Before the Federal Census of 1790*, pp. 4–5, 156–7.

PAGE 272. Byrd's comment: William K. Boyd (ed.), *William Byrd's Histories of the Dividing Line*, p. 72. Varied groups in North Carolina: Ashe, *History of North Carolina*, I, p. 254, 265–6; Marcus Lee Hansen, *The Atlantic Migration, 1607–1860*, p. 49.

PAGES 273–4. Elder Pratt's comments: Salley, *Narratives*, pp. 199–200.

PAGE 274. Scottish settlers: Wallace, *History of South Carolina*, p. 341. Silk from Purrysburgh: *Ibid.*, p. 338; Meriwether, *Expansion of South Carolina*, pp. 32–5. Amelia and Orangeburg: Meriwether, *Expansion of South Carolina*, pp. 42–4.

PAGE 275. Woodward and Westo Indians: Crane, *Southern Frontier*, pp. 19–20.

PAGE 277. Trails of the traders: *Ibid.*, p. 39.

PAGE 278. Yemassee War: *Ibid.*, pp. 162–86.

PAGE 280. Turbulence in North Carolina: Andrews, *Colonial Period*, III, p. 255.

PAGES 281–2. Church established in North and South Carolina: Ashe, *History of North Carolina*, I, pp. 155, 196–7; Wallace, *History of South Carolina*, I, pp. 172–8.

PAGE 283. Blair's comment: Hugh T. Lefler (ed.), *North Carolina History Told by Contemporaries*, pp. 45–6. Byrd's comment: Boyd, *William Byrd's Histories*, pp. 72, 96.

PAGE 284. South and North Carolina become royal provinces: Andrews, *Colonial Period*, pp. 245–6, 266–7. Carteret refuses to sell: *Ibid.*, p. 246.

PAGES 285–6. Manigaults: *Dictionary of American Biography;* Hirsch, *Huguenots in South Carolina*, pp. 229–32.

PAGE 286. Eliza Lucas: Harriott Horry Ravenel, *Eliza Pinckney*, passim.

PAGE 287. Population of Charleston: Carl Bridenbaugh, *Cities in the Wilderness*, p. 303. Glen's report: Bowes, *Culture of Charleston*, pp. 9–10.

PAGES 288–9. Education in South Carolina: Colyer Meriwether, *History of Higher Education in South Carolina*, U. S. Bureau of Education Circular of Information No. 3, 1888, pp. 15–17; Bowes,

References

Culture of Charleston, p. 39; Wallace, *History of South Carolina*, p. 194.

PAGES 289–90. Education in North Carolina: Charles Lee Smith, *The History of Education in North Carolina*, U. S. Bureau of Education Circular of Information No. 2, 1888, pp. 22–31.

PAGE 290. Libraries in South and North Carolina: Wallace, *History of South Carolina*, pp. 195–6; Bowes, *Culture of Charleston*, p. 56. Stephen B. Weeks, *Libraries and Literature in North Carolina in the Eighteenth Century*, Annual Report of the American Historical Association of the Year 1895, pp. 177, 189–91.

PAGES 290–1. *South Carolina Gazette*: Bowes, *Culture of Charleston*, pp. 70–2. Music, Art, and the Theater in Charleston: *Ibid.*, pp. 102–3, 105–8, 109.

PAGE 292. Lord Cardross: Crane, *Southern Frontier*, pp. 28–31. Sir Robert Montgomery: *Ibid.*, p. 210–11; Coulter, *History of Georgia*, p. 12.

PAGE 293. Sir Alexander Cuming: Crane, *Southern Frontier*, p. 278–80.

PAGE 294. General Oglethorpe: Coulter, *History of Georgia*, pp. 14–16.

PAGE 295. Hope for silk culture: *Ibid.*, p. 57. Diversity of immigrants: *Ibid.*, pp. 24–9.

PAGES 296–7. Land tenure: *Ibid.*, pp. 51–3. Opposition to slavery and rum: *Ibid.*, pp. 55–6.

PAGE 298. George Whitefield: *Ibid.*, pp. 67–8. Comment on Christian Gottlieb Priber: From contemporary account in *The South Carolina Gazette* quoted by Verner W. Crane in "A Lost Utopia of the First American Frontier," *Sewanee Review*, XXVII (1919), pp. 48–61. See also Wallace, *History of South Carolina*, pp. 363–5.

PAGE 299. War of Jenkins' Ear: Coulter, *History of Georgia*, pp. 40–50.

PAGES 299–300. Comment on lawyers: *Ibid.*, p. 71. Comment of Tailfer: Patrick Tailfer et al, *A True and Historical Narrative of the Colony of Georgia in America*, pp. iv–v.

CHAPTER VII

PAGE 302. Burke's comment: From *An Account of the European Settlements in America*, quoted in *The Cambridge History of the British Empire*, I, p. 4.

PAGES 303–4. Population figures: E. B. Greene and Virginia D. Harrington, *American Population before the Federal Census of 1790*, pp. 4–6.

PAGES 307–8. Author of *Essay*: Anon., *An Essay upon the Govern-*

[353]

ment of the English Plantations on the Continent of America (1701), Louis B. Wright (ed.), pp. 48–9.

PAGE 311. "Join or Die": Gipson, *The British Empire*, V, p. 125. Albany Congress: *Ibid.*, pp. 113–42. Chief Hendrick: *Ibid.*, pp. 119–20.

PAGE 312. Governor Dinwiddie: *Ibid.*, p. 112.

PAGE 313. Braddock: Stanley Pargellis, "Braddock's Defeat," *American Historical Review*, XLI (1935–36), pp. 253–69.

PAGE 315. Quakers: Wayland F. Dunaway, *A History of Pennsylvania*, pp. 126–7. Expulsion of Acadians: Gipson, *The British Empire*, VI, pp. 282–5. Acadians in South Carolina: David Duncan Wallace, *The History of South Carolina*, II, pp. 16–18.

PAGES 316–17. Abercromby: George M. Wrong, *The Conquest of New France*, pp. 196–7.

PAGES 317–18. Quebec: *Ibid.*, pp. 215–37.

PAGES 319–20. *Essay: An Essay upon the Government of the English Plantations*, pp. 37, 55–6.

PAGE 324. Kalm's comment: *The America of 1750: Peter Kalm's Travels*, I, pp. 18, 131, 341, 344.

PAGES 324–5. Williamsburg; Virginia women: *Burnaby's Travels*, pp. 33–4, 57, 63.

PAGES 325–6. Trade of Pennsylvania: *Ibid.*, pp. 91–3.

PAGES 326–7. Rhode Islanders: *Ibid.*, pp. 127–8. New Hampshire: *Ibid.*, pp. 146–9. Philadelphia's culture: *Ibid.*, p. 96.

PAGE 328. King's College: *Ibid.*, p. 112. Redwood Library: *Ibid.*, p. 120. Cambridge and Boston: *Ibid.*, pp. 133–9.

PAGE 330. Franklin's comment: *The Autobiography of Benjamin Franklin*, John Bigelow (ed.), pp. 222–3. Jews in New York: *The America of 1750; Peter Kalm's Travels*, I, p. 129. Synagogue in Newport: *Burnaby's Travels*, p. 121.

PAGE 332. Weakness of colonies: *Ibid.*, pp. 150, 152–5.

PAGES 334–5. Gadsden's comment: R. W. Gibbes, *Documentary History of the American Revolution . . . 1764–1776*, p. 8.

INDEX

[i]

Index

Index

Cabot, John, 4, 6, 162
Calef, Robert, 158; *More Wonders of the Invisible World*, 158
Calicut (India), 4, 16
California, 25
Callowhill, Hannah, 241
Calvert, Benedict, 96
Calvert, Cecilius, 66–70, 76–9
Calvert, Charles, 96
Calvert, George, 65–70, 191, 212, 215, 221
Calvert, Leonard, 66–70, 76–7
Calvert, Philip, 79
Calvinism, *see* Puritanism
Cambridge (Mass.), 136, 150
Cambridge Press, 155
Cambridge University, 37, 116, 117, 150
Camden (N.J.), 195
Campbell, John, 154
Campbell, John, Earl of Loudoun, 316
Canada, 9, 54, 203–5, 306–18
Canada Company, 54
Canary Islands, 140
Cape Ann, 114
Cape Breton Island, 307
Cape Cod, 101, 106
Cape Fear River, 54, 264, 265
Cape Henlopen, 177
Cape Horn, 25, 26
Cape May, 164, 197
Cape of Good Hope, 3, 163–4
Cape Verde Islands, 5
Capitalism: influence of Quakers, 242; relation to Puritanism, 38–9
Cardross, Henry, Lord, 292
Caribbean, 5
Carolana, *see* Carolinas
Carolina, A Brief Description of the Province of, see Robert Horne
Carolina . . . and the Natural Excellencies Thereof, see Thomas Ashe
Carolinas, 7, 8, 11–12, 194, 260–92, 303–7; Anglicanism, 281–3, aristocracy developed from landed gentry and rich merchants, 285ff.; became a royal province, 283–4; early settlers, 263, 265–6; education, 288–9; eight proprietors, 261,

Carolinas (*continued*)
284; Fundamental Constitutions, 261–3; Indian wars, 278–9; introduction of rice, 270; land claims, 261; land and commerce the basis of wealth, 267–8; libraries, 289–90; music, painting, theater, 291; political unrest, 279–81; population elements, 271–3; printing, 290–1; promotion literature, 264–5; slave holders became the aristocracy, 269; sold Indians as slaves, 268–9; trade with Indians, 277, 281
Carter, Robert, of Corotoman, 84, 90–2
Carteret, George, 194–6, 260, 284
Carteret, Philip, 195
Cartier, Jacques, 5
Carver, John, 107, 108
Castiglione, Baldassare, *Book of the Courtier*, 40
Catholics, 201, 210, 330; English, 54; French, 9–10, 205; in Jerseys, 196; in Maryland, 66–8, 78–79, 96; in Virginia, 78; Spanish, 10–11
Cato, Major, see Cicero
Cato's Moral Distichs Englished in Couplets, see James Logan
Causton, Thomas, 300
Cavaliers, 70 1, 89
Caxton, William, 19
Cecil, William, 31
Celebes, 26
Chambers, Ephraim, 252
Champlain, Samuel, 54
Chancellor, Richard, 20
Charles I, 41, 42, 66, 67, 103, 261
Charles II, 72–3, 77, 82, 137, 142, 143, 159, 190, 192, 212, 213, 261
Charles Town (S.C.), 265–71, 273–9, 282–92, 298, 300, 315, 322
Charles Town Free School, 289
Charles Town Library Society, 290
Charleston (S.C.), *see* Charles Town
"Charter of Freedom and Exemptions," 170
"Charter of Liberties and Privileges," 199
Charter of 1701, 235–6
Chauncy, Charles, 129

Index

Index

Index

Index

Index

Index

Index

Index

[xi]

Index

Index

Index

Index

Index

Index

Index

Index

The text of this book was set on the Linotype in Janson, a recutting made direct from the type cast from matrices made by Anton Janson some time between 1660 and 1687. Janson's original matrices were, at last report, in the possession of the Stempel foundry, Frankfurt am Main.

Of Janson's origin nothing is known. He may have been a relative of Justus Janson, a printer of Danish birth who practised in Leipzig from 1614 to 1635. Some time between 1657 and 1668 Anton Janson, a punch-cutter and type-founder, bought from the Leipzig printer Johann Erich Hahn the type-foundry which had formerly been a part of the printing house of M. Friedrich Lankisch. Janson's types were first shown in a specimen sheet issued at Leipzig about 1675. Janson's successor, and perhaps his son-in-law, Johann Karl Edling, issued a specimen sheet of Janson types in 1689. His heirs sold the Janson matrices in Holland to Wolffgang Dietrich Erhardt, of Leipzig.

478